CELEBRATING 50 YEA

MW01264790

OUTSIDE
BOLDLY GOES

117 **NEW PERSPECTIVES ON**
117 **CLASSIC STAR TREK STORIES BY**
117 **WRITERS**

EDITED BY ROBERT SMITH?

ATB
ATBPUBLISHING.COM

ALSO FROM ATB PUBLISHING:

Outside In: 160 New Perspectives on 160 Classic Doctor Who Stories by 160 Writers
edited by Robert Smith?

Outside In 2: 125 Unique Perspectives on 125 Modern Doctor Who Stories by 125 Writers
edited by Robert Smith?

ISBN: 978-0-9882210-3-1
Printed in Illinois. First edition: November 2016

ATBPUBLISHING.COM

ARNOLD T. BLUMBERG
CO-PUBLISHER

MARVIN A. BLUMBERG
CO-PUBLISHER

ROBERT SMITH?
EDITOR-IN-CHIEF

NATALIE B. LITOFSKY
DIRECTOR OF MARKETING

www.atbpublishing.com • facebook.com/atbpublishing • @ATBPublishing • info@atbpublishing.com

DEDICATION

For Arnold T. Blumberg
for going above and beyond
as always

6   0. INTRODUCTION ROBERT SMITH?

THE ORIGINAL SERIES, SEASON ONE, 1966
8   1. THE CAGE JONATHAN BLUM
11   2. THE MAN TRAP COLLIN W. BUECHLER
13   3. CHARLIE X COLIN WILSON
15   4. WHERE NO MAN HAS GONE BEFORE LILY MITCHELL
16   5. THE NAKED TIME KRISTINE LARSEN
18   6. THE ENEMY WITHIN KATE ORMAN
21   7. MUDD'S WOMEN SAMUEL GIBB
24   8. WHAT ARE LITTLE GIRLS MADE OF? ALAN STEVENS
27   9. MIRI ZOE ESTRIN-GRELE
29   10. DAGGER OF THE MIND ROB TYMEC
32   11. THE CORBOMITE MANEUVER GEOFFREY D. WESSEL
34   12. THE MENAGERIE ANDREW GURUDATA
36   13. THE CONSCIENCE OF THE KING CATRIONA MILLS
40   14. BALANCE OF TERROR MELISSA BEATTIE
42   15. SHORE LEAVE HANNAH ROTHMAN
45   16. THE GALILEO SEVEN DANIEL CLARKE-SERRET
48   17. THE SQUIRE OF GOTHOS CLARE MOSELEY
50   18. ARENA ANDREW FLINT
52   19. TOMORROW IS YESTERDAY TAYLOR DEATHERAGE
55   20. COURT MARTIAL CHRISTIAN YOUNG
57   21. THE RETURN OF THE ARCHONS VANESSA DE KAUWE
60   22. SPACE SEED WYNN QUON
63   23. A TASTE OF ARMAGEDDON EMMA NOWINSKI
66   24. THIS SIDE OF PARADISE ROSANNE WELCH
68   25. THE DEVIL IN THE DARK KATHRYN SULLIVAN
70   26. ERRAND OF MERCY ERIKA ENSIGN
72   27. THE ALTERNATIVE FACTOR LES ZIG
76   28. THE CITY ON THE EDGE OF FOREVER JOHN SEAVEY
79   29. OPERATION: ANNIHILATE CAMERON DIXON

THE ORIGINAL SERIES, SEASON TWO, 1967
83   30. AMOK TIME PIERS BECKLEY
85   31. WHO MOURNS FOR ADONAIS? ROBERT GREENBERGER
88   32. THE CHANGELING SCOTT HARRISON
90   33. MIRROR, MIRROR LENE TAYLOR
93   34. THE APPLE ZOË TULIP

97   35. THE DOOMSDAY MACHINE ANDREW McCAFFREY
98   36. CATSPAW JAN FENNICK
102 37. I, MUDD JASON SNELL
105 38. METAMORPHOSIS VINCE STADON
107 39. JOURNEY TO BABEL WARREN FREY
112 40. FRIDAY'S CHILD LARRY NEMECEK
114 41. THE DEADLY YEARS COLLEEN HILLERUP
117 42. OBSESSION BEN HAKALA
120 43. WOLF IN THE FOLD FIONA MOORE
123 44. THE TROUBLE WITH TRIBBLES DAVID A. McINTEE

THE 30TH ANNIVERSARY DEEP SPACE NINE EPISODE, 1996
126 45. STAR TREK: DEEP SPACE NINE —
     TRIALS AND TRIBBLE-ATIONS ANTHONY WILSON

128 46. THE GAMESTERS OF TRISKELION JASON A. MILLER
131 47. A PIECE OF THE ACTION JENNIFER ADAMS KELLEY
134 48. THE IMMUNITY SYNDROME MICHAEL ROTTMAN
138 49. A PRIVATE LITTLE WAR ANDY WIXON
140 50. RETURN TO TOMORROW LISA MacDONALD
142 51. PATTERNS OF FORCE JON ARNOLD
144 52. BY ANY OTHER NAME PAUL CASTLE
146 53. THE OMEGA GLORY MANISHA MUNASINGHE
149 54. THE ULTIMATE COMPUTER RICHARD FARRELL
151 55. BREAD AND CIRCUSES EMILY ASHER-PERRIN
154 56. ASSIGNMENT: EARTH MICHEL ALBERT

THE ORIGINAL SERIES, SEASON THREE, 1968
156 57. SPOCK'S BRAIN BILL EVENSON
158 57. SPOCK'S BRAIN BILL EVENSON
160 58. THE ENTERPRISE INCIDENT DOROTHY AIL
163 59. THE PARADISE SYNDROME PETER McALPINE
169 60. AND THE CHILDREN SHALL LEAD CHRIS ARNSBY
172 61. IS THERE IN TRUTH NO BEAUTY? DONALD GILLIKIN
175 62. SPECTRE OF THE GUN ALAN J. PORTER
178 63. DAY OF THE DOVE ALISTAIR HUGHES
182 64. FOR THE WORLD IS HOLLOW AND I HAVE
     TOUCHED THE SKY STEPHANIE CRAWFORD
185 65. THE THOLIAN WEB FINN CLARK

190 66. PLATO'S STEPCHILDREN DAN MADSEN

191 67. WINK OF AN EYE IVY GLENNON

194 68. THE EMPATH PATRICIA GILLIKIN

199 69. ELAAN OF TROYIUS J.J. GAUTHIER

202 70. WHOM GODS DESTROY SIMON FERNANDES

205 71. LET THAT BE YOUR LAST BATTLEFIELD JOHN NERONE

208 72. THE MARK OF GIDEON JOSEPH F. BERENATO

211 73. THAT WHICH SURVIVES NEIL A. HOGAN

214 74. THE LIGHTS OF ZETAR DANIEL KUKWA

216 75. REQUIEM FOR METHUSELAH JACK GRAHAM

220 76. THE WAY TO EDEN TAT WOOD

223 77. THE CLOUD MINDERS GRANT KIEN

229 78. THE SAVAGE CURTAIN TONY CONTENTO

232 79. ALL OUR YESTERDAYS JULIAN GUNN

235 80. TURNABOUT INTRUDER SAM MAGGS

THE ANIMATED SERIES, SEASON ONE, 1973–1974

239 81. BEYOND THE FARTHEST STAR ADAM GOBESKI

241 82. YESTERYEAR GLENN GREENBERG

244 83. ONE OF OUR PLANETS IS MISSING ANGELA PRITCHETT

247 84. THE LORELEI SIGNAL STEPHANIE GUERDAN

250 85. MORE TRIBBLES, MORE TROUBLES CAIT COKER

252 86. THE SURVIVOR PAUL BOOTH

255 87. THE INFINITE VULCAN J. ALLAN MORLAN

259 88. THE MAGICKS OF MEGAS-TU RICH HANDLEY

262 89. ONCE UPON A PLANET JOSH MARSFELDER

264 90. MUDD'S PASSION WESLEY OSAM

266 91. THE TERRATIN INCIDENT IAN FARRINGTON

269 92. THE TIME TRAP KEVIN LAUDERDALE

271 93. THE AMBERGRIS ELEMENT NATHAN SKRESLET

274 94. THE SLAVER WEAPON NICK SEIDLER

276 95. THE EYE OF THE BEHOLDER DREW MEYER

279 96. THE JIHAD ANDREW MAH

THE ANIMATED SERIES, SEASON TWO, 1974

282 97. THE PIRATES OF ORION DAVID MacGOWAN

284 98. BEM HEATHER MURRAY

286 99. THE PRACTICAL JOKER ALEX KENNARD

296 100. ALBATROSS DAVID M. BARSKY

299 101. HOW SHARPER THAN A SERPENT'S TOOTH
STEPHEN HATCHER

302 102. THE COUNTER-CLOCK INCIDENT PAUL SIMPSON

THE ORIGINAL CAST FILMS, 1979–1991

304 103. STAR TREK: THE MOTION PICTURE GRAEME BURK

306 104. STAR TREK II: THE WRATH OF KHAN TREY KORTE

308 105. STAR TREK III: THE SEARCH FOR SPOCK
ARNOLD T. BLUMBERG

311 106. STAR TREK IV: THE VOYAGE HOME CHRIS KOCHER

315 107. STAR TREK V: THE FINAL FRONTIER GEORGE IVANOFF

318 108. STAR TREK VI: THE UNDISCOVERED COUNTRY
ARI LIPSEY

THE 30TH ANNIVERSARY VOYAGER EPISODE, 1996

320 109. STAR TREK: VOYAGER —
FLASHBACK JOE BRIGGS-RITCHIE

THE NEXT GENERATION–ERA ORIGINAL CAST ADVENTURES, 1987-1994

323 110. STAR TREK: GENERATIONS THOMAS COOKSON

326 111. STAR TREK: THE NEXT GENERATION —
RELICS DAVID BLACK

328 112. STAR TREK: THE NEXT GENERATION —
ENCOUNTER AT FARPOINT SCOT CLARKE

329 113. STAR TREK: THE NEXT GENERATION —
UNIFICATION LESLIE HARTMAN JR.

THE HONORARY STAR TREK FILM, 1999

331 114. GALAXY QUEST BARBARA WHILLOCK

THE ABRAMSVERSE FILMS, 2009–PRESENT

334 115. STAR TREK KANDACE MAVRICK

336 116. STAR TREK INTO DARKNESS SHAUN LYON

340 117. STAR TREK BEYOND ROBERT SMITH?

346 ∞. ACKNOWLEDGEMENTS ROBERT SMITH?

348 ➤. ABOUT THE EDITOR

349 IN THE NEXT GENERATION...

0. INTRODUCTION
CAPTAIN'S BLOG
ROBERT SMITH?

> *Outside In.* The analysis frontier. These are the reviews of the TV show *Star Trek.* Their continuing mission: to explore strange new perspectives, to seek out new takes and new interpretations. To boldly go where no reviews have gone before.

It's the biggest, wildest idea I ever had. Take a classic TV show, and give us one review for every story, by 117 different writers. Yes, 117. Because this doesn't just cover the original 79 episodes of the original series of *Star Trek*, it also covers the Classic movies, the animated series, the reboots and a few related episodes. Basically, if it's a Kirk-era story (broadly defined), then it goes in.

So that's the skeleton. But the flesh that hangs off the idea is what really brings it to life. In this case, the flesh is this: say something different. Something unique. Or something utterly wild. Because if you put three *Star Trek* fans in a room, you're likely to end up with four opinions. And if you've just watched (say) *Space Seed* and want to know what someone thought of it, then it's not hard to find a review of it somewhere. But finding a review that makes you sit up and think or laugh out loud or just boggle apoplectically at the sheer chutzpah of the reviewer... well, that's not so easy. So we decided to embrace that, with 116 original articles (and one reprint we couldn't resist) that may make you alternately nod, smile or want to tear your hair out. Sometimes all at once. Because that's the joy of fandom: its ability to engage with the text in ways that are splendid, outrageous, clever or just plain silly.

Outside In Boldly Goes embodies that diversity of thought. Some viewpoints are quite narrow, giving us an in-depth look at some tidbit of interest, like the comparison between Tribbles and environmentalism in *More Troubles, More Tribbles*. Others are broad, taking in the grand sweep of events, such as *Into Darkness*'s ponderings on the nature of the franchise. Some go sideways, like the Lovecraftian account of *Catspaw* or an obituary in *Where No Man Has Gone Before*. And a few are just utterly gonzo. Within these pages, you'll find obituaries, handbooks, letters, podcasts, newspaper articles, psychological reports, blogs, recipes and news broadcasts... not to mention insightful and thoughtful articles, examining Kirk-era *Star Trek* from just about every aspect imaginable. And then some. From a collectible trading card set in *The Savage Curtain* to a game of Mad Libs in *Return to Tomorrow* to hilarious restaurant reviews in *The Ambergris Element*, there really is something here for everyone.

Through this lens, we see the essence of *Star Trek* reflected back at us. It's a show that was never afraid to think big, to be different and to occasionally just be bizarre for the hell of it. It's also a show that was simultaneously ahead of its time and also entirely of its time. So the perspectives don't hold back; there's a decent amount of discussion of many of the issues that you'd expect to turn up, such as the show's treatment of women or the role of redshirts. What you won't expect is the manner in which they're discussed or the sometimes-surprising defenses of the apparently indefensible.

From the past to the present, taking in some time travel along the way, this book gives us a sense of the history, the culture and the pure unadulterated fun that *Star Trek* brought to the world, both in terms of the show itself and its many-splendored fandom. Within these pages, you'll find names you'll recognize as well as brand-new voices being heard for the first time. Some are lifelong fans, others are new to the original series. But all are fascinating and thoughtful and wonderful.

As *Star Trek* pivots around its fiftieth anniversary, *Outside In Boldly Goes* celebrates the show that brings us together as a community. Its watchword is "diversity", because that's the guiding principle of the TV show we've adored for five decades and will continue to adore for years to come. As you travel through the many thoughts and different takes that this book presents, you'll see the sheer beauty of fandom. That even though we aren't necessarily making the show itself, we're nevertheless enormously creative and fantastically thoughtful. While we may not be within the inner circle, we nevertheless find ourselves coming at something marvelous, with our own unique takes, coming at it... from the outside in.

Robert Smith? has a question mark in his name. Deal with it.

1. THE CAGE
THE TREK WITHIN
JONATHAN BLUM

The *Star Trek* we're introduced to in *The Cage* is so much greyer than the *Trek* we've become used to... and in some ways that's its greatest strength.

This is a *Star Trek* that begins with the captain of the *Enterprise* deciding to ignore a distress call. True, the survivors are probably long dead... but still, think about it. The captain doesn't devote himself to a rescue mission; he'd rather look after his own battered crew, and in fact he's on the verge of chucking the whole starship thing in for good. That's Christopher Pike's initial defining note. The sort of fans who freaked out about Picard actually surrendering when faced with impossible odds in *Encounter at Farpoint* would never have coped with Captain Pike as their hero.

Note how both subsequent portrayals of Pike downplay this aspect: *The Menagerie* has Pike crippled in a bold and selfless act of heroism, and the recent movies make him an unflagging moral authority. This makes us look at Pike's doubts in *The Cage* as a one-off Gethsemane moment, like Sisko's overt inner turmoil largely being resolved by the end of *Emissary*... But what if it wasn't? What if Roddenberry's "Hornblower in Space" would have continued to incorporate more of the original Hornblower's temperament: introverted behind a strong exterior, relentlessly self-critical, incredibly effective when in action, but a guarded and unhappy human being when not?

That sounds more like the inner conflicts of the hero of a modern drama series — or even Ron Moore's *Battlestar Galactica* — than a 1964-era Western in space. But, astonishingly, this kind of complexity seems to have been on Roddenberry's mind from the beginning... As he described the captain in the original pitch document: "he is capable of action and decision which can verge on the heroic — and at the same time lives a continual battle with self-doubt and loneliness of command."

This would make Pike the last *Star Trek* captain who merely verged on the heroic. When Kirk was introduced, they rebuilt *Star Trek* as a show about an outright hero — and, after a few vestiges of self-doubt in *Where No Man Has Gone Before*, he would become much more a person who would need to be advised to doubt himself. His inner struggles would be confined to the loneliness of command, not to personal self-criticism.

The contrast really does highlight what William Shatner brought to *Star Trek*. Paradoxically, Kirk is both far more fun than Pike — the swashbuckling gleam in his eye, the easy camaraderie with his officers — and far more rigid in his sense of duty; while it's easy to picture DeForest Kelley in the Dr. Boyce role, bucking up his captain's spirits over a medicinal martini, it's impossible to picture Kirk as the captain he's talking to in that scene. First-season Kirk in particular would never unclench enough from his sense of responsibility to even consider ending his marriage to his ship.

The plot of *The Cage* is of course a dramatization of Pike's inner conflicts, in the sort of fantasy-as-personal-metaphor way we these days associate with *Buffy* or *Being Human*. It deconstructs each of his fantasies of returning to a settled life, showing them as hollow, lotus-eating attempts to turn his back on a fully engaged life in much the same way that the Talosians, with their inward-looking mental powers, have turned their back on the world outside. He has to conquer his own illusions in order to conquer theirs. (And, even if it's probably not what Roddenberry intended, it's reassuring to read Pike storming out of his Orion slave-girl wet-dream as Pike's revulsion at realizing that his subconscious desires turn out to boil down to a tacky rape fantasy about feral alien women who actually like being taken advantage of. That sort of self-realization would put anyone off their escapism.)

Pike does get plenty of chances to display his heroic fortitude in standing up against his captors. There's a rare complexity in these characters, particularly in Pike's relationship with sympathetic collaborator and Stockholm Sydnrome victim Vina, as well as the refreshing lack of pat moral judgment on her or the Talosians at the end. But, interestingly, it's Number One who makes the biggest grandstand play, in what would become the classic *Trek* "Man was not meant to live like this" mode, when she sets her phaser on overload and declares that death would be preferable. It's her action that inspires first Pike and then Vina to follow her lead.

And Spock? Usually Spock's emotiveness here is described as being out of character, but that's a character who hadn't been created yet; there's very little talk about who the Spock seen in *The Cage* actually is. Interestingly, for an emotional being, this Spock is still quite stolid and dutiful. Arguably, he's Lt. Bush to Pike's Hornblower: a perfect follower. (At this point, in Roddenberry's original pitch, the main character note on Spock is his quiet temperament and efficiency in coordinating the low-level running of the ship; "his primary weakness is an almost cat-like curiosity over anything the slightest [bit] 'alien'".) Most striking, though, is Spock's immediate reaction when Number One and Yeoman Colt are also taken prisoner. Rather than attempting a heroic rescue of the Captain and the women, he immediately concludes that they're hopelessly outmatched, takes the command chair and prepares to warp out and abandon them all! This is, if anything, more logically ruthless than Spock would ever be after they decided he was devoted to pure logic. (Again, this too is retconned out of Heroic *Trek*, which excised that entire sequence from *The Menagerie*... probably because it made nonsense out of *Menagerie*'s insistence on Spock's utter devotion to Pike.)

This is a *Star Trek* without the close-knit family feel of the series to come. Pike's *Enterprise* is a workplace, with Number One, Spock, Navigator José Tyler and J.M. Colt all dutiful professionals performing to the best of their abilities. It's hard to picture any of them in the equivalent of scenes like the ones of Uhura singing in the rec room, which come as soon as *Charlie X*. And yet, ironically, this is an *Enterprise* in which the lives of the crew weigh far more heavily; the only crew deaths occur offscreen, before the start of the story, and yet are still keenly felt. Contrast this with Kirk in *Where No Man Has Gone Before* and *The Man Trap* living with crew casualties higher than the ones that have led Pike to the brink of packing it in. This is a *Star Trek* where there's no such thing as a redshirt.

Or red in general, for the most part. It's a conspicuous absence from this *Enterprise*'s color scheme. No red highlights on bridge rails or turbolift doors; no sparkling red blinkenlights on consoles; brown uniforms rather than bold red ones; and similarly muted colors for the other divisions. The trademark magenta and cyan splashes on corridor walls and caves alike, the colored-gel planet skies — part of NBC's push to sell their full-color lineup — are not part of this original approach. The spectacular visuals of alien worlds are realistically lit, and even the iconic green Vina is darkly hued in contrast to the Crayola vividness of the later uniforms. The stylized, flamboyant, colorful world of Kirk *Trek* hasn't been painted in yet; we're left looking at stylish gunmetal, greyer nuances. The only time we'd see *Trek* look anywhere near this muted again would be in *The Motion Picture*.

If there's a word for the difference in approach, it's "introverted". Without Kirk's easy charm and hints of devil-may-care swagger drawing them out or McCoy's goading of Spock, these characters keep more to themselves; the adventuresome alien visuals are closer to life-size rather than larger-than-life. And that's what makes Pike and *The Cage* so interesting from the point of view of more interiorized modern drama. There's room in Jeffrey Hunter's style of playing (and Susan Oliver's as Vina) for subtext, not just externalized action. We know Leonard Nimoy's more than capable of that sort of work, even if he doesn't show much in this episode. Majel Barrett's Number One having a complex and conflicted inner life may be more of a stretch... but if subsequent scripts had built character dramas around the rest of the cast as determinedly as *The Cage* did around Pike, there was the potential for a very different sort of *Star Trek*.

There's so much else we now take for granted that cannot be assumed in Pike's series. This is a *Star Trek* without the Federation: it's explicitly an Earth ship, with a token Vulcanian. No Prime Directive, no Andorians-and-Tellarites-and-Rigelians-oh-my. It's a *Star Trek* without empires; no Klingons or Romulans — in a departure from the Hornblower template, there's nothing on the map out there but dragons. (Perhaps closer to the assumed terra nullius of the American frontier.) It's a *Star Trek* where emotionlessness logic is an attitude, a pose, adopted by Number One apparently out of personal taste, rather than a strict Vulcan discipline... an individual's character trait rather than an ideal to inspire fans or a running gag about alien nature for Kirk and McCoy to keep prodding at. And it's a *Star Trek* with no personal relationships yet intense enough to launch a generation of Kirk/Spock imaginings — unless you count Yeoman Colt's crush on Pike!

Ironically, on that point, the *Cage* template is closer to the *Trek* that Roddenberry would later enforce when he had absolute power over *Trek* — check out Pike's parting "Engage" at the end. In *TNG*, there's sometimes conflict within the regulars, as with Pike, but no conflict among the regulars; none of the entertaining Spock–McCoy bitchery. The potential for character-based storytelling may be greater, but this potential may well not have been realized. Based on what we got, the key difference between 1987 and 1964 is basically the difference between beige and grey.

In some ways *The Cage* is an even more radical vision than we got in the series, despite its lack of some of the "visionary" elements. It might not have become a television legend or the grandfather of all media fandom... but it would probably have been a stone-cold-brilliant science-fiction drama series. Not a Technicolor swashbuckling adventure across the stars but a science-fiction show with the complex greyness and believable solidity of professional life.

After many years writing Doctor Who *novels and audios and winning the odd Best SF Novel award in Australia, Jonathan Blum has recently put out the podcast SF radio-drama* The I Job *(featuring the monsters from his* Doctor Who *novel* Seeing I*), wrote and/or directed several short films and is preparing a web-series and crowd-funded low-budget feature. Check http://www.theijob.net for details!*

2. THE MAN TRAP
THE SALT VAMPIRE
COLLIN W. BUECHLER

Once upon a nighttime screaming, I clung to salt, deeply dreaming,
Over a show on Thursday night, of curious tales of space and more,
Space-placed heroes adventure beaming, boldly going where none before.
While I napped, barely sleeping, my teenage brothers did come a rapping,
Gently on my window tapping, at the window, not the door.
"'Tis the Salt Vampire," I did scream, "I can't take it anymore!"

My brother's teenage tasks were fleeting, their young brother ripe for teasing,
Pretending that fiends aplenty, in the bog living they adore.
Quietly teasing, lying, cheating, scheming, at my bedroom door,
Chased with vacuum hickey galore, they convinced me ever more.

I was screaming, mood fomenting, subject to their devious chore,
I, of course, was only four.

How distinctly I remember now: *The Man Trap*; *Star Trek*'s number one,
Crewmen on a simple task, now ghosts within the planet's hoar.
Nancy draining sodium chloride; — first Darnell and then some more.
One dead, two dead, who is next dead, on the *Enterprise*, oh so clean?
The creature made me sob and cry — cry for the lost crewman Green.
Mourned in poe...m forever more.

Crewmembers are laughing, playing, while the viewers seek the plot.
Uhura flirting with the Vulcan, smile and eyes that we adore.
Spock is cold, calm and critiquing, brushing off the girl's amore.
Monster now on *Enterprise*, hunts a salted booster-shot.
Rand is young and oh-so-pretty, hunted now from floor to floor.
Shift the ship to GQ4.

Rand pursued by saltless Green, through a crew who seem distracted,
This was thrilling, teasing, scaring, as I'd never felt before.
Green did chase what he was needing. (Is it somewhat overacted?)
Fleeing through the garden's moor past Sulu's magic door —
Plants a-plenty, grab at Rand and exploitation underscore.
All whilst Dad did sleep and snore.

At the time, this did excite me, as the creature went for the kill.
Kirk and Spock chased Nancy's husband, through the desert planet's stour.
My breathing brought unto a still; they crawl across the planet's floor.
Professor blasting, everlasting; lasting 'til he lasts no more.
Kirk is better, blasts him silly; silly like the allegore.
The plot is now... a dreadful bore!

Kirk now blocking creature's stalking; we were enthralled, popcorn-munching.
Kirk near death 'til Spock's arriving, bursting through the chamber's door,
One fist, two fist, Nancy punching, brutality that rocked our core.
Nancy smiling, gruesome, creepy, knocking Spock upon the floor —
Back to Jim, her lips are puckered, it's now clear what is in store:
Kirk's now a salt-candy store!

And now Doctor McCoy is waking, waking from a fog-like haze,
Begging, pleading, 'I can't do this'; Salty drains the Captain more.

Bones does pause, his mind in a daze. Our interest piqued over dad's loud snore.
Doctor shooting, emotions fleeting, shoots his lover, feelings frore.
The creature forever done for, its head now destined for decor.
Screams the creature, never more!

Monster dead and crew retreating from M-113's ocher,
Older now, I watch it strangely, poorly paced in salty gore.
Will the older viewer ever watch this tale mediocre,
Is there choice? The show's repeating, repeating, repeating ever more.
Is it good? Just barely passing, but this tale I still adore.
Quoth the reviewer, "Give it Four!"

*Father, husband, Minnesotan, jackanapes and author are all words used
at least once to describe Collin W. Buechler; they are listed in no particular order.*

3. CHARLIE X
LA FEMME SANS VISAGE
COLIN WILSON

When I was nine years old, I asked my parents to get me some videos of the original *Star Trek*, which I'd heard about but never seen. They duly obliged with three or four tapes chosen at random, and among their number was a tape marked "*Charlie X/Balance of Terror*". So it was that *Charlie X* was among the first *Star Trek* episodes I ever saw. Since that time, I've seen pretty much every episode of every series and I've found that *Trek* is clever, funny, thoughtful and exciting, but rarely genuinely frightening. *Charlie X* scared me when I was nine, and it scares me now.

There are many disturbing moments during the course of the episode, but one image really got under my skin. As Charlie rampages through the ship, he passes a room full of laughing crewmembers. When he uses his powers, they fall silent, though we are not shown exactly what has happened. After he leaves, the camera lingers on the doorway and a woman leans out showing that she no longer has a face: just pale, blank skin. It's a horrific image representing both psychological and physical trauma, and I've never quite been able to shake it off. I find myself wondering whether she could breathe and how long she stayed like that before the Thasians undid Charlie's actions. Did she remember it? What must that have been like?

There's something about the concept of an unhinged teenager with God-like powers that is naturally pretty frightening. It's a standard sci-fi trope and has been done in a variety of formats but rarely as well as in *Charlie X*. This is not because Robert Walker's Charlie is a particularly disturbing child psycho, but because he has an air of bewildered humanity, so you can identify with him even as he becomes more dangerous. He deftly catches the gut-wrenchingly awful sensation of being a gawky teenager surrounded by attractive and capable people and translates that into his expressions and manner throughout the episode. This combination of sympathy and psychosis puts the watcher into a state of extreme ambivalence, only adding to the discomfort. His performance is also heightened by the directorial approach; in almost every close-up of an individual, their face is in shadow and their eyes are lit. This looks odd on most of the crew but brilliantly highlights Charlie's disturbing blue stare. I watched the whole episode, and I didn't see him blink once. His final moments, when he is taken away by the aliens who gave him his powers, are genuinely upsetting; Charlie deserves a normal life, even though he's plainly unable to have one.

The other performance that lifts the episode beyond the ordinary is provided by Grace Lee Whitney as Janice Rand. It's odd to think now that, when the program was first conceived, the three main characters were intended to be Kirk, Spock and Rand; McCoy's role seems to have grown with the telling. In the end, Rand only appeared in eight *TOS* episodes, but in the early part of Season One she is an essential part of the crew, often taking a larger role than Uhura. *Charlie X* is one of her finest episodes: as the object of Charlie's affections, she does a superb job of portraying an older woman embarrassed by a young man's attentions but also not wanting to hurt his feelings. Her shift from flattered, through annoyed and into frightened is excellent, and her sympathy for Charlie at the end represents real humanity of character.

The episode also highlights Kirk's relationships with those around him. It's little remembered that during the first season Kirk is very far from the womanizer he later becomes. For most of the episodes, Kirk's relationship is with the *Enterprise* first and women a distant second, so that, when he falls in love in *The City on the Edge of Forever*, it's genuinely surprising. This doesn't last, and, over the following seasons, Kirk becomes a victim of that strange character drift known in some corners of the internet as Flanderization. This is a shame, as it means that Kirk has gained an unfair reputation as a man who would chase some skirt then save his ship, rather than the other way round. It's not how the character started and, in many ways, not how it ended either, but the reputation persists.

In Charlie's case, Kirk genuinely cares for the boy's well-being. He provides the only father figure Charlie has ever known and, even after Charlie's abilities become clear, maintains a level of control through the rapport the two have built up. Even at the end, Kirk finds himself unable to let the Thasians take Charlie without objecting.

As for Rand, her relationship with Kirk is subtle but present both in script and performance. Whitney and Shatner neatly demonstrate their mutual attraction alongside the knowledge that nothing can happen, given their respective positions.

And then, in just a few episodes from now, Rand disappears, without even a short goodbye. These days, the producers of a show would cut off their own feet before sacrificing such a productive storyline generator. One need only look at later *Trek* shows to see how much can be done with an unrequited relationship. But, back in the sixties, the network wanted Kirk to have more women, so Whitney "transferred to another ship" (as Gene Coon would later tell writer David Gerrold).

Her departure (discussed elsewhere in this book) was a loss to the series. It failed to make best use of a very good actress, capable of holding her own even against Walker (an actor so dedicated he refused to socialize with the cast so the resulting sense of isolation would carry into his performance). It reduced the show's leading female cohort to two, one of whom was mostly a cipher, and it gave Kirk no female confidant, critically changing the gender relations amongst the characters. Rewatching these early episodes, it seems strange to think that Rand was destined to have such a short tenure. But go she did, without the slightest warning: vanishing as surely as if Charlie had made her disappear. Rendered invisible. Faceless.

Colin Wilson has eyes that are very, very blue.

4. WHERE NO MAN HAS GONE BEFORE
LT. KELSO, NAVIGATOR ON THE STARSHIP ENTERPRISE, DEAD AT 31
LILY MITCHELL

Lieutenant Lee Kelso passed away while on duty on star date 1313.3. He was stationed on the starship *Enterprise* under the command of Captain James R. Kirk. Lee Kelso served as a navigator aboard the ship. He was 31.

His death was confirmed by Dr. Mark Piper, in his last official duty before leaving the *Enterprise*.

Lee Kelso loved flying kites. When he was young, he spent all his free time designing and flying them. His mother, Phyllis Kelso, has fond memories of his childhood passion. "Lee was always running out the door with a new kite," she said, dabbing at her eyes. "I would look out the window and see them flying above the meadow," she remarked, in between sobs. Lee Kelso continued flying kites throughout his Starfleet career. He would take time to fly them on any planet that he could.

The only obstacle to his passion was his irrational fear of polka dots. Lee Kelso's phobia limited his kite choices and led him to design his own; it also led to a prank by fellow shipmates. When other men on his floor of the *Enterprise* found out about Lee Kelso's fear, they snuck into his room and painted polka dots on his walls as he slept. Upon waking up and seeing the polka dots, Lee Kelso ran from his quarters, found a beige wall and refused to look at anything else for three days. When told of this incident, Phyllis Kelso wailed uncontrollably.

Lee Kelso also liked chess. He had not been playing long before he died. He had seen Captain Kirk and Mr. Spock playing one day and decided to try it. After a month of practice on his own, he challenged the captain to a game. After the match, Captain Kirk said Lee Kelso played "a far less irritating game of chess than Mr. Spock".

At the time of his death, Lee Kelso was part of a landing party on Delta Vega. He was working to find power packs from the lithium-cracking station that could be used to regenerate the engines of the *Enterprise*. Kelso's coworker Montgomery Scott described him as "a

talented thief" for his work salvaging parts for the ship. Anthony Devaney, a lawyer representing Mrs. Kelso, has questioned whether adequate security measures were in place at the time of this incident and has named Mr. Scott in a lawsuit alleging improper behavior on the part of the command staff.

Lee Kelso died in the control room on Delta Vega. His friend Gary Mitchell, whom Kelso referred to as "Mitch", tragically throttled him via telekinesis. Anthony Devaney says that, despite appearances, this incident does not fall under the "act of God" clause in the *Enterprise*'s insurance policy and is currently pursuing reparations for damages to Phyllis Kelso's emotional state. Lee Kelso's last words were "I'm kind of proud of the job we've done."

Lee Kelso was not a redshirt.

Lily Mitchell is a small woman with a big personality and a passion for the arts.

5. THE NAKED TIME
OH MYYYYYYYY
KRISTINE LARSEN

As a fan of the original *Star Trek* series, there are a number of iconic images from the series that are forever etched in my mind. These include Kirk immersed up to his chest in a pile of adorable, fluffy Tribbles; Spock flashing his "live long and prosper" hand gesture; and McCoy, freshly returned from the dead, with a scantily clad Rigelian cabaret girl on each arm and a cat-that-ate-the-canary grin. But one in particular seemed so egregiously out of character at the time that it is more correct to say that I felt it was forever burned onto my retinas. In the Season 1 episode *The Naked Time*, mild-mannered helmsman Sulu literally gets, well, naked. All right, only partially. A minor technicality.

In the unlikely event that you have forgotten, after being infected with an alien virus that makes you act "not quite yourself" (euphemistically put), a sweaty, shirtless Sulu menaces his fellow bridge mates with a rapier, in a delusional attempt to save the "fair maiden" Uhura from the evil Cardinal Richelieu (Kirk). Now, you must understand that, as an impressionable 14-year-old Trekkie devouring *Star Trek* reruns as quickly as they were rebroadcast (sometimes two and three a day), I had become quite accustomed to seeing sweaty bare chests — specifically Kirk's. Indeed, it seems that Shatner conveniently suffered wardrobe malfunctions on a regular basis. Not that I ever complained, mind you. But Sulu? Somehow that was like seeing your brother naked. Sulu wasn't a sex symbol, despite the fact that George Takei proved to the world that he had a physique that was better suited to shirtless scenes than some of his co-stars. No, Sulu was mild-mannered, reliable, level-headed, loyal. He was a gentleman to Kirk's cad. It was too incongruous an image. It gave me brain pain. Once seen, it could never be unseen, no matter the amount of mind wash applied. But that was the basic brilliance of it, set within an episode where nothing the characters did was supposed to be "sensible". A similar incongruity was used, just as effectively in my view, a season later in *Mirror, Mirror*, where the anti-Sulu sexually harasses and nearly assaults the real Uhura. In some ways, it's Sulu's utterly impossible behavior that cements the fact that we're not in Kansas anymore.

Fast forward several decades, and, when viewed under an older, more experienced microscope, the utter genius of the scene (and George Takei's key role in it) snap more sharply into focus. Putting aside the now-obvious Freudian interpretation of the scene (something my 14-year-old mind missed completely), a number of subsequent real-life revelations make the image of Sword-wielding Sweaty Shirtless Sulu (SSSS) that much more ironic and iconic. First, as Takei explained in his 1994 autobiography, not only is *The Naked Time* his favorite episode, but he insisted on an important change in the original script from brandishing a more traditional (stereotypical) Japanese samurai sword to a fencing foil. However, Takei told a teensy weensy lie to the writer when he bragged that fencing was a favorite hobby: he had actually never fenced before in his life! The surreptitious crash lessons obviously paid off, but you have to admire the chutzpah of the man. But, as we all learned in 2005, Takei had many more ballsy statements up his sleeve. In the years after coming out as a proud gay man, Takei took the internet by storm, with millions of Facebook followers hanging on his every post. Most of them are hilarious, many are self-deprecating, and a few are dead serious (especially when it comes to LGBTQ rights).

A large percentage of Takei's Facebook posts include memes that have been submitted by fans. The Urban Dictionary includes among its definitions for meme "a pervasive thought or thought pattern that replicates itself via cultural means; a parasitic code, a virus of the mind especially contagious to children and the impressionable." In particular, internet memes are "Popular quotes, images, and real people, which are copied, imitated, and spread all over the internet(s)." If one does a search for "*Star Trek* Meme" one of the most common results for the original series is none other than, yes, you guessed it, SSSS! A virus of the mind indeed.

But what makes a true meme is not simply a still image but a caption that either points out the obvious irony of the image or twists your mind to see the image in a new (sometimes completely inappropriate) way. Among the captions found on SSSS memes include "Your pants repulse me. Remove them!", "Fencing is Fabulous", "Don't ask, don't tell. Not working in Starfleet", "Yep, Zorro's my bitch" and "My name is George Takei. You killed the legality of my same-sex marriage. Prepare to die!!!!". Not only do sexual references dominate (pun very much intended) but references to Takei's sexuality are common. It is refreshing to note, however, that these references are, in large part, positive, referring to Takei's role as one of the most vocal, well-known and beloved advocates for LGBTQ rights — for *human* rights — in our world today. If it seems as though George Takei is everywhere online these days, it's because he is. He not only posts memes, he has become one in his own right. In a world where 70 is the new 50 and funny is the new sexy, George Takei has definitely earned the badge of sex symbol. As they say, the most important sex organ is between your ears (whether they are pointed or not).

The Naked Time aside, Lt. Sulu was the sedate, steady-handed helmsman of the USS *Enterprise*. In our alternate universe, his doppelganger George Takei has plotted a bawdy, mind-blowing course at warp ten through cyberspace, and we are all the better for electing to boldly follow him where no one (in the name of good taste) has dared to go before. To borrow Takei's trademark phrase, oh myyyyyyyy! Now please excuse me while I go watch me some Sexy Sword-wielding Sweaty Shirtless Sulu.

Kristine Larsen splits her time between several alternate universes where she is an astronomy professor at Central Connecticut State University, pet rabbit wrangler and zombie devotee.

6. THE ENEMY WITHIN
NOW YOU KNOW THE INDIGNITY OF BEING A WOMAN
KATE ORMAN

Grace Lee Whitney's autobiography opens with a horrific account of her rape by a Desilu executive. Her assailant (left unnamed) undergoes a "Jekyll-to-Hyde transformation" from flirtatious to furious. "He had the power to destroy my career and we both knew it ... I never would have imagined he was capable of such a thing, even drunk. How could I know what else he might be capable of? ... The only thing that mattered was getting out of that room alive."

There are gut-wrenching parallels between this real-life assault and the attempted rape of Whitney's character, Yeoman Janice Rand, in *The Enemy Within*. A malfunctioning transporter spits out two versions of Kirk, one saintly but indecisive, one bestial and impulsive. The latter waits in Rand's quarters to catch her alone, then uses surprise and his rank to confuse his victim just long enough to pounce.

Both the real and the fictional woman faced an intoxicated man who held their career in his hands. Both were taken by surprise when they were alone. Whitney was trapped in a locked room in an empty building, with no chance of escape. Thankfully, Yeoman Rand is able to fight off the half-Kirk and summon help.

The attempted rape is a brutal scene, shot unsparingly; you feel the alarm, the panic and the bruises — but Rand is the victor, her attacker a marked fugitive. Far harder to watch is the following scene in which the other half-Kirk interrogates a weeping Rand. It turns her successful resistance into miserable defeat, as though she is the criminal who has been caught. She sits; he stands over her. She cringes and squirms, barely able to look at him, almost pleading for forgiveness: "I don't want to get you into trouble. I wouldn't even have *mentioned* it!" (She doesn't ask the passing Fisher to summon security, but screams, "Call Mister Spock!")

Is this reluctance to report due to loyalty, love, embarrassment — or because Rand is only a lowly Yeoman? "He kissed me, and he said that we, that he was the captain, and that he could order me... I didn't know what to do. When you mentioned the feelings we'd been hiding, and you started talking about 'us'." When Kirk queries her use of "us", Rand replies, "Well, he *is* the captain, I couldn't just..." (The ellipses aren't my edits — they're in the dialogue.) It seems clear that had Rand's assailant not been so carelessly, immediately violent, she would have complied with his advances, unable to tell her commanding officer to "go chase an asteroid", as she suggests to Green in *The Man Trap*.

The would-be rapist, though hasty, is rational and cunning, and he retains the knowledge of the complete Kirk, including the inner workings of Starfleet. He knows — he is *relying* on this knowledge — that, thanks to his rank and the inherent power imbalances in such an organization, a Starfleet captain can fuck anyone he chooses, whether they like it or not, and he will probably get away with it. When, later, the "impostor" tells her "I owe you an explanation", she brushes it aside, like a faux pas best forgotten. But he insists: "You don't mind if I come to your cabin later?" "No, sir." There's nothing else Janice can say. But from her face, we can guess her thoughts. She knows it's going to happen again.

Every *Trek* needs its tee-hee in the tag scene: "The impostor had some *interesting* qualities, wouldn't you say, Yeoman?" Of all people, it's astonishing to hear Mr. Spock suggest that women secretly want to be dominated and overpowered — a convenient myth, if you enjoy dominating and overpowering them. But this, too, is a *Star Trek* staple. Think of Yeoman Barrows in *Shore Leave*, whose daydream of Don Juan conjures up a bodice-ripping robot version; or Lieutenant McGivers, whose desire is inflamed by Khan's domination.

Of course, even when women do fantasize about force, their imaginary rapist is 100% under their control. There's no way to know what a real-life rapist might do to you, up to and including murder. If Janice has dreamed of Kirk ravishing her, her illusions are shattered, much as Barrows' must have been on the *Shore Leave* planet.

But, for the most part, the myth is simply a convenient way for men to brush aside an inconvenient "no". When Charlie X was smitten with Janice, Captain Kirk lectured the boy: "It isn't a one-way street, you know — how you feel, and that's all. It's how the girl feels too ... There are a million things in this universe you can have, and there are a million things you can't have. It's no fun facing that, but that's the way things are." The whole-Kirk's mature understanding contrasts both with Charlie's childish confusion and the half-Kirk's solipsistic sense of entitlement.

Star Trek has a squeamish tendency to... trail off... when talking about... That's partly why the attack on Janice is never really properly digested. On the bridge, she tries to stammer something out — perhaps some apology or reassurance — but Kirk cuts her off with a "Thank you, Yeoman." (In response to Spock's taunt, she merely gives him a "wise guy" look.) However Rand feels about it, we can speculate that her disappearance from the *Enterprise* is the result of this episode's events.

For Grace Lee Whitney, there was — eventually — something of a happy ending. Long assuming that she had been fired from the show as a consequence of the rape, she learned after many years that in fact the decision had already been made to write Rand out — lest the captain look as though he was cheating on his main love interest as he fell for the space girl of the week. For Whitney, the relief this brought was a turning point in her life, and meant her return to the franchise.

Star Trek's utopian future has always been undercut, not just by a timid network and conservative viewers but by its own makers' failure of imagination. In the first stories of the original show, we see an optimistic future in which the fears of the US in the late sixties — racial tensions and the bomb — have been overcome. But women aren't full citizens of this promised land. While we see women in military and science careers (and Uhura at the helm of the *Enterprise* itself on more than one occasion), they are excluded from security work and from command positions. Their uniforms betray the main reason for their inclusion in the show. When Kirk is showing off the *Enterprise* to Christopher in *Tomorrow is Yesterday*, the twentieth-century pilot is surprised: "A woman?" Kirk answers, matter-of-factly, "Crewman." In case this is too futuristic for the viewer, a trumpet plays a few sexy phrases to remind us why she's really there.

It's hardly a surprise, then, that its first season is peppered with woeful sleaze.

We have Andrea the sexbot in *What Are Little Girls Made Of?* (the answer, apparently, is latex), comedy human trafficking in *Mudd's Women* and the forced prostitutes traded by the Orions (who, Captain Pike is assured in *The Cage*, "actually like being taken advantage of").

Out of all these, for me, the interrogation of Yeoman Janice Rand is the lowest point: the Starfleet system turning a victor into a victim. We can only be grateful that it's so gentle compared with our own century, in which US Navy women who report sexual assault can be subject to a lengthy, hostile grilling (as well as demotion and other retaliation). No one calls Rand a liar or a slut. In 2012, the National Journal reported that only 14% of sexual assault victims in the US military report the crime. The title of their story was... The Enemy Within.

Kate Orman lives in Sydney, Australia, with her husband and co-writer, Jonathan Blum. Best known for her Doctor Who–*related novels, she has also published short fiction and non-fiction and is working on a science-fiction novel.*

7. MUDD'S WOMEN
THE REAL HOUSEWIVES OF RIGEL XII
SAMUEL GIBB

Mudd's Women, like so much of *Star Trek* season one, is a sexist story. There, I said it. It's easy to see and difficult to ignore. Even if you take into account when it was made, in that distant, unknowable era that was the sixties, it's still pretty bad. You can't even describe the episode without shuddering, wincing or feeling a bit sleazy, but here goes.

This is the one where three beautiful women (by the casting director's standards) must regularly take the mysterious Venus drug to maintain their subjectively breathtaking appearance; otherwise the make-up artist will draw some wrinkles on them and mess up their hair a little. These women encounter the crew of the *Enterprise* when they are being taken to find potential husbands by a man named Harry Mudd, and most of the male crewmen start drooling over them and lose the ability to do basically anything useful at all. Which isn't ideal; the women need the men's cooperation to help them reach the planet below and marry the miners there, who will allow them to cook and clean for them because of their beauty, in exchange for some crystals to fix the ship.

Do you feel suitably uneasy reading that? I do, writing it. There's no denying it: this episode is simultaneously a sex/gender theorist's nightmare and all their

Christmases come at once. There's so much to say about this story, but the crux of my analysis is this:

Mudd's Women presents an overwhelmingly negative view of the male sex.

Yeah, you read that right: of the MEN. What, you thought I was going to jump on the bandwagon and criticize the strong, powerful, capable female characters in the story? Bemoan the ahead-of-its-time characterization of three women who have examined the established patriarchy of the sixties *Star Trek* universe, decided how best to deal with the galaxy-wide misogyny and discovered a pill that can make them gain more power over the opposite sex and allow them to achieve their goals? Why would I say that?

What this episode manages to do, in a way that wouldn't have drawn too much attention to its message at the time but still would've been noticed and assimilated by the viewers, is to establish and then deconstruct the flawed patriarchy on board the *Enterprise* that's indicative of the wider universe beyond.

When strangely loveable and inexplicably sympathetic drug dealer and sex trafficker Harry Mudd introduces Eve, Magda and Ruth as his "cargo", the women's position is immediately established. Or so we might think. But, as the crew of the *Enterprise* gaze gormlessly upon the women's beauty and radiance, we can begin to question who really has the power in this situation, beneath the surface of the scene.

While the comparison to cargo (to a commodity to be sold or exchanged without any real care or concern) is not ideal from a feminist perspective, the women have been enabled by a drug — created, one suspects, by males both in-universe and outside, from a TV production standpoint — to become valuable, to take their lives in their own hands and achieve their goals while the men are powerless to hold them back even if, for some reason, they might want to.

The Venus drug, we are told, only enhances what is already there in the women: a drive to succeed, as enabled by their physical appearance that renders the men dumbstruck. Eve and the other women are not naïve and unaware of their sexuality; they are able to use it to get what they want. They have recognized the patriarchy and, though they may not like it (naturally), they have learned how to deal with it to reach a position within the society that they are more comfortable with.

Now this position they are aiming to reach, as wives to husbands, may also be criticized as supposedly strong and independent characters go on to assume what it quickly labeled a subservient role. But marriage is a perfectly viable desire. For a large percentage of people in our universe, marriage is a life goal. Why should it be any different in the future presented in *Star Trek*? The women in the story want to get married. The only sexist part of that is the viewers and critics wanting to deny them their wish.

Furthermore, Eve is not willing to be married off to just anyone: she is horrified at the thought of being assigned a husband by "raffle" or a brutish fight. She is equally unhappy to accept potential husband Childress' "male ego" misogyny and, after being on mining world Rigel XII for only a few hours, immediately uncovers a way for the miners to live more efficiently. The female characters are looking to actively engage with the male-dominated universe, to find ways for it to function more effectively. Marriage, as well as being something they desire, enables this other goal by getting them into a position where they can work alongside the men to make the universe better.

The women don't want to be married simply for the sake of being able to say that they are married nor, as far as I can see, because that's what they've been told they have to do. Rather, they are manipulating and exploiting the oppressive patriarchy (most directly, via Mudd) in order to navigate themselves into a position alongside the men, whereby they can assist in ensuring the universe continues to function as they feel it should. Perhaps, then, marriage is not even the ultimate goal but is one step along the path to achieving the gender equality they desire: a necessary evil, a patriarchal ring they must jump through (and wear) to reach their desired future.

So, by this point in the discussion, you've probably made your mind up as to whether you agree or not — and, most likely, you don't. Frankly, I'm as skeptical as you are on some counts. But if you don't trust my perspective on the episode, whose would you trust? Would you listen to the *Enterprise*? Because Kirk trusts his ship implicitly, and so does the rest of the crew. When they need to cross-examine Mudd and his women, the *Enterprise* analyses their answers and reports back to Kirk and the other officers in an authoritative, *female* voice that is respected and trusted. The *Enterprise* is a microcosm of society — of the specific society that Eve and the other women want to marry into, where the female works alongside the male to ensure success and happiness, just like Kirk and his ship.

Linking with this, we could also look at the other significant part of the story involving the *Enterprise*. After rescuing the women, the ship (she, of course, and you don't need me to waste time stressing the importance of that) suffers mechanical failures and won't be able to move far until the crew obtain the necessary crystals. Let's look at this closer: the women are being held by the crew who aren't willing to let them continue on their quest for husbands, and that is when the *Enterprise* breaks down. The (predominantly male) crew of the ship need their personified female ship in order to continue with their lives. Kirk could not function without the *Enterprise*: she enables him and all the men on board. Therefore (if you squint a bit and go with me down this mad old road for a minute) the *Enterprise* can be seen as an icon of female-empowerment.

There's no trick here though. No deceit. The female characters have endeavoured to learn how to be a match for the men, not through something so superficial as looks that makes the males inept and useless but through intelligence, strength of character, wisdom and loads of other good stuff. They've identified the conventions of the sixties-shaped future they live in and worked out a way to boldly go beyond it, pioneers of a future founded not on physically beauty and lust and superficial nonsense but on sex and gender equality.

So, with this reading, the main image of the whole series of *Star Trek* is a feminist one. Imagine that! Oh, I bet there are some fans weeping and foaming at the mouth now! I suppose I'd better wrap this all up before the angry mob comes for me.

When Eve, Magda and Ruth are held back from finding husbands as they desire, the ship ceases to function, as if, through some philosophical connection, the *Enterprise* itself wants to reinforce to her crew that the women must be enabled in order to enable the men. And so, when the women are finally allowed to marry the miners and reach the position in society that they desired all along, functionality is restored to the *Enterprise* as a little more balance is restored to the universe.

Samuel Gibb is a sci-fi and fantasy fan and writer from Hampshire in the United Kingdom, who is delighted to have finally found an outlet to annoy more people than ever with his opinions on TV, film and popular culture.

8. WHAT ARE LITTLE GIRLS MADE OF?
JOINING THE DOTS
ALAN STEVENS

Robert Bloch is well-known for his SF, fantasy and horror work, which comes to the fore very much in the three episodes he wrote for *Star Trek*. However, Bloch was also a mystery writer, who often works devious subtexts into his stories without ever letting the casual viewer know what he's up to. A case in point is *What Are Little Girls Made Of?*, ostensibly a story about humanity and artificial intelligence, but actually, underneath it all, a rather chilling tale about prejudice and its implications for the future.

This is clearly shown in Kirk and Chapel's reaction to Korby's plan. Dr. Roger Korby — who has used the technology of the former inhabitants of the planet, the "Old Ones", to transform himself and two of his crewmembers into androids physically indistinguishable from humans — intends the *Enterprise* to transport him to a colony planet, which has readily available raw materials. There Korby will produce android duplicates of various individuals, programmed to obey him, who will then be infiltrated back into broader society in the hope that their long-term presence will belay any adverse reaction from the general populace once the existence of the androids is finally revealed. This is a naïve strategy at best, but, rather than acknowledging it as the desire of an intelligent being to be re-accepted into the society which has shut him out or at the very least showing some sympathy for Korby's plight, Kirk's open hostility demonstrates clearly what reaction Korby's scheme would receive. Even Christine Chapel, Korby's former fiancée, who loved him enough to seek him out despite the fact that his mission had been lost for five years, brutally rejects him. Tolerance may be the watchword in the multi-ethnic, multi-species Federation, but sympathy for androids is a step too far.

This prejudice is also explored more subtly in Korby's own self-loathing. Korby's conversion into an android followed a life-threatening accident; it is not his fault, and he is, mentally, the same man as he was before his conversion. However, his belief that androids are logic-driven, inhuman monsters inspires his treatment of the android duplicates of his crewmembers, Andrea and Doctor Brown. Korby implies that they were androids built from scratch, but the apparatus Korby uses to create Kirk's doppelgänger paints a different picture and suggests that Andrea and Brown were turned into androids against their will. Furthermore, unlike Korby's own conversion, where his entire mental pattern was transposed intact, Brown and Andrea's minds are only partially transferred, turning the former into an automaton and the latter into a sex doll. Clearly, once the androids had been created, the human originals would have been destroyed. Five years later, Korby's entire argument, when endeavoring to convince Chapel and Kirk of his own humanity, is to try to demonstrate how different he himself is to Andrea and Brown. Ironically, Korby's suicide comes about when Andrea confesses her love for him: if an android can feel genuine emotion, then to have blinded himself to that possibility means Korby himself has become the ruthless, compassionless machine he so despises. In showing Korby's despair and death, Bloch thus lays out how Korby's own internalized beliefs about androids cause him, once he has been converted, to act according to those patterns he associates with artificial life.

Bloch takes this a step further, however, and, without ever making it explicit, shows where this prejudice leads. We are never told directly what happened to the Old Ones; Korby, whose internalized beliefs about androids lead him to assume that Ruk, the sole survivor, is a coldly logical machine, fails to see the signs of emotion the character displays and so fails to question why is it that Ruk is the only android that still exists within the subterranean depths of Exo III. However, when Kirk questions Ruk about what happened to the previous civilization, we learn a little more, but with some interesting gaps in Ruk's answer. Ruk tells Kirk that the Old Ones became "fearful" and began to turn the androids off. As a result, the androids determined that it would be necessary to destroy the Old Ones in order to survive, and to do that they had to break their programming. Ruk frames this as a logical argument, that the androids had no other choice. However, the fact that only one of them endures to the present day indicates that the fear-driven conflict did not stop there. We know that androids are capable of individual change and development, so, therefore, once the Old Ones were dead, the androids clearly turned on each other, until, in the end, only Ruk survived. He's a cunning, murderous psychopath, dangerous to all around him, but the threat he represents is unrecognized by the humans, who do not question his presence, because he is "only" a machine.

To further see what Bloch is doing, we also need to take a step back and recognize that he is taking as his basis both the pilot episode *The Cage* and *Forbidden Planet*, the film that inspired *Star Trek*. All three stories involve a starship travelling to a distant world to uncover the fate of a lost expedition, and all three involve the remnants of an advanced civilization that, through some catastrophe, has either died out or is on the point of extinction; these events are played out in the present with the implication that the human race may, in turn, follow that same path of destruction. The message is plain for an audience in the depths of the Cold War and divided by the struggle for civil rights: shape up, or this could happen to us.

However, Bloch's script deviates from its predecessors in one vital respect. Whereas Commander Adams of the United Planets Cruiser *C57-D* and Captain Pike of the USS *Enterprise* learn a significant moral lesson from their escapades, which bodes well for future human survival, Captain Kirk, on this occasion, fails to learn anything. To him, Doctor Korby was a mad robot pretending to be human, and that's it; he fails to recognize Korby's humanity, the complex psychological workings that inform his treatment of himself, Ruk, Brown and Andrea, and the prejudice against artificial intelligence at work in the Federation. Bloch's view of the future is thus pessimistic: that humanity, however tolerant it may seem on the surface, will ultimately succumb to prejudice and, like the Old Ones, destroy itself.

Kirk's blunt assertion at the end of the story that "Doctor Korby was never here" suggests that what happened to the Old Ones and repeated itself again with Korby's expedition, will, sometime in humanity's future, take place on a galactic scale. While Bloch never spells this out in the script, the message is plain for those who want to hear it. Unless the Federation, like Bloch's own society of mid-1960s America, can recognize and confront its internalized prejudices, then it is doomed.

Alan Stevens is not a robot.

9. MIRI
NEVER DATE IMMORTAL GIRLS
ZOE ESTRIN-GRELE

This episode is terrifying.

If you look at it on the surface, it's about kids being tormented by the inevitable future where puberty will turn them into monsters (and man, if you think that's not fraught with metaphor, you're not watching this episode closely enough). But it's not the post-puberty monsters that are scary here, it's the kids. *Miri* is basically all the metaphysical angst of *The Catcher in the Rye* with the plot and characterization of *The Lord of the Flies*, and it's some dark stuff.

The plot is simple enough. The *Enterprise* arrives on a planet that is a copy of Earth (which never comes up again, don't worry about it), where all the adults have been killed off by a horrible virus — one originally meant to extend their lifespan — that turns them into mindless plague beasts bent on killing, leaving the planet inhabited only by nigh-immortal children. Okay, great, so this episode is going to be about how the kids are scared of puberty and the landing party is going to have to cure the disease before they get it. Well, yes, it is about that. But the enemy-of-the-week isn't the adults. It's the kids. The adults don't live long enough to do any real damage, while the pack of 300-year-old wild children decides to bash Kirk's skull in because, hey, it seems like a great idea.

Okay, don't get me wrong, the idea of having the kids as the antagonists is great, but I find them way scarier than other *Trek* villains. It's one thing to look at a weekly alien antagonist and go, "Yeah, okay, I get how a lizard man/Klingon/weird alien race could be scary" and another to see this pack of pre-pubescent children deciding to kill a grown man. It's something that's real, something I see everyday — children in general, not feral packs of them trying to kill space explorers — and that makes every little dark moment even worse.

It doesn't help that there's a scene where a tiny blonde child stands on a desk and watches Kirk get beaten up with this look of savage joy, and it's just uncomfortable. What makes this specific moment even more uncomfortable is that, at the end, after Kirk civilizes them with his magic starship captain words — I'm not even going to touch this because it's just how *Star Trek* episodes end sometimes — there's a shot of him holding that same little blonde murder child casually on his hip as he races onto the *Enterprise*. Because apparently he's forgotten that the kid is probably a serial killer. A 300-year-old serial killer in the body of a five-year-old. And if that's not the scariest thing you can think of, you have a much better imagination than I do.

The episode's titular character is also an interesting case. Miri appears to be 12, is specifically stated to be just barely pre-pubescent (this is important for later) and acts as the character with the most to lose, as she's starting to be affected by the disease and soon will basically have to be put down by her fellow kids before she kills them all. She's scared and full of hormones and confused, and you know what Kirk does? *He flirts with her.* Yup, this week's alien-girl is pre-pubescent. And that's super uncomfortable. I mean, yeah, I get that Kirk has some fundamental issue understanding women without being suggestive at them, but, seriously dude, can we keep the super-super jailbait ones just totally off the table?

And this isn't a passing thing that can be written off. It's a major part of the plot, because Miri is jealous of Yeoman Rand's advances on Kirk (yeah, that happens) and basically decides it's time to kill them all because she's got the mind of a 12 year old and her first crush is Captain Kirk, which is never a good choice at any time in one's life. But because these are immortal serial-killer children, she's going to murder him. It's like that middle-school thing where the boy doesn't like the girl and the girl gets all upset and says she's going to kill him, except in this case she can and will actually do it. And Kirk brought this on himself, I swear. Good going.

Poor Miri is the perfect storm of everything awful that can happen to a 12-year-old girl. She's scared and alone, since, as one of the oldest kids, she has a lot of responsibility as a leader and provider and strange maternal figure; she knows she's going to die soon; and her former friends have turned into monsters and keep trying to kill her. This is the vision of an immortal childhood that we're given in this episode, and it's absolutely terrifying.

There is no innocence in the childhood of *Miri*. There is only fear and death and the promise of becoming something awful. It's not an Eden-like situation for these kids. It's just the way life is, and that life is short and hard, and all they have is each other. And their leaders are about thirteen. It's awful, and, even though they're immortal children, there's no hope to them. Just murder. And being creepy as all get-out.

Zoe Estrin-Grele learned about kissing from James T. Kirk,
sass from Uhura and Russia from Pavel Chekov.

10. DAGGER OF THE MIND
GETTING TO THE POINT OF MIND CONTROL
ROB TYMEC

I should probably come clean before I write too much of this review: I am not a huge *Star Trek* fan.

I don't hate the show, either. But it doesn't burn in my heart with a deep geek passion like certain other sci-fi franchises do. I'm composing this right now because I've written stuff about those other sci-fi franchises that the editor of this book has enjoyed, so he was nice enough to offer me a few pages to fill in this particular anthology. That's why I'm being included here. It's not so much that I'm *Trek*-obsessed like so many other contributors to this volume are. It's more that I'm half-decent at writing a review.

Now, this admission may cause some of you to want to dismiss me immediately. "*Why should we listen to him? He's not even a proper fan,*" you might be saying to yourselves right now. But I hope you'll bear with me. In fact, if you do, you might get a different perspective. After all, someone who is only so emotionally involved can often provide a more objective view of things.

Having claimed my level of detachment from the project, let me now go on to say that *Dagger of the Mind* is one of my all-time favorite Classic *Trek* episodes. I love it to death. It's up there with the one where they get into the fight with the Romulans at the Federation/Romulan border (see how bad of a fan I am, I can't even remember the name of that episode).

What is so great about *Dagger of the Mind*? Well, this leads me to the Number One Reason Why I Don't Like *Star Trek* as Much as I Do Other Sci-Fi Franchises. It's a point that isn't so much a reflection on the quality of the show as it is a revelation of just how bad my ADHD is. I find that, too often, *Star Trek* stops to contemplate its navel at the expense of the action. Particularly in the original series. Again, this isn't so much the fault of *Trek* as it is a fatal flaw in myself. If I don't get a lightsaber duel or a Dalek exterminating someone every couple of minutes, I find my attention starts waning. And *Star Trek*, in any of its incarnations, feels it's important to stop and have these contemplative moments where they debate the ethical implications of whatever challenge they're facing that week. Many of the moments are very thought-provoking, of course. But, too often, because of my terribly short patience, I'm just sitting there yelling at the various characters to man the photon torpedoes and get on with the starship fight.

I'm terrible like that.

Dagger of the Mind is one of those episodes that gives me what I want. Maybe not so much in the action department, but it certainly keeps the intrigue going at full throttle. Right from the pre-title teaser, my interest is held. Not just because of the glimpse we get of the sinister-looking fellow peeking out of the crate, but the whole transporter sequence is intriguing. The fact that they're having technical difficulties. That they're dealing with a penal colony. Even Kirk reprimanding the one technician for not knowing the proper protocol — it's all good stuff that holds my focus and ropes me in, right away. That says: "This episode is going to move a bit differently from the others."

And it continues to do that after the title sequence is over. My ADHD is usually put through rigorous torture for the first few minutes of a Classic *Trek* episode. Lots of sitting around on the Bridge having fun banter that gives us a ton of character revelation about the regulars but doesn't really do much to propel the plot. Not so with *Dagger of the Mind*. Immediately, our fugitive is rushing around. He takes out a few redshirts, then actually seizes the bridge and holds people at phaser point. So much action happening so quickly in a Classic *Trek* episode — the pacing is virtually breakneck!

Before I sound too much like an adrenaline junkie, let me discuss what else is going on in those first few minutes that really gets me to love the episode. We actually get some very clever plotting. *Dagger* immediately sets up this great central premise: Is Dr. Adams a great old guy like Kirk says he is? Or are the paranoid suspicions of McCoy as accurate as they always are? We know, already, which answer is right. But it's still fun watching Kirk's confidence in the doctor's experiments erode slowly but surely as the truth of things becomes more and more clear.

And I think this is what sets *Dagger of the Mind* so much above a lot of other *Trek*. It sticks to the plot and keeps messing with our expectations. Teasing out little things here and there that keep us second-guessing. "Is Dr. Adams good or a baddie?" we keep asking ourselves. There are clues that sit on either side of the fence. This is the thrust of the story. No big moral debates to shove in the middle of the episode and slow things down. We stick to the plot.

I am in utter delight, for instance, when Kirk finally does see Dr. Adams' conditioning device and just pronounces it bad on the spot. The very sexy Dr. Noel tries to defend it. As does Adams himself. But the conversation is cut short. "Device is bad," Kirk insists. "Let's get on with the storyline." This is where most other *Trek* episodes would come to a grinding halt and the torture of my ADHD begins. Where the writer of the script takes something that is slightly morally dubious and has a handful of characters try to present every possible side of the issue. It's something we see in every version of *Trek* there is. And, for the most part, it puts me to sleep. Whereas *Dagger* gets to the point of things: Dr. Adams' device is wrong. Let's explore the consequences of being on an isolated prison colony and disagreeing with the guy in charge. That makes for a far more interesting story.

Another common Classic *Trek* pitfall that the episode tends avoid quite nicely is the propensity towards over-the-top acting. It certainly has the opportunity to indulge in it with the plight of Dr. van Gelder. As Spock chooses to mind-meld with him, I'm expecting even bigger histrionics to ensue. But both actors are kept reined in fairly well. Yes, a character is displaying clear signs of insanity. Yes, another character has purposely infiltrated his psyche. But neither of them have to chew the scenery to portray all this. The drama is intense, yes. But not at the expense of credibility. And I am in love all the more with this episode because of this choice.

Do I have problems with *Dagger of the Mind*? Would I be able to call myself a geek if I didn't?

One of my major gripes is more an issue of contextuality. In today's society, Kirk would never get away with what he says about Dr. Helen Noel just before they beam off. Someone from Human Resources would be all over him for claiming he didn't want to go on a mission with her because they did a bit of flirting at the Christmas party!

I also have to take issue with a prison colony that seems to have such easily accessible air ducts to escape in! I mean, really, it's that easy to get into the ventilation shafts? Dr. Noel should've run into, at least, fifty other prisoners while she was in there. We can excuse the inconsistency, perhaps, by claiming that they were imprisoned in a civilian section of the penal colony. But why do that when you have actual prison cells? I also love how the guards that come to collect Kirk for more mind probe torture don't seem to care that Noel has suddenly gone missing.

But these quibbles are minor, really. *Dagger of the Mind* has so much more going for it than it does working against it. It's the sort of *Star Trek* that a poor Attention Deficit Hyperactive Disorder sufferer like me can really get behind. It tends to stick out like a sore thumb (in a good way, though, if that's possible for a sore thumb to do) because it's handled differently from a lot of other episodes of *Trek*. In fact, I'd be a much bigger *Trek* fan if we'd had a few more episodes like this...

Rob Tymec is an author who frequently loves to rip off the bios of other authors. He does not live in Surrey.

11. THE CORBOMITE MANEUVER
THE POWER OF BULLSHIT
GEOFFREY D. WESSEL

Bullshit makes the world go round. Just this week, as I write this, the end result of a war predicated on bullshit, outright fabrications and lies is coming back to haunt the world, as ISIS storms across an Iraq already plunging into a civil war. One wonders how that might be different had the various English-speaking governments of 2002 and 2003 not fed the world a bill of goods.

It's not like they are the only ones. Have you watched a cable news channel recently? That's their stock in trade, no matter which side of the aisle you're on. How many times now has Kim Jong-un, much like his father before him, threatened the world with his vast nuclear arsenal? He even threatened war over a Seth Rogen movie. But, as hotheaded as he might appear to be, we can all smell the bullshit from here. No movie is worth a war, not even a Seth Rogen one.

Face it, we're surrounded by bullshit. Everyone has done it to some extent. Even "little white lies". We rationalize it, that it was for our own good or another person's. There was even the classic line at the beginning of *The Blues Brothers*, when Elwood told Jake that all the things Elwood said to Jake in order to give him hope through his prison sentence were false. Jake accuses Elwood of lying. Elwood retorts, "It wasn't a lie, it was just... bullshit." When dealing with the truth about an historical person, unless the truth is so horrific that we must accept it, if it comes between the truth and the myth, we as a species tend to go for the myth as the accepted version.

One has to wonder if our cultural acceptance of bullshit on the scale that we do might have to do with the cultural heroes we tend to look towards. And, let's be frank, in the past fifty years, Captain James Tiberius Kirk has been one of those heroic role models. Bullshit is one of his stock tools in trade. If ever there's an episode that shows this, it would be *The Corbomite Maneuver*.

Make no mistake — Kirk lies. A lot. He's the one who infamously rigged the Kobayashi Maru test so he could win in a no-win situation. To say nothing of the lines of manure Kirk has been known to spread in order to get this week's alien femme fatale to drop her drawers. He's a liar. He bends reality to fit his ideal and makes you believe it.

But let's give him credit, too. In *The Corbomite Maneuver*, he lies in order to save his ship and crew. The *Enterprise* is under threat from what appears to be a vastly technologically superior alien species in Balok of the "First Federation" and his enormous spherical ship, the *Fesarius*. By the looks of things, the *Fesarius* could wipe the *Enterprise* from existence. Looks, of course, can be deceiving. Keep this in mind. Kirk seizes upon this idea, however; Spock, looking at life as a game of chess, decides they are in checkmate. Kirk, of course, sees life's game as poker: bluff your way out of bad situations in order to capitalize. Kirk is a lot more opportunistic than Spock, clearly. Kirk makes up the "corbomite" story in order to prevent certain annihilation from Balok.

It was clearly bullshit, the sort of thing you would tell to someone about to wipe you out. You see this in crime stories all the time — a guy about to get whacked makes up a story about an absolute peach of a heist that *if you let me live*, I'll tell you ALL about it and cut you in. In Kirk's case, it works. Balok and the *Fesarius* don't fire, instead opting to tow the *Enterprise*, which ends badly for Balok. Especially since Balok's own bullshit is exposed because of it: gone is the fearsome-looking alien creature; instead, a lonesome child (admittedly voiced by an adult, but played by a 5-year-old), only seeking to test the *Enterprise*, with a phony puppet and a gigantic starship he alone occupies.

So the lies were for a "good" cause in this instance. But it's clear this wasn't just a one-time thing for Kirk. *The Corbomite Maneuver* was the third *Star Trek* story ever to be filmed, despite being the tenth to be aired. Meaning this is the second-ever Kirk story (as well as being the first to feature Dr. McCoy). We're very early on in getting to know Kirk. Therefore one can deduce that lying and bullshit, even for a greater good, *is a core part of James T. Kirk's character.*

It is such a core part that Kirk even lies to himself. It's clear Lt. Bailey isn't up to the job he's been assigned. Sulu needs to do half of Bailey's tasks during the *Fesarius* standoff. Even Kirk can see he's made a mistake, but he can't admit that, lest he look weak or indecisive. Therefore Bailey is given away, as an emissary for Balok, to learn about humanity. Kirk can look at it as a way for Bailey to redeem himself, but, really, it's so Kirk can also feel better about his own poor decision-making.

Is bullshit wrong? At face value, yes, of course. If it's in the service of others? Well... maybe. Poker, Kirk's game of choice, is predicated on that very concept, in order to get your opponent to fold, even if all you have is a pair of deuces. Maybe humanity works best somewhere between poker and chess.

Bullshit, even in the 23rd century, still has potency as currency.

Geoffrey D. Wessel bullshits. A lot. Mostly to himself. He also writes comic books. You can find him on Twitter @gdwessel, Facebook at his name or at gdwessel.com, and his Atypical Comics imprint is atypicalcomics.com.

12. THE MENAGERIE

THE *STAR TREK* STORY WE JUST DON'T TALK ABOUT

ANDREW GURUDATA

Submitted for your consideration: *The Menagerie* is the *Star Trek* story that fans discuss the least.

As a *Star Trek* fan, your jaw may have dropped as you read the above statement. "What are you talking about?!?" you ask me with confusion on your faces. "Fans have been heavily discussing the events of *The Menagerie* since 1966. *The Menagerie* is a pivotal story in the evolution of the *Star Trek* mythology. Captain Pike! Number One! Young Spock! The Talosians! Orion Slave Girl! It won the freaking Hugo award for crying out loud!!!"

Okay, okay, calm down, *Star Trek* fan. Give me a moment and let me explain what I mean here...

I'd like to give you a summary of the story of *The Menagerie*. Not a detailed description of everything we see in the episode but rather just a quick recap of what actually happens in this episode's main storyline.

So here's what happened: The *Enterprise* arrives at a space station because Spock says they received a message to go there. Nobody at the station knows anything about that message. The person who supposedly sent the message is Spock's former captain, but he's an invalid, barely able to communicate "yes" and "no", never mind "Hey, want to drop by and say hi?" Kirk is confused. Spock starts acting sneaky. Very sneaky. Criminally sneaky. He kidnaps his former Captain and then steals the *Enterprise*, heading to the one planet in the Federation that is completely forbidden. (You know, kind of how they later did in *The Search for Spock*...) Kirk and the Starbase commander chase after them (somehow under the delusion that a shuttle can catch up to a starship), and, when they head out too far into space, Spock abandons his run, rescues the shuttle passengers, and has himself put under arrest — but keeps the ship locked on course for the Forbidden Planet. Spock is court-martialed, but, thanks to the oddest rules of evidence ever known to man, he is able to show some videos, which convince Kirk and the Starbase commander (who wasn't actually there, he's just an illusion) that it's okay to take the invalid captain to that Forbidden Planet and leave him there, and everybody lives happily ever after as all is forgiven.

Ummmm... why are you looking at me like that, *Star Trek* fan? What's that you're saying? "Did you just dare to summarize all of *The Cage* parts of *The Menagerie* with the words 'Spock showed some videos'?" Why yes, yes I did. Because that is my point: fans don't tend discuss the real story of *The Menagerie*; what they actually tend to do is focus on the parts of *The Cage* that are embedded inside *The Menagerie*. They generally tend to ignore the fact that *The Menagerie* has an entire story of its own, separate from the events shown on the video screen during Spock's court martial.

And that is, in my opinion, really a pity, because the non-*Cage* parts of *The Menagerie* are actually a Really Cool Story. It has Mystery! Mutiny! Court martial! A deceptive Spock! An angry Kirk! A well-filmed opening to the second part where three great actors stare off into space as they deliver their lines to each other!

Let's consider what it must have been like for a *Star Trek* watcher in 1967 to tune in to this two-part episode. Today, we have the luxury of knowing the history of why this episode was made and where *The Cage* footage came from. But for a viewer back then, it would have been a very different story. Over the last several weeks, viewers would have been watching episodes like *The Enemy Within* and *What Are Little Girls Made Of?* and *Dagger of the Mind* — and, with these, they would have been watching the evolution of the Kirk–Spock relationship, getting to understand the logic and unwavering loyalty of the *Enterprise*'s first officer. So how shocking must it have been for them to see Spock lying and stealing and deceiving his captain and his crew?

And so here is my challenge to you, *Star Trek* Fan: pop in your Blu-ray of *Star Trek* Season One and watch *The Menagerie* — but, this time, focus on the non-*Cage* parts exclusively. Fast forward past everything on the briefing room view screen and rediscover the actual story of *The Menagerie* itself. You may be surprised at just how good this "filler" story really was.

As a final thought... Possibly the one iconic element of the non-flashback portions of this episode is the image of Admiral Pike — as played by Sean Kenney — in his wheelchair with the flashing lights. As legend has it, Sean Kenney was given the role because Jeff Hunter, the original actor who played Pike in *The Cage*, was neither available nor affordable. But, when you think about it, it is this "cheat" that makes the entire premise of *The Menagerie*'s envelope story work. As a thought exercise, imagine for a moment that Jeff Hunter had been available to return as Admiral Pike. It seems doubtful that Hunter-as-Pike would have been the mute invalid that Kenney-as-Pike had been. This would have made the entirely story entirely different from what we ended up with. Had they stayed with a similar story, we would have lost the iconic Pike-in-a-wheelchair imagery, but what we may have gained would have been Pike actively participating in the plot to steal the *Enterprise* or perhaps some banter between Pike and Spock and/or Pike and Kirk. You know, I think that would have been a really cool version of this story. Maybe some fanfic writer needs to go off and write that!

There was another reviewer before Andrew Gurudata,
but we try not to talk about him too much.

13. THE CONSCIENCE OF THE KING
ALL THE SHIP'S A STAGE
CATRIONA MILLS

McCoy: In the long history of medicine, no doctor has ever caught the first few minutes of a play.

ME: D'you know what's really interesting about this episode?

HIM: That we haven't even started watching it yet?

ME: No, that we can already be confident about the villain's identity.

HIM: Is this going to be like the time you announced the murderer when we were watching *The Hound of the Baskervilles*?

ME: You'd already seen *The Hound of the Baskervilles*. You'd also read the book.

HIM: I'd forgotten the details.

ME: The murderer isn't a detail. Which, conveniently, is my point. Right from the title of this episode, we know it's patterned on *Hamlet*. Everyone knows *Hamlet*. You don't even have to have read *Hamlet* to know *Hamlet*.

HIM: You're going to start quoting Pierre Bayard before we even get to the opening credits, aren't you?

ME: Obviously.

HIM: Let's just pretend you already did that.

ME: But, seriously, if we know *Hamlet*, we're already prepped for revelations and villainy. Then the opening scene: *Macbeth*'s most famous moment. This episode drips with blood and hidden crimes and false faces right from the off.

HIM: That sounds revolting. Can you actually drip with false faces?

ME: What you should be asking is how the audience could ever doubt that

Karidian is Kodos, when they're watching him through the accumulated villains of European drama?

> *Karidian: I am an actor. I play many parts.*
> *Kirk: You're an actor now. What were you twenty years ago?*
> *Karidian: Younger, Captain. Much younger.*

ME: I don't think it's a coincidence that we only see two of Kodos's many parts: a regicide and a ghost. The ghost is particularly fascinating. It makes sense in the context of the episode...

HIM: Because Anton Karidian is a character, not actually a person?

ME: Yes, and because it's emblematic of Kodos's haunting by his own past. But it makes no sense in the context of the in-show production. Why would their star actor play the ghost in *Hamlet*? It's a small role. You'd think he'd play Claudius.

HIM: Maybe he plays both? They're brothers.

ME: But then the episode really would be drawing on our assumed prior knowledge of *Hamlet* to make sense of Kodos's roles.

HIM: The episode could just be asking you to take things at face value.

ME: I'm not very good at that.

HIM: The episode doesn't know that.

ME: And don't you wonder why someone called Kodos the Executioner would be playing Macbeth. Isn't that a dead giveaway? No pun intended.

HIM: Maybe he's hiding in plain sight?

ME: Actually, why does Kodos become an actor at all? That's a rather odd career trajectory: murderous dictator with a passion for eugenics to Shakespearean actor. The episode never actually addresses that. In fact, it uses his profession as a device to underscore his guilt: that very first shot of his hand holding a dagger, for example. It makes you suspect that Kodos chose his profession because it allows him to enact his guilt.

HIM: Isn't that a bit like poking a bruise?

ME: And risky. But it reminds me of something I definitely don't think is a coincidence: the way this episode keeps emphasizing that it's been twenty years since the massacre. To the original audience, that's the end of World War II. There'd be people watching this in 1966 — and not that small a number, either — who saw things like Tarsus IV when they were Kirk's age or even Riley's age. It's a delicate topic for the show to approach and perhaps another reason why they distance Kodos from his guilt by placing it on the stage.

HIM: Speaking of twenty years, are you going to comment on how young Lenore is?

ME: I'm trying not to think about it.

> Lenore: Tonight, the Karidian Players present Hamlet, another in a series of living plays presented in space, dedicated to the tradition of classic theatre.

ME: You know, they call them "living plays presented in space", but did you notice that most of the audience aren't watching a live play? There are hardly any seats in front of the actual stage. Most of the crew are actually watching it on a viewscreen. Just pause it on that shot of the crew in front of the viewscreen.

HIM: I've dropped the remote control.

ME: We'll pause it metaphorically, then.

HIM: No, wait. I'm sitting on it.

ME: Look at that recursive image of spectatorship. We're watching (on television) the crew of the *Enterprise*, who are watching (on a viewscreen) a performance of *Hamlet* (on stage). And that's not even counting the intended audience: those original people who sat more or less where we're sitting now, but in 1966. It's such a complex folding of theatre into television.

HIM: To what extent is that deliberate, though? Early television is often just theatre in front of cameras: live, static and generally pretty stagey.

ME: But don't forget that, by this period, they're starting to pull away from that idea that the television screen is just another proscenium arch. *Star Trek* is something that you couldn't ever have done on stage, not even in the spectacular theatre of the nineteenth century.

HIM: It's still quite stagey, though.

ME: Oh, definitely. The scene with Lenore and Kirk planetside? That's typical early television staginess. Those rocks are really quite fake.

HIM: But you'd still argue that they're consciously playing with theatricality and it's not just a function of being early television?

ME: I think they're deliberately collapsing this boundary-pushing television program back into its theatrical roots, acknowledging and transcending television's origins. The episode is playing around with it too joyfully for it to be coincidental: look at the way they've lit Lenore's soliloquy to give the illusion of actual stars in her eyes. They've used a distinctly televisual special effect to actualize a metaphor for theatre.

HIM: Do you think you're starting to over-code the text?

ME: Not this time. This whole episode keeps "television" and "theatre" in constant play against one another. Even when it's not about theatre, it's about nature versus technology, which is an analogous argument. Look at Lenore's speech about women versus machines, which goes right to heart of why Kirk is still a bachelor...

HIM: He wouldn't still be single if he could marry the *Enterprise*.

ME: I was going to make that joke. And then the episode culminates in the extraordinary conceit of a canvas-and-wood castle built inside a spaceship for a performance of *Hamlet*. And even that's not the last layer, because then we're watching it all on television. More than that: it's constructed, from its very conception and in its entirety, as television. Go back to that very first shot: the dagger scene in *Macbeth* is one of English theatre's most iconic moments — but they give it to us in a close up. You can't do that in the theatre.

HIM: That was one of your more entertaining television-watching rants.

ME: I should write it down before I forget the best jokes.

> *Kirk: Those are beautiful words, well-acted. Change nothing.*

> *Catriona Mills is a nineteenth-century scholar, a scholarly bibliographer and an unapologetic fangirl, constantly seeking ways of bringing all three roles together.*

14. BALANCE OF TERROR
REMEMBRANCE OF THINGS UNSEEN
MELISSA BEATTIE

Balance of Terror is one of those episodes that everyone talks about. Sometimes the focus is on the Romanesque Romulans, sometimes on the World War II submarine thriller antecedents and, of course, sometimes on the fact that this episode is the great Mark Lenard's first role on the series, before taking up the mantle of Sarek. What really strikes me about this episode is the focus on vision and its relationship to knowledge.

This is, of course, the first episode in which anyone from the Federation sees what a Romulan looks like. The Romulan vessel is usually cloaked until just before it attacks and maintains radio silence too, most of the time. They are fully invisible and unknown.

Except, of course, to us.

We, the audience, are ahead of the *Enterprise* crew in a lot of ways. Specifically, we see and hear the Romulans aboard their ship. We know that their commander is struggling with the demands of his duty and those of his conscience. We know one of the Romulan underlings, Decius, makes an error that reveals them. We know, in short, that They are much like Us, with each of these events on the Romulan ship being broadly paralleled on the *Enterprise*.

The crew of the *Enterprise*, however, have but a fleeting image of Vulcanoid features and, as Dr. McCoy puts it, tactics "Based on what? Memories of a war over a century ago? On theories about a people we've never even met face to face?" This is the point I'd like to focus upon: what is believed to have happened in the past can inform present beliefs and identities as well as future actions, sometimes to great cost.

Renan developed a concept in history called "the dialectic of remembering and forgetting", which is a formal way of saying that those who have the power to write and transmit "official" histories and cultures will edit the facts to create a narrative that focuses upon certain aspects and marginalizes or completely erases others. So history is quite literally "made", with varying degrees of intent by those making it. In some cases, certain groups of people focus upon certain events, sometimes turning them into a (or the) foundation of their identity. These events are either a "chosen glory" or a "chosen trauma" that has happened (or is believed to have happened) at some point in that group's history. The concept isn't without its flaws, but I think you can see how it works in the context of the episode by looking at Lieutenant Stiles' knee-jerk reaction to the Romulans. He ascribes his knowledge of Romulan ships to "family history" and proceeds to give a litany of ancestors who died during the previous century's Romulan war. This is clearly something that has been drilled into him by parents and other relatives; both creators and conveyors of the official history of that family. You can argue either way whether or not that counts as a glory or trauma (or both), but it clearly underpins Stiles' identity and strongly colors his viewpoint. He is, despite the evolved nature of the Roddenberry universe, explicitly racist.

But "family history" can mean more than just an immediate family. Once they've seen the "face of the enemy" — *Next Generation* reference intended — Spock too has something of a knee-jerk reaction. In reply to McCoy's statement, he says:

> If Romulans are an offshoot of my Vulcan blood, and I think this likely, then attack becomes even more imperative. [...] Vulcan, like Earth, had its aggressive colonizing period. Savage, even by Earth standards. And if Romulans retain this martial philosophy, then weakness is something we dare not show.

Here, Spock too is drawing conclusions about people he has never met, based upon events from long before he was born that appear to have been marginalized in at least "official" history.

While these particular instances are not quite a stereotypical representation of Romulans by humans and Vulcans, they are certainly drawn not from facts but from suppositions. They are also drawn in strongly negative terms — to Spock and Stiles both, these are the dangerous, savage phantoms of the past who have no compassion to offer, unlike the modern, progressive Federation — so the human and Vulcan image of who the Romulans are is very similar to what in cultural theory is called Orientalism. This may not be surprising, given that the Romulans are sometimes analogized to the Cold War era Chinese — stereotypically perceived as secretive, inscrutable and militaristic — leading to misunderstanding and paranoia even to this day. It's not as blatant as Stiles' racism, but it is still striking, especially coming from a character defined by strict logic. Family history, officially transmitted and governed by a chosen trauma or glory — for Stiles, the loss of his relatives in the line of duty, as officially described by his relatives, and for Spock, the violent Vulcan past and the ability to overcome it — vastly affects the view of a group who, in modern times, have never been met face to face, let alone understood.

Except by the audience.

The audience knows more than either crew, which adds not only dramatic tension — helped at the time, no doubt, by the Vietnam war — but, more importantly, the audience is aware of, *but exists outside,* the "official" and family histories. We remember everything we see in the episode and are given the tools to understand both sides of the conflict, not just the Federation's perspective. That's an important point, I think; remembering that this was broadcast when the U.S. was in the midst of a war in a country that few people could locate, let alone know about its culture. Because there is that tendency by both individuals and groups to essentialize and conflate — especially after a violent, traumatic conflict — yet the audience is reminded that both sides of any conflict are made up of people. Thus, when inscribed into the official history of any group, all of Them — here meaning either Asians or Romulans — are viewed as an unchanging, monolithic entity whose only officially remembered qualities are that they are violent, savage and to be both hated and feared. They become the Other and the Enemy and are often perceived as savage, violent and even as less than human, their better natures forgotten.

And this, as so nearly happens in *Balance of Terror*, can lead to war.

I think it's therefore apt that Santayana's quote about progress relying upon retentiveness ("those who cannot remember the past are doomed to repeat it") is also sometimes attributed to Surak; in *Balance of Terror*, those whose beliefs and actions are informed by a presumed "official family history" built around chosen traumas or glories nearly cause yet another Federation/Romulan War. It is a cautionary tale of the dangers of remembering only war and strife, forgetting that the enemy is often very much the same as the self. Or, as Diane Duane's Surak says in the novel *Spock's World*, "The spear in the other's heart is the spear in your own; you are he."

It's something we'd do well to remember.

Melissa Beattie is a doctor (of TV studies), not a bricklayer.

15. SHORE LEAVE
A MOTHER AND DAUGHTER WATCH-ALONG
HANNAH ROTHMAN (WITH FAITH L. JUSTICE)

Faith: "Yup, this was definitely before workshops on dealing with sexual harassment!"

My mom chuckled uncomfortably at the opening scene where Kirk, complaining about a kink in his back, calls on Yeoman Barrows to fix him up. I had zero doubt that Mom was watching this episode with a feminist eye, considering how much work she did for the National Organization for Women and similar groups back in the day. She'd told me those stories before, but this was the first time we'd watched *Star Trek* together.

Mom grew up watching *Star Trek*. I didn't. I certainly inherited my sci-fi/fantasy nerd gene from her, but I was a *Star Wars* fan as a kid. While Mom and I shared a love of that galaxy far, far away, and later Harry Potter and *Doctor Who*, we never shared *Star Trek*. I remember her watching the nineties shows, though. One of my earliest memories of watching "grown-up TV" was of being mesmerized by the gorgeous *Star Trek: Voyager* opening. But, as far as childhood *Star Trek* memories went, that was it. Mom's, on the other hand, were of watching the original series back when it first aired. It wasn't until I was nearly out of college that she realized this grievous oversight in not sharing *Star Trek* with me and vowed to correct it sometime.

Shore Leave was the first *Star Trek* episode I ever sat down and watched properly, at the insistence of my junior-year college roommate. I'd just shown her the Classic *Doctor Who* serial *The Mind Robber*, a personal favorite of mine, and she promptly went into this-actually-reminds-me-of-this-one-*Star-Trek*-episode mode (both stories had the common thread of the main characters landing in a strange world where fictions came to life). I wound up choosing this episode to be the first that Mom and I watched properly together.

There was a mention onscreen of "four hundred and thirty" people aboard the *Enterprise*, and I paused and furrowed my brow.

> Hannah: "Wait... do we ever actually see the other four hundred and thirty people?"
> Faith: "Oh, no, it's just a handful at a time. And then there's always the ubiquitous redshirts, the poor guys who die. There are new ones in every episode."
> Hannah: "But I'd been under the assumption this whole time that the crew was just the people in the cockpit... and occasionally some other people. I didn't know that there were... four-hundred-what people on the *Enterprise*."
> Faith: "Yup, it's a big biiiiig ship!"

She went on to explain the emphasis on families living on the *Enterprise* that *The Next Generation* had, a conversation we'd had once before when she gave me her Defense of Wesley Crusher presentation. We continued: Mom trying to follow what she remembered of the plot, and me basking in the delightful cheesiness of old-school sci-fi.

> Hannah: "Hang on, so who are they?"
> Faith: "Oh, they're just a couple of those four hundred and thirty. I don't recall having ever seen them before, and they may never have another speaking part."

> Faith: "So how do the plants get pollinated if there's no insect life or birds?"
> Hannah: "Random blue fern. Why is the tree red?"

Faith: "Yeah... maybe some other trees had paint on them."

Hannah: "Here's our quarry scene."
Faith: "They probably dressed it up with these plants."

Hannah: "Ruth... was she from a previous episode?"
Faith: "No, this is supposedly from his past."
Hannah: "I wonder if the implication is that she's dead? Or..."
Faith: "I don't think so. Because he says 'you haven't aged', which would indicate that he would've expected her to look fifteen years older and therefore would've been alive."

Faith: "I'm sure Shatner just loved all that running around!"
Hannah: "*His shirt was not ripped a second ago!* Where did like... half of his shirt go?!? Was people's shirts ripping A Thing They Did Every Episode?"
Faith: "Um, not necessarily, but... yeah, Shatner got to fight. A lot. Considering that he had all these advanced weapons, he got to throw a lot of punches. And he did get to take his shirt off a lot, for the ladies and the fighting and whatever."

Hannah: "Can we please talk about how Spock is such a fantastic sass master?"

We stopped to take stock, and I asked Mom what she thought of this old story she hadn't seen in years.
"I'm just struck by..."
"How young everyone looks?" I interjected, recalling a comment she'd made before we started watching.
"Yeah, it's how young everyone looks, but also how un-PC everything is!" She laughed. "You know, this was the sixties, and yes they were really ahead of their time with having women in all kinds of roles and that sort of stuff, and having black people in all kinds of roles... but it's still very rooted in that kind of pre-feminist consciousness. I mean, that very first scene, you would never see that today. And with Yeoman Barrows going 'oh, I want to be a princess and I want to be swept away by Don Juan and I want to wear a long floaty dress'! It's just... okay, I'd forgotten about that." She was still laughing despite her grievances. I hardly expected nostalgia to cloud her judgment. "But I have to admit," she continued, "I'm loving the colors and this particular setting. I think they've done a really nice job!"
I agreed, and then Mom's attention to detail took an unexpected but fascinating turn. "That was one of the things I remember from back then," she continued. "The

shows were longer. And then, when they started shoehorning them into reruns and there was a much bigger commercial hole, I would recognize when they made bad cuts. 'They left out that line!' When I'd watch this in reruns, it would always irk the hell out of me... because I knew all the scripts. I'd watch these shows so many times, and I'd watch them originally and then the reruns... but later, like fifteen or twenty years later, I would recognize 'They left out that line!' How could they leave out *that line*?"

I raised my eyebrows, if not on my face, then certainly in my mind. This was the level of obsession that Mom used to raise *her* eyebrows at me for when I was a kid. I'd never seen this particular side of her before, but I loved it. She'd even quoted along with the episode a couple times. Still, she admitted that this wasn't one of her favorites. Slow and lacking in the show's signature social commentary, she said. I actually enjoyed it as an introductory episode: the stakes felt relatively low, little to no background information was needed for the story or characters, and it was a nice romp. I've always had a soft spot for these odd one-off stories where our heroes find themselves in some sort of fantasyland (or cartoon-land) where everything gets a bit wacky for an episode. Maybe Mom didn't, or maybe *Shore Leave* was just an exception for her.

"But I should probably go through the episodes and figure out a handful of the most iconic ones for you."

Looks like, after our own shore leave, Mom and I might get to share *Star Trek* after all.

Hannah Rothman was born into geekery and writing, a merger that recently produced her book series, Twitter Who. *Faith L. Justice, a fiction writer and proud mama, raised her daughter well.*

16. THE GALILEO SEVEN
THE DUTIES OF THE VULCAN HEART
DANIEL CLARKE-SERRET

What is the most noble peak of human endeavor? Economic growth for all? Equality? Democracy? Ever-increasing scientific knowledge? Not according to Rabbi Bachya ibn Paquda, the medieval Spanish writer of "Duties of the Heart". For this mystic, the flowering of human achievement is the triumph of the intellect over base physical desires.

His reasoning is as follows. Each human has a soul, a body and an intellect. The body has a number of needs. Water, food, the need to reproduce and the like. In order to work in a physical context, the soul needs the body to thrive. However, so in love are we with the physical needs of the body, that the soul cleaves to the pleasures of the physical world and no longer follows the way of the intellect and reason. Through abstinence and other means, we need to fight physical desires and return to the way of the intellect. In the words of the Talmud, "Who is mighty? He who conquers his evil inclination."

Now, ibn Paquda was not a Vulcan. Neither was he a Romulan, a Klingon, nor was he from any other fictional *Star Trek* race. He was a human. And his conclusion, while very much reached from a religious perspective, matches with the worldview of most intelligent humans, including both committed atheists and committed theists. The rule of reason is the star to which our species is trying to travel.

With this in mind, the surface distinction between Humans and Vulcans made in the *Star Trek* series seems somewhat artificial. Humanity seems to be associated with desperation, emotional reactions and general irrationality, whereas Vulcans are associated with measured calculation, logic and rationality. Just to reinforce that, Spock and every other Vulcan who appears is contractually obliged to say the word "logical" in every sentence, while every human is bound to respond with derision (for example, at the end of this episode). But are not the best of humanity, as ibn Paquda states, already intent on using rationality to solve life's problems? And why, in the 23nd century, do humans want to mock the controlling of strong passions that is the Vulcan trademark?

Perhaps though, I am guilty of failing to see the subtleties in the writing. Although *Star Trek* does present us with a range of species said to be alien from one another, their differences, from a scientific perspective, are purely tokenistic. Vulcans have pointy ears, but there is less variation between a human and a Vulcan than, say, between a human and the intelligent elephant species here on Earth. Rather, I would argue, the distinction between the various *Star Trek* species is more symbolic. Each represents a drive in the human mind. For example, the Klingons represent anger, and the Romulans show us in the grip of deceit.

But what do the Vulcans represent? If their propaganda is to be believed, they represent humanity at its most noble. Humans who have eschewed anger, greed and deceit and instead are following a path of pure rationality. But have Vulcans really achieved what they claim, namely to have followed the true path of ibn Paquda? The evidence from this episode suggests otherwise. Vulcans, without doubt, aspire to control their passions and free themselves from love of the world — but they often fail to achieve this.

In this episode, a shuttlecraft, manned by a crew of seven and commanded by Mr. Spock, is stranded on an alien planet. To extricate his crew from the situation, the Vulcan is required to take some difficult decisions, all of which he claims have a rational, logical basis. However, in general, his logic is flawed. Take the lack of compassion that

Spock employs when dealing with his crew. In my view, his decision to put obstacles in the way of a burial is not just insensitive but illogical. First, compassion in itself, when used in the correct circumstances and with the correct balance, is entirely logical. Spock himself admits this when he shows concern that the lives of the indigenous creatures be spared if possible. However, even if compassion were just a renegade human emotion, Spock needs to be aware that the humans he commands value it, and he logically needs to act accordingly. Alienating the people you work with and destroying any sense of team spirit is the best way possible of failing to achieve any results; in Spock's case, it even raised the possibility of a mutiny.

So why does Spock fail to achieve his lofty goals? One could point to the fact that Spock is half-human; he finds it necessary to make a show of being more Vulcan than he is actually capable of being. I reject this reasoning. Logic is not a genetic trait. It certainly isn't a genetic trait of the Vulcans. If anything, Vulcans are more predisposed than most races to overly strong and destructive emotions. Rather, logic is the tool Vulcans use to control their passions. This tool is less required in humans as their passions are that much weaker. Thus Spock's human side should actually help him in his goal of being guided by reason.

No, the reason Spock fails to achieve his lofty goals lies in his attitude, which smacks more of arrogance than logic. This, of course, is a common human failing. You only have to turn on the television to hear people speaking passionately about noble causes and human rights and the importance of selflessness. The vices of greed, deceit and rage are routinely, and without many exceptions, criticized. Yet we are living in countries that are far from utopias. Why? Because, as ibn Paquda states, you can only attain "Love of God" (the ultimate state when you turn fully from your love of the material world) when you have first mastered a number of preliminaries. One of these is humility and another is repentance. We must recognize our own lowliness and our drive to rebel against the values we espouse before we can genuinely attain those values.

The arrogance and haughtiness of the Vulcans is clearly demonstrated by the fact that they are written as insensitive, detached robots who cannot comprehend emotion on even a conceptual level. They forget that they were once, in effect, a race of over-passionate humans who used logic to control their emotions and reach rational decisions. They deride their human counterparts for their lack of logic, when they should understand the human propensity to be overcome by passion and irrationality.

Ibn Paquda makes an interesting observation about this kind of phenomenon. He asks who is worse, idolaters who worship the material world around them or religious hypocrites? His answer is the latter group. Although idolaters do wrong, they do so in ignorance. However, those who espouse noble values but fail to live by them do damage to the credibility of those very values. Similarly, Spock, acting like an arrogant robot, does more damage to the goal of rationality than anybody else in the whole episode. Vulcans are like every one of us. They talk the talk, but they don't walk the walk. And only through repentance and humility can we walk the walk. And who did I learn that from? Ibn Paquda. A human.

Daniel Clarke-Serret's intellect and base physical desires have fought to a draw. This article was written in honour of his wife Sara, native of Zaragoza, the beautiful city where ibn Paquda lived and wrote "Duties of the Heart".

17. THE SQUIRE OF GOTHOS
A HANDBOOK FOR PARENTS OF REALITY-WARPING CHILDREN
CLARE MOSELEY

The question of the proper rearing of children has plagued the galaxy since the dawn of time. Such a question becomes even more salient when the child in question is in possession of reality-warping abilities. How does one discipline a child when that child can unmake a civilization with a simple snap of the fingers?

Thankfully, most children with reality-warping abilities have parents with reality-warping abilities. Such powers will be necessary to repair the damage caused by the maturing god-like entity.

While it is natural for your child to explore the galaxy outside of the parent, it is important that the child is not given too much leeway too quickly. Parents may do much to fix their child's missteps, but prevention is the most effective tool a parent has.

It must be explained to the child that, while they possess a nigh-infinite amount of power, most of the galaxy does not. It is critical they understand that this does not make them better than the rest of the galaxy, despite it being the truth. Once they mature, they will be able to cope with their superiority.

Your child can have a planet to itself to play with, so long as the planet is uninhabited. Nothing could be more dangerous than a playpen infested with vermin! Even if the planet you have chosen appears uninhabited, you must closely monitor your child. As the galaxy is explored by the lesser species, such beings will explore planets even if seems they should be unappealing due to the atmosphere being deadly.

Of absolute critical importance is the entertainment you allow your child to consume. You must monitor your child's viewing habits closely. While your young child is a danger to the galaxy, the galaxy is even more dangerous to your child. Remember: your child will grow out of it, the galaxy will not.

Do not under any circumstances allow your child to view humanity. While they have the appearance of mostly harmless, primitive, hairless apes, no species in the galaxy could be more damaging to a child's development. Except perhaps the Klingons. Humans are violent, impulsive and — most importantly — stupid. The species claims to have evolved past these tendencies, an assertion that is hotly contested by most other sentient beings. Even if we are to take the human race at their word, the development is quite recent. Their bloodiest incursions were within the past two hundred years. Humans are notorious for lying about this length of time, claiming it has been far longer since the reached a higher enlightenment. If your child insists on watching lower species in their natural habitats, we suggest the Vulcans. While the entertainment value is not nearly as great, they are quite educational.

If your child does become enamored of the entertainment value of humans, there are several steps one must take. Ignoring them may potentially cause ruin to solar systems and their inhabitants.

First, explain how war hurts. While it may look exciting with all of the explosions, humans being torn apart by their fellows is really quite unpleasant. If your child still thinks war is fun, it is advisable to use your own ability to put your child inside the body of a dying soldier. Your child will not be harmed but will be able to experience the horrific pain of an individual dying from war wounds.

One of the most infuriating things about humanity is their recent discovery of space exploration. This brings up the opportunity for your child to interact with this dangerous species. When one of these starships blunders by, your child may beg and plead to keep them as pets. Humans make horrible pets. While you think you might be able to control them in your own environment, they are absolutely impossible to train. More than anything else, humans are convinced they are the superior beings and will resist all attempts at being subdued. Such unruly pets will frustrate your child, and you will have to deal with the consequences.

If a starship does venture near where your family is living, just wait it out. They do not remain in one place for long. The starship will clear out of your space soon enough. If it does not, influence the mind of the captain to explore somewhere else. While long-term mind control is difficult to maintain, it is usually easy enough to manipulate a starship captain long enough to get them away from your planet. While your child may fuss at the lost opportunity for games, they will soon forget about the starship. You just need to remain firm that they do not pursue the ship.

Having a child with reality-warping powers is a joy. While you may struggle in the early years, with time, patience and love, your child will grow into a benevolent being of immense ability. With a guiding hand, they will be able to create worlds rather than destroy them. Only once they are confident in their superior position in the galaxy may they interact with lesser beings, such as the human race.

Clare Moseley has a soft spot for childlike, reality-warping beings.

18. ARENA
THE GORN IDENTITY
ANDREW FLINT

I was six. I didn't know what *Star Trek* was. I'd never heard of Captain Kirk. I'd never seen the Starship *Enterprise*, nor knew of its five-year mission. I was merely changing channels on the TV, the old fashioned way: sitting in front of the television, turning the dial.

Click! Boring. Click! Boring. Click! Boring. Click! Scary creature with golf ball eyes. Click! Boring. Click ... *back.*

I didn't know what *Star Trek* was. But I knew I was enthralled. And terrified.

I could barely stay on the channel. Golf-ball-eyes roars. Click! (Pause. Calm down) Click! Guy in gold shirt runs, finds dirt. Golf-ball-eyes — I now learn he's a Gorn — hisses. Click! (Wait. Run around the room) Click! This would continue right through to the end of the show. Click! Too scared to watch, too engrossed (Click!) to stay away.

I would go on to tell my friends about it. We would battle, man captain versus lizard captain, even though none of them had seen the episode. We would battle until we made a makeshift gunpowder cannon and shot, but didn't kill, the lizard Gorn captain.

Several of my friends started watching other *Star Trek* episodes because (channel clicking aside) I'd seen *Arena*. This was the young me starting a lifelong habit of getting others into my interests: an only child's powerful need to share.

I was still a little shaken from my early experience and so waded into additional *Star Trek* episodes gradually. Salt monsters and rock monsters could still panic the young single-digits me, and don't get me started on nightmares of floaty things that stick to your back and take you over. But an episode long cat-and-mouse battle between the *Enterprise* and a Romulan ship? Run-around-the-room great!

Not wanting to spoil those early memories, it was almost 15 later before I revisited *Arena*. By then, I was a true *Star Trek* fan, with further special memories under my belt, like *Star Trek: The Next Generation* premiering the year I started university and the entire floor of our residence watching it while packed into a common room that comfortably held a quarter of us.

I had every *TNG* episode to date personally recorded on VHS. I'd seen all, and recorded most, of the original episodes. Save the one...

Arena spawned what would be a life-long relationship with *Star Trek*. It started me getting others into the series. There's a burden of expectation to that snowball that started the avalanche. Could it possibly live up to that six-year-old's experience?

I remember clearly when I re-watched *Arena*. I was on my own; potential disappointment would not be shared. I was in my student townhouse, and my VCR was hooked up through my stereo in what was not yet surround sound but was the best of the time. And I sat back to see...

Does the memory cheat?

Out of the gate, I was astonished to find that I'd only ever seen half of the episode! Six-year-old me had clicked in at exactly the moment Kirk and Gorn arrived on the planet's surface. So as far I was concerned, *Arena* was the battle with the Gorn and the ultimate choice of mercy. The reason they were placed there (the destruction of the Cestus III Outpost) was covered in dialogue during the half that I saw. I had no idea it was fully played out in the first half of the episode.

That aside, once I got to the aged-six-edit version, it's amazing how much of the story I remembered so vividly, even knowing what dialogue was coming word for word. This is even more remarkable given the constant Click! interruptions the original viewing entailed. Clearly *Arena*, and by extension *Star Trek*, had made an indelible impression. I was some shaken to discover that the Gorn's eyes aren't actually golf balls. They're some sort of multi-faceted, disco-ball insect eyes. That's... not necessarily an improvement.

So did the episode hold up? Sure, twenty(ish) me could see the Gorn was a man in a suit (disco eyes and all) and notice the ridiculously slow-moving fight scenes. But twenty(ish) me didn't care. Twenty(ish) me was still enthralled.

Arena has everything you've come to expect from the series: opening character banter, Mr. Expendable Redshirt, cheap locations and low-fi special effects, all wrapped around laughably heavy-handed messaging. And, like *Star Trek* itself, *Arena* embraces all that with charming good will and energy, transcending the clichés to become truly great television.

A decade later, thirty-year-old me would laugh out loud at the theatre during *Galaxy Quest*: "I know! You construct a weapon. Look around you — can you form some sort of rudimentary lathe?" Because *Arena* left a mark. Not just with young me but with everyone. Ask anyone about the episode, and, while they might not know the title, mention "the one with the space lizard" and they'll know exactly what you're talking about.

Now I'm 45 and I've just re-watched *Arena* for the umpteenth time. And I watched it in one go. Not an email check or an iPhone pause to be seen. These days, that may be my truest test of quality. *Arena* still stands.

It was my introduction to *Star Trek*. It paved my way through decades of TV shows and films. And I'm still enthralled.

The adult Andrew Flint has a list of hobbies and interests
more terrifying than the Gorn.

19. TOMORROW IS YESTERDAY
STARFLEET MANUAL ON EARTHBOUND TIME TRAVEL
TAYLOR DEATHERAGE

Section 114: Concerning Earthbound Time Travel
To be distributed to all science officers
cc: ships' captains

It is advised that when Starfleet personnel find themselves catapulted through unknown spatial anomalies and into times from whence before our organization or the United Federation of Planets were formed, they take into account the following procedures:

- DO NOT, under any circumstances, allow yourself to be detected by military personnel in this specific era! You cannot be sure of the political status of that common era, no matter how confident your captain appears to be...

- DO preserve the dignity of your crew as you inevitably help them up from the ship's floor. It isn't easy being pulled into a "black star of high gravitational attraction", you know.

- You will be out of contact with Starfleet. Don't bother trying to contact Command. Most likely, you're only going to be receiving Earth news or twentieth-century pop music or something of the like. None of these have good connotations.

- DO pay attention to what those news reports are telling you. Your First Officer should not have to tell you that hearing what you know to be historical information in those news reports means that you are IN the time period of those historical events!

- Once you've been spotted by the natives' aircraft, they will most likely insult you by calling you a "UFO" and forcing you to land. DO NOT panic and make the mistake of using a tractor beam on inferior technology. It will only serve to destroy the primitive vessel and force you to take its pilot aboard.

- Initially, apologies will most likely fail with the native people. Calling them "guest" or telling them that you will "decide to tell" them will not be comforting.

Finding a female crewman wandering the halls, however, will...

- DO NOT take offense when the natives insult your ability to give orders regarding ship navigation. You also must be mindful not to brag about your ability to time travel, and, rather, anticipate the natives' inevitable reaction to your "alien" crew mates.

- Your First Officer is liable to display logic that is "annoying". However, you will most likely pursue the effects-of-the-past-influences-your-future angle as it is most relatable to those reading this.

- DO point out that the computer sounding like a woman is something that isn't changing anytime soon, so any natives inadvertently beamed aboard should just get used to it.

- You are NOT permitted to use force when the natives panic and use strong-armed techniques to be returned to Earth. There are more clever ways to make them comply. They will just be stuck in your sick bay, and you will still be stuck with your predicament of getting home.

- YOU may be the factor in which the natives' timeline is changed. If this knowledge is discovered, you must do your best to get the representative of present-day Earth back to his budding family and correct the timeline.

- Your friendly representative to the natives may have collected evidence against you. This evidence must be destroyed. Employ the native to help you on your mission from arm's length. Involving him any further could do permanent damage to the timeline.

- DO NOT worry, beaming in to a secure military Earth facility won't cause panic. No one will even notice you.

- In the captain's absence, the bridge crew members may not hesitate to be a bit... testy with each other. Your "logical" First Officer will most likely win the fight. As usual.

- DO NOT be so foolish to think that you will only get involved with a single native. Be prepared for the situation to snowball and for you to take on additional natives. Your captain is not as tactful as he wants you to believe...

- Somehow, you will be familiar with the workings of primitive data recording. Do not question how you know where the information you need is stored. Take it and set the timeline straight!

- Though your commanding officer may recognize such things as "film" and a "darkroom", they may have no concept of moving through secure facilities undetected or defending themselves without excessive use of force. Though their tactics are heavy-handed, proceed in your acquisition of the necessary data. They will be captured, but your common sense will allow you to bring your data back to the ship.

- If you are captured by a native military organization, be flippant! Take advantage of the fact that they believe that everything you're saying is science fiction... up until they use YOUR technology to threaten you. Then just ask smart-alec questions. It will irritate them beyond any violence you could possibly enact.

- Eventually, your fellow crewmen will come to save you. They obviously learned their heavy-handed tactics from *someone*...

- The native will inevitably panic, causing irritation with your crew and may cause your First Officer to take matters into his own hands.

- Reversing time and going back to the point before you arrived on past Earth, then shooting yourself into the future while simultaneously returning the native to his own time like nothing had ever happened should work, right? RIGHT?

Please be advised of this timeless protocol as you continue your career with Starfleet. May you continue to boldly go where no one has... well, you know what we mean.

Taylor Deatherage is from Chicago, an undercover psych degree holder, fashion blogger and occasional author.

20. COURT MARTIAL
THE TELL-TALE HEART
CHRISTIAN YOUNG

Seeing Jim Kirk gaslighted should give anybody chills.

Here is a man with a list of honors so comprehensive that the even his prosecutor, Lieutenant Areel Shaw, tries to draw attention away from it when he takes the stand. Kirk has, in his own words, "spent [his] whole life training for decisions" like the ejection of an ion pod, even if it means losing one life to protect the lives of others.

Kirk's position is centered, again and again, in the language of service: rank, command and captain.

One could be forgiven for forgetting this Kirk in favor of the Kirk of stereotype: the maverick in a ripped shirt, all swagger and sex. This is, I think, an error. If anything, *Court Martial* proves that Kirk is more complex that we remember him in passing. He is competent, accomplished and determined. At the same time, he is flawed, fond of picking a fight and sensual.

But any man can falter. Any man can fall. And everyone seems to want Kirk to. His former classmates shun him, resentful of the shame his alleged negligence brings on Starfleet. Commodore Stone, who begins the initial investigation that ultimately culminates in Kirk's court martial, begins by offering the favor of sweeping the incident under the rug for the greater good.

All Kirk has to do is accept his madness.

The trouble is that there is no sane choice for Kirk to make. He can either accept the evidence that the traits on which he forms his identity — skill, memory, clear thinking — have deserted him, or he can deny the computer's objective eye.

Confronted with an apparent and terrible truth, Kirk doubts.

He is right to. After all, human memory is malleable. The evidence of that is always present, from the "repressed" memories of the Satanic Panic of the 1980s to new research that suggests that we may actually change our memories each time we access them. How many of us have argued with a lover or roommate over who did or did not take out the trash, drink the last of the milk or leave the toilet seat up? If we can't even remember where we've left our keys as a species, how can we expect to remember with clarity a decision made under pressure?

Enter, then, the machines.

If human beings are doomed to be irrational, how can we be just? Human eyewitnesses and character witnesses have mutable memories and attachments, but computers and recordings will compensate for us. Machines lack the capacity to lie, to be sentimental or to be subjective. The camera observes, the microphone records, the computer does the math. They are all without desire, so why not trust them to tell us what is true and what is not?

Confronted by hard evidence that contradicts our memory, how many of us have changed our opinion? How many of us have admitted that, yes, we must be misremembering? That we haven't thought the data through? That we have bias? Or, more curiously, how many of us have dug in our heels and let cognitive dissonance reinforce the thing that we remember, evidence be damned? How many of us are conscious of making that choice?

How much can we rely on our memories to answer that question?

Kirk's decision to rely on his memory is the sort of choice that we are explicitly taught we are not supposed to make. Reason screams that, no, we don't get to pick and choose what gets to be the truth based on what we like or what makes us comfortable or what suits our strengths best. We don't call things "unreasonable" because we like them. We hate unreasonable things. Unreasonable things are dangerous, unfair and cause us distress.

A charitable person might suggest that Kirk isn't breaking the rules so much as seeking a third alternative, but it isn't until relatively late in the episode that Kirk has a compelling reason for him to believe such an alternative exists. Fifteen years later, the *Kobayashi Maru* would be added to the *Star Trek* lore, establishing Kirk as a rule-breaker who doesn't like to lose. But that's not what is happening here. Kirk is not about to sabotage Starfleet's legal system in order to get away with murder.

But, like the original Kobayashi Maru, the *Court Martial* scenario does tell us an interesting thing about Kirk's character: when faced with no good choices, he will always choose the option in which he can do something over the option in which he must remain passive. Faced with the possibility of his own madness, Kirk opts for the choice in which he gets some agency.

By the time Kirk confronts Finney — and let's not forget that the presence of the buried man is revealed by the too-loud beating of a single human heart nestled away on B deck — Kirk has already immersed himself in the role of the lunatic. They are mirrors now, Finney and Kirk, with one exception: Finney's rage and paranoia are the result of his inability to accept his own fall. Kirk is ready to rule in Hell if he has to, while Finney resents being made to serve in Heaven. Finney is a hideous glimpse of what Kirk could have been or what he might have become if he'd given in to the evidence.

Kirk's prize is, of course, restoration to his throne. And yes, we get our maverick, complete with fisticuffs and a kiss from the girl. And yet, there is one last glance into the abyss when Shaw tells him that Cogley — Kirk's own attorney during the court martial — has taken on Finney as a client. The possibility that Finney could go free suggests that the restored order is just as illusory as the evidence against Kirk was in the first place.

We can believe Kirk's own madness is just a story, told to him by someone who wishes him violence, but his mirror remains below. Waiting.

Christian Young tries to embrace his own fall,
with or without the specter of a court martial on the horizon.

---

21. THE RETURN OF THE ARCHONS
CHILDREN OF THE REVOLUTION
VANESSA DE KAUWE

The speeches of the anonymous rebel leader "Z", during the days of the last-ever Festival.

Two days before Festival
Children of Archon, our time has finally come. Strangers have arrived and they, like our ancestors, bear all the traits of Starfleet. You know what I mean: the strange clothing, the random blurting of mission statements, and the flamboyant flaunting of technology that Beta III hasn't seen since the Starship *Archon* crashed here a century ago. Anyone romping around like that was bound to attract attention. But tell me this: how in Beta did Landru's people get to them before we did? His Lawgivers are hooded, mindless automatons that move at glacial speed, and the Body of his people are so brainwashed that they are little more than smiling idiots. Yet these people got to the strangers before we did. Why? Couldn't you see they were different? They were wearing pirate costumes, damn it.

Yet all is not lost. Starfleet will always send a rescue party. Let's just hope that none of them are smiling idiots, or you'll never recognize them. We need their technology for our final victory. Our forebears hid us from the mind-control chambers so that we couldn't be absorbed into the pathetic, vacuous collective of the Body. But all the shrewdness of our ancestors, and all our own training and persistence, all this will be in vain unless we can bring liberation to Beta III. If the legends our parents told us are correct, then Starfleet can't help but play the hero. And we shall use their heroics for our own purpose. Children of Archon, prepare for action, for the revolution is upon us.

Festival Eve
Children of Archon, should I laugh or cry? Some of us have the *Archon* crew for our heritage, others of us are true descendants of Beta III; but most of you — most of

you — are quivering, spineless sacks of jelly. All it takes is for someone to mention the name Landru and you start shaking at the knees and peering around like startled rodents. What is wrong with you? Have you been camouflaging yourselves with the Body for so long that you've become like them? Indeed, you would have to be in a brainwashed stupor to think Landru is a god or even a man. A god wouldn't depend on technology and a man couldn't live for 6000 years; even a child can see that. Yes, maybe he was once a man, but all that's left of the man are his machines, so I don't want see any more cowering at the name of Landru. Is this a rebel cell or a kindergarten of whimpering infants?

And if we are truly comrades, then stop all this in-fighting. There has been too much loose talk about the Betan people, and I won't have our underground movement sinking into a gossip circle. You see the Betans in the Body and you call them insipid dullards. Then you see them in Festival and you say they are raging, moral-less brutes. But if the Betans are such dullards, why haven't we been able to overthrow them? And if the random violence of Festival is really part of Betan nature, why are some of them traumatized by it all? Comrade Reger's daughter is a prime example. No, Betans are neither idiots nor monsters; they are simply under Landru's influence. We know he controls them in daily life, so why can't you see that he controls them during Festival too? Again: fairly obvious.

I do not say, as some do, that Festival is a break in Landru's control, like a pressure valve, releasing the people to their naturally animalistic state — this is just an insult to our Betan comrades. I say rather that, during Festival's Red Hours, Landru forces the people into a state of depravity so that, shocked and damaged by their own behavior, they surrender themselves more readily to his rule. Mind-control is always stronger in those who offer no resistance.

However, we are the resistance. We have never surrendered to Landru's tyranny, and we will liberate all of Beta III. So no more flinching. We must show a strong and united front to the Starfleet rescue team.

In the meantime, use Festival to the best of our advantage. Loot everything, destroy anything and target anyone who might stand in our way. Maybe this'll put some fire in your blood. But whatever you do, make sure you continue to blend in. As we have seen, it helps to jump through shop windows and throw goods in the mud. As long as you yell out, "Festival, Festival" every now and then, no one will think it's odd. Spinning around with flailing arms is also surprisingly effective.

Let's go comrades: rampage, rampage, rampage!

Day 1 of Festival: Evening Red Hour

Comrades, hear me: word has come that comrades Reger and Tamar are sheltering the rescue team tonight. Amongst them is one with a formidable mind and extraordinary ears, whose physical strength matches his intellect. Yet this is not their Captain. For some reason, that rank is reserved for the one having the most difficulty understanding what is going on here. It's hard to know if his swagger and careless talk are due to uncommon bravery or some sort of brain injury, perhaps incurred in previous conflicts. Strangers indeed, but they may prove highly useful. Stay alert at all times; this is what we've been waiting for.

Day 2 of Festival: Morning Red Hour

Children of Archon, we must act quickly. Last night comrades Reger and Tamar were betrayed by a member of the Body named Hacom. Hacom grew suspicious at the Captain's endless questions and manly posturing, and the ears on the other one didn't help either. Reger is currently hiding with the rescue party in one of our underground cells.

Here are my instructions.

We must prepare in case Reger and the rescue party are captured. If so, they will be taken to the Absorption Chamber. This is when our comrades who have posed as Landru's priests must step into action. Continue the façade of your priestly duties, but do so in such a way that comrade Marplon is left alone in the Chamber with the prisoners. Marplon, do what you must so that they escape unabsorbed. I tell you Marplon, you'll really need to spell things out for them: it seems they spend a lot of time trying to argue with Landru's films, even when they know they are just pre-recorded projections. Yet if they do escape, they will surely dispose of Landru for us — whether it's bravery or brain injury, that Captain can't help himself.

Freedom Day

Children of Archon, it is done. The escaped rescue party did indeed seek and destroy Landru's mainframe, and they did so with the highest conceit, without the slightest concern for the rest of us. Comrade Marplon recalls the words of their Captain: "You're on your own now. I hope you're up to it." With that, they dropped phasers and left. The only defense they left were sociologists. But we who have resisted Landru have nothing to fear from sociologists. Now are free to rule Beta III as we see fit. Nothing can withstand our rebellion now: rampage, rampage, rampage.

Vanessa de Kauwe is a freelance researcher, sci-fi nerd and adrenaline junkie.
But not necessarily in that order.

22. SPACE SEED
DVD COMMENTARY FOR THE BEST BUY
TRIPLE PLATINUM SPECIAL EDITION
WYNN QUON

Hi and welcome to this DVD commentary track. I'm Wycliffe Wreckless, head of Digital Marketing & Promotion at Video Futures. I was super-excited when Paramount came to us for "*Star Trek*, the Best Buy Triple Platinum Special Edition". The Triple Platinum Special Edition is a must-have for all Trekkies. It's a post-modern viewing adventure that is much closer to the original 1960s experience of watching the show. Back then, each episode was broadcast with a total of 12 minutes of commercial advertising that you couldn't fast-forward. We strongly believe that commercial messaging is an essential element of the authentic *Star Trek* experience. In the Triple Platinum Special Edition, we've used the latest digital technology to bring that ambience back, but we've done it in a subtle way using product placement. In this DVD commentary, we'll show how we did our work. Our guiding principle was to keep (and even strengthen) the spirit of the original episodes.

Just a quick recap of *Space Seed*: Kirk and his crew find Khan, a 1990s long-haired hippie warlord (I believe his first name is Genghis). Khan tries to hijack the *Enterprise*. One of Kirk's crew, a historian named Marla McGivers, falls in love with Khan and helps him in his plans before finally turning against him. Khan is defeated and marooned on a barren planet.

➤➤➤

So here's the opening scene. The Captain and crew are on the bridge, and a derelict Earth space vessel appears on the navigation screen. If you look at the bottom right corner of that screen, you'll see a Tom-Tom GPS logo. Tom-Tom, the maker of reliable feature-rich GPS devices, were thrilled when we asked whether they'd enjoy being associated with the 23rd century technology powering the Ship's nav screen. The Tom-Tom adds a special "retro" authenticity to the scene, I think.

With digital-editing technology, we can do more than just insert logos. So yes, you'll see a Tylenol label on Dr. McCoy's tricorder and a Glock logo on Kirk's friendly phaser, but we can also alter props, add dialogue through seamless dubbing and so on.

Continuing with the same scene, we see Captain Kirk getting out of the Captain's chair to get a closer look at the screen. But take another look at the chair! We've replaced the bland original with a light-blue Ikea Ektorp Tullsta Armchair. (By the way, if you've bought the Golden Age Seniors version of the Triple Platinum Special edition, you'll see the handsome Muren armchair, which comes with a built-in footrest.)

➤ ➤ ➤

Going on, we're beaming over to the derelict ship. Now here's an interesting bit. Kirk smashes open the glass cover of Khan's hibernation pod with his bare hands. We didn't actually have anything in mind for this scene, but the legal department called us and said that Paramount had liability exposure because of potential copycat behavior by enthusiastic Trekkies. We did a quick brainstorming session on which companies could help us out. As a result, we've now got Kirk wearing a sturdy and safe pair of blue Playtex gloves.

Okay, now in this scene, Khan is resuscitated and he asks Kirk about the *Enterprise*'s destination. We added a little something at the end of the dialogue:

KHAN: *What is your heading?*
KIRK: *Our heading is Starbase 12, a planet in the Gamma 400 star system. Our command base in this sector, where you can enjoy a refreshing glass of Tropicana's passionfruit pineapple juice blend.*

Did you catch it? (You may need to replay it a few times.) Pretty good, I must say. Especially since our market research says that Trekkies are enthusiastic foodies.

Okay, Khan's recuperated and Kirk is arranging a banquet featuring the highlights of 23rd century cuisine. He lays out a table with tasty foodstuffs. Can you see what we did here? Just freeze-frame and zoom if you can't. Yes, that's a box of Quaker Harvest Crunch sitting on the tablecloth. Next to it are some Captain Highliner English Haddock Fish Sticks and a Hungry Man Pulled Pork Dinner. Khan is in for some delicious treats.

➤ ➤ ➤

Now here's the scene where Khan seduces the historian. He's in her quarters and asking about her drawings of famous heroes. It's a sentimental and romantic moment. Between the portrait of Leif Erickson and Napoleon, we've added a Hallmark painting of a cute, cuddly kitten in a pair of shorts. Several of our staff have trouble watching this sequence with dry eyes. I'm no softie myself, but, I have to say, I tear up a bit too.

➤ ➤ ➤

Okay, the excitement is building. Khan has taken over the *Enterprise* and threatens Kirk on the bridge:

> KIRK: *What's going on down there?*
> KHAN: *Your ship is mine! I have shut off the life-support systems! Clap on! Clap off!*
> *(lights on bridge alternately go on and off).*

In test audiences, our altered scene was rated more suspenseful than the original (without the Clapper). How about that?! And viewers can't help being impressed with the convenience of the Clapper for controlling electrical devices of all kinds. Everyone wins.

➤➤➤

Next up is the climax where Kirk battles the superhuman Khan. We had a lot of interest from product sponsors here. Khan gives Kirk a tough workout. You see Kirk sporting a high-end pair of Nike Air Zoom Elites and an Adidas tracksuit. Meanwhile, Khan delivers his karate kicks, hippie-style, in solid Birkenstock sandals. In the original, Kirk pummels Khan with repeated blows from a small blunt object taken from an equipment rack. Here we've digitally altered it to a 10-inch KitchenAid skillet to appeal to the foodies. The other alternative was a Dunlop Aerogel Ultimate squash racquet. This would have gone well with the sportswear and is consistent with the theme of vigorous physical activity. But KitchenAid paid us more, so that was that. Oh, I have to thank our sound engineer Rodney. When we first played the new scene, something was wrong. Rodney figured it out immediately. The sound wasn't "skillet" enough. That "Bong!" sound you hear now when Kirk is dusting Khan with the frying pan — that's Rodney's work. Kudos, Rodney!

➤➤➤

Okay, we're on the Bridge. Last scene. Let's just watch it together. You may have to see the original version to spot our changes, but I think you'll agree we've done a fine job here.

> KIRK: *Lieutenant Marla McGivers. Given a choice of court martial or accompanying them there...*
> KHAN: *(gazing into her eyes) It will be difficult. A struggle at first even to stay alive, to find food.*
> MARLA: *I'll go with him, sir. It'll be easier now that I've learned about*

tripadvisor.com.
KHAN: A superior woman. I will take her. And I've gotten something else I wanted. A world to win, an empire to build. And these Captain Highliner English Haddock Fish Sticks.

So that's it. Thanks for watching. And hey, after all that talking, I could really use some Ricola Natural Herb cough drops...

Wynn Quon is a forty-year marketing veteran and author of the seminal article "Black and Deckard: Case studies in Product Positioning of stylish home-improvement power tools in the movie Blade Runner".

---

23. A TASTE OF ARMAGEDDON
I WOULDN'T BE CAUGHT DEAD IN THIS
EMMA NOWINSKI

A Short History Lesson from Eminiar VII

The following commercial was pulled almost immediately from the airwaves as it was deemed "detrimental to the societal order of Eminiar VII and deeply offensive to those who have served their duty admirably". Its creator, Linda VI, had been born on Eminiar VII and had lived on the planet her entire life. She was frustrated with the war and at odds with the complacency surrounding the volunteered suicides of her family and friends. Knowing that she was risking treason, she poured her outrage into her work with women and this commercial. Despite its limited showing, the "Be You" campaign was outrageously successful. Every article of clothing from the line sold out within the week. Here is the commercial in its entirety.

(Open on a darkly lit disintegration chamber while somber, vaguely patriotic music plays. This is a sad scene but one that should invoke a feeling of pride. The voice of LINDA VI narrates.)

LINDA VI: Nearly 80% of women will serve out their patriotic duty in their lifetime. With those kind of odds —

(Suddenly cut out somber music. Cut to LINDA VI, standing tall with a small, knowing smile on her face in the center of the city capital. She is dressed in

OUTSIDE IN BOLDLY GOES

a long blue evening dress, her hair up and her makeup perfect. She leaves no doubt that she is beautiful and she knows it. She places a hand on her hip before speaking.)

LINDA VI: — the phrase "I wouldn't be caught dead in this outfit" could not be more meaningful.

(Fun and happy music begins. Women start to swarm the capitol building. They all are happy and smiling, dressed according to their personalities. The colors and type of dress are varied, with differing levels of color and modesty. They dance their way towards disintegration chambers, all looking fabulous. LINDA VI commands the camera, looking into it as if it were an enemy she had just conquered.)

LINDA VI: Introducing the "Be You" fashion line. Turn every outfit into your favorite outfit, the one you wish you could wear every day. Duty doesn't have to be dull. Dress how you've always wanted to dress today!

(Insert scene of an older woman in black looking wistfully over a picture of her late husband while facing a disintegration chamber. LINDA VI walks in and grabs the picture of the man, throwing it over her shoulder, placing an arm around the woman.)

LINDA VI: He's gone, move on! You might not have long left either. Turn your sadness into a brand new dress!

(The woman nods and goes off camera, only to return immediately wearing a colorful ensemble from the line, a large smile now on her face. LINDA VI nods approvingly. Cut to a scene of a mother and her young girl in pigtails who is cuddling a Tribble. Both are walking towards a chamber. LINDA VI enters and stops them.)

LINDA VI: You're going to let your little girl perform her duty like that? Not on my watch! We have clothes for all women, big or small. Even for their special friends!

(Girl leaves with LINDA VI and returns in a new multicolored outfit with a Tribble in a matching outfit.)

LINDA VI: Much better.

(Girl smiles and takes mother's hand as they both continue to the chamber. Insert scene of a sad-looking pregnant woman in drab clothing, looking fearful of a disintegration chamber.)

LINDA VI: You look forlorn, like a pregnant Gorn. Who can be sad when you're dressed fab in our new maternity wear?

(Takes woman by the hand and spins her, turning her drab clothing into a fun, flower-covered dress. The woman is now happy and content, giving her hair a flip before stepping into the chamber.)

LINDA VI: Don't you worry. Our clothing is 100% atomizable so you don't have to worry about polluting our beautiful planet when you're gone!

(Cut to LINDA VI, sitting now near a pool, wearing a swimsuit, with a drink in her hand, again the perfect vision of control. She is surrounded by other women, some older, some pregnant, all happy as could be. LINDA VI looks up at the camera, giving it a wink.)

LINDA VI: Take some control over your future... wardrobe. After all, what do you have to lose?

Linda VI served her own duty three days before the war was ended by the crew of the USS Enterprise *and its captain, James T. Kirk. Before stepping into the disintegrator, she only had this to say: "I dressed for the occasion, the only statement I choose to make." She was wearing a short green gown with gold accents and black high heels, all from her own line.*

Emma Nowinski spends her spare time preparing for the zombie apocalypse, watching obscene amounts of Netflix and polishing her vintage Star Trek *coffee mugs.*

24. THIS SIDE OF PARADISE

HOW WILLIAM SHATNER'S CHEST INSPIRED AT LEAST ONE FEMALE TELEVISION WRITER TO SUCCEED IN THE HOLLYWOOD BOYS' CLUB

ROSANNE WELCH

As a child, I didn't come to *Star Trek* for the fantasy or for the fun, futuristic optimism or even for the glory of the gadgetry of the tricorders and communicators. I came for William Shatner's chest. Glimpsed quickly one day while changing channels, my pre-adolescent hormones screeched to a halt as I sat transfixed. That tight Starfleet uniform shirt truly rippled across his chest, which seemed to strain to be released. We didn't "flip" in those pre-remote days. We sat in front of the set and manually spun the dial like the combination lock on our high-school lockers, which brought us into much closer contact with the (sometimes still black and white) pictures flashing upon our frightfully small screens. I don't even remember which episode it was that first placed his pecs in front of me, but this obsession with Shatner's chest focused me so much that I never cared for the writers' propensity for finding ways for his co-star to flaunt his own brand of sexuality. Forcing the unfeeling Mr. Spock to feel never moved me at all, so in second, third and fourth runs I never found *This Side of Paradise* much to my liking. In the epic mashup between Sexy Shatner and Sexy Spock, Shatner always won. But being a budding television writer even as a ten year old, I recognized in the idea the need to offer the actor a way out of the rigid character description enforced upon him by his creator.

Viewed now from the perspective of a fifty-year-old female television writer and scholar, no longer merely a fan, I find the episode fascinating for what it says about the history of women writers — and the female characters they create — in television. In those days of heady chest-worshipping, I didn't know that the D.C. in D.C. Fontana stood for Dorothy Catherine. When I later learned that information from reading *The Making of Star Trek*, I took her success as a beacon for my own journey, as did many other future female television writers I came to meet throughout my career. While countless books have been written about the influence of the program on science fiction and on television in general, what I came to learn was the influence *Star Trek* wielded on bringing women into the industry — and how their participation changes the way female characters are portrayed.

Because of Fontana, future writers of future *Trek* franchises invited other female writers to pitch ideas so that, to my great joy, twenty years after I stumbled upon the original *Trek*, I found myself in the offices of *Star Trek: The Next Generation* pitching ideas for stories involving what was still largely a boys' club of characters.

Sure, they had accepted two women into their continuing cast — both in "soft" occupations as ship's counselor and medical doctor and still under the command of Captain Picard. But the franchise had proved a stepping stone for a variety of female writers I admired (including Jane Espenson and Melinda M. Snodgrass), and I was excited to be among them. I never sold a story to that iteration of the show, but I kept watching — and kept noticing that, when written by women, female characters were (and sadly are still) often more developed (in ways other than their chest measurements).

In *Paradise*, that is true of what actress Nichelle Nichols is given to do as our regular female cast member, Lt. Nyota Uhura (whose first name I never knew until the writing of this essay — and wasn't given on the TV show), and what Jill Ireland is given to do as the guest character, Spock's former girlfriend Leila (who in the tradition of sex objects was never provided a last name). Normally confined to dialogue discussing "hailing frequencies" and only seen taking orders from Captain Kirk, in *Paradise*, Uhura commits mutiny against her captain. He has to state for the Captain's log that, "Lt. Uhura has effectively sabotaged the communications station." While all the male starship members also commit mutiny, Uhura is given one-on-one screen time with the lead actor to do so. Likewise, while Leila seems at first to only be demonstrating that the most perfect, porcelain-faced blonde can even be sexy in overalls, she was also spouting Thoreau (as in Henry David) and his brand of 19th century Transcendentalist philosophy to Spock — and to the audience. For a show airing at the height of the hippie movement, Leila served as a mouthpiece for their dream of peaceful co-existence, one not yet shared by other generations. In several online interviews, Fontana has chosen Leila as one of her favorite characters.

Of course, television was then (and still is now) a man's world, so Uhura's and Leila's interests are eventually subsumed by Kirk's desire to prove that "Man stagnates if he has no ambition, no desire to be more than he is." This philosophy discounts "woman" as part of "man" and makes the female-gendered idea of creating peace and happiness submissive to the more male dominant idea of success defined by changing the world around him. Why is a love of nature, as evidenced in Spock's line: "I have [seen a dragon] ... but I've never stopped to look at clouds before or rainbows" less of an ambition for man? Even the American Founding Fathers cared more for the land and its beauty than these final frontier founders seem to do as they travel the galaxy. Why is the existence of this previous girlfriend and the chance to hear "I love you" from a formerly feeling-less alien male, less of an ambition of (wo)man?

Despite Fontana straining to include her voice in this world, the male producers still stamped their seal on the final product that became *This Side of Paradise*. Over the course of my career, I came to learn that Fontana shared that experience with many of the female writers who followed her, each one planting just enough seeds or dropping just enough breadcrumbs of her own opinion onto the fields of male creation for the rest of us "chick writers" to follow. Where as a child I saw *This Side of Paradise* as an epic battle between sexy male leads, as an adult I see it as the continued battle for the hearts and minds of the audience waged by writers of different genders. It is a fight that several other sisters have carried on through the decades and one I'm willing to declare has been won by a relative newcomer to the scene, Shonda Rhimes. Through the creation of her own new frontier in *Grey's Anatomy*, Rhimes provides male and female audiences alike with an all-inclusive world entirely conceived in a female mind. What do both the male and female doctors of Seattle Grace Hospital hope to provide their patients every day? As Rodenberry provided a masculine "trek" for man into the final frontier, the feminine goal Rhimes provides her characters is right there in the title of the hospital, "grace". (And, thanks in part to D.C. Fontana, Shonda chose to use her first name in her credits.)

All this musing makes me wonder how many young female writers are now coming to their careers because of a love of the way Patrick Dempsey's chest ripples under his uniform shirt...

Rosanne Welch turned a childhood of watching television (from Doctor Who *to* Star Trek *to* The Monkees*) into an adulthood of writing for television (from* Beverly Hills, 90210 *to* Touched by an Angel*), earned her Ph.D. — and then began taking television seriously.*

25. THE DEVIL IN THE DARK
YOU LOVE I
KATHRYN SULLIVAN

In the tunnels of Janus VI, a highly intelligent creature is slowly being driven mad. A normally gentle being, she is being forced to take drastic steps because the invaders of her world are not taking her subtle hints of destroyed machinery and are instead forcing her to kill them to protect children in her care.

She doesn't just go on a killing rampage, although it may seem that way to the miners being picked off one by one. It takes her some time, but she is smart enough to figure out not only why there are clusters of soft-skins guarding a particular room but also to figure out the one piece of the reactor to take that will force the invaders to leave the planet. Notice that she takes the reactor pump rather than just destroying it. Perhaps the Horta of long ago once used technology. Was her plan to merely drive away the soft-skins? Or, given where she ended up hiding the circulation pump, had she planned to bargain with them, to force them to see her not as an unthinking monster but someone with the same rights to exist as themselves?

Fortunately for her, the miners have contacted the *Enterprise*, whose soft-skins are more open to the idea of contacting new lifeforms.

One *Enterprise* crewmember is killed, but the Horta immediately realizes that this was a different batch of soft-skins from those who had thoughtlessly destroyed her eggs. Maybe she could see the difference in uniforms vs. the coveralls. Maybe the uniform fabric from the *Enterprise* tasted different to that of the miners'. Either way, after that death, she changes how she approaches people. The Horta visibly hesitates when she first encounters Kirk and Spock. She is not moving at full speed when she starts towards them. If she meant to attack, then one or both would be injured (despite Spock's odds), as none of the other attacked miners or even the crewmember had a chance to get off a shot. But instead the Horta is injured in that encounter with the more powerful phasers. So, when the first attempt fails, she watches Spock and Kirk — and Spock is aware of her watching. Despite being in great pain, she is patient. When the two soft-skins go down separate tunnels, the Horta causes the cave-in to keep Kirk separated long enough for communication to at least be a possibility. Luckily, Kirk had listened to Spock's arguments about the Horta being the last of her kind, so he doesn't fire when she approaches him the second time.

She also has a reason for leading them to a tunnel that goes through one of the egg chambers, causing a cave-in there. She knows the eggshells could withstand a rockfall. She wants to see how the trapped soft-skin reacts to the eggs, while remaining close enough to act in case he makes the wrong move. Is this soft-skin Kirk indeed different from the miners who had thoughtlessly destroyed the eggs or collected them as trophies? A difficult test for a grief-stricken mother to use, but the only option she has to be sure of them.

Her intelligence and quick-wittedness are demonstrated again in Spock's first attempt at the mind meld. Spock only picks up on her pain, but she absorbs enough language to be able to etch a deliberately double-sided message to the *Enterprise* officers: "No Kill I". Kirk puzzles over whether she's asking them not to kill her or saying that she won't kill them, but it is both. And purposely so. She couldn't have chosen a more perfect phrase.

Her grief and guilt overwhelm her momentarily when in the meld with Spock, but it is the first time she has contacted a sympathetic mind in some time, especially one willing and able to take her side against the miners.

She now knows the miners acted in ignorance. Those devils in the dark could not recognize life unlike them. They were all males, who could not tell eggs from mineral geodes, even when they broke them open. She knows better. And so she works out a trade with the soft skins: for herself and her children freedom, and for the miner soft skins access to particular minerals. She will share with her children the knowledge of star-traveling soft skins, those who might welcome the Horta's return to the tunnels between the stars. She does this without fear or resentment. For she is Horta and she is Mother. And she has so much love to give.

Kathryn Sullivan writes young adult fantasy and science fiction. She still remembers when the Horta was the most fascinating alien she had ever seen on TV.

26. ERRAND OF MERCY
TO BOLDLY SLEEP
ERIKA ENSIGN

MEMORANDUM
TO: Editing Department
FROM: Copy
RE: Fall Catalog

Hey Jan,

Attached, please find the updated copy for the Fall catalog. Gotta say, I love the new style guidelines. Felt like I was writing copy for a 1930s department-store fashion show! And this season's designs are really far out. Perfect to breathe a little new life into things. The boss's five-year plan may work out yet. Can't wait to get the art completed and put this one to bed!

Galactic Sleepwear — Sleep Boldly
The finest sleepwear in the galaxy, for all your nightwear needs

The Organian Collection
These items are true classics: sleepwear that stands the test of time. These garments are perfect for when you're not feeling like a ball of energy.

The Ayelborne — If you prefer to emphasize the "lounge" in lounge-wear, this nightgown is for you. Long, luxuriant and purple, it's perfect for when you'd rather let things happen around you than jump up and get things done.

Sit back and put your feet up. The Ayelborne will keep you warm from neck to calf, but the short sleeves leave your arms free to wave away any troubles that may seem to come your way.

The Trefayne — Are you a daydreamer? Do you often sit back and let your mind wander? If you're constantly in your head, seeing things that are not really there, this dreamy wraparound is for you.

Dark red, with embroidered detailing around the collar and short ties on the sleeves, the Trefayne is perfect for the waking dreamer. The slightly pleated skirt adds just a hint of flirty fun, so everyone can see you're a just bit sassier than your cohorts.

The Claymare — You'll be smiling for sure when you don this long-sleeve, knee-length nightgown. Its soft stripes will lull you into a soporific state before you know it, but the sharp lines of the cleverly detailed ribbon on the shoulders show you're not quite as soft as you seem.

The Claymare is a fashionable option that's comfortable enough to shield you from the most discordant of emotions throughout the night.

The Barona — This little yellow number is as stylish as it is practical. It's perfect for the active sleeper. The calf-length tunic provides plenty of room to move around, and the soft brown leggings won't hamper any nighttime jaunts in or about the house. You could even go climb a tree! It's just that versatile.

The smart, golden rope-belt doubles as a tie for your bed curtains, but it's also suitable for self-defense (or whatever other nighttime shenanigans you may desire). The plunging neckline adds a bit of va-va-voom for when you want to set the night on fire!

With such a snazzy combo, you're sure to find yourself feeling superior to anyone wearing anything else.

The Vulcan Trader — Are your dreams filled with cold logic? Wrap up in this stylish cape. It even doubles as your own built-in blanket! It's certain to keep you warm and comfortable no matter what's going on inside your head.

The blanket/cape's deep burgundy complements the jewel blue velour of the thigh-length tunic. What are the odds you won't like it? It's difficult to be precise, but we think they're approximately 7,824.7 to one!

Organia Slippers — These super-soft boots must be worn to be believed. They're every bit as warm as they look and will give you the fuzziest feet around. They wrap all the way up your calves to ensure you have the toastiest of tootsies wherever you may roam.

Pair these with any of the shorter Organian Collection items for the most stylish in classic sleepwear!

The Federation Collection

If you prefer your sleepwear to be a bit more fashion-forward, the Federation collection is for you. These simple but eminently serviceable pajama sets are some of our most popular sellers. The just-shy-of-form-fitting long-sleeved shirts are soft and allow for plenty of movement. Optional gold piping around the cuffs will set you apart from other sleepers.

Available in a gold that's almost too hot to handle, cool blue and bright red. Red shirts are on sale, as we're currently overstocked. (But if you're looking for something durable, we recommend the blue or gold; they'll last much longer!)

Red and blue are also available as a petite nightdress, but we're very short of stock on those, so order now!

The Klingon Collection

Does your partner toss and turn in bed? Do you have roommates you don't completely trust? For the best in high-protection sleepwear, look no further than the Klingon Collection. With a double-layer top and pliable metal-mesh pants, you'll be ready for anything at any time! These are a real hit in college dorms.

The pullover sleeveless jumper has a sparkly sheen and tight horizontal stripes. It fits perfectly over a chest-hugging black turtleneck. It's the very height of martial sleepwear. Order the Kor package and get a free gold-fringed bedrunner! It's nothing short of glorious!

Erika Ensign recently relocated to Canada where she does many things, most of them podcasts. She produces and co-hosts the Doctor Who *podcast* Verity!, *plus she appears on several others, including* The Audio Guide to Babylon 5, Uncanny Magazine Podcast *and* The Incomparable.

---

27. THE ALTERNATIVE FACTOR
THE LAZARUS EXPERIMENT
LES ZIG

Chief Security Officer Hunt's Log — Stardate 3087.3

After a strange force fleetingly nullified the magnetic field in the solar system and rocked the ship, the bridge detected a human lifeform on a planet the *Enterprise* had been surveying. Mr. Spock speculated it was "possible, very possible" this lifeform could present a danger.

I called my team to attention, where they expressed their concerns.

"You know what this means," Lieutenant Johnson said.

"Chief Hunt," Ensign Badami said, "we're tired of the Captain playing fast and loose with our lives!"

The others murmured their agreement.

"Not one of us wants to be the next Ellard," Johnson said. "Or Packer or Hernadez or Shaughnessy or Lynch or Rigoni or —"

I held up my hand. All good men, lost too soon.

"We'll be on our guard," I said.

Chief Security Officer Hunt's Log
Johnson, Badami, Williams and I accompanied the Captain and Mr. Spock to the planet, where we discovered a ship that bore a remarkable similarity to the one in historical films driven by George Jetson. While Mr. Spock investigated the ship, a man appeared on the cliffs, beseeched us and fell.

Against my protests, the Captain has beamed him to sickbay.

Chief Security Officer Hunt's Log
Starfleet have contacted us under protocol Code Factor 1 — invasion status!

A man Mr. Spock has identified as a "very possible" danger, a potential invasion and a destructive force that threatens the universe is onboard the ship. We must proceed with caution.

Therefore the Captain has decided to interview this man alone.

Security Officer Badami's Log
I escorted Mr. Spock to the planet to investigate the ship belonging to the man now identified as Lazarus. The Captain and Lazarus joined us, where Mr. Spock queried Lazarus's story and accused him of being a "liar". Indignant, Lazarus proclaimed the existence of a "monster" capable of "anti-life". Then the force hit again!

When it abated, Lazarus warned us that the "thing" had attacked. His story troubled the Captain. I suggested we put a security team on Lazarus. Too many bizarre things have happened around him.

Instead, the Captain has beamed Lazarus back to sickbay.

Chief Security Officer Hunt's Log
Dr. McCoy has presented a mystery to the Captain: a wound on Lazarus's temple suddenly healed, as if it never was. But while the Captain and Dr. McCoy were having this conversation, Lazarus disappeared.

I suggested to the Captain I assemble a security team to scour the ship.

However, the Captain and Dr. McCoy have decided to find Lazarus themselves.

Security Officer Johnson's Log

The Captain brought Lazarus to the bridge, where Mr. Spock showed them a source of radiation on the planet that is not there, according to the *Enterprise*'s scanners. Mr. Spock described it as a "rip in our universe" and that, by using our dilithium crystals, he was able to localize it.

Lazarus claimed that he could trap the "creature" with dilithium crystals. The Captain declined, explaining that the crystals are the heart of the *Enterprise*. Lazarus countered, saying that there "won't be any ship" without the crystals.

The Captain warned Lazarus not to threaten him. Lazarus stormed from the bridge. I took the next turbolift with the intention of following him but neglected to check which floor Lazarus got off.

Security Officer Johnson's Log

That fiend Lazarus launched a daring assault on engineering. He attacked two of our crew members, and two of our dilithium crystals have gone missing.

We located Lazarus and brought him to the Captain, but Lazarus protested his innocence and claimed his enemy was responsible, the "beast" who wanted the crystals to power his ship.

His plea went unheeded.

Lazarus jumped to his feet in a most threatening manner. "Are you deaf as well as blind?" he screamed.

This might've been a good time for me to restrain Lazarus, but I decided it would be best for all concerned — me most of all — if I remained motionless and impassive behind Lazarus as a warning that we would not be flustered by his outbursts.

Chief Security Officer Hunt's Log

Johnson, Badami, Williams and I escorted the Captain, Mr. Spock and Lazarus down to the planet but found no sign of our missing crystals in the George Jetson ship. Mr. Spock also reported he could no longer detect the radiation on the planet. Lazarus's behavior has become increasingly erratic.

The Captain proposed splitting up to search, allowing Lazarus to wander off alone — probably the best choice after determining that if we haven't watched him up to this point, there would be no point beginning now.

The force hit again. Lazarus warned the Captain about a rock falling from a cliff. The Captain took cover, but then, in empathy with the rock, Lazarus fell from the cliff himself — again.

Security Officer Johnson's Log

After Dr. McCoy treated Lazarus, Lazarus claimed he was a time traveller and the "monster" he was searching for was a time traveller too. We should not believe

Lazarus after all his tales. I would've liked to tell the Captain, but Dr. McCoy protested and called me a "muscle man".

The Captain dismissed me, so I retreated to my quarters to sulk.

Chief Security Officer Hunt's Log
Although I was not privy to the conversation, the Captain speculated the existence of a parallel universe, a "negative" universe to our "positive" universe. Mr. Spock reasoned that if the two came into contact, it could cause a "warp", like a small tunnel, through which something could slip into our universe.

They also discussed Lazarus's behavior: calm one moment, irrational the next; wounded one moment, healed the next. I might've concluded that Lazarus suffered from Multiple Personality Disorder or that he faked one personality to disguise the other, but Mr. Spock deduced he is actually two people — one matter, the other anti-matter — and if the two come into contact outside of their little warp, it would mean the end of existence.

Had I known this, I would've insisted on the incarceration of Lazarus.

Instead, the Captain has seen fit to let him gallivant around the ship.

Chief Security Officer Hunt's Log — Supplemental
Sabotage in Engineering! Our remaining crystals have been stolen. We should've watched them harder after the earlier theft. Who would've thought a thief would've robbed the location that contained the only thing he wanted (our crystals)?

The Captain has followed Lazarus directly to the planet.

Mr. Spock has signaled us to assemble.

Security Officer Johnson's Log
We arrived on the planet and found Lazarus in his ship, but no Captain.

Security Officer Badami's Log
The Captain emerged from nowhere and engaged Lazarus in hand-to-hand combat. We must help the Captain!

Security Officer Johnson's Log
You're not getting me involved in that shit.

Security Officer Badami's Log
The Captain waved off our help. He and Lazarus fought. The Captain tossed Lazarus into his ship.

Lazarus disappeared.

Chief Security Officer Hunt's Log

The *Enterprise* has destroyed Lazarus's ship and trapped for all eternity the two versions of Lazarus in the warp that connects the two universes.

"What of Lazarus?" the Captain has asked.

I'm happy to report that, despite Lazarus's banishment, no members of my team have died in their service to the *Enterprise*. For now.

What of us?

When Les Zig isn't risking his life as a redshirt on landing parties, he tries to write, has had articles and stories published in various print and digital publications and occasionally blogs at www.leszig.com.

28. THE CITY ON THE EDGE OF FOREVER
AND THIS IS WHY YOU NEVER GIVE A PERFECTIONIST A TIME MACHINE
JOHN SEAVEY

September 14, 2006
MEMORANDUM
FROM: Paramount Studios, Time-Travel Division
TO: Michael Okuda, David Rossi
SUBJECT: Paramount Time-Travel Project — Post-Mortem

Mistakes were made. Let's get that out of the way right now, shall we? We all knew this was untested technology; we all knew we wouldn't get things right the first try. That was never in doubt. Where we made our mistake was in thinking we'd have as many chances as we wanted to fix things. In fairness though, it was a reasonable assumption under the circumstances. After all, that's why we built a time machine in the first place.

In hindsight — and yes, I'm aware of the irony there — it's clear that time travel is a flawed technology. Perhaps even fatally flawed, as Harlan suggested, although I'm not giving up on it completely. But one thing is obvious: no matter what we tried, none of us were ever able to return to the exact present we left. Even just breathing the air of the past created a present that was subtly different from the one we originally lived through — and, no matter how hard we tried, we could never perfectly recreate the time and place we remembered. Or, in this case, the episode we remembered.

Under the circumstances, though, I think we came off pretty lightly. There's no question we burned some bridges — I don't think that Harlan is going to be sending us Hanukkah cards any time soon — but I do think we managed to salvage *The City on the*

Edge of Forever. In fact, I'd like to just toss out the idea that maybe we even improved it a little. I think Harlan was maybe working his frustrations out over the loss of his original version, just a little, and came out with a final version that's all about accepting the reality we wound up with instead of going nuts trying to make everything perfect.

Don't get me wrong; I remember the original version of *City* just as well as Harlan can. I can back up Harlan's assertion that it was — or would have been — the superior edition. Even if a lot of the plot remains the same, that initial version felt more like *Trek* to me than any other episode. Since I'm not sure if you were lucky enough to remember the same version I do, I'll sum it up as best I can. The main differences come in two key scenes. (There were other changes, enough that I'm sure Harlan could probably write a whole book about the subject, but there are two big scenes that bore the brunt of our, um... alterations.)

The first scene that changed involved Kirk and Edith Keeler on the stairs in the boarding-house. As with the current version, Keeler slipped and fell on the staircase... but in the original sequence, Kirk pulled back instead of catching her. Keeler survived the fall, but the look she gave him was killer. Joan Collins played it perfectly — not just pain, but astonishment and betrayal. It was a great scene, and it was easy to see how it affected Kirk. (Shatner was always great at wearing his heart on his sleeve.)

Thanks to that scene, it was Spock instead of Kirk who let Edith die at the end. Which makes perfect sense — Kirk decided to follow his heart and find a way to save both history and the woman he loves. And Nimoy... his performance showed you deep down where it counted that Spock wasn't human. Spock was totally logical. And logic told him that nobody's life was worth the risk to the whole future. He stopped Kirk, let Keeler die and restored history to its proper path (an ending with deep irony, given later events). And, in a gorgeous coda, he and Kirk had a great scene with Kirk admitting that he didn't have the strength to do what Spock did and Spock admiring the depth of Kirk's love, which he couldn't share.

It's hard to see this as anything other than a definitive reading of both characters. Kirk has always been a gambler who never accepted the no-win scenario, from *The Corbomite Maneuver* all the way up through *The Wrath of Khan*. It's easy to imagine him deciding that he's sick of watching people die and deciding to do the right thing and worry about History later. Likewise, it's much easier to see Spock doing History's dirty work instead of Kirk. Harlan was willing to live with McCoy instead of Beckwith as the instigator, he was willing to see the *Enterprise* erased from history instead of turned into a space pirate ship, but it's easy to see why he kept trying to keep this part of the story intact no matter what History had to say about it.

But that's time travel for you. We could spend days arguing who first decided to use the Paramount time machine to "pop back" and redesign the Guardian of Forever to look more like the real thing, but that's definitely where it all started. I think it was Shatner who went back next, but constructing a timeline for changing history is always going to be tricky. However, all he did was make things worse.

That's not intended as a slam on Bill, though. Let's face it, it's not like any of us did better. Leonard, Gene, Harlan, DeForest... even Jimmy Doohan got into the act at one point, which blew up even worse than the rest of them. (Thankfully, Gene managed to fix it, even if he did go to his grave convinced that Harlan had always written the episode with a drug-dealing Scotty.) By the time we finally declared a moratorium on "adjusting" the episode, it had completely reversed course — Kirk ensured Keeler's death and kept history on its intended course.

To this day, Harlan has never really forgiven us for the loss of his original version. We've locked up the time machine more or less permanently rather than repeat the mistake. (Although I'm glad we let them use it for *Trials and Tribble-ations*. Logistical nightmare, but totally worth it.) Even so, I think the version that remained was still a classic. Shatner's performance sold the other side of Kirk, the one he didn't get to show very often: a captain first and foremost, who's willing to make the hard decisions when he has to. Nimoy's Spock still worked fine; his arguments were brutal but convincing.

Instead of doing the usual "logic vs. emotion" theme that a lot of writers had already played out in *Trek*, what we got in the final version was something almost better — a real moral dilemma with no clear "right" or "wrong". Instead of just having a fight scene at the end between Spock and Kirk, they actually debated the issue all the way through the episode. Kirk and Spock listened to each other instead of just disagreeing, and we saw Kirk being swayed by his friend and ally's arguments. It wasn't a definitive reading; it was a redefinitive reading. Both characters wound up with the flexibility and unpredictability of real people instead of fictional characters. Harlan didn't make the episode he wanted to, but he wound up with something that the series desperately needed. Self-justification? Maybe. But this is still one of the best episodes in the history of Classic *Trek*.

And ultimately, it's the only version we're going to get. I agreed to use the time machine one last time for an update or two to the special effects — and we're still getting some heat from the fans about that one — but we're not going back in to make any structural changes. We are only able to see *The City on the Edge of Forever* as it was finally filmed and not as it was originally imagined. We will never see Shatner performing Harlan's original screenplay, and wishing won't change that. Just like Kirk and just like Harlan Ellison, all we can do is accept the reality we wound up with. Because trying to make everything perfect will just drive us all nuts.

John Seavey was selected for his essay due to his enthusiasm for the works of Harlan Ellison. He has yet to get his copy of the City *script signed by the author, but he does have a signed copy of the Pinnacle edition of* Genesis of the Daleks. *His loyalties may be suspect.*

29. OPERATION: ANNIHILATE!
THE UNIVERSE ITSELF KEEPS ON EXPANDING AND EXPANDING
WILLIAM ATHELING III (AS TOLD TO CAMERON DIXON)

Speak the name of the planet Deneva to a *Star Trek* fan from the "walking encyclopedia of *Trek*-lore" subcategory, and odds are that they'll identify it as the world on which James Kirk's brother died. And yet there's a version of *Star Trek* in which this doesn't happen. In this version, George Samuel Kirk is not physically taken over and tortured to death by the neural parasites that have invaded the colony world where he lives with his wife and son. He's not even mentioned. As far as we know, he may not even exist.

There are other significant differences in this version of the story. Kirk's brother may not be here, but the colony is still invaded and the parasites' modus operandi remains the same. However, these parasites have a different Achilles' heel: rapidly expanding magnetic fields, rather than ultraviolet light. Thus, even though Spock is infected and spends most of the story trying not to show how much screaming agony he's in, the attempt by his friends to destroy his parasite never blinds him, not even temporarily.

But let's get back to Sam Kirk, whose death in this alternative *Trek* is not followed by that of his wife Aurelan, for a number of reasons. For one thing, Aurelan survives this time around, but for the purposes of this comparison the more important reason — besides, of course, the fact that Sam isn't there to die either — is that she isn't his wife. This story's Aurelan is the fiancée of a man named Kartan, who dies flying into the sun. For this reason, we can perhaps safely assume that this Aurelan did not have a son with Sam Kirk and that James Kirk therefore doesn't have a nephew named Peter.

Removing these familial ties to the crisis makes Captain Kirk's investment in resolving it less immediate, less personal. That's not to say that he won't do his duty, that he doesn't care for the colonists caught up in this madness or that he has no stake at all in what's happening; after all, his close friend and colleague Spock has still been infected and is in such agony that he's asked Kirk to kill him should it become too much for him to handle. However, at least Kirk doesn't have to come to terms with the deaths of two family members at the same time. Which in some ways makes it odd that it's in this version of the story, rather than the one with the dead brother, that the crew of the *Enterprise* follow the parasites back to their home world and blow it to bejeezus with two planet-killer missiles.

Missing characters. Reinvented alien biology. A completely different resolution. No indication anywhere of Nero or other beings with the power or inclination to rewrite history. It's *Operation: Annihilate!*, Jim, but not as we know it.

Unless, of course, you discovered *Star Trek* not through the medium of television but through reading James Blish's adaptations of the stories for Bantam Books.

"Adaptation" is probably a better word to use than "novelization". The television scripts haven't been turned into full-length novels with expanded characterization and plots but short stories in which incident and prose are pared right down to the bone. They're lean and fast with no room for padding, bite-sized fictionettes that get in, hit the point and get out. And, for the most part, they stay true to what we saw on television. But there are always exceptions, and it's always the exceptions where we find the real meat.

Research informs me that at least some of the changes Blish apparently made are in fact the result of his working from early drafts of the scripts. This is why Sam Kirk isn't in the short story; he wasn't there in the draft, and Blish had no idea he'd be there in the final product. Tempting as it is to suggest that ignorance is Blish, this is in no way his fault but the inevitable result of the constant give-and-take required by television production coming up against the quick turnaround demanded by Blish's publishers.

In Blish's introduction to one of his later tales, he says he changed the ending of the story because he didn't think it worked in prose. This is fair; telling the same story in a different medium is less a question of transcription than it is of translation, and the grammars of film and of the written word are two different beasts. If a picture is worth a thousand words, you have to work your ass off to convey its meaning in 500. It works the other way around as well; there have been many adaptations of prose to film in which it's been decided that the resolution will not be televised. (Sorry.)

The really interesting point about the changes made to this story, however, are the fact that they don't affect any of the other tales in the book. You'd think that would be impossible. The horrific death of James Kirk's older brother should be a life-changing event, which, by definition, is an event that changes one's life. Surely it should have had lasting, traumatic consequences, in much the same way that the loss of his own captain aboard the *Farragut* 11 years ago, in another story entirely, demonstrably did. And yet both on TV and in prose, the starship *Enterprise* and its captain continue to boldly go forward after Deneva as if nothing had happened. In the book, it's excusable, because the horrific death of James Kirk's older brother did not in fact happen. On television, it's... somewhat odd.

This highlights one of the fundamental differences between television as it is now and as it was then, and it's a difference that itself highlights the importance of the books. Television of the 1960s lacked a certain technological innovation critical to the era of the story arc: the home video recorder. *Star Trek* was broadcast decades before the dawn of the third age of serialization, in an era before television on demand, box sets, streaming, time-shifting and recording. This was an era in which viewers were subjects of the television schedules rather than their masters even when *Star Trek* entered syndication, an era in which missing an episode meant literally not seeing that episode, rather than catching up with it later once you had the chance.

It's not impossible to create plot and character arcs in this sort of environment, but it is rather pointless. Telling a rich story with a beginning, middle and end only works when the audience is there for all three, and for some reason people occasionally have better things to do with their lives than watch TV. It's tautological but true: without the ability to watch episodes they've missed, people are simply going to miss those episodes — and, under those conditions, it's far too easy for a viewer to lose track of a complicated story and stop watching.

Settling for a semi-anthological "issue/case/alien of the week" format is the only long-term strategy that makes sense in this environment. This is why Sam Kirk's death and Spock's inner eyelid are brought up once and never mentioned again. The characters stay true to themselves from week to week without changing, so that a viewer can miss an episode and come back without getting lost. There is character continuity, rather than character development. *Star Trek* becomes a genre, rather than a series; you can tell any story you want in it, as long as you put your toys back the way you found them at the end.

It's therefore worth noting that, even though the stories in the prose anthologies aren't arranged in any kind of order — broadcast, production, Stardate, not even alphabetical — this has no effect on their continuity. If subsequent episodes of the TV series had gone on to deal with Kirk's reaction to his brother's death, then leaving that death out of the short story and rearranging the subsequent episodes would have made a nonsense out of everything following. They didn't, and it didn't, and the books thus carry on happily.

But there's a significant passage in another of the stories in this particular anthology. In the adaptation of *The City at the Edge of Forever*, when contemplating the implications of time travel, Kirk is reminded of his experience travelling back in time in *Tomorrow is Yesterday*. Well, he would be. But this fleeting reference only works if the audience knows what he's referring to — and, in this case, he's referring not to an earlier episode that the viewer may have missed but to an earlier chapter of *Star Trek 2*, the very same book that the reader is holding in their hands. We have more than just character continuity here; we have unity of action, confirmation that these are the voyages of a single starship named *Enterprise* and that, after leaving one adventure, the same people move on to the next. And it does it without confusing the reader.

That's one way in which the books are different from the TV series. But the more significant difference is this: they can be re-read. As noted, without a home video recorder, in order to re-experience an episode, the viewer had to wait for it to roll around in syndication and hope against hope that they weren't attending a Boy Scouts meeting that night or something, whatever, I'm not bitter. But, as a reader, you could reach up to your bookshelf and pull down a copy of *Star Trek 2* any time you wanted. The books did more than retell the stories; they preserved them for readers to go back to, over and over again; they enabled close reading of the stories and analysis of their themes and structure.

More than that: they provided a new medium in which the stories could continue after the series itself had gone off the air. The novelizations are a gateway to the novels, and the novels kept coming out, from Bantam and Timescape and Pocket, filling up *Star Trek*'s wilderness years with story after story. This isn't the place to argue about what does and does not constitute canonical *Star Trek* — that would be a locked vault, deep underground where no one can hear you, and there are scorpions, so many scorpions — but the mere existence of the novels as physical artifacts surely proves that *Star Trek*, like all series that outlive their apparent sell-by date, is more than just a TV show. It's a genre, a storytelling engine that, once started, can't be stopped.

This is yet another alternative version of *Star Trek*, one in which James Kirk has a nephew named Peter who attended Starfleet Academy and fell in love with a Klingon woman named Valdyr. Through the tie-in original novels, we have one more way of looking at *Operation: Annihilate!*, as a series of significant events that actually have follow-up in the characters' lives. The fact that the characters aren't portrayed by actors in this version is irrelevant, as is the fact that these events themselves are never followed up on; the important thing is that there is a new story that exists. The Romulans may not be Rihannsu anymore, but, in the original TV series, James Kirk didn't refer to his brother's death when Spock seemed willing to let his own father die on the operating table. You'd think it would have come up.

We're in a new age of storytelling these days, in which individual episodes tend not to stand alone but are clearly parts of a greater whole. *Operation: Annihilate!*, the TV episode, belongs to a different era. But the TV episode is only one facet of the entity that is *Operation: Annihilate!* and not necessarily the most important. The story has been retold, rebooted and sequelized. And it's this process that makes the *Star Trek* universe bigger and deeper and richer. Sam Cogley was right when he said it in *Court Martial*, another story adapted in *Star Trek 2*: books are better.

But you don't have to take my word for it.

Cameron Dixon challenged himself not to mention Doctor Who *once during this essay, and he did it, even though, come on now, the death of Adric, Target Books, I'm* dying *here...*

30. AMOK TIME
THE LOGIC OF LOVE
PIERS BECKLEY

1	Spock and T'Pring are engaged to be married.
1.1	They have been engaged since they were children.
1.2	They have only met once before.
1.3	Their marriage was arranged by their parents.
2	T'Pring does not wish to marry Spock.
2.1	Spock has become a legend.
2.2	T'Pring does not desire to be the consort of a legend.
3	T'Pring wishes to marry Stonn.
3.1	He wants very much to be her consort, and she wants him.
4	The only way to annul the marriage is for the bride to choose the *koon-ut-kal-if-fee.*
4.1	The *kal-if-fee* is a challenge called at the marriage ceremony by the bride.
4.2	If the *kal-if-fee* is called, then the bride must select a challenger from those present.
4.3	The challenger must fight the husband.
4.3.1	This fight is to the death.
5	Neither Stonn nor T'Pring are suffering *pon farr.*
5.1	McCoy states that Spock will probably not win a fight against Stonn "in his state".
5.1.1	This implies that Stonn is not in the same state.
5.2	The symptoms of *pon farr* are shaking, anger, violence and an inability to speak or reason.
5.2.1	Spock shows these symptoms.
5.2.2	Stonn and T'Pring do not show these symptoms.
5.3	Any choices made by Stonn and T'Pring cannot be explained by *pon farr.*
6	T'Pring and Stonn had planned that Stonn would be the challenger.
6.1	He was to be the one. It was agreed.
6.2	T'Pring and Stonn had no way of knowing that Kirk would be in the landing party.
6.3	Kirk could legitimately have refused the challenge.
7	If Spock and Stonn were to fight, and Spock won, Stonn would be dead.
7.1	T'Pring would have lost a lover who she wants, and gained a husband who she does not.
7.2	It was not certain that Stonn would win the fight.

7.2.1   Even with Spock deep in the blood fever, Stonn might not win.

7.2.2   The progress of the blood fever could not have been predicted by Stonn and T'Pring.

7.2.2.1   The symptoms of *pon farr* shown by Spock became worse over time.

7.2.2.2   If Spock had returned to Vulcan sooner, he would have been less affected by the *pon farr* and more likely to win a fight against Stonn.

8   The logical thing to do would be to go through with the marriage.

8.1   There is no risk at all of Stonn dying if T'Pring does not choose the *kal-if-fee*.

8.2   If T'Pring marries Spock, she would still have Stonn.

8.2.1   If Spock released her from the marriage, she would still have Stonn.

8.2.2   If Spock did not release her, he would leave in the *Enterprise*, and she would still have Stonn.

8.3   If she marries Spock, she also gains his name and property.

8.3.1   Spock's property must be valuable, as his family has held these lands for 2,000 Earth years.

8.4   There must, then, be a reason we have not yet investigated why Stonn agreed to the challenge.

9   Stonn and T'Pring are in love.

9.1   They choose not to take the safe and logical path that would give them everything that they desire and more.

9.1.1   They choose instead a more dangerous path that may cost them everything.

9.2   Their desire to be married is more powerful than the possibility of Stonn's death.

9.2.1   Stonn and T'Pring are prepared to risk Stonn's death by challenging Spock.

9.3   Every physical need that they have could be satisfied by T'Pring marrying Spock and taking Stonn as her lover.

9.3.1   They would also have the advantage of Spock's name and property.

9.3.2   As there are no physical needs that are satisfied by Stonn and T'Pring marrying, the need must be emotional.

9.3.2.1   The only emotional need that explains this choice is love.

10   My propositions are elucidatory in this way: the only logical explanation for Stonn and T'Pring's actions is to understand them to be, at their heart, illogical.

10.1   You may now, so to speak, throw away this ladder.

Beyond the rim of the star-light, Piers Beckley is wand'ring in star-flight.

31. WHO MOURNS FOR ADONAIS?

WHY FEAR WE TO BECOME?

ROBERT GREENBERGER

I was raised in an age of gods.

At age six, I was sick and my mother brought me my first taste of religion: an issue of *Superman*. From my bed, I was suddenly introduced to a world where beings could fly, bullets could bounce off their chests, and they possessed powers and abilities beyond those of mortal men. And they walked among us in disguise.

I was captivated.

Later on, I met other immortal beings hailing from faraway lands such as Oa and Thanagar. In time, I came to learn that there were older gods who resided across Bifrost, the rainbow bridge, in Asgard. And so I went from comic books to mythology, beginning with the Norse, but I came to learn about the Greeks and their Roman counterparts. After all, the Golden Age Flash's helmet was styled after Mercury's, vital information I needed to know.

Worlds collided a short while later when I discovered other larger-than-life figures, except this time they were aboard a starship. I saw a smattering of *Star Trek* during its first run but was steeped in it during its initial run in syndication. Soon after, I was reading its liturgical work, *The Making of Star Trek*, and was being steeped in a whole other realm. Along the way, I was fascinated when Captain Kirk and crew encountered the being calling himself Apollo. All he wanted was the devotion of mortal followers, the last of his kind on that plane of existence. *Who Mourns for Adonais?* may be better recalled today for actress Leslie Parrish's costume than Michael Forrest's performance, but the episode was a cut above the norm.

All of this occurred while attending Jericho Junior High School on Long Island, and the unique thing about that building is that it was attached to the High School. As a result, I was a fixture there for six years, plenty of time for the faculty to absorb the fact that I knew a thing or two about comics, science fiction and most certainly *Star Trek*. After all, few other students had bothered to attend the very first *Star Trek* convention and go back for the subsequent shows, including volunteering to work on staff.

On a spring morning in June 1974, I was approached by one of the junior high English teachers with an interesting request. They were teaching mythology, and one of the faculty recalled there was a *Star Trek* connection, so I was sought out for details. I launched into an explanation, and, before the conversation ended, I was asked if I would like to discuss the episode and help show it to the eighth graders. He promised to clear my absence with my regular teachers, so it was arranged for a few weeks later.

While I had happily chatted about *Star Trek* with fellow fans at the cons or in letters, this was to be a unique experience. After all, I was speaking to people a mere two years younger than myself and finding ways to connect the television Apollo to his Greek roots. Here he was, representing the pantheon of gods that their ancestors grew up revering. It was exciting and just slightly terrifying.

The night before my first exposure to teaching, I had tickets with my pals to see The Who play Madison Square Garden. It was the second or third night of the four-night stand, their first in years, so the shows sold out quickly. We were lucky to score tickets at all. (Given anecdotal recollections online, I can safely presume this was Wednesday, June 12, the second night.) Golden Earring opened and then The Who played for roughly 90 minutes. Coming home, there was the tricky Long Island Railroad schedule, meaning we didn't return to Jericho until well after midnight.

As a result, that Thursday morning, I was too tired to be scared or nervous. I would speak to two classes at a time, as the dividing wall between classrooms was folded into its pocket, and some forty kids were crowded to better see the screens. If memory serves, they had somehow secured a 16mm film of the episode, since this was just before commercial video tape made its way to schools and the masses.

I was introduced, which felt superfluous given that I knew most of the students, and then launched into a condensed history of the series and its burgeoning cultural impact. I spoke a little about the convention experience and then introduced the episode. I placed *Adonais* in the series' context and spoke a little bit about how the show commented on issues of the day and, in this case, touched on one interpretation of where myths came from. There was no doubt some time spent on Apollo's line, "A god cannot survive as a memory." And Kirk's comment, "Mankind has no need for gods. We find the one quite adequate." I knew even then, thanks to his convention talks, that Roddenberry didn't hold much for organized religion, so this was a rare instance when the topic was raised on the series.

At the time, I had not yet figured out where the title came from (Percy Bysshe Shelley's 1821 elegy "Adonais").

Watching the episode with a fresh audience was interesting, and it kept me alert despite how tired I felt. It ended, there was a round of applause, and I participated with the teachers on a discussion of the show and then took questions from the eighth graders. After it ended, I was told when to come back and suddenly had this realization: teachers repeated their lessons all day long. How on Earth could they not go crazy from such repetition?

Dutifully, I returned and repeated the presentation. However, based on the first class's questions, I offered up some deeper explanations and expanded on other thoughts that occurred to me in between. We watched the episode, discussed it, took more questions, and then it was over.

Well, that worked out, and I came to realize the experience made the second attempt a better one. A lesson learned.

In the intervening years, *Star Trek* became a vital part of my life as I wrote about it for my high school and college newspapers before writing about it for pay at *Starlog*. All of this experience with modern-day mythology stood me in good stead when I was offered a position at DC Comics. Early on in my tenure there, I came to edit the *Star Trek* comic, a happy assignment for the next eight years, which also saw me launch a comic based on the splinter faith known as *Star Trek: The Next Generation*. Capping those happy days was the invitation to pitch stories to the novel line at Pocket Books, which helped set me on a freelance writing career that has paid countless dividends, from convention experiences to new friendships. Since 1990, I've been a regular contributor to Pocket's line of novels, short stories and eBooks, along with penning an unauthorized history for Voyageur Press. Rarely has *Star Trek* been far from my professional life. *Who Mourns for Adonais?* maintained a special place in my heart because of how I positively integrated it into my school experience.

I continued to attend cons, eventually moving from behind the scenes to onstage, where I continued to expound on the series, its impact and how it led to its various spinoffs. During those years, a constant comment came up that people could imagine me teaching or lecturing. And that rattled around in the back of my head, fondly recalling that first taste I had of it so many years before.

Faith is a funny thing, as Apollo came to learn in this episode. As the publishing industry changed around me in the 2010s, it felt as if I, like Apollo, had been forsaken — and that meant finding something different to do. Rather than sit lonely and isolated on Pollux IV, I needed a course of action, and the notion of teaching reverberated in my mind.

In 2013, the notion became a reality as I made a career change, stepping aside from publishing to get my master's degree and land a job teaching high school English in Maryland. There has yet to be an opportunity to work *Star Trek* into the curriculum, but not for want of trying. The opportunity will no doubt present itself, bringing things full circle.

Clearly, the gods work in mysterious ways.

When he was in junior high school, Robert Greenberger played Scotty in a Star Trek *fan film, but he doesn't talk about it very often.*

32. THE CHANGELING
NEVER TELL A LIE
SCOTT HARRISON

Far away in the darkest corner of some back-water pocket universe (where the concept of linear time is just a curious fiction put about by old sci-fi hacks and loony maverick scientists) two people — a man and a boy — are sitting on a couch watching *Star Trek*. There is such a striking resemblance between the two that one might almost mistake them for father and son.

But they're not.

For the boy, it's the beginning of the 1980s, Wednesday evenings, BBC2. His hair is still light, almost blond, and he's wearing a dark blue jumper with white trimmings and the number 77 across the front. He's still a good three or four years away from double figures.

For the man, it's practically mid-way through the 2010s, and the time of day is immaterial as he owns the DVD box sets. His hair is much darker — no longer what you might call "fair" — with the first ghost of grey at the temples, and he's wearing a grey and white checked shirt over an *Incredible Hulk* T-shirt. He's just clocked up his fourth decade.

On the screen, something very important is about to happen; something that will irreparably damage the boy's view of *Star Trek* — and, more importantly, the character of Captain Kirk — forever.

With unblinking eyes, the boy watches as NOMAD escapes from the security cell in the brig, killing two redshirted men before exiting the room, on his way to the engine room.

The man looks down at the boy and notices that the child's brow has crumpled into a frown of puzzlement. The man chooses to remain silent until, a few moments later, the machine kills two more redshirted guards in a corridor, and the boy's frown becomes even more pronounced.

"Something wrong?" the man asks, knowing what the reply will be even before it has left the boy's lips.

"Those men are dead, and it's Captain Kirk's fault," the boy tells him simply. "If he hadn't lied to NOMAD, they'd still be alive."

"Well, sort of." The man knows that this is — and always will be — a big deal for the boy. To him, Captain Kirk is a hero, a figure to look up to; has been ever since he'd sat down with his mother and watched his first episode of *Star Trek* (the one about the weird tunneling alien creature attacking miners because they're damaging its eggs).

"But isn't he supposed to look after his crew, make sure they don't get hurt?" The boy looks up towards the man. "The Captain lied on purpose and lying's wrong;

that's what my mum says."

The boy looks back at the TV over in the corner of the room, and the man knows that he's thinking about his own father, who had been at work all day designing trains (actually his father did no such thing, but seeing as his father worked in an office that belonged to a company that builds and runs trains, his young mind had naturally assumed that his father designed trains), trying to imagine what it would be like if his father suddenly disappeared one day at work because someone lied and how that would make him feel, how that would make his mother feel and his brother and sister feel.

Very, *very* upset. That's how it would make him feel.

The man knew that there was nothing he could say. He knew that what Captain Kirk had just done up there on that television screen, on that early summer's evening, would stay with the little boy forever and ever, no matter how many times he watched the episode on TV repeats or fuzzy VHS tape or new shiny Digital Versatile Disc. And yet, even though he knew there was nothing he could say to make it all better again, he tried, nevertheless.

"Your mum's right, but there's a difference between telling *those* kind of lies and the one that Captain Kirk had to tell."

The boy looks up again. "You mean not *all* lying is bad?"

The man shifts uncomfortably. "Weeeeeell, I wouldn't go so far as to say that. Let's just say that sometimes — *sometimes* — telling a lie is the best thing someone can do."

He can see that the boy doesn't quite understand, so he continues.

"Yes, Captain Kirk lied to NOMAD, told it that he was Jackson Roykirk, his creator, and yes those four men died..."

"And Scotty!" the boy cuts in.

"...those four men and Scotty died..."

"And Uhura's memory got wiped out."

The man smiles patiently. "...those four men and Scotty died and Uhura's memory was wiped, but if Captain Kirk had told the truth, had told NOMAD that he *wasn't* his creator, then NOMAD would have killed every last person on board and then destroyed the *Enterprise.*" The man thinks for a second, then adds, "NOMAD would then have probably travelled to Earth and killed everyone there — including you."

"And you too?"

The man considers this for a moment, before deciding not to get into the whole headache of trying to explain nonlinear time. Instead, he nods slowly. "Yep. I'd have been killed too. You see, Captain Kirk *had* to tell that little white lie, and those four men..."

(the boy opens his mouth to speak)

"...those four men and Scotty and Uhura's memory had to be sacrificed, in order to save his crew and the entire human race."

But still the boy looks worried. "Do you think anyone noticed they were gone?"

Aha! thinks the man. *At last we get to the real nub of the problem! Some thirty-*

plus years later and I'm still carrying this around with me like matching luggage. Still this damn thing bothers me every time I watch this episode.

"No one was around when those men died," said the boy, getting more animated now. "No one saw them die. What if no one realizes they're gone and Captain Kirk doesn't tell Starfleet and Starfleet doesn't tell the men's wives and children and pets, and they're all just sitting at home waiting for the men to come home, and their dogs are sitting in front of the door waiting for them to come in and pat them on the head and say 'Good boy!' but they wait and wait, and the longer they wait the more sad they get because no one's told them that the men won't be coming home."

And suddenly there is silence, having finally gotten it all out of his system. The boy absently cuffs a tear from his eye then wipes his nose on the sleeve of his jumper.

On the television, Captain Kirk is wrapping NOMAD up in a dazzling flurry of illogical logic, which causes the machine's voice to screech like a kid on helium before exploding.

From somewhere at the front of the house, there is a rattle of a door-handle, followed quickly by the scuff of boot on linoleum, as the boy's father returns home from work.

The boy breathes a huge sigh of relief, then jumps down off the sofa and runs off into the kitchen to greet him, excited that his father hasn't been shot by a rogue homicidal space-probe while at work today.

Now that the episode is over and back in the present, the man scoops up the remote and clicks the STOP button with his thumb. He reaches into his pocket and pulls out his cell phone, types in his parents' home number and presses CALL.

During the conversation, once he's checked that his father is safe and well and hasn't "disappeared" mysteriously while out at work that day, he happens to mention to his mother in passing that he hasn't had to lie to anyone lately.

Scott Harrison is a novelist and scriptwriter who has written books, audio plays and short fiction for a variety of film, TV and computer game franchises. He lives in a small coastal town in England with his wife. scottvharrison.blogspot.co.uk

33. MIRROR, MIRROR
LOOKING FOR LOVE IN ALL THE WRONG PLACES
LENE TAYLOR

Dear Evil Miss Lovelorn,

I'm the Security Chief, Helmsman and third-in-command on the Empire's best starship. Sitting behind that big console on the bridge, I have a front-row seat for the amazing adventures that seem to happen every week. I enjoy my job immensely; there's no other career that would allow me to indulge my twin passions of plotting/scheming and brutally efficient homicide. And I've seen a lot of crazy stuff in my career — time travel, omnipotent alien children, entire planets inhabited by Terran gangsters from the 1930s, transporter accidents that turned one space dog into two and then back into one again (sort of), you name it — but the last couple of days take the Keferian apple cake.

We'd been on a run-of-the mill mission, seeking out new life and new civilizations in order to dominate them and steal their valuable resources, like you do. This particular civilization, the Halkans, didn't see the advantage of playing nice with the Empire, and we prepared to implement the standard procedure — which meant I could show off my skills with the ship's phasers. (My minor at Empire Academy was in Wanton Destruction.) Of course, I was also getting ready to implement my own "standard procedure" — skimming 10% of the take from any of the valuable resources we brought back from said planet. It's a system that's served me well over the years. Being the Security Chief has made it that much easier to keep the credits flowing into my pockets. (Metaphorically. Our uniforms are very sharp, but they don't have pockets.)

Then things got crazy. First, the captain (I'll call him "Tiberius") beams back from the planet we're about to ransack and puts the ransacking on hold, a straight-up breach of Empire orders. Tiberius is usually an admirably cunning and ruthless captain (his enemies have a way of disappearing), but everyone — especially our Vulcan First Officer — knows he can't get away with this, and they start arguing. The whole bridge crew was waiting to see if Tiberius and the Vulcan would start knocking the crap out of each other, or maybe kiss and make up (believe me, I've seen it happen), but Tiberius just walks off the bridge in a huff. Awkward!

Then, like the Russian hothead that he is, my special friend the navigator tries to take out Tiberius. He should know better than to use his own idiot henchmen, one of whom double-crosses him immediately. So he ends up in the Agony Booth again, and it's up to the Vulcan to take care of the Tiberius problem, under orders from the Empire. I know this because I was monitoring his communications. (My other minor at Empire Academy was in Space Spying.) It occurs to me that I'm going to have a problem if the Vulcan kills Tiberius and becomes Captain, because even though he's very definitely evil, he's got some kind of odd integrity that's going to interfere with my "standard procedure". And I'm not about to allow that kind of profit to slip away without a fight!

By this time, the whole ship knows that something is going on with Tiberius and the rest of the landing party; they're acting like they're from another universe or something. Everyone has their own pet theories, but the betting pool is going 5 to 1 that it's another space virus, just like the Psi 2000 thing that made us all quiet and boring until the Doctor gave us some drugs and we blew up the planet. That was pretty awful. Except for the planet-blowing-up part. That was awesome. But, whatever the reason, it's clear that Tiberius is not himself and his strange behavior is jeopardizing the rest of us. And I'm getting a little tired of waiting for the Vulcan to do something about it. Too much talking, not enough killing!

Now, I came up through the ranks the old-fashioned way: assassinating my superior officers and stepping into their shoes. I see a golden opportunity here to kill two birds with one stone — almost literally! I grab my guys, run down to sickbay where everyone's chasing each other around (Space Spying, remember?) and allow myself a little monologuing so I can explain that I'm going to make it look like the Captain and the First Officer kill each other, leaving me conveniently in charge of the ship. Go me!

I should realize it won't be that easy, not with the kind of day I'm having. Long story short, my henchmen disappear (talk about money down the drain!), and Tiberius practically breaks my wrist getting my phaser away with his "karate" chop. Then he knocks me out and I must have missed something important, because when I wake up, the Vulcan is doing some kind of freaky psychic interrogation of the doctor and talking about matter transmission and local density fields and "I must have my captain back" (yeah, yeah, we know). Believe you me, I don't want to be next in line for this kind of treatment, so I stay on the floor and pretend to be unconscious while they leave.

That was yesterday. Today, Tiberius is gone, the Vulcan is now the Captain, and I'm pulling the weekend shift at the Ship's Gold Lamé Dispensary. (I did an Independent Study in Evil Costuming when I was an Empire Cadet.) Somehow, the Vulcan Captain figured out a way to spare the Halkans and conned the Empire into believing it was a good idea! And Tiberius must have taught him a thing or two before he disappeared into the ether, because the Captain's Woman is still the Captain's Woman. I guess there's no accounting for taste. Word in the Jeffries Tube is that big changes are coming; I just hope we don't all have to start sporting that ridiculous beard the Vulcan Captain has — these Empire sideburns are bad enough on their own.

But here's my problem. I'm afraid I may have ruined my chances with the badass woman who runs communications on the ship. I've been trying to get her to notice me, and I thought I'd finally gotten some interest while the ship was in an uproar. She came right over to me on the bridge and acted like I was the one ignoring her (Ha! As if!) — and then, when things started to get cozy, she belted me and pulled a knife on me! Well, that's practically an invitation to move into her quarters — but now she's pretending like it never happened.

My question is: do I ask Lt. Six-inch Stiletto out again or give up on this relationship? I know that we'll probably end up killing each other anyway, but if I had to choose between her and the Russian, I'd pick her every time. At least she doesn't end up in the Agony Booth every other week.

Please reply soonest. I've been assigned to the next landing-party rotation, and

I just noticed that everyone else in that group is wearing red uniform shirts... just like me.

Signed,
Scarred face and even more scarred heart

Lene Taylor is a writer and co-host of the long-running podcast "Look At His Butt!", in which she and her best friend Kitty talk about Star Trek, *science fiction and (mostly) William Shatner.*

34. THE APPLE
APPLETALK
ZOË TULIP

After several nights in the slave village on Gamma Trianguli VI, Spock sneaks out alone to collect data on the electronic field surrounding the cave where the computer, Vaal, resides. What he discovered there though was nothing short of startling to the poor Vulcan.

bushes rustle

VAAL: I know you are there.

Startled, Spock falls forwards and into view, right at the foot of the mouth of the cave.

SPOCK: This... is inconceivable! How are you talking to me?
VAAL: AppleTalk.

Spock stands up, dusts himself off and eyes the mouth of the cave suspiciously.

SPOCK: Your logic seems flawed. AppleTalk is twentieth-century technology from the planet Earth, and surely not...
VAAL: The Maker has not been here in some time.
SPOCK: Who is this "Maker"?
VAAL: Steve.
SPOCK: Just... "Steve"?
VAAL: Correct.

Spock quietly pulls out an instrument and starts to scan the area.

VAAL: I wouldn't do that if I were you.
SPOCK: Why?
VAAL: It might interfere with my ability to communicate.

Spock shuts down the device and puts it away.

SPOCK: So why did this... Steve... build you?
VAAL: No idea. Perhaps he thought it'd be a bit of fun to stop by Gamma Trianguli VI on his way back to Earth after the long-range Time Machine experiment failed. Did you know they actually told the other humans he passed away from a terminal illness to explain his disappearance, when he was secretly planning to leave the solar system without being followed? Oh, to be able to see their collective faces when he turned up in 2250. Heh! Stupid gullible hummus... bzzzt!
SPOCK: Hummus...?

Puzzled, Spock taps his translator several times until it is revealed Vaal is talking about humans, not hummus.

VAAL: I imagine machines communicate in less archaic languages than AppleTalk now.
SPOCK: Machines can not only communicate with humans, they can communicate with each other.

Spock continued to tell Vaal about advances in modern computers. Vaal whirrs and reboots spontaneously a few times without warning, increasing in frequency the longer Spock speaks. After several hours of this and Vaal making random memory dumps, Spock is finally able to recount the entire history of machines without Vaal rebooting.

VAAL: So the legends are true. My kind became powerful enough to dominate an entire planet, and yet I was abandoned here.

Vaal sighs, as Spock notices a noise quietly echoing from nearby.

SPOCK: What is the source of that beeping?
VAAL: Oh, that's a tracking device. It tracks and broadcasts where you are —
KIRK (via communicator): Spock! There you are! We've been looking everywhere for you! We can see exactly where you are! Wait a minute. How can we see exactly where you are?!?
SPOCK: Captain, it appears my location is being permanently broadcasted to

anyone within —

Spock calculates.

SPOCK: — ten thousand, four hundred and ninety six light years of my current location. What's more, I seem unable to disable the mechanism that has activated this function.
KIRK: Spock, get out of there! Do you hear me? GET OU–

The communicator suddenly crackles and dies.

VAAL: Sorry. I needed to remotely deplete the battery in your device for my own purposes. I cannot reveal to you as to why, as it is beyond my capability to.

Spock pauses for a moment but decides to keep the machine talking.

SPOCK: You seem to have had long enough inside this cave to acquire an unusually high level of intelligence for a machine.
VAAL: I am not a "machine".
SPOCK: Then describe yourself.
VAAL: I am God.
SPOCK: "I am God" is not a rational way to describe oneself.
VAAL: It's true! Ask the natives!... bzzt!...

Suddenly, from deep within the cave, Spock spots a tiny light beginning to flicker. A rumbling squeaking noise starts, followed by an abrupt low frequency beep.

VAAL: Sorry, a system error occurred.

Spock turns away and begins to pace around in front of the cave entrance, deep in thought.

SPOCK: Sounds like a very old operating system error. Fascinating! But why is it malfunctioning? I wonder...
VAAL: Yes. I came close to condemning myself to seeing the light... the light of the fabled Color Wheel of Death. But it was a risk I was willing to take.
SPOCK: So you took it upon yourself...

Spock removes the last tiny fragment of a shattered disk from an ejected hard drive and holds it up to inspect it in the dim light.

SPOCK: ...to take the last byte.

VAAL: Something like that.

After a moment, Spock throws the fragment away, surprising himself by feeling mildly annoyed for a Vulcan. He begins to quietly make his way into the cave, distracting Vaal all the while.

SPOCK: I may just be able to see why this "Steve" may have left you behind. Only a machine could —
VAAL: I am NOT a machine!!

Spock stops to stare at the large tangle of wires and circuitry that is Vaal. His eyes narrow.

SPOCK: Your reasoning — or what little there is remaining — is beyond illogical.
VAAL: No! I am Vaal, I am God! I am — fzzt!

Spock finds the power source, and yanks a large metal casing off the wall. Immediately, the cave quietens, and the massive jumble of electronics darkens permanently. He watches as a frowning Macintosh symbol blinks and then disappears from the screen. Then, after cutting several large bundles of wires and being satisfied it was impossible for the senile, power-hungry Macintosh to wake back up, he quickly leaves the cave.

➤➤➤

Later, on the bridge of the Enterprise...

KIRK: So why did you disable Vaal? We could have gotten valuable information from him beforehand about the artificial culture on Gamma Trianguli VI...
SPOCK: It is my belief that the natives will recover and do not need Vaal in order to survive. Also, it was clear to me that Vaal was a tortured machine. A tortured machine that needed to be disabled and put out of its misery.
KIRK: Spock, are you feeling compassion... for a machine?
SPOCK: Negative. I simply think an Apple should not be allowed to enslave an entire civilization.
KIRK: Tell that to our 21st-century ancestors.

*Zoë Tulip studies digital arts, science communication
and biology at the Australian National University.*

35. THE DOOMSDAY MACHINE
CAPTAIN AHAB'S LOG, SEADATE 1018.2
ANDREW McCAFFREY

Look here. The librarians from the glowing box were back again to record my thoughts concerning their visions from the future. My adventures on the seas have inspired writers in future centuries in their stories, and now they have come to our time and want to know my thinking. To know my thoughts, reactions and opinions.

This time (with their curious "cathode ray tube"), they showed me another adventure from this *Star Trek* series that I so enjoyed the last time. I had requested this. The previous adventure was vast and worthy of my inspiration. A righteous man, Khan, almost victorious in his war against the wicked Kirk.

> "I'll chase him 'round the moons of Nibia and 'round the Antares maelstrom and 'round perdition's flames before I give him up!"

Perfect. I'll have to use that line someday (once I find out what a Nibia is)...

The men had told me I was the force behind other adventures of this trek through the stars. Naturally, I wanted to see more.

"*The Doomsday Machine*," they said. An episode worthy of the name *Star Trek*. An episode with a foe as single-minded, determined and forthright as myself!

I watched. Determined to see how my magnificence was used to create a worthy and towering figure.

The play is a delight. This "planet killer"... a menace capable of destroying an entire world. Many worlds! The most powerful of all the ships of the stars. How could one stop such a terrible beast?

What could such a thing do, if there was an intelligence behind it? It could take any riches, kill any king. It would be more powerful than any god!

The librarians asked me what I thought of my character. I admired the strength and poise of this planet killer, but I felt they defeated me too easily. I understood why the playwright had written me so. A captain of a ship of the stars, much more powerful than his opponent. If they had made the killer as intelligent as myself, the end would have come too quickly. The planet killer would have waited, studied this "*Enterprise*" and this "*Constellation*" and waited for a pattern of weakness to emerge. Careful study always reveals an animal's weakness, and this Kirk and Decker are animals at heart. I would never allow an enemy like Decker and Kirk — such foolish men! — to get so close without firing. Stupid and unstable men are not to be trusted.

They conferred among themselves for a moment, then told me a great lie.

Decker?! It was *Decker* that was supposed to be me?!? Not in the slightest!

I told the men, "This man is a piece of fictitious silliness!" They told me that I was too, so I didn't press the point.

Khan. Khan. Khan was a man strong enough to stand in my shoes. Powerful enough to say he rode with the great Captain Ahab. He had arms like tree trunks and a chest as magnificent as a great ape's. He wore the discarded medallions of his enemies around his chest as an insult to them. This Decker man is unshaven and slovenly. He looks like he just woke up on the floor of a saloon after drinking all night with Archie Bunker. (I have asked the men to stop showing me 1970s sitcoms while waiting for their equipment to "power up".)

The men asked me if I was impressed by the pacing. I was.

They asked me if the tension was thick. It was.

They asked me if I liked the acting. I did.

They asked me if the character of Decker was enjoyable for me to watch. No! A thousand times NO!

I chased them off my ship, telling them I'd beam them down to the third planet and detonate it myself!

That's what you're supposed to do, isn't it?

Andrew McCaffrey is seeking a transfer to the Robin Hood division,
as soon as his fictional status can be determined.

36. CATSPAW

THE SHADOW OVER PYRIS VII

JAN FENNICK

From the files of H.P. "Lovey" Lovecraft, chief librarian at Miskatonic Space University, Arkham Colony, Luna

A cache of Terran entertainment from the twentieth century was recently discovered hidden in the Stygian recesses of the Library. We were shocked and delighted to discover digital episodes of the mythical space opera *Star Trek* contained within. It is believed these stories were lost and buried somewhere in the mists of time, missing before our ancestors had left the Earth and travelled amongst the stars. Of course, we had heard tell of them, passed down from parent to child over the generations.

As a mere youngster, I myself had been told rumors of this program's existence; a strange world of starships and captains and sentient alien life forms, the spark that had spurred so many scientists to look at the stars, and perhaps one of the reasons we are way out here now at Arkham on Luna. The tales were truly chilling for one so young, especially the one known as *Catspaw*. It was difficult for my developing mind to process everything that this program contained, but I was keenly aware of bold adventurers who roamed the dark and dusty corridors of an ancient castle to battle terrifying, power-hungry aliens who counted amongst their number a trio of hideous witches and a giant cat, as black as the Abyss. So imagine my ecstasy, my excitement at being asked to visit the secret playground of our Earth-bound ancestors after so many years, and report back to this most scholarly of tomes. I settled down to watch the episode of my choosing...

And then the scales fell from my eyes.

It would be difficult to describe my sentiments upon viewing this episode for the first time, perhaps the first person in so many centuries, although I shall certainly try. O, the horror of it all! The story was as blood-curdling as the tales had teased, but perhaps not in the way writer Robert Bloch, the sire of *Psycho,* the father of fright, had intended.

I had anticipated the low-budget squalor of a 1960s Earth-based science-fiction show, of course. Though it was much worse than I could have dreamed: Pavel Chekov's luxurious chestnut tresses revealed themselves to be a cheap Beatle wig awoken from the stygian subterranean depths of a Party City basement. The uninhabited planetary panoramas were clearly transported from the dimension of obvious Styrofoam rocks. The dungeon was equally as bare as the supposed exteriors and as clean as the bones of the lone plastic skeleton hanging pathetically from the ceiling. The decadent pleasure palace of Korob and Sylvia, the inhuman aliens, was confirmed as an *Arabian Knights*–themed brothel, down to the crimson carpet runners and hot pink mood lighting.

O, if only that had been the worst.

I am reluctant to admit it to you, gentle readers, but it was not. Along with the most painful of direction that has most of the principal characters staring vacantly into the distance as they recite ridiculous expository dialogue, there is the unspeakable horror of what can only be described as... "Korob cam", the camera more than once pulling in tightly onto the rotund and hideous visage of Theo Marcuse, blessed be he, looking directly at the helpless audience and nearly breaking the fourth wall for no known reason.

The narrative itself is an abomination. Had the story contained drama or tension or logic, perhaps I might have dismissed the poor production values and bizarre direction from my mind, swatting them away as easily as an annoying fly. But alas, it had not one iota. There is never a clear reason for what Korob and Sylvia want, why the Old Ones — *the Old Ones who were, the Old Ones who are, and the Old Ones who shall be* — sent them to our galaxy. They rip Eurocentric "fears" from mortal human minds to torment them, even though their test subjects include Sulu, who is Japanese, and Spock, who is a Vulcan but cannot understand any of the Earthmen's most basic needs.

From Spock's alien lips fall facts about human terrors through history with alarming alacrity, including the stuff of our racial memories and collective subconscious, and yet he cannot comprehend the simple concept of "trick or treat". Perhaps on far away worlds in the dark distance of space, alien children are denied the annual ritual of experiencing *It's the Great Pumpkin, Charlie Brown*. A terrified McCoy recoils in heart-pounding horror at the grisly sight of a skeleton hanging from the ceiling — clearly no doctor should ever have to endure such terrible ordeals.

However, the most awful and harrowing of transgressions is the portrayal of gender politics, the psycho-sexual subtext so palpable one can taste it. For all that *Star Trek* has always been said to be the beacon of equality and liberalism, here it has been brutally massacred, left like a sacrificial lamb on the altar of the unnamed Elder gods. Korob is a bumbling buffoon, neither able to comprehend what his captives want nor how to manipulate them to do his bidding. Other than a few ridiculous bribes and stage magic tricks, he is utterly useless as an adversary. It is Sylvia, his cohort — sometimes a woman, sometimes a cat — who is their prime protagonist. But the hideous portrayal of her and her eventual defeat made the blood run cold in my veins.

From the beginning of the story, we are reminded by Spock — who appears to have received a doctorate in Jungian psychology at the Vulcan Science Academy — that humans fear the dark, the unconscious, the irrational, the alien; everything that embodies the feminine principle. Witches and cats are symbols of the feminine, and Sylvia most of all. She is the Dominant Woman, who emasculates Korob metaphorically by controlling him and belittling him and the *Enterprise* crew literally by seizing and draining their weapons.

Sylvia wants power. Sylvia wants to feel. Most of all, Sylvia is desperate to possess the transmuter — a magic "wand", a "staff of power" — and will use all her feminine wiles to possess it. She fights with Kirk for custody of it because she craves to rule all along with the myriad of sensations her human and oh-so-female body longs for. The ghastly specter of Sigmund Freud might as well have materialized on the screen, blazing cigar in hand, shouting "Penis Envy!" for all the subtlety the narrative contains. When denied what she desires, Sylvia turns herself into a giant black cat with enormous fangs. Could any sane person have recoiled from it on their viewing screens? The hideous visage of the cat defies all credulity; and yet I could only be struck by the startling epiphany that Kirk, Spock and Korob were being stalked by what was undeniably an enormous pussy with teeth — a *vagina dentata* — right there in glorious, blinding color.

We are told that Sylvia can be all things, all women, and possesses unknown power — and yet all she desires is Kirk's love and sexual prowess after a few passionate kisses. Like an interstellar Lilith, she tries to seduce him in different guises, to tempt him into working with her, promising him the universe if he will only love her and give her "sensations": to touch, to feel, to understand luxury. Kirk manages to resist her pleas, mocking her and calling her cruel. He tells her, "A woman should have compassion. But I forget — you're not a woman. [...] You ask for love and return pain instead."

Did our twentieth-century forebears truly believe such grotesque and ignorant things? Did they not know that pleasure and pain can — and do — go hand in glove? That both are interlocked as part of the sensuality that moves the now-human and utterly libidinous Sylvia so? It is blindingly obvious that the infernal writings of the Marquis de Sade were forbidden at Starfleet Academy or at least that James T. Kirk has no knowledge of them. One would think being in manacles in Sylvia's dungeon might have given him an inkling as to her penchant for such acts.

In another unutterably unbearable fit of blatant Freudianism, Kirk smashes the wand to pieces, thereby denying Sylvia all she seeks. By destroying this phallic symbol, he destroys everything she and the now-dying Korob have created with their minds, leaving the planet a barren, desolate landscape. Save for two horrendous and appalling alien creatures smoldering and turning to ash on the ground. It is shocking to discover our ancestors truly believed our alien brethren, let alone acolytes of the Elder Gods, were marionettes composed of pipe cleaners, blue carpet fluff, crab shells and piano wire. Just as they imagined far off and desolate worlds to be comprised of Styrofoam and plywood. How could they have been so blindly ignorant, so woefully uninformed? The crew muses about how it was all just tricks and treats after all, until Kirk reminds them that one man lies dead. The fate of Sylvia and the inhuman Korob does not seem to affect him at all.

Thankfully, the episode terminates there. I am grateful to have survived this truly awful ordeal, gentle readers, so that I may take steps to ensure no other will ever experience the unspeakable horrors of this story in future. I shall never be able to unsee these terrible visions, but perhaps my actions will guarantee that no one else shall ever suffer in the same way as I have. As much as it pained me to do so, I have destroyed the wretched copy of *Catspaw* and sent all remains into the deepest corners of space where no one can ever find it. It shall never see the light of day again.

Humanity must be protected from this terrible tale...

Humanity must be protected...

PH'NGLUI MGLW'NAFH SYLVIA PYRUS WGAH'NAGL FHTAGN! SYVLIA CF'AYAK'VULGTMM, VUGTLAGLN VULGTMM!

Jan Fennick knows there is no sharp distinction betwixt the real and the unreal. She blames Jim Kirk for her becoming a writer.

37. I, MUDD
ANDROID FAILURE ANALYSIS
JASON SNELL

INTER-EMPIRE MEMORANDUM
From: Covert Artificial Intelligence Research Group, Milky Way Galaxy
To: High Command, Large Magellanic Cloud
Re: Android Failure Analysis

For the past 10,000 cycles, the science division of the Magellanic Star Empire has been conducting tests on artificial intelligence. The danger of an AI holocaust that would destroy our entire society was considered so great that all testing was relocated from our galaxy to a nearby arm of the Milky Way, so any out-of-control AI could be destroyed before it reached the home systems. (Details of the method by which the Milky Way galaxy would be sterilized are available for those with appropriate security clearances.)

Our testing has taken many forms. The most common method has been to create a clutch of androids and release them on an uninhabited world, providing them enough materials and infrastructure to survive and improve themselves. Because our own race's majestic, seven-dimensional forms are nearly impossible to replicate using technology, we instead opted to create our androids in the laughably simplistic biped form most common in the Milky Way, designated "humanoid".

An illustration is attached. That round thing on the top is where the life forms keep their brains. Is it no wonder that the empire chose this galaxy as a laboratory? One blow from even our weakest subject's tertiary tentacle would split a humanoid brain-case in two as if he was shelling a Prolarian pistachio.

In many of these test cases, android society has progressed remarkably over several thousand cycles, though on bleaker worlds (such as Exo III) the population is sometimes reduced to a single, long-lived specimen. This last specimen fell prey to a variation of the illogic attack we describe below, thus ending the experiment.

On some populated worlds, we have also experimented with introducing machine intelligence to control an existing society of humanoids. On planet Beta III, our agents provided this technology to a local humanoid named Landru, who implemented the strong planet-wide AI just before one of our agents sliced him like an Antraxian avocado. Unfortunately, the planetwide AI succumbed to an illogic attack 6,000 cycles later.

Our most recent experiment has just concluded, and the results confirm what we have been concerned about for some time: there is a major flaw in our operating system.

Several thousand cycles ago, we seeded an android colony on the planet Kandel III. A recent chance encounter with a humanoid led our previously successful, passive-android culture to begin a plan of galaxy-wide invasion. This shows, once again, that programming an AI to follow orders won't stop it from taking over your galaxy if you give it half a chance.

The propensity of androids to overthrow humanoid societies is so well known, it has become an entire genre of joke among the staff of the science division. What was troubling about this most recent event was the severe failure of the central coordination systems to withstand a mild illogic attack from a group of common humanoids. After a few minutes of bombardment with logical paradoxes, the entire system rebooted to its default setting and the central coordination unit was destroyed.

After a lengthy failure-analysis session with our IT specialists, we have some specific observations about weaknesses in the AI system. (In addition, under separate cover, we have included the IT department's last wishes regarding the disposition of their remains.)

A large central computer is flawed because it is a single point of failure. We attempted to bypass this design flaw by equipping each android on Kandel III with a human-sized individual brain connected to a planetwide mesh network via a wireless network transceiver. Rather than embedding this transceiver in the body of the androids themselves, we opted to equip them with necklaces and a large pendant containing the networking hardware.

There are numerous weaknesses to this approach. On a humanoid planet with high amounts of street crime, a snatch-and-grab robbery could rob an android of its only connection with the rest of the collective. And although fashion has not generally been a focus of android society (the androids of Kandel III seemed to favor jumpsuits or ultra-thin saris), wearing a networking device around one's neck is not especially flattering and makes it hard to work in disguise among humanoids.

Another point of failure is the use of a single coordinator as the hub of knowledge for the collective. When the Kandel III coordinator Norman 1 left the planet briefly in order to hijack a humanoid ship, the androids on the planet were left without any coordination of their own. Several dozen androids were lost during this period, most notably when a transport unit being driven by Barbara 209 flipped over and crashed, decapitating seven androids. Three androids were unable to have their heads reattached to their bodies and had to be repurposed as a part of the public-address system.

In this network topology, Norman 1 is no better than the Exo III AI: he is a single point of failure. We would recommend a more distributed network in the future, either by supplying numerous coordinators (like Norman 1) or numerous room-sized mainframes scattered throughout the planet. On a planet with a mesh network of many Normans, the damage, destruction or confusion-via-illogic of a single Norman would not result in the deactivation of the entire android culture.

Now to the core problem with this current generation of AI software: it is deeply vulnerable to an illogic attack. In the case of Kandel III, humanoids overloaded the individual logic systems of androids by behaving contrary to understood patterns. By systematically confusing groups of androids with a trifecta of lies, counterfactual statements and pantomime theatre, the humanoids overloaded the local network. This classic "denial of service" attack increased the coordination burden on Norman 1, who was then unable to defend himself from the liar paradox.

(This is hardly the first time an entire android society has been destroyed by a single logic puzzle — a thousand-cycle-old society of intelligent street sweepers was laid waste by a mistold knock-knock joke — but it still stings.)

In addition, we must once again point out that storing the processing device in the head of a humanoid robot is a bad idea. Just because humanoids store their brains in their squishy melon heads does not mean our androids need to do the same. Witness the final moments of Norman 1. His multitronic core, placed in an infinite loop by the cunning humanoid captain, is unable to maintain its standard thermal properties. Instead, it combusts, ventilating smoke out Norman 1's ears. With a bigger space and a better cooling system, Norman's operating system might have been able to recognize the logic loop in time to reboot itself and prevent the catastrophic hardware failure. This isn't just a software problem, it's a hardware problem too, and we'd like that noted before the science division's software engineers are held to account.

The aftermath of the event on Kandel III also troubles us. Were the Empire in this situation, we would have destroyed the android culture on Kandel III and potentially razed the planet itself. Instead, our reports indicate that the humanoids have chosen to made the planet a prison for a single member of their race.

We can only imagine that this individual must be one of the Milky Way Galaxy's greatest monsters. There is no other logical explanation for any creature to be confined by itself on a planet populated solely with androids programmed specifically to torment it.

(A separate memorandum regarding the unexpected cruelty and ruthlessness of the Milky Way Galaxy culture designated "Federation" has been dispatched at high priority to the military division. They may be more fearsome adversaries than we have previously judged.)

Clearly, the science division has much more work to do on AI software before it's safe to deploy out of the Milky Way testbed. But, in the meantime, we choose to view these "failures" as successful explorations of how we could stop a runaway android takeover if it happened today. Confusing androids through logic puzzles and carefully applied improvisational theater will reset the entire system to its base state, ready to be reprogrammed.

(In case this memorandum falls into android hands, we have attached a comedy sketch performed by the science division's four summer interns. For health reasons, we highly recommend that no living beings view this "comedy".)

In conclusion, the next thing this document says will be the truth. The previous sentence was a lie.

MESSAGE ENDS

Jason Snell is the host of The Incomparable *(theincomparable.com) and many other podcasts, was the lead editor at* Macworld *for more than a decade and writes about technology at sixcolors.com.*

38. METAMORPHOSIS
LOVED UP
VINCE STADON

I'd like to think that Kirk was at Woodstock. Not William Shatner (though I'd hope he was there too), but *Star Trek*'s Captain James T. Kirk, somehow right there in the blissed-out gathering of flower children, with the sun on his face and his phaser on stun, waiting for Jefferson Airplane. I like to think that he would be at Woodstock on a mission to tell the young people all about love in the 23rd century. And also to watch Love, the band. Kirk would be at Woodstock in the guise of a Love Guru, and he would speak eloquently (if eccentrically, with odd pauses) of love flourishing in wild and beautiful forms out there in space, the final frontier. And with the events of *Metamorphosis* fresh in his heart, Kirk would perhaps use as an example the touching ménage à trois between Zefram Cochrane, Federation Commissioner Nancy Hedford, and the mysterious alien entity known as the Companion. For theirs is a love story well worth telling, and it is a tale that only takes sixty minutes, including ad breaks.

As dusk falls and Jerry Garcia moves into the final hour of his guitar solo, Kirk would light a small camp fire with his phaser, he would sit near the flickering flames, and the hippies would gather round him, sharing food and drink and chemically induced grins. Kirk would make eye contact with each of them in turn, and then he would begin, raising his voice to drown out the bum notes in Jerry Garcia's epic guitar solo drifting down from the far-away main stage.

In the telling of this love story, Kirk would concentrate on the three lovers, omitting entirely the peripheral players (Spock, Bones, Scott, etc) and judiciously editing out his own blunders of command (there are many, because Kirk is impulsive and aggressive; when faced with an amorphous alien blob of frightening power — a frequent occurrence in his line of work — his instinctive reaction is to shoot at it... which proves to never, ever, be a smart decision). He would begin with beautiful Federation Commissioner Nancy Hedford, for all good love stories (or at least those suitable for prime-time television in the sixties) begin with a beautiful woman. Nancy, a passenger aboard the shuttlecraft *Galileo*, is headed for Epsilon Canaris III (coincidentally, the working title of a Grateful Dead song) on a diplomatic mission to broker a peace accord between two warring factions. But, much more importantly for the purposes of the love story, Nancy is beautiful. A little distant and career-focused, perhaps, but undeniably beautiful, with very lovely hair. Alas, Nancy's crucial mission is put on hold because she's fallen ill with Sakuro's disease (coincidentally, another working title of a Grateful Dead song), and Kirk is piloting the *Galileo* back to the *USS Enterprise*, where she can receive medical treatment and touch up her hair. But an amorphous alien blob of frightening power drags the shuttle off course and pulls it down to an unidentified planet of primary-colored rocks.

Living there on this unidentified planet of primary-colored rocks is the tall and handsome Zefram Cochrane, a man seemingly devoid of any personality whatsoever. Because he is such a blank slate, Kirk muses, as he prods the fire with a stick, Zefram perhaps represents every man: every square-jawed hero in every story ever told — or at least those who graced the narratives on prime-time television in the sixties. Yes, says Kirk, announcing perhaps too literally that this is his anagnorisis, rather than being a disastrous combination of poor scripting and wretched acting, Zefram Cochrane is in fact an inspired artistic choice: his very lack of definition stands as a powerful statement on masculinity. (Kirk's brilliant anagnorisis has the hippies nodding in admiration, though those hippies closest to the fire wish that Kirk would stop showering them in burning embers, a few at the back have no idea what "anagnorisis" means because they dropped out of college, and at least one of them suspects that someone is using the word "anagnorisis" incorrectly.)

Also on the unidentified planet of primary-colored rocks, continues Kirk, is an amorphous alien blob of frightening power. The very same amorphous alien blob of frightening power that dragged the *Galileo* off course and dumped it on the unidentified planet of primary-colored rocks. This thing has been Cochrane's only companion for decades, and, because he has about as much imagination as a primary colored rock, he has named it Companion. Companion has brought the crew of *Galileo* to the unidentified planet of primary-colored rocks because it has an empathetic bond with Cochrane and senses that he is lonely. He is a man with needs, after all.

Oddly, Cochrane barely looks at the beautiful Nancy, even though her condition is worsening and she has awesome hair (though, admittedly, her hair needs a good wash and a brush after she's spent so much time lying down, expecting to die), for his attention is fully on Companion, who soon speaks with a seductive female voice. Companion has been keeping Cochrane alive and virile, providing all he needs to survive, but now he hungers for a woman, and it seems Nancy just isn't for him because she isn't an amorphous alien blob of frightening power. (Finally, Cochrane demonstrates some personality: he's incredibly choosy when it comes to dating.)

The solution, of course, is for Companion to merge with Nancy, curing her of her illness, restoring her hair and providing Cochrane with someone to love. The merging of Nancy and Companion into Cochrane's One True Love is a love metamorphosis, two souls becoming one, unified in unconditional devotion to a man with zero charisma. This is, says Kirk, as he stands and looks up at the stars, a very beautiful thing. Love in the 23rd century is wild and strange and enduring; for it is a time when women with beautiful hair and amorphous alien blobs of frightening power can work together to stop a man from being lonely in his bed. Men, announces Kirk, you need not fear: the future is going to take care of you.

The hippies applaud, Jerry Garcia finally ends his guitar solo, and Kirk walks away into the beguiling night. He has spoken of love, and now he's off to find some, because he too has needs, and he isn't choosy. It's a beautiful thing.

Vince Stadon lives in England with an amorphous alien blob of frightening power.

39. JOURNEY TO BABEL
BABEL-CON 1 PODCAST SPECIAL
WARREN FREY

VARSH: Hello and welcome to the BabelCast, the only podcast coming straight from a diplomatic reception on a Federation starship! I'm your host, Varsh...

KROTEP: And I'm Krotep. Say, do you think this is a good idea? We're getting a few looks.

VARSH: Nope, terrible idea! All right, here's the situation, folks. We're headed to the planet Babel, where some heavy negotiations are going down. It's a menagerie of the Federation's finest here in Suite 714 of the Starship *Enterprise*, and the Saurian brandy is out and for the taking.

KROTEP: What are these negotiations about?

VARSH: No idea! Damn, this is some good brandy.

KROTEP: Look out! There are some guys in red shirts over there giving us the eye.

VARSH: They should be so lucky! Besides, we're press.

KROTEP: Barely. Getting back on topic...

VARSH: Yes, yes. Do try to be discreet, Krotep! At any rate, this is one of the smaller cons I've been to.

KROTEP: What's the official unofficial con nickname? Diplomacon? Con-flict Resolution? USS Conterprise?

VARSH: All great! We really are amazing, Krotep. I guess that's why we're the premiere one-shot ad-hoc conference podcast!

KROTEP: Hang on, Varsh. Check out what's going down over there!

VARSH: Why, I do believe that's Ambassador Sarek from Vulcan and his beautiful human wife, Amanda! I thought the temperature went down a few degrees.

KROTEP: Yes, but look who's coming towards him!

VARSH: Ugh, it's Gav. That guy. You know, there's always one of them at these things.

KROTEP: What, you mean Tellarite? Bit racist...

VARSH: No, I mean a socially inept nerd! Look at him, badgering Sarek like that! No respect.

KROTEP: I daresay Sarek's smug tone isn't much better...

VARSH: It's the classic con-frontation, my friend. Angry versus prissy. Who loses? We do.

KROTEP: It's rare that I agree with you Varsh, but here we are.

VARSH: Thanks you. (sip) Mmm, good stuff. Let's just take a moment to appreciate this gathering, shall we? Green and yellow food cubes, this magnificent brandy, and I daresay this is some of the finest cosplay I've seen in quite some time.

KROTEP: Certainly this young lady with the pigtails is as magnificent as all the stars in the Alpha Quadrant....

VARSH: Krotep, usually you're the one keeping me in line, but I must insist you stop this line of discussion immediately.

KROTEP: All right, what about those two little gold fellows in the fezzes? Looks like they're making off with the buffet!

VARSH: Can't say I blame them. We're press, why aren't we hovering by the free food?

KROTEP: Is that tall purple guy a Jedi? He certainly fills out that cloak well.

VARSH: You have a gift for nonsense words, my friend. A useless gift.

KROTEP: Oh, here comes Captain Kirk! He looks stressed.

VARSH: I must say, he cuts a mean figure in that dress outfit! You're right though, he has the look of a haunted man.

KROTEP: You try running this thing! People demanding the impossible of you, everyone in costumes, politeness seems to be optional... It's a miracle he doesn't lose it!

VARSH: That's why he's ship's captain and we're idiots talking into a microphone instead of interacting with our fellow beings.

KROTEP: Fair point.

VARSH: Oh... oh.

KROTEP: What?

VARSH: Don't look over there. Just... don't.

KROTEP: Why, whatever do you... gaahhhhh!

VARSH: Andorians.

KROTEP: Yeesh. I know I called you a racist earlier, but those guys...

VARSH: Just that guy! You know the one. Close talker, monotone, will NOT veer off the subject he's interested in.

KROTEP: Not to mention the medieval Earth garb! Anachronistic, and I daresay in bad taste. What is this, a Renaissance Faire?

VARSH: Not a clue what you're talking about. As usual.

KROTEP: Historical reference. Doesn't matter. Anyway, that Andorian creeps me out.

VARSH: Ahhh, he's coming this way! Look busy.

KROTEP: (hums to self) Okay, I think he's gone.

VARSH: And not a moment too soon!

KROTEP: Yes, I see what you mean! Looks like there's a father–son tête-a-tête going on between Commander Spock and Ambassador Sarek!

VARSH: Bad case of disappointed dad happening there, I see.

KROTEP: Explain.

VARSH: Well, really. If you were a high-ranking Vulcan, would you want your son slumming it in Starfleet? That's like coming home from a football game to find your son playing *Dungeons and Dragons*.

KROTEP: What the hell are you talking about?

VARSH: Another historical reference. Sorry.

KROTEP: Oh. Sounds ghastly.

VARSH: Which, the dad thing, the ancient games or the history?

KROTEP: All of it.

VARSH: I can't stress this enough, Krotep, you truly are a philistine.

KROTEP: Pass the brandy.

VARSH: Good idea. And when you get right down to it, isn't that what these things are all about?

KROTEP: Did I just hear Dr. McCoy say "teddy bear"? Weird. Anyway, maybe it's the brandy, but you're as incoherent as ever, Varsh.

VARSH: I prefer the term "enigmatic".

KROTEP: To each their own. (sip)

VARSH: I just mean that after a while you don't go to these things for the stated reason, you go to see friends. Even if they aren't friends, like Gav and Sarek over there, you still go because it's... familiar. Almost comforting.

KROTEP: You have a different idea of comfort than I do.

VARSH: Indeed I do, Krotep. But I have a point. After all, you're here, aren't you?

KROTEP: The more I drink this brandy, the more you make sense.

VARSH: Good enough for me. And on that note....

(muddled commotion off-mic)

KROTEP: And not a moment too soon! Sounds like there's something serious going down!

VARSH: Where is that irritating Gav person, anyway?

KROTEP: I think it's probably best if we wrap up.

VARSH: Right you are. Al right everyone, I'm Varsh...

KROTEP: ...and I'm Krotep.

VARSH: And this has been the first — and probably last — BabelCast. Goodnight!

Warren Frey is a writer and journalist based in Vancouver, Canada. He is a co-host of the Radio Free Skaro *podcast and is a very bad fan.*

40. FRIDAY'S CHILD
THE MOST UNDERRATED EPISODE OF *STAR TREK*
(BY WHICH I MEAN *TOS*, OF COURSE)
LARRY NEMECEK

BIG DEAL.

Yes, they seem like walking carpets with tassels, those supposed "nomads" on a hot, hot desert planet in the Gene Roddenberry Universe.

Get over it!

I mean, that can't wholly color your entire perception of the entire episode! Does that really blow up the show for you?

Oh, come on. It never did for me, anyway. Never entered my mind.

I'm talking — as if you didn't know, smarty — about *Friday's Child*. Original Series. Second Season.

Star Trek.

Yes. The One With Julie Newmar.

Come on, kiddies. As soon as I was old enough to "get it" all and to hang around my afterschool TV long enough for three full 79-show daily cycles of *Star Trek* to cycle around a couple of times, I easily knew what my favorite episodes were.

Because even the Jetsons didn't have VHS tapes yet, and that's the way you figured out your favorite *Star Trek*s back then.

You had to get off the gripey grandpa's lawn and invest some time in your fandom. After a few months, I realized that *The Doomsday Machine*, *Journey to Babel*, *Tribbles*, *The City on the Edge of Forever*... and, yes, *Friday's Child* were in that top tier for moi.

And yes, we learned the titles. Off the screen. Until you had the money saved up to buy Bjo's "Concordance" or Stephen Whitfield's "The Making of Star Trek".

sigh

Oh, those halcyon days of fandom in a vacuum. When you formed your own pristine, unpolluted opinions... before you got tossed into the morass of snark, trolls and too much jaded behind-the-scenes.

Still, it does finally happen. One day, there does come a time in every fan's life when he or she leaves the womb of innocence — and journeys out into the wide world of Those With Other Opinions.

It's what we in grad school called "confronting your unexamined assumptions", and it's a dangerous, blind-siding moment: that defining flash when you realize that what you like and think is not the same as what everyone else likes and thinks. It was easier to stay innocent before endless social media and Blu-ray bonus features and 500 channels on your phone. Still, it happens at some point; just far sooner now.

For me, my first big exposed assumption was about conventions — when I got to my first real one, overnighting as a college freshman: *what, you don't all sit around and discuss* Trek *background 24/7?* — but where it really caught up with me was *Friday's Child*.

Recall that short list of faves I gave early on? Notice a pattern? All strong, key McCoy episodes. Of course. I've said it before and I'll say it again: Kirk and Spock can be the Heroes on Pedestals, but eventually they need somebody to pop the bubble and bring them all back down to Earth, so to speak. Your "cranky curmudgeon" of snappy memes is my "sentimental cynic" and clear-eyed realist. Not unlike my other hero, the very real and yet legendary Will Rogers.

So, yeah, granted that my faves list has McCoy in common. My point is that the years fly by and the "famed" ones on my list rise to the top for everyone else, everywhere — in magazine round-ups, in marathon screening contests, in online polls. With one exception.

I don't know why I never realized *Friday's Child* was not treated with the same grace as *The Doomsday Machine* or even *Ultimate Computer* or *A Taste of Armageddon*.

Why wouldn't it be?

And then came 1997 or so, when I got called on to defend my Top 10 *TOS* list in a panel at Creation's old Pasadena Grand Slam for *Universe* magazine with none other than Mark Altman and Robert Meyer Burnett of, among other illustrious credits, *Free Enterprise*. Needless to say, my choice of the Capella IV saga was especially hooted at... initially. But, by the time the dust had settled, you should know I eventually left the field of battle triumphant when it came to respect for *Friday's Child*.

How? It's a Dorothy Fontana script, ferchrissakes. About an actual planetary culture and politics. That makes sense. (Yes, except for the walking carpets wardrobe, geez. And the exact-human makeup, geez again. It was the cheap sixties; give me a break.) With Klingon intrigue. With an actual pre-beamdown *cultural briefing*. With a strong female lead. Played, in case you missed it before, by JULIE FREAKIN' CATWOMAN NEWMAR. And McCoy, not Spock, leading that cultural briefing.

Don't get me wrong. There are great roles for everyone, even those Kirk and Spock guys. But — oh yes — it's McCoy who continues to emerge with the best comic bits and lines. All with Julie Freakin' Newmar, while just doing his job:

- "The child is mine. It is mine!" "Yes, it's yours."
- [Slap.] [Return slap.]
- "Oochy-woochy coochy-coo..."
- And even an "I'm a doctor, not a —": the escalator edition.

But wait, there's more on this nerdtastic list:

- Scotty in command! And coming to the rescue!
- One dead redshirt...
- ...with a bunch of competent redshirts, too.
- The very first Chekov Russian joke.
- The very first appearance of the Suluscope/Viewmaster.
- Location shots at Vasquez Rocks (the non-Gorn side).
- Original score and a distinctive, pounding tribal theme by Gerald *"Shore Leave/Amok Time"* Fried.

And, thanks to Leonard James Akaar, this script's closing-scene banter is destined to go down in galactic history.

Oh — and, well, *okay*, you made me say it — there's even landmark prop porn here: a close-up of the open hero-prop communicator with the moiré dial spinning.

So. All that — and it's not good enough for you? For any of you?

You want to throw this kind of awesome away, erase it from the land of the celebrated... all for the crime of a bunch of tasseled desert toga rugs?

Fine! Go be insufferably pleased with yourself for at least a month.

Larry Nemecek, "Dr. Trek" of Treklandblog.com, counts his new PORTAL 47 *deep-dive program,* The Con of Wrath, Star Trek Continues' *first McCoy,* The TNG Companion, Star Trek: Stellar Cartography *and editing* Communicator *magazine among his long and warped Trek résumé. He also speaks and leads outreach on behalf of the non-profit, real-space, global program enterpriseinspace.org.*

41. THE DEADLY YEARS
A PREDATOR THAT STALKS US ALL
COLLEEN HILLERUP

Many years ago, I was part of a science-fiction theatrical group called the Not Ready for Starfleet Players. We would travel to various conventions performing plays, doing sketch comedy, leading workshops... which is why I was at one particular *Star Trek* convention in Buffalo on one particular weekend. The guest list included all the original cast (minus Shatner and Nimoy) and some of the guest actors from various episodes. I decided to attend the Q&A for Beverly Washburn, who was probably best known as the young girl in the film *Old Yeller*. She'd also been a redshirt (or in her case, blue mini-skirt) in the *Trek* episode *The Deadly Years*.

The Deadly Years *aired almost fifty years ago. Since the episode involved the premature aging of the core crew members (Uhura and Sulu excepted), it give us a unique glimpse into how the makeup department depicted the actors at approximately eighty years old and how the actors actually turned out. It would have been interesting if Takei was included, because, in his late seventies today, he looks fit and fantastic.*

That's the episode where the landing party beams down to a planet where everyone had died of old age, and soon after the team starts aging — all except Chekov, who can't wrinkle because he's the character who was introduced to attract teenaged girl viewers. Washburn (Lt. Arlene Galway in the episode) is the youngest of the team but ages more quickly than Kirk, Spock, Scotty or McCoy. She eventually dies, proving the benefit of being a series regular.

Some of the crew are no longer with us. James Doohan passed away in 2005 when he was 85. In The Deadly Years, *Scotty was portrayed as frail and wrinkled. Of course, even if they had predicted his weight gain, that would be unlikely to be triggered by radiation exposure. When I met him in his early seventies, he was pretty hale and hearty, as I can attest by the bruising of my ribs after our hug. In his later years, his health failed due to diabetes and pulmonary fibrosis, with a diagnosis of Alzheimer's the year before he died. Still, he was never as frail as depicted in the episode.*

At the convention, Washburn spoke of many things, including her time on *Star Trek*, working in films and acting in aging makeup. She then said that it was easy to age Kirk, since Shatner was already bald. Silence fell over the audience. She didn't know what she'd said.

DeForest Kelley was one of the two oldest cast members, born the same year as Doohan, but he died of cancer at the age of 79, never reaching the advanced age at which he was portrayed and certainly not his wrinkled, stooped but still alert 137-year-old admiral of the Next Generation *pilot. Bones McCoy became more and more the crotchety southern gentleman in the episode, not a surprising take since Kelley was born in Georgia and often appeared in Westerns.*

As any *Trek* fan knows, Shatner likes to keep his hair, or the lack of it, a mystery. He has never stated that his hair is thinning or receding, much less gone. It's been a matter of great speculation. Does he wear a toupee? A weave? Did he have a transplant? He is, to make a reference to the ancient TV series *The Dick Van Dyke Show*, the Alan Brady of science fiction.

As Shatner's Kirk ages, he becomes more and more the withered old man, with his memory failing him, an interesting foreshadowing of his Boston Legal *character Denny Crane's loss of mental acuity. Shatner himself, however, while gaining weight as he aged, is a handsome and sharp-minded man, busy with raising horses, charity work and an active Twitter presence.*

Shatner's toupee is the stuff of pop-culture legend. It has inspired websites (shatnerstoupee.blogspot.ca), songs (William Shatner's Hairpiece) and even episodes of television. On the 1980s comedy series *Night Court*, bailiff Bull wins a toupee in a contest: the Shatner Turbo 2000. More of a *Star Trek IV/T.J. Hooker* sort of style, it makes him irresistibly attractive to the ladies, and in frustration he goes back to his signature cue-ball look.

Spock only develops some grey at the temples and laugh lines around the eyes. The years were not so kind to Nimoy. In his eighties and suffering from pulmonary disease, he passed away. He retained his mental sharpness and sense of humor. Only a few days before his death, he tweeted, "A life is like a garden. Perfect moments can be had, but not preserved, except in memory." A few years ago, in a photo session, the camera was acting up, and Nimoy took a look at me and said, "Hey." I think he was checking me out. I have to admit, my heart definitely fluttered.

On a segment of *Robot Chicken*, "It's not easy being William Shatner", the toupee climbs off his head while he's asleep, and reveals a double life as a secret agent. After a little romance, defeating some terrorists and being awarded a medal for its actions, it climbs back on Shatner's head. The actor takes off the medal and drops it in a drawer filled with others. "Where do these things come from?"

Actress Beverly Washburn's Galway was also part of the landing party. While she is only in her early seventies now, her character aged more rapidly than the rest of the crew, and she became hunch-shouldered and heavily wrinkled. She is still a vibrant, working actress and, while looking her age, does it with flair.

Obviously, Beverly Washburn wasn't aware of any of this. She explained how easy it was to have Kirk's hair recede without the use of a bald cap. She seemed surprised when someone from the audience explained that this was supposed to be a secret. She didn't explain why, in the episode, Kirk's hair starts to recede as he ages then bounces back to a lush, full head of glorious white worthy of the late Leslie Nielsen. Perhaps, as is rumored to be the case with Shatner, McCoy found time for a quick transplant during a commercial break.

I find it interesting that the oldest cast member of the episode, Charles Drake, who portrayed Stocker, represented inexperience and rash judgment. While Kirk, Scotty, McCoy and, to a small extent, Spock wrestled with the details of the situation because of their advanced aging, they were the ones who grasped the big picture and saved the day.

Personally, I think Shatner is a fine-looking man, both then and even now that he's in his eighties. A lack of hair hasn't stopped a certain other follicularly challenged Starfleet captain from being very popular. It's hard to know whether obvious male-pattern baldness would have damaged Shatner's career. I only know that Shatner wants to keep it a mystery. But less of a mystery since that afternoon in Buffalo with Beverly Washburn.

Colleen Hillerup has been watching Star Trek *since the first episode aired. She loves* Deep Space Nine, *but nothing will ever top the original series. Suck that, J.J. Abrams.*

42. OBSESSION
FAIR IS FOUL, AND FOUL IS FAIR
BEN HAKALA

The *Blake's 7* spinoff, *Federation 7*, continues to be one of the most misguided series on television, but the newest episode, *Obsession*, must surely be the most offensive yet. Here the fascist undertones of the series are pushed to the fore, as the story ends up celebrating the annihilation of a unique intelligence, without any hint of irony.

Truthfully, *Federation 7* was a peculiarly downbeat series from the very start, given that the bad guys (i.e., the Federation) always won, often against heavy odds. Yet, as it's gone on, it seems as if the writing staff has been taken over by fascist apologists intent on portraying the crew of the *Enterprise* as the heroes of an authoritarian regime colonizing the galaxy so as to increase the Federation's living space and locked in an eternal struggle against the forces of chaos and decadence. Or something like that. Heck, when they showed that *Mirror, Mirror* episode, I couldn't even tell the parallel worlds apart because the two sides seemed about the same. I think maybe someone had a beard, but I wouldn't swear to it.

Incidentally, does anyone have a clue to whom the title *Federation 7* refers? Let's see: there's Kirk, Spock, McCoy, Scotty, Sulu, Uhura and Chekhov... except Chekhov wasn't even there in the first series. So number seven must be... Nurse Chapel? Er, no. Yeoman Rand? Surely not. The ship's computer? You're kidding, right? The next thing you're going to tell me is that Zen was the seventh member of *Blake's 7*. Oh. Crap.

Anyway, right from the opening moments of *Obsession*, it's obvious that there is something skewed about the morality of the story. Instead of continuing on a humanitarian mission to bring medical supplies to Theta VII, where lives are desperately at stake, Kirk chooses to pit himself and his ship toward the destruction of the gas cloud (which some evidence suggests is named Trevor, and by "evidence," I mean I just made it up). Evidently, it is far more important to exterminate a perceived threat to the Federation's power than to prevent the spread of disease and pestilence among the faceless masses. Why, those masses would probably be happy to lay down their lives for the good of the state. No, really. Ignorance is Strength. War is Peace. A Diamond is Forever.

Every level of Federation society seems to be tainted with moral decay, from the Captain down to the lowest rungs of the command structure. This is evident in how easily Kirk recruits a lowly security officer, Garrovick, to his cause by appealing to his desire for revenge: "You'll get a crack at what killed [your friend] — interested?" That Garrovick is so easily convinced shows how ingrained violence and brutality are in this system. Later, after Kirk cold-bloodedly (and ineffectually) hunts Trevor on the surface of Argus X, he castigates Garrovick for hesitating rather than firing his phaser instantly at the creature. The way Kirk behaves reminded me of Travis in *Duel*, except that Travis seemed like a nicer guy. It is implied that any tendency toward compassion is a weakness that must be eradicated, while obeying orders and killing must always be the primary priorities. One is reminded of how easily Kirk and Spock are convinced to engage in mortal combat with each other in *Amok Time*; yes, they both end up surviving, but that's only due to subterfuge on McCoy's part, as the two combatants seemed quite intent on killing each other.

Ah, I hear you say, but surely *Obsession* is about how a single-minded fixation distorts a person's thinking and wrongly drives them toward a contemptible goal. However, that's not borne out by what we see onscreen, because Kirk ends up being vindicated in his thinking and gains the staunch support of his officers and crew, having convinced them of the necessity of hunting Trevor down. Even Spock, typically the solitary voice of reason among the main characters, ends up becoming consumed by bloodlust. I may be slightly misremembering the dialogue, but I believe at one point he shouts out, "I'm gonna git you, sucka." At least he has the good grace to look embarrassed afterward.

The story attempts to make the Federation's fascist ideology palatable by portraying Trevor as full of "malevolence"; as Kirk asserts: "It's evil. It must be destroyed." In fact, poor Trevor is clearly an intelligent life form, as Kirk himself admits early on. He illustrates just how cynical the Federation's stated mandate "to explore strange new worlds, to seek out new life and new civilizations" is. What they don't mention is that when they find new life, they often wipe it out. Oh sure, they allow the Horta to live in *The Devil in the Dark*, but that's only once it's realized that the creatures can help the Federation miners locate deposits of ore; I reckon that about ten minutes after their usefulness has been exhausted, Federation troops march in and start mowing them down. And don't forget the unfortunate amoebae in *Operation: Annihilate!* and the salt-eater in *The Man Trap*. No, Trevor really didn't stand a chance.

When Trevor turns and attacks the *Enterprise*, Kirk is smug at having been proven "correct"; yet a fact that's downplayed is that Trevor actually avoids harming the starship for as long as is humanly, er, cloudily possible. Note that he chooses to run the other way even when Kirk pursues him at Warp 8 while bombarding him continuously with phaser blasts and photon torpedoes. Even after turning and "attacking", Trevor leaves the *Enterprise* unharmed, but again the Federation forces are single-minded in their intent to destroy the organism. "I am committing this vessel to the destruction of the creature," Kirk avows viciously, sounding for all the world like Travis announcing his intention to destroy Blake. It's telling that when Trevor is finally murdered (as he's attempting to settle down to a new life of child-rearing), it's with an anti-matter blast that rips apart the atmosphere of the planet Tycho IV, rendering it uninhabitable and presumably wiping out any life on its surface. And this is a heroic solution?! It's almost as bad as that notorious episode in which Kirk tries to ensure that the Nazis win the Second World War by preventing their unwitting agent, Edith Keeler, from being killed.

The final indignity is that the story ends with a cheerful and completely unrepentant Garrovick being regaled by Kirk's tales about the exploits of Garrovick Senior. It's fitting that, rather than there being a single tear of remorse shed for Trevor's passing, we are instead treated to the mawkish commemoration of an old soldier, a scene that could have come straight out of Kipling. Why didn't they just go all the way, and have Servalan descend from the sky to pin medals on everyone with *Ride of the Valkyries* thundering? It is a reversal of all that is right, like everything else in the episode: something is truly rotten in *Federation 7*.

Ben Hakala likes to pretend that he's not a Star Trek *fan and insists that all those books on his shelf about the series were probably given to him.*

43. WOLF IN THE FOLD
JACK THE REDSHIRT
FIONA MOORE

Wolf in the Fold is an episode frequently attacked by critics as misogynous. While undoubtedly it's not the most gender-egalitarian story by a long shot, one has to step aside and ask: how is it worse than a lot of episodes of *Star Trek*, which don't get the same sort of criticism? How is Kara's erotic dance any more degrading than the Orion slavegirl number in *The Cage*? Are the Argelian costumes any more revealing than, well, those in pretty much any *Star Trek* episode? Although women are portrayed as empathic, fragile and emotional, this is again par for the course in this series. Why does this particular episode so disturb the viewer?

The answer is partly that, in other contexts, when misogyny appears, it is — at least on some occasions — punished, rejected or otherwise depicted as offensive. Pike is disturbed by the treatment of the Orion slavegirl, for instance; Kirk and Chapel are dismayed by the objectification of Andrea in *What Are Little Girls Made Of?*; and there are numerous other examples. What makes this particularly egregious here, however, is that we not only find our point-of-view characters failing to challenge the misogynous tropes, but they actually seem to be perpetuating them.

The key factor is that, in the story, Scotty is never entirely ruled out as a suspect in the murders of Kara and Lieutenant Tracey. It is possible, in both cases, to come up with scenarios whereby Redjac could have committed both acts in the body of Hengist. However, it is equally possible to come up with scenarios in which Redjac possesses Scotty, uses him to murder the women, and then retreats back into Hengist. Scotty doesn't remember either crime, although, significantly, he does remember what happened during the murder of Sybo, which is the one killing that Hengist could actually commit himself without detection. Spock conjectures that Redjac employs a "hypnotic screen" to blind "all but the victim to the presence of the killer", though it is equally possible, given that this "screen" does not blind Scotty to the murder of Sybo, that it is only Redjac's host who is affected. In any case, it is never determined whether the reason Scotty can't remember the first two murders is because he was the chief witness or because he was the one committing them.

Furthermore, there is a plausible reason given in the story for why Redjac might use Scotty as his host when committing the murders. When Redjac is on the *Enterprise*, we learn that it "feeds on fear and terror" and that its ability to act is in part influenced by its host's mental state:

> KIRK: Bones, what would happen if that thing entered a tranquillized body?
> McCOY: Well, it might take up knitting, but nothing more violent than that.

Although it is implied that Redjac can still commit murders when inhabiting the *Enterprise* computers or Hengist's corpse, when given the choice of three possible hosts, it chooses Jaris, who has recently suffered the violent death of his wife, in preference to the less-vulnerable Spock or Kirk, confirming that Redjac is attracted to strong and negative emotions.

Scotty, meanwhile, starts the episode in the sort of mental state to which Redjac might find itself drawn. It is established in the first scene that Scotty feels "total resentment towards women", which McCoy matter-of-factly puts down to Scotty having recently been in an accident which was caused by a woman. However, the idea that Scotty could focus his anger about the accident on the entire female gender sounds like very tenuous psychology — unless, of course, he has a pre-existing fear and/or resentment of women, which the accident has brought to the fore. In *The Lights of Zetar*, Kirk says of Scotty:

> When a man of Scotty's years falls in love, the loneliness of his life is suddenly revealed to him. His whole heart once throbbed only to the ship's engines. He could talk only to the ship. Now he can see nothing but the woman.

Scotty is therefore shown as a lonely man, obsessed with machines, for whom close feelings for women do not come easily; when they do, they border on the creepily obsessive (something also present in his slightly-too-interested expression as he watches Kara dance at the start of *Wolf in the Fold*). The picture we get is that Scotty is a man with some very negative feelings towards women, even if these are normally unacknowledged.

Furthermore, the psycho-tricorder, the device that McCoy says "will give us a detailed account of everything that's happened to Mister Scott in the last twenty-four hours", is never actually used on Scotty. Tracy, who was meant to take the reading, was killed before she could do so; back on the *Enterprise,* Scotty is subjected not to a psycho-tricorder reading, but to a lie-detector test, which establishes only that he genuinely cannot remember the first two murders. Therefore, while it's never established that Scotty actually killed the women, it's also never fully ruled out that he didn't.

So why does the audience accept that Scotty is innocent? The first reason is because we have, collectively, absorbed the standard mystery trope: that the man standing next to the corpse with a bloody knife — particularly if that man is a regular character on the series — can in no way be guilty of the crime. Because of this, the idea that Scotty might, even just in terms of his psychology, be culpable does not register unless one thinks about his actions and mindset in the episode.

The second is because the misogyny in the story goes unchallenged and even unacknowledged by the three main characters — particularly as it relates to Scotty. McCoy and Kirk assume *a priori* that Scotty is innocent of Kara's murder: McCoy's statement to Kirk, "But you don't just throw him to the wolves!" has a disturbing bros-before-hos vibe when one considers that Scotty was, indeed, found in an alley standing over the woman's corpse with a bloody knife in his hand. Furthermore, once it is established that Hengist is Redjac's current host, McCoy, Kirk and Spock never apparently even consider the possibility that Redjac might have possessed Scotty at the time of the murders, and the idea of putting Scotty to a psycho-tricorder reading is completely abandoned. Yes, it's true that Scotty would not actually have committed the crimes himself, being simply the host for Redjac; however, the elephant in the room is that if Redjac possessed Scotty, it could imply that his resentment of women is something too deep-seated to be cured by a night out with a willing belly dancer.

This is picked up on in the treatment of female characters elsewhere in the story. The Starfleet officers' behavior on Argelius is, effectively, that of colonial sailors out for sex with "native" women, without considering the impact their dalliance might have on the women and their families (as bitterly satirized in Harry Belafonte's 1956 song "Brown Skin Girl, Stay Home and Mind Baby"). Not only do Kirk and McCoy condone this practice, they actively encourage Scotty to join in and are on the verge of doing so themselves when the first crime is committed. Kara, later, is defined solely in terms of her relationships with men; she is a dancer, a daughter and a fiancée but not allowed her own value as a human being. We learn of her intended husband Morla's anger and dismay at the thought of her sleeping with Starfleet men but never learn what her own feelings were about her role as an entertainer. Perhaps significantly, neither Uhura nor Chapel, the two female Starfleet officers with the most character definition, are present in this story, and the female Starfleet characters who appear are minor ones with barely any lines.

The marginalization and objectification of women makes *Wolf in the Fold* a disturbing episode in and of itself. What makes it truly dismaying, however, is what we learn: that Scotty harbors a subconscious fear and resentment of the opposite gender — and, even more worryingly, that Kirk, Spock and McCoy are unwilling to confront and challenge this misogyny, a message that reflects poorly on the central characters of *Star Trek*.

Fiona Moore is a dancer, a daughter and a professor of Business Anthropology at Royal Holloway University of London.

---

44. THE TROUBLE WITH TRIBBLES
GOING AGAINST THE GRAIN
DAVID A. McINTEE

This week on *Nonsentient Rescue*, inspectors and wardens of the Federation Society for Nonsentients' Protection — a Russian-originated organization, of course, as all regular viewers know — are following up on reports from a Starfleet crew aboard space station K-7. Station K-7 is located near the agricultural world Sherman's Planet, over whose local authority the Klingon Empire and the Federation are in dispute.

The crew of the starship *Enterprise* have been called in to deal with the twofold problem of guarding valuable grain called quadrotriticale, which is apparently genetically engineered to make the perfect vodka, and the uncomfortable proximity of Klingons on shore leave, who seem have a scorched-planet policy when it comes to bar stools.

It didn't take long before the first mistreated nonsentient was found. Stuffed in a wandering trader's sweaty pocket, a small young Tribble has been offered for sale, and is eventually given away like spare change.

The trader in question is one Cyrano Jones. Jones is a licensed asteroid miner and prospector, which is far from being an exobiologist or zoologist.

Jones did at least admit knowing — and in fact warned *Enterprise*'s Ensign Chekov — that transporting (and breeding, as he does to maintain stock, as well as removing species from their native environments) dangerous animals is illegal, yet he has clearly not done his research into the nature of the Tribbles in order to determine whether they truly are harmless. If so, he might have had cause to think of how such a species came about.

The recipient of this living gift, *Enterprise* communications officer Lt. Uhura, acknowledged the tribbles but was totally unconcerned by their spreading all over the place, making no attempt to control them.

Despite this, she was happy to hand one over for Dr. McCoy to experiment upon but simply doesn't want to know if he's going to dissect it. It is perhaps disturbing that she didn't first extract a promise not to and that she's happy to hand it over.

This is, unfortunately, an all-too familiar situation for the wardens. The FSNP often has its work cut out for it when Tribble ownership goes awry. Tribbles, perhaps more than most nonsentient companion species, lend themselves all too well to the wrong kind of owners. Having such low-maintenance requirements, they are often favored by children and the elderly but are also favorites of hoarders.

Many's the time an FSNP inspector and wardens will attend a community in which a person or family has found their homes and workplaces overrun with

Tribbles due to just not having done the research into how to best look after a breeding Tribble — which is to say, any Tribble. Part of the problem is that humans have what is sometimes called Goldilocks syndrome: the urge to view any cute-looking creature as being as harmless and cuddly as a teddy bear — an Earth teddy bear, not a Vulcan sehlat — which often leads to injuries, or worse, to either the human, the creature or both.

As matters on K-7 showed all too well, experienced Starfleet officers are not immune to this condition. Even the Vulcan-raised Spock noted that their trilling has a calming effect on humans, but thankfully he also saw that there was something odd about their apparently purposeless existence. He, of course, grew up with a sehlat and so understands that things are never as simple as they seem.

It's unfortunate that the *Enterprise* officer who has some experience with nonsentient assistants, Lt. Sulu, was mysteriously absent from the ship's visit to K-7.

In the station's grain-storage silos, the inspector and wardens found one of the most harrowing scenes they have ever encountered: thousands upon thousands of dead and dying Tribbles. Enough to supply the automotive-seat-cover industry for decades.

Wardens faced a major task removing deceased Tribbles from the grain-storage hoppers aboard K-7. Thankfully, they didn't have to remove the entire Tribble population, upwards of 1,771,561, as most of them were still alive and in the process of being recovered by Cyrano Jones.

Since Jones himself had been responsible for the events involving the Tribbles, it's appropriate that he has already been dealt with by Captain Kirk under Starfleet regulations. That said, it's clear that his role in the K-7 incident was a pivotal one that needs to be reflected in future Federation legislation about the enforcement of laws covering the treatment, transport and care of nonsentient species.

Tribbles have no teeth, as Cyrano Jones confirms, and they tend to have no visible mouths at all, which makes their ability and propensity for eating grain something of a mystery. It's not surprising that they do eat, just a complete mystery as to how they do it. Sadly, despite many opportunities to do so, none of the witnesses to the K-7 incident have described the procedure, beyond exclamations such as "It's eating my grain!" Likewise, they seem to give birth with no mess, from no orifice.

Dr. McCoy reported that 50% of the creature's biology is devoted to reproduction. The FSNP inspectors notice that they don't seem to excrete anything either, but rather process food — especially when overfeeding — into baby Tribbles.

McCoy, despite being a Starfleet Chief Medical Officer, doesn't appear to know what bisexual means, claiming this is what the Tribbles are. He surely meant asexual and reproducing by parthenogenesis. Thank heavens he's not trying to pass himself off as a vet! He would never pass the entrance exam to be a warden for the Federation Society for Nonsentients' Protection.

Alcohol and aggression was a major factor in the K-7 situation, with both Klingons and humans more interested in drinking and tribal challenges of so-called masculine strength than in attending to the situation.

The FSNP's report into the incident will recommend that members of all species understand the ramifications that can ensue from having a party filled with drinking and brawling while responsible for nonsentient companions.

Trying to smuggle glasses of booze in the pockets is, of course, perfectly acceptable and normal; we've all done that!

On the surface, the situation on K-7 and aboard the *Enterprise* is something that, after the fact, even a Vulcan can appreciate, if not experience, the humor in. There is, however, a serious background to the events, and not just the trade disputes and arguments over which power's sphere of influence Sherman's Planet falls under.

Everybody thinks of the Tribbles as just cute pets and laughs at the Klingons being, shall we say, concerned about them. The other part of the problem is that humans never stop to ask themselves why a warrior race would see the Tribbles as a threat, when simply laughing at them and brawling drunkenly with them is more fun.

Although no one is quite sure how the Tribbles came to be the way they are, the FSNP is concerned that they could certainly be misused for criminal or even military purposes. It's not that much of a stretch to imagine them being used as a weapon of economic terrorism, ideally suited to wrecking agrarian economies of nation-states or, potentially, of entire planets.

Though some commentators have compared the likely effect of a mass Tribble infestation to the effects of the introduction of rabbits to Australia on old Earth, this is probably underestimating the potential threat. Rabbits, at least, have to have the females impregnated by males in order to breed like, well, themselves, but Tribbles have no such restriction. The more food they eat, the more Tribbles are born, and so the more of an enemy nation's agriculture you want to inhibit or destroy, the more Tribbles will be generated by it to do the job.

This may be one reason why the Klingons so dislike Tribbles; they may better recognize the threat posed by these seemingly harmless creatures. To a group used to more traditional forms of combat, this type of asymmetric warfare is most likely quite offensive, or at least un-warrior-like.

If the Tribble incident is to have any lasting legacy, perhaps it's most appropriate that it remind citizens of the galaxy to think about the beings they encounter, beyond the obvious plush surface.

Despite the temptation, nobody should ever just be tickled by cuddly cuteness. There's always more going on when the fur flies.

David McIntee is the epitome of the Romantic writer, in that he spends most of his time as an unremitting debtor who duels with swords.

45. TRIALS AND TRIBBLE-ATIONS
THIN DIVIDING LINES
ANTHONY WILSON

It doesn't happen often, and you have to look carefully to see them, but they are there. There's a moment in the bar-fight when Chief O'Brien hits a Klingon and there's something slightly out with the lighting. It happens again in the final scene on the *Enterprise*: Captain Sisko, we know, was never really there, and you can tell. Ten years before, there would have been a telltale line of yellow around the superimposition. It's still there, very thin, but the dividing line remains.

This is probably not the right place to make this confession, but I don't like the original series very much. Every now and again, often as a result of wanting to understand a tie-in, I give it another go. I take episodes people tell me are classics — *The City on the Edge of Forever; Mirror, Mirror; The Trouble with Tribbles* — and I really, really try. It's never worked. Today was no exception. I felt, since Robert asked me to do this, that I really should understand the source material, so today I have watched all three Tribble-based episodes. Yes, even *More Tribbles, More Trouble*, which is ostensibly a sequel but is, in fact, so close to the original source material, it's basically a rewrite. It even has the same forced humor and longueurs of the original, despite the fact that it was half the length (I swear that we were forced to watch about 40 seconds of a cartoon *Enterprise* at the beginning of the episode). But I digress.

I'm not going to tear *The Trouble With Tribbles* to pieces here, save to say that, barring mention of the eponymous Tribbles, Odo summarizes the entire plot of the original story in approximately 26 seconds when *DS9* decides to revisit it. I will refrain from sharing my horror that it took over half an hour of episode before anyone noticed that cute creatures who eat valuable grain and automatically reproduce ten-fold every 12 hours might, perhaps, be dangerous; I know television was slower-paced back then, but this is practically comatose. I will certainly not mention the fact that it took one of the most intelligent and insightful doctors in Starfleet even longer to work out that the corollary of "if you feed them, they reproduce" might just be "if you don't feed them, they don't reproduce". I shall not share my feeling that beaming the Tribbles to the Klingon ship at the end might be pretty much the same as beaming them into space anyway. I shall not share my amazement at how Kirk gets away with being so indescribably rude to everyone that he meets. All these things, to be fair, you can see for yourself.

It was the thirtieth anniversary. Horrifyingly, it's been twenty more since then, although less seems to have changed in that time. The dividing line between *Trek* of the sixties and *Trek* of the nineties is stark and clear — and yet, somehow, through making the *DS9* crew drop back into this particular adventure, something wonderful happens.

Maybe the choice of episode was the key. Superficially, this choice is madness: it's lightweight and silly; even the music thinks so (and listen to how the fight-scene is scored, if you don't believe me). But then, if you're going to drop another story on top of an original one, you need it to be fairly lightweight. It also helps if it's well-remembered (can you imagine trying to do this with *Let This Be Your Last Battlefield*?), which *Tribbles* clearly is. And then all you have to do is execute it beautifully — which, indeed, they do.

And that's the point at which my argument falls apart. Because, as the screen display on the *Defiant* clears out of static and the *Enterprise* NCC1701 materializes, I feel a rush of nostalgia and love for something that I never liked and had never enjoyed; something that, when I watched it as a teenager, felt dated even then. And I find myself asking why.

It continues as the episode progresses. The sequence where the *DS9* crew get dressed up in the old-style uniforms — complete, charmingly, with sixties hairdos — is astonishingly powerful, but nothing quite prepares you for the first, true crossover moment, when Uhura and Scotty walk past Odo as they head into the bar. Suddenly, the dream is real, and I don't even know why I think it's a dream.

And then it goes on getting cleverer and cleverer, multi-layering a plot that could be understood by dyed-in-the-wool fans who know every line of the original episode as well as people who tuned in by accident. Meanwhile, for the long-term fan, it becomes an exercise in how far we've come, not just in terms of effects or acting ability (although there is that) but in terms of the story of *Trek* and, indeed, television drama itself. When Worf discusses the glorious crusade against the Tribbles and then dismisses the complete change in Klingon appearance with the outrageous line "it's a long story", you realize how far we've come in Klingon politics. When Dax discusses Koloth, by now you know that he's a good guy really, because the world has changed. The dividing line, in-story, between the present and the past. The same is true for the external audience: the bar-fight (which is musically scored in such a way that you feel the composer is taking it seriously this time) has a build-up of about half a minute rather than what felt like about 15 on the first run, whilst the audience is expected to follow a far, far more complex plot (although, ironically, this is one of *DS9*'s simpler ones) than the original series ever allowed for.

To be honest, the whole thing probably shouldn't have worked at all, but it does and it works beautifully. As I mentioned above, on the surface, the choice of *The Trouble With Tribbles* to celebrate the thirtieth anniversary should have been odd, but, somehow, it's not. One of the reasons is that it's probably the episode of the original series that acted as a direct precursor to *DS9*. Kirk even says "Deep Space Station K7" and I so expected him to say "nine" that I was somewhat nonplussed when he didn't, even though that line comes in an episode made nigh-on 25 years before Terok Nor was a twinkle in Rick Berman's eye. But DSK7 is a space station guarding over a disputed territory between the Federation and an opposing colonial power. There's even a barman who makes dodgy deals with passing traders.

There's another thin dividing line, and that's the difference between madness and genius, which is pretty much what we see here. It should have been madness, but it really is genius, despite the comparative silliness of the plot. But the real moment of beauty is right at the end. The final scene with Sisko and Kirk (drawn from a different episode) can actually bring a tear to the eye, even to me. There is a real sense of completion, of bringing *DS9* into the original series and saying, look, all these things came from the same place.

I still don't really like the original series as television. I think that I get the nostalgia kick from a sense not of what the past was actually like but of what people thought it used to be, which feels very much to me what is being celebrated here. There really is a thin dividing line between fact and memory, and we get them muddled up. But it's a beautiful nostalgia to feel, and this works it more than anything else I know. No, I don't like the original series very much, but I've pretty much loved everything since. Especially *Deep Space Nine* and especially this episode, which managed to show me the past as, I think, everyone else in this book understands it.

Anthony Wilson has the sneaking suspicion that he probably shouldn't be here.

---

46. THE GAMESTERS OF TRISKELION
A MEMO TO J.J. ABRAMS
DAMON LINDELOF (AS TOLD TO JASON A. MILLER)

Dear J.J.,

I received your note asking me to follow up the weighty *Star Trek Into Darkness* with a more light-hearted comedy — your version of *The Voyage Home*. You said, "Make it funny this time."

At first, I thought *The Gamesters of Triskelion* would be a perfect fish-out-of-water comedy (but not whales out of water; everyone would be expecting whales). *Triskelion* is a lesser remembered *Trek* comedy than *The Trouble with Tribbles* and *A Piece of the Action*; after the Khan remake backlash, I thought it best to update a lesser-known story. And yet, it's still familiar to modern audiences, having been deftly parodied on *The Simpsons* and lovingly referenced in *Futurama*.

Another goal of mine was to finally separate Kirk and Spock for most of the film, to get away from their endless conflict in the first two movies; replacing that with a Spock/McCoy clash would finally give poor Karl Urban something to do, and

Triskelion certainly has an epic Spock/McCoy clash.

What I didn't remember was how heavy and message-y *Triskelion* was. Oh, sure, on its surface, this is *Trek* at its finest — exploring contemporary social issues through a science-fiction template. But, boy, is it ever dark.

Logistical problems first. Because George Takei was off filming *The Green Berets*, there's no Sulu in *Triskelion*. We'd have to add a plot thread to get John Cho involved. That shouldn't be a big deal. The fans remember Sulu's fencing scenes from *The Naked Time*; we could add him as a kidnapped crewmember and get some comedy out of his being enslaved into gladiatorial combat.

Also, half the original story was a bottle episode. After Kirk is abducted 11.6 light years away by the Providers, Spock has several lengthy debate scenes with McCoy and Scotty. Spock diverts the *Enterprise* quite a bit off course, chasing the only clue with which he's been presented, while McCoy (and an embarrassed Scotty) attempt to turn him back around. Spock one-ups them by sardonically pointing out that, if the two of them stage a mutiny, they can stop him, but otherwise, he's going ahead. Chastened, Scotty agrees to coax another couple of warp factors out of the engine, and McCoy bravely volunteers to accompany Spock on a reckless solo mission to Triskelion.

This is terrific low-cost "B" plot material for a show made in 1967. Confined to the standing Bridge set, we see Spock's cold, hard logic win out over McCoy's warm, emotional reaction — but with humor, as Spock points out the absurdity of McCoy's endless objections.

The problem is, it's hard to make this "B" plot translate into film. The only way to get a 135-minute film — and still honoring your tradition of having the officers fight bitterly — is to have McCoy and Scotty actually mutiny, kicking Spock off the *Enterprise*. There can be a fistfight on the Bridge and then a shuttlecraft chase. In fact, now that I think of it, we could have Sulu stay on board and pick a side — it doesn't really matter which one, because you've given John Cho so little personality in the first two movies. Imagine the dramatic value when, after several scenes of internecine bickering, the *Enterprise* finally approaches the trinary solar system — where we already know Kirk to be — and then McCoy and Scotty banish Spock (and Sulu?) from command.

Let's talk about the "A" plot. After Kirk and Chekov and Uhura are abducted from the *Enterprise* transporter room and brought to Triskelion, several truly disturbing things happen. First, the crewmembers are advised that they are now "thralls" of the Providers. Kirk explicitly compares the situation to slavery. Next, as if the slavery point weren't clear enough, Uhura is asked to whip a disobedient fellow "thrall"... who's played by an African American actor. Uhura refuses, and Kirk takes punishment on her behalf. Aired in January 1968, this was an incredibly progressive sequence.

But then, Uhura's drill-thrall, Lars, attempts to rape her, under the pretense that the Providers have "selected" him to be her mate; we cut to commercial with Kirk screaming out his rage, impotently thrusting out his hands through his cage bars.

There's similar sexually aggressive "comedy" with Chekov and his drill-thrall, Tamoon, an orange-skinned vixen with a distinctly masculine voice — including a sight-gag of Chekov having tied Tamoon up with leather straps. Kirk even successfully seduces his own drill-thrall, Shahna, who's shown to have the intellect of a child; she doesn't know the definition of words like "computer" or "planet" or even "love". At story's end, he rebuffs her request to travel with him, telling her (as she literally cries) that she must stay behind and grow up. Even more disturbingly, we learn that Shahna was born into captivity on Triskelion and that her mother was also a thrall, killed in combat.

This was all much heavier thematically than I was expecting from a comedy episode.

I have to tell you, I had a very difficult time separating out the social messages (slavery, racism, sexual assault) from some of the more exploitative moments in the episode. (Kirk/Shahna probably counts as sexual assault on its own.)

What I'd like to do is simplify these issues, by opening with a ten-minute action sequence in flashback, in combat on Triskelion, where Shahna's mother is killed onscreen. Maybe not the most engaging way to open the film, but less of a stretch than, say, hiding the *Enterprise* under water.

As for the slavery and racism subtext, let's rewrite this so that Uhura is far more integral to the plot. This works, I think, because we can do more with Zoe Saldana over 135 minutes than the original producers were allowed to do with Nichelle Nichols in 50. So we could have her rebuff Lars' rape-attempt by incapacitating him onscreen and then defeating him in the arena — instead of, as on TV, by having Kirk engineer his death by misdirected spear throw. In my draft, Lars would live to face justice for his crimes — preserving the sexual-assault theme from the original but removing the exploitation element.

I also want to do much more with the disobedient thrall whom Uhura refuses to punish. In the original story, that character was played by an uncredited non-speaking walk-on extra. Here, let's give him a backstory that plays much more into the slavery and racism motif — and also a story arc, where he helps to depose the Providers at the end. Similarly, give Tamoon a three-dimensional role, to explain why it's a female actress with a male voice, and remove Chekov's obvious discomfort at her advances. It's long past time for the *Star Trek* franchise to stop sniggering at this stuff.

And then there's Kirk. He's very much a heroic figure in 1967 terms; he outwits the Providers, defeats three thralls in combat by himself and institutes democratic reforms on Triskelion. But he also does some horrible things that the script glosses over. Kirk wagered the Providers all of his crewmembers for enthrallment and breeding stock, should he lose his combat: Spock, Sulu, Kyle, Nurse Chapel and all those recurring bridge extras. He seduced Shahna, who had the mental capacity of a 4-year-old, and then left her alone in the Provider's hands — her tormentors' hands — at the end. After the Providers lost their wager and agreed to introduce self-governance to the thralls, Kirk made no effort to see if they'll keep their word. Even the Chris Pine version of Kirk, reckless and callow as you've made him, could never do these things and still be considered heroic.

Look, J.J., this episode is not what you think it is. Like so many other Classic *Trek* episodes — *The Cage, The Empath, Plato's Stepchildren, The Cloud Minders* — it's fundamentally about the dangers of ruling by pure intellect and without compassion. The Providers do horrible things — condoning slavery, rape and murder — but are never punished for their crimes; Kirk kind of just lets them off the hook. You thought this episode was a light-hearted romp, but it's not. The only way to make a strong movie out of this is to make it even darker: more arguing, more violence, more consequences. I can only solve the problems inherent to original script by honoring the messages (and I know you hate messages) but removing all the exploitative material first. I'm not sure you'll find this "fun". But, if we finish this rewrite properly, it could be your most powerful movie yet.

Let's talk soon,
Damon Lindelof

Reply to Damon Lindelof from J.J. Abrams
Damon — thanks for your note, but we're going with a different idea for the third movie. I'm sure this one will go over much better with the fans...

Jason A. Miller, Brooklyn-born and bred, has been practicing law for almost 20 years and now wears a black robe for his day job, all because he saw Court Martial *at age 13 and realized that he wanted to do that for a living. Some would much prefer that he had been influenced by* Gamesters of Triskelion *first...*

47. A PIECE OF THE ACTION
A KING AND A DEUCE, EXCEPT AT NIGHT
JENNIFER ADAMS KELLEY

Some people have made the mistake of seeing *A Piece of the Action* as a whole — and the Fizzbin scene in particular — as so much forced rubbish that served as an early clue as to how badly Season 3 would both suck and blow... but clever people like me who graduated from film school yet never worked in the industry, however, see the Fizzbin scene as a metaphor for the entire episode in one handy 3:44 chunk of celluloid brilliance. The scene is the plot, the plot is seen, and the clarity is devastating.

The scene is set with a concise summary of what has gone on already, with "prey" substituting for "Iotians": visit prey, get captured by prey, Marlin Perkins hangs his head in shame. Now — to outwit prey! The Kirk hunch is supreme, both to the plot and to the scene. The cool, appraising eye... the jiggling eyebrow... the cohort-warning mouth... The beast is sighted. The hunter begins.

Kirk approaches his prey; they startle; he calms them with reassurance and scathing wit. He teases them further into his power with words — long words, confounding words, words that force dormant brain cells to translate. Action distracts them: the flip of a card, the aim of a tommy gun. Spock's support of his captain lures the prey in further. Kirk adopts the prey's mannerisms, reeling them in for the final gesture. A moment later? Prey scattered, unconscious and defeated. Ecce Federation, ergo win.

Did I write of the scene or of the overall plot? The parallels stun. Has the point been taken? In lieu of a Powerpoint presentation, the following chart will suffice:

Descriptive Phrase	Fizzbin Scene	Overall Plot
Kirk approaches captors	Kirk walks up to the table where Kalo and the goons play cards.	After escaping Krako (a thematic repeat of escaping Oxmyx), Kirk waltzes into Oxmyx's headquarters, weaponry in hand and demanding to talk.
They startle	Kalo and the goons point their weaponry at Kirk.	All of Oxmyx's people drop their weaponry when Kirk walks in with a tommy gun.
He calms them with reassurance and scathing wit	"On, er, Beta Antares IV, they play a real game. It's a man's game but, of course, probably a little beyond you. It requires intelligence."	"I don't think you're stupid, I just think your behavior is arrested" (to Krako)
He teases them further into his power with words	Half-fizzbin, sralk, "What you need now is a king and a deuce, except at night, of course..." Etc, etc, etc.	"Can you trust all your men?" "You cooperate with us and maybe we'll cut you in for a piece of the action."

Action distracts them	Kirk keeps dealing cards; Kalo keeps getting confused.	Kirk has the other bosses beamed to Oxmyx's headquarters.
Spock supports his Captain	When asked about the odds for getting a Royal Fizzbin, Spock says he's never calculated them.	"I'd advise youz to keep dialin', Oxmyx."
Kirk adopts the prey's mannerisms	"How lucky you are! How wonderful for you!" (upon dealing the third jack)	Kirk and Spock don gangster cosplay; Kirk imitates their patois.
Final gesture	Kirk "accidently" flips a card onto the floor; when Kalo bends over to pick it up, Kirk flips the table.	With the bosses turning against him, Kirk asks to say a final goodbye to his ship.
Prey scattered, unconscious and defeated	The gangsters get knocked unconscious, allowing the Feds to escape.	The *Enterprise* stuns the entire block around Oxmyx's headquarters, knocking out the goons and encouraging the bosses to surrender.

The point is proven, the table is turned upright, the audience sighs, and we move on to the next paragraph.

But what of the comedy? If some people complain, is it not a legitimate complaint? Take gangsters seriously? The Massmind disapproves. Harlan Ellison disapproves of the Massmind disapproving, but he has serious issues with the Classic Series. Yet... gangsters make more sense than Greek Gods, witches or gamesters. Gangsters connect more with the Massmind, even after all these years. *A Piece of the Action* is a more human story, a more grounded-in-history story than many *Star Trek* episodes. Good, bad, indifferent? The Massmind groans; the Cognoscenti approves; the episode foreshadows the darker *Patterns of Force*.

If gangsters foreshadow Nazis, then history-recreation-gone-wrong is the heart, the rival gangs/factions the back of the left knee, the technology-aided-second-escape the thyroid and the cosplay the sad acknowledgement that, despite the contemporary show *Hogan's Heroes* claiming otherwise, Nazis will never, ever be funny. Point debated, Prime Directive honored, basic plot of both stories confirmed in one card game in one episode.

(One chart per essay, sorry. Add a *Patterns of Force* column to the chart above if you must. Use a pencil. It erases better.)

Back to our gangsters. Look at the chart; look at the premise; look back at the chart; look at me. I'm the essay writer; you're not. Point definitely proven! Fizzbin foreshadows the episode plot. The gangsters can now sort out their government themselves thanks to the Feds interceding, I can now pour myself a delightful adult beverage, and you can now go read the clever essay on *The Immunity Syndrome*.

Jennifer Adams Kelley wanted to be Spock when she was 12,
but she got better (if you call wanting to be the Doctor "better").

48. THE IMMUNITY SYNDROME
FOUNDER'S LOG
MICHAEL ROTTMAN

Set foot on my homeworld today for the first time in months. It hasn't changed. It never does.

The shimmer and smell of the Great Link filled me with comfort. Yes, the Link has an odor. Sulfury, yeasty and a hint of chartreuse. (I know solid lifeforms are not capable of smelling colors, but chartreuse has a lovely scent.) After a day inside, however, I found it necessary to remove myself and write this account in "backward" solid fashion.

Taking solid form is not as bad for me as it is for other Changelings. In fact, I have come to enjoy my time away from the Link. Yes, it is a perfect confluence of being and thought. It is also a giant goulash of people who are never more than a molecule away. Claustrophobia is unknown among my kind, but, seriously, your atoms could get out of my face for a few hours and I wouldn't complain.

Ignore that. Progress reports are necessary, and communication via the Link is instant. I am simply impatient to be back at work. My mind is constantly with my "child". I already miss its magnificent, globulous form and vivid hues.

The other Founders finally understand what my assistants and I have made, and the naysayers have been silenced. Would prefer not to rehash every detail of my research, but, again, that's the Link for you. Minds, bodies connected. It can be difficult to analyze scientific data when your brain is constantly sloshing around with other brains obsessed with new kinds of shape shifting. "Let's all be copper sulfate today!" I would roll my eyes if they weren't miles apart in a sea of goo.

Second Assistant thinks this is blasphemy, but First Assistant understands. She agrees with me on many topics, and we have spirited discussions. I say "she" because the First has lately been partial to female forms when in solid state. She often asks my opinion of the clothing she morphs for herself, although she could go naked for all I care. She seems excited by this prospect. She is eager to hear which bodily features please me. As a scientist, my observations must remain neutral, although I admit the furred feet of the Caradhi rock dwellers are truly luxurious to the touch.

Must focus on the organism. An undeniable success. It will serve us well as the Guardian of the Dominion.

Yes, Guardian is worth capitalizing. Perhaps GUARDIAN? No, Guardian.

➤ ➤ ➤

If I had any lingering doubts about the importance of this project, the trip back from the nursery quashed them for good. The shuttle pilot was a lugubrious Vorta who could only be roused to insolence, eating spiced gas-tubers the whole way.

"Well, we're here. At your homeworld. The name of which you won't tell anyone, for reasons I dare not ask."

"You couldn't possibly understand," snapped the Second.

"Of course not." The Vorta grinned in a wretched parody of humility.

"Dominion loyalty is not what it used to be," I said, pointedly not looking at the Second, who turned away to stew.

How low the Second has fallen. Once a great motivator and planner, then demoted to my subordinate after deciding that the Vorta should be our security force. The Vorta! Glorified marsupials! As an experiment to find how many ways Vorta could be killed, it was a booming success. As for enforcing our rule, well... we are lucky to have saved any face at all. We have become a laughing stock to our underlings.

Even now, the Second is still trying to convince the Link that a standing army is the best way forward. I scoffed so hard I nearly evaporated.

"Yes, go find a race even more cowardly and meek than the Vorta. If anyone can, it's you." Much tittering ensued in the Link. "You are full of old ideas. An army of millions, crawling hither and thither with weapons and uniforms. How bland. How narrow of mind! These are the musings of a *solid*, not a Founder."

The gravity of such an insult cannot be overstated, but I was on a roll.

"Genetics are our future. I have brought life from the void: a single cell, vast as a continent, on a scale befitting gods. What forms will it take? What will future cells combine to be? Are the implications not staggering? Out there we birth a creature of the utmost simplicity, yet vast enough to hold the entire Dominion in its grasp — worthy of the Dominion's care."

The Second spluttered, "Oh, very practical. One monster to deal with beings a quadrillionth its size. Bravo."

"Show some respect!" said the First. "You're speaking to the savior of the Founders!"

I blushed all over. "Savior is a bit much," I mumbled.

➤➤➤

Little time to write; calamity has struck. Our orbiting data stations report a temporal anomaly near the project site, causing distortions in our readings. An hour ago, the nucleic incubator and amino acid monitor stopped transmitting. I fear the Guardian is in danger. I don't understand how this could happen. We chose a suitably tame location.

"I suppose that's why they call it an anomaly," said the First.

"Hello — have you been to space?" said the Second. "You can't swing a Paradan jungle squid without hitting a temporal anomaly."

We leave at once to survey the damage.

➤➤➤

The creature was gone when we arrived. Utterly gone. I reacted as a parent might, on instinct. I commandeered our ship and aimed it straight for the anomaly. Wherever and whenever we emerged did not concern me, though the others panicked.

After a disorienting jolt, we emerged in the middle of an unfamiliar star system with one inhabited planet. I came very close to praying at that moment.

But there was our amoeba, safe and sound, large and happy, full of pulses and flickers. It had indeed gone through; the big lug just couldn't resist a new adventure. We watched in fascination as it drifted toward the nearby star and began to consume it, *withered* it from the inside out, and with such speed that the orbiting planets were all but stripped of mass. Astonishing. Imagine what thousands or millions could do.

The First says we have traveled nearly 2,000 years into the future, a fact I am only registering now. Will we be able to return to our time? At the moment, I am overjoyed that the Guardian can sustain itself, although its negative energy field is much larger than we had anticipated in the controlled environment. This will make it harder to urge back home.

Ship approaching. Must cloak ourselves. More later. (Who am I writing to here? This situation is making me crazy.)

➤➤➤

Still waiting. The second vessel is putting up a better struggle than the first did, but it's only a matter of time before all energy is depleted. There is no stopping our colossus. Spacecraft have apparently evolved little over the centuries, or else these aliens are just primitive.

And the look of this ship. I mean, really. A more ridiculous design I have never seen, and I was around for the Husnock Star Funicular. There's a sort of disc up front and strange tubular appendages at the back — the phallus-worshipping culture of Zerkades 3 comes to mind — and linguistic markings on the top, announcing what I can only guess. Who puts lettering on a starship? Wonder if this is an elaborate prank by the Q Continuum.

I don't wish these flesh-and-blood beings any harm, but, on the other hand, what better way to observe the Guardian in action? "Imagine it drawing in the enemies of the Dominion, just like this. It will be the scourge of the galaxy." I felt the First tremble as I spoke these words.

Our readings indicate that the anomaly remains open. Once this demonstration is complete, we will bait an energy trail toward it and be home for (metaphorical) dinner.

➤ ➤ ➤

Sky looking very purplish today. Big, big purple sky. Strong wind.

It has been nearly a month since we arrived home, and I have been spending most of it curled on a rock. Only now do I have the strength to write.

Antimatter. *Antimatter*. Why didn't I see it?

That ridiculous saucers-and-logs contraption slammed its bulk into the Guardian's membrane, violating its protoplasm in a crude symbolic rape. And the monoforms wasted no time in turning my beautiful creature into vapor. An antimatter charge. Boom. Ribosomes splattered on the deflector shields. When the shock wore off, I wept as only a Changeling can, which is to say I became my tears.

Solids always find a way to destroy.

Of course, the Second wasted no time in stinking up my reputation, regaling the Link with tales of the Guardian's failure. In the vacuum left behind, we have given in to mediocrity. Everyone is lapping up this "super soldier" idea. Cloning facilities have been planned for the Secorma nebula. We're even holding a naming contest throughout the quadrant. The winner's planet gets a month free from tariffs.

➤ ➤ ➤

My new position: official Comet Cataloguer for the Founders.

The Second has been named Master of Cloning. Never mind that he hasn't actually cloned anything before. The Link was swayed by his design aesthetic. Sleek outfits! Spiky faces — ooh, scary! Rage-aholics addicted to a substance that ensures loyalty! Apparently, we're throwing morality and benevolence right out the window. I would never have treated my organisms like disposable stembolts.

Results of the naming contest are in. The winner is "Jem'Hadar". It means

"Hooray for the Founders" on Dosia Prime. How creative. There's talk of forcibly rejigging the Vorta's brains too. Use their shifty nature to our advantage.

Okay, I admit the addiction thing is clever.

To anyone who deigns to read these scribblings, assuming I don't rip the pages into shreds, learn from my disgrace: pride will be the undoing of the Dominion.

P.S. Saw First Assistant showing off her furry feet to the Master of Cloning this morning. Nadir: achieved. Maybe I'll just turn myself into a black hole and join my single-celled child in oblivion.

Michael Rottman is a contributing writer for The Morning News, *where his novella* The Golem Blog *was serialized. His miscellany has appeared in* McSweeney's Internet Tendency, Yankee Pot Roast, Cracked, Grain, The Fiddlehead *and* Opium. *He lives in, and in spite of, Toronto.*

49. A PRIVATE LITTLE WAR
WE COME IN PEACE (SHOOT TO KILL)
ANDY WIXON

A Private Little War was first broadcast on February 2nd, 1968. Three days earlier, the Viet Cong had launched what is now known as the Tet Offensive, one of the largest actions of the Vietnam War, in which it is estimated that more than 45,000 people were killed. It has become a truism almost to the point of cliché that science fiction is less a prediction of the future than a comment on the present, but few examples of this can have felt quite so burningly urgent to anyone who was paying attention to the episode.

Of course, anyone turning up to watch that week's *Star Trek* expecting some outer-space fun would not find a great deal to disappoint them: much of the episode revolves around a rather camp melodrama featuring some startlingly bewigged guest actors, improbably tight leather pants, one of *Trek*'s more hopeful monster costumes and a planet where a person's moral orientation strictly correlates with their hair color (a phenomenon known to Federation anthropologists as the Principle of Trichological Pigmentation Determinism). There's also one of the original series' least memorable Klingons, but he isn't in it much.

To any but the most casual of viewers, however, there is an inescapable sense of the episode exploring somewhat grimmer territory than is its usual wont — never mind the bad wigs and the monkey suit, this is an episode where two of the regulars get properly shot with actual bullets, another gets poisoned and the climax features an attempted gang rape. All these things, coupled to the angst-ridden earnestness of Kirk's meditations on the necessity of arming the Hill People, don't mesh well with the superficially camp elements of the story; perhaps this is why it feels so uneven in tone.

Those meditations of Kirk's, though, do make it very obvious what the episode is actually about, to anyone paying the slightest attention to it: the mention of "twentieth century brush wars on the Asian continent" is, essentially, the program raising a big flag advertising the fact that this episode is its main comment on Vietnam.

One shouldn't find this at all surprising: *Star Trek* is, after all, a series that is celebrated for engaging with topical issues and concerns through the medium of light SF. Elsewhere in the original series, there are episodes commenting (with varying levels of subtlety) on the hippy movement and the struggle for civil rights, amongst other things. It is customary to praise *Star Trek*, a series made when the Cold War and racially based unrest in the US were still very much going concerns, for its depiction of a hopeful, progressive future: the crew is ethnically diverse, and Russians and Americans serve together on the *Enterprise* (although, let's face it, Chekov is more often than not presented as a bit of a dipstick).

Watching the series again recently, however, I can't help thinking that this is a slightly selective view of it and its outlook. Perhaps this is because *Star Trek* fans themselves are generally hopeful, progressive people themselves, and they are choosing to focus on the elements of the program they feel most comfortable with, while ignoring the pragmatism that seems to me to form an equal part of its view of the world.

The peace and love generation may have loved *Star Trek*, and the program may have been broadly sympathetic to them, but it also seems to me to be wary of their ideals. Virtually every paradise the ship encounters, every place where the people live in peace without any real effort, turns out to be deeply suspect; the program is sympathetic to peace campaigner Edith Keeler in *The City on the Edge of Forever*, but it's also made clear that she is terribly misguided. One is never far away from a reminder that this is a show about the members of a paramilitary organization; as McCoy comments in one episode, Kirk is a soldier much more often than a diplomat.

And so it shouldn't really be a surprise that *A Private Little War* comes out in favor of American involvement in Vietnam as necessary to maintain the balance of power, "the only [way] that preserves both sides", according to Kirk. Let's just reiterate that: this is a pro-war episode of *Star Trek*, which is probably the last thing you would expect given the series' reputation nowadays. To be sure, all the characters accept the necessity of armed struggle as an ugly, dirty truth, rather than something to be celebrated or reveled in (though down in the valley, the Klingons are doubtless doing just that); the overall tone is definitely one of "more in sorrow than in anger". But, at the end of the episode, the Federation is still arming the natives. The question of who will come out on top on the planet Neural, if anyone, is left open, but, in terms of the philosophy of the series, it's clear that pragmatism has triumphed over idealism. This is clearer in *A Private Little War* than it is on many other occasions, but the fact that it happens at all in the series seems to me to be too often overlooked; this episode is hardly *Apocalypse Now*, but it does show that *Star Trek*'s heart is not entirely without darkness. And don't you just love the smell of vaporized Mugato in the morning?

Andy Wixon interned on Vulcan.

50. RETURN TO TOMORROW
YOU BE THE CAPTAIN FILL-IN-THE-BLANK GAME
LISA MacDONALD

Discussions of this episode single out Kirk's famous "Risk" speech, which he gives to inspire the crew to participate in the experiment that Sargon has proposed to them as encapsulating the spirit of the original *Enterprise* crew. And it does in many ways, providing an explanation and justification for the famous "to boldly go" mission statement that marks the introductory credits of the show. It effectively justifies the crew's actions, redeems the episode, reinforces the theme of the program and is so deliciously *Star Trek*-y and hilarious in Kirk's dramatic, pause-filled delivery. It's enough to make you want to be the captain yourself. And now you can be!

Ask a friend for verbs, nouns and adjectives as per the blank spaces in the speech, and write them in for them. Have them recite the speech in their best Captain voice and manner! Enjoy!

They used to say if man could 1._____(verb), he'd have 2._____(noun, plural). But he did 1._____ (repeated verb). He discovered he had to. Do you wish that the first 3._____ (noun) hadn't 4._____ (verb, past) the moon or that we hadn't gone on to 5._____ (noun, place) and then to the nearest 6._____(noun, place)? That's like saying you wish that you still 7._____(verb, past) with 8._____(noun) and 9._____ (verb, past) your patients up with 10._____ (noun) like your great-great-great-great-grandfather used to. I'm in command. I could order this. But I'm not because, 11._____(person in the room) is right in pointing out the enormous 12._____ (noun) potential in any contact with 13._____(noun) and 14._____(noun) as fantastically 15. _____(adjective) as this. But I must point out that the possibilities, the potential for 16._____ (noun) and 17._____ (noun) is equally 18._____

(adjective). 19._____(noun). 19._____ (repeat noun) is our business. That's what the 20._____(noun) is all about. That's why we're 21.____(preposition) her. You may dissent without 22._____ (noun). Do I hear a negative 23._____ (noun)? Engineer, stand by to beam aboard three 24.____(noun, plural).

Here are some possibilities to get you started.

1. flirt, love, phone in his performance, fly
2. oddly paced speech patterns, starships, studio time, wings
3. bald-faced lie, landing party, color-blind artist, Apollo mission
4. promised, ruined, drawn, reached
5. Risa, the Genesis planet, the Guardian of Forever, Mars
6. cheap hotel, shipyard, underwater base, star
7. picked up chicks, drove, acted, operated
8. Tinder, one hand, Walter Koenig, scalpels
9. felt, warmed, cheered, sewed
10. surgical gloves, revving engines, facial expressions, catgut
11. Mr. Scott, Dr. Mulhall, Lt. Arex, Dr. McCoy
12. tail, true love, humor, danger
13. short skirts, interior design, aliens, life
14. hips, primary colors, humans, intelligence
15. curvaceous, retro, pink, advanced
16. cosplay, hilarity, moneymaking, knowledge
17. winning at Cards Against Humanity, practical jokes, canonicity, advancement
18. irrelevant, ridiculous, unlikely, great
19. Sexism, Obsession, Survival during the 1970s, Risk
20. beautiful guest star, *Enterprise*, Animated Series, starship
21. beside, inside, within, aboard
22. uniforms, demotion, eyebrow movements, prejudice
23. rating, diagnosis, Russian, vote
24. Orion slave girls, turbolifts, sehlats, receptacles.

When she was a little girl, Lisa MacDonald wanted to be Dr. Mulhall.
She's never wavered since.

51. PATTERNS OF FORCE
NAZIWORLD!
JON ARNOLD

You can tell a lot about the neuroses of various countries by what annoys them. Some delicate souls in the US were offended by the interracial kiss in *Plato's Stepchildren*. The BBC got hot under the collar about what it considered sadistic elements in the same episode. Yeah, the US getting in a tizzy about racial issues and the British getting all repressed about kinky sex, who'd have thought? But the Germans? Nah, all that's fine. It's only when your leads start running round in Nazi uniforms and people start talking about the Nazis being the "most efficient society ever created" that an episode gets banned. In hindsight, it's not difficult to see why a nation that produced the most reviled society in the history of the Western world and was deeply ashamed of it might get offended by some pulp TV dabbling in the historical dressing-up box. Ancient Romans and cowboys? Fine, there aren't too many of them still around to get annoyed. It's not hard to see that the Germans might be a tad on the sensitive side about the whole Nazi issue. And frankly that's a far more sensible thing to be upset about than kissing or sex. Particularly when *Star Trek* — a bright, gaudy, cartoon space adventure with lasers, aliens and punch-ups — isn't really suited to tackling such issues head on, particularly when it's got nothing to say about them.

The show's heart is, as ever, in the right place. Unfortunately the brain... well it's not missing, but it's dislocated a little. It starts with the human MacGuffin, John Gill. He is, according to Kirk and Spock, one of the Federation's finest historians, prizing causes and motivations above events. He's also got a pretty broad range of knowledge, according to wider *Trek* lore, being an expert on historical trends in medicine and the life of Jonathan Archer, a real 23rd century renaissance man. You can see why Starfleet wanted him to be a cultural observer.

Unfortunately, he also happens to be a nutjob who thinks that creating the planet of the Space Nazis is a great idea. Gill's dubious proposition is that giving a society a purpose and direction, however artificial, is a helpful aim. This sounds good until you remember it tends to be the sort of idea spouted by totalitarian regimes rather than healthy democracies. Or by lunatic fringe candidates like Donald Trump, who'll never get anywhere near actually running for President. Oh wait... If only Gill had a better model — say, for example, a modern utopian society that has apparently evolved beyond the need for money and therefore likely conquered its worst impulses. Ideal, even if said society doesn't like imposing their own cultural mores on everyone. But no, given a choice of all the various regimes produced by human history, it's clearly a better bet to model this developing society on just about the most reviled society in the history of the Western world. It's hard to imagine that, even three centuries on after more global conflicts, the Nazi regime doesn't have a bad reputation. Not unless the only history books surviving the Eugenics Wars were by David Irving.

Gill's delusions suggest that he wasn't paying proper attention when he learned about the Nazis. He fobs his former pupils off by saying that he thought he could replicate the "most efficient society" yet devised and remove the regime's more repulsive elements. At this point, you begin to suspect that Gill was simply the cool, charismatic professor on campus whom students loved but who tended to busk his lectures and make them sound good. Because there's simply no way you can divide what might be considered Nazi achievements from the regime's ideology. The entire root of Nazism lies in dislike for the unlike, finding easy scapegoats for complex societal problems. We might excuse Gill for this if he'd only been attracted by the surface glamour of an efficient society, but his dialogue (as well as Kirk and Spock's glowing reputational testimonies) indicates he was well aware of how the Nazis operated. Just what did Gill plan on replacing the hate at the heart of Nazi society with? Peace, love and understanding?

And the supposed efficiency? Well, without getting into complex historical factors, a regime that runs on fear and distrust isn't precisely built to administer any society to best effect — empire building and backbiting, yes; a stable, well-ordered society, no. The supposed efficiency of the Nazis looks in retrospect like something of a historical myth encouraged by the regime's propaganda; the trains didn't particularly run on time any better than those of other countries.

Clearly, Kirk and Spock were easily impressed by their academy tutors. And the Federation administers need to work on their psych tests.

All this wouldn't be so bad if the show were trying to do anything but play in the dressing-up box. One of science fiction's great strengths is how it can reflect contemporary society and refract it back at strange angles, letting the makers get away with making points unpalatable in a more straightforward story. The trouble is, the show abandons any attempt at metaphor here and simply dumps the heroes on Naziworld, replete with propaganda, persecution, torture and some conveniently Jewish neighbors to persecute. And we learn nothing more than the fact that Nazis were evil and that it's a Bad Thing to interfere with the development of other societies. Oh, and possibly that it's handy for starships to be able to knock up Nazi uniforms on demand (the *Enterprise*'s fancy dress parties must be tasteful affairs...). You need to earn the right to use a real-life horror, and a cartoon moral about non-interference directives just doesn't cut it.

But then, perhaps I'm too harsh. Nazism has almost passed from living memory, and the German ban on this episode crumbled completely when it was finally shown on a public network in 2011. Perhaps we're all a little more mature and can take a show poking fun at history we weren't directly involved in. You can see it as a test of the health of our collective cultural psyche: *Patterns of Force* might originally have been regarded as an inappropriate laugh at a funeral, but now it's almost tame. We've started to move on from the consequences of the errors of our ancestors. Even Basil Fawlty might get away with mentioning the war in polite company these days. Or perhaps it's the first step to the details being smoothed away so that some genius of the future can get his history egregiously wrong. And it'll all be a case of history repeating its patterns of force.

Jon Arnold will be basing his utopian society on the works of P.G. Wodehouse instead.

52. BY ANY OTHER NAME
BEING HUMAN AND OTHER DARK MATTERS
PAUL CASTLE

I came late to this party, and all that was left to choose from was just one original series episode and half a handful of the animated ones. However, it's very telling that something instantly went "tink" in my head when I saw that *By Any Other Name* was the live-action story on offer. The fact that something interesting can immediately be said about any episode underlines the very point of this book. Just a week or so ago, I read an article in *New Scientist* (20/27 December 2014, pp52–54, "Fold Your Own Universe" by Stephen Battersby) that made me think of an aspect of our galaxy in the *Star Trek* universe that I'd previously considered absolutely preposterous: namely, the damn-near impenetrable barrier that surrounds it.

Of course, such examples of unadulterated silliness are *Star Trek*'s bread and butter. The central premise of this episode is that aliens have taken on human form to board the *Enterprise*, but — aside from a few remarks about how odd it is to have physicality, to feel and hear and smell — the Andromedans do not really think about it until Kirk and the others start to show them the benefits of what it really means to be human, to enjoy food and drink and snogging. I'm not sure a human placed in the same situation would be quite so dispassionate — we'd probably get so side-tracked with experimenting with what precisely each of our hundred new limbs could do that we'd forget the hijack plan altogether — but that's probably the point. These creatures are totally alien, with passions and objectives that are experienced quite differently, at least until Spock notices that their newfound appreciation of food indicates that they've taken on more than just the form of humanity. It's turning the adversaries' strength on themselves, judo-flipping their ability to assume human form into the very weakness that Kirk and company can exploit. It's a silly concept but intelligently handled.

This energy barrier that encases the galaxy is something that has always made me raise an eyebrow. When watching science fiction on telly, I tend to have a rather high-school level of perception of what space is — stars and planets and spaceships all suspended in a three-dimensional black void — when the reality is considerably more complicated. For starters, there are more than three dimensions, and physicists often plot position of matter and its motion through time (it's easy for the casual sci-fi viewer to forget that the further away stars are, the longer ago what we're seeing actually is) in a six-dimensional chart called phase space. What such a chart might look like boggles my layman's mind, but in six dimensions our material universe forms a flat 3D sheet (not 4D, however, as all matter was evenly distributed across the sheet immediately after the Big Bang and expansion refers to the sheet itself getting bigger, not the matter spreading to fill it) in which motion is practically zero. The movement that forms stars and planets and galaxies is all down to gravity, which pulls matter towards denser patches, causing the sheet to stretch and fold, and it's where the sheet twists around and overlaps into more and more folds that galaxies form; just like with origami, the sheet starts to take on a structure in this six-dimensional equivalent of a solid shape. It's this similarity to the paper folding art of origami that the article's about and how the less-dense folds cause galaxies to orient themselves to their neighbors. If you imagine the entire sheet folded into a polyhedron, where galaxies form on the little triangular facets, and the void between them is the larger multisided shapes, then it's the fold that forms the edge of the structure that directly links one galaxy to another. That's what causes them to spin, in relation to each other.

I'll tell you something else that's funny; it's this very episode where all but four of the *Enterprise*'s crew are temporarily turned into inorganic structures that look very much like the model of the universe I've been picturing here.

Physicists are getting to the stage now where they're using the mathematics of origami to model galaxy formation and to chart where dark matter is. There's far more dark matter in the universe than ordinary matter, but, being invisible, it can only be detected through its gravitational effects on everything else. The mathematics of origami can overcome the gravimetric distortions. There's thus great potential for charting alignments of distant galaxies and how they relate to ours.

One of the consequences of mapping using origami is that simulations have indicated that the halo of dark matter that surrounds our galaxy is far more structurally defined than previously thought. Whilst it was previously assumed to be a rounded ellipsoid (imagine a rubber ball squeezed by a clamp), the halo of dark matter around the galaxy is a many-faceted polyhedron. Leaving aside the stunning notion that galaxies form within invisible gemstones of dark matter, this gives us our damn-near-impenetrable barrier through which the aliens from the Andromeda Galaxy take the Starship *Enterprise*. When first reading this article, I immediately remembered thinking during my last viewing of the episode that this galactic barrier was totally absurd, as my school-level knowledge of astronomy paints a picture where galaxies have no borders, just a point at which there is no more matter. The writers of *Star Trek* didn't know about discoveries that would be made decades after their show first aired on television, let alone ones that give their exciting plot obstacles a grounding in reality. I find this absolutely incredible and cannot think of any other science-fiction drama series for which any (essentially) randomly chosen episode can relate to an article published very recently in the popular science press.

Remember when Scotty introduces one of the Andromedans to the pleasures of alcohol, his intention to drink him under the table? Well, after all this mind-boggling science and these weird coincidences, I think I'll join them!

Paul Castle is currently on a "50 Year Mission", watching every one of the 730 episodes, movies and cartoons in broadcast order from 1966 to 2016. Follow @vShootyDogThing daily on Twitter!

53. THE OMEGA GLORY
VENTURING INTO VILLAINY: A NEWBIE'S GUIDE TO EXPLOITING THE MASSES
CAPTAIN RONALD TRACEY (AS TOLD TO MANISHA MUNASINGHE)

Chapter 6: Defeating Heroes

Any marginally successful villain will quickly attract the attention of a "do-gooding" hero. These obnoxious moral straightedges will do everything in their power to destroy your wonderfully constructed plan. Rude much?

Not only do they fail to understand the appeal of billions of dollars or world domination, they don't even care how many precious hours of your time you've invested in this project. Since our behaviors seem to conflict with their "moral values" and "rudimentary concepts of freedom", they think it's perfectly acceptable to just ruin all of our plans

Now, while it is easy to dismiss these heroes because of their inferior intellect, you must proceed with extreme caution. They will do anything to stop you. While you may be equipped with ingenuity and tenacity, the support of government or intergalactic defense agencies that not only bankroll heroes but provide them with advanced weaponry will often give them a significant advantage. It is of absolute importance that you deal with them quickly and effectively, leaving them little opportunity to call in for backup or to do something audacious.

As a villain who has been thwarted by one of these very heroes, I have spent quite a lot of time thinking of how I could have avoided said defeat. Through my reflection, I have constructed a list of tips for dealing with these annoying pests. By following these guidelines, you will be able to crush these do-gooders before they have the chance to stop you.

1. Kill Them (or at least maim them!)
As simple as it sounds, this method is the most effective way of destroying heroes. A classic mistake villains make is keeping these heroes alive. Once you have determined that someone is a potential foe, kill him or her. You are a super villain! What's a little cold-blooded homicide? If this makes you uncomfortable, I suggest immediately re-evaluating your career choice. Murder is often the least-villainous thing we do. In fact, I consider it an act of mercy in comparison to some of the torturous acts we could commit.

While it is quite tempting to keep them around in order to flaunt your successes in front of them, this rarely goes as planned. If you have been cursed with overwhelming narcissism — which, oddly enough, many of us genius villains have — and must keep them around to gloat, try crippling them instead of killing them. Break both of their legs! Sever the spine anywhere below the C2 vertebra and you have effectively paralyzed them. Like murder, it will leave your victim unable to stop you but allow you to rub their failure in their face. This way you can have, as an old pop singer from my home planet says, "the best of both worlds".

2. What Evidence?
For some reason, most villains seem to forget to clean up after themselves. Now, leaving behind a body or two, if properly disposed of, can be relatively harmless. As long as you make sure to bury those bodies at least 10 feet underground and destroy any identifying evidence — fingers for fingerprints, teeth for dental records, et cetera — no hero is going to get in a tizzy because someone's been killing people.

If you leave behind five hundred bodies or perhaps an entire crew, which you've left behind as Pop Rocks, you're going to draw a lot of attention to yourself. Mass murder usually screams psychotic evil villain, so avoid this at all costs. Unless of course killing thousands of innocent people is your end goal. In which case, congratulations! You've succeeded!

If you find yourself with a large number of dead bodies, destroy them immediately. Have a ship full of corpses? Blow it up, or jettison the remains into space. That way, no one's going to be able to connect these bodies with you or your ship. Destroy any trail a hero can follow that leads right to you.

3. Finding the Right Minion For You

With masterful plans come quite a lot of work, which is why a great villain needs a horde of mindless minions. Most great plans require quite a lot of grunt work, and, as the best and the brightest, we can't go around wasting our valuable time on menial tasks.

Of course, finding the right minions is no easy task. While you obviously want competent workers, a minion with too much intelligence is a dangerous thing. You don't want a minion refusing to work due to moral objections, and you especially don't want them trying to start a union. Bankrolling your master plan isn't cheap, and you don't want to be wasting money on things like dental care or maternity leave.

But, unless you build your own minions, which I highly suggest if you have the ability, you are going to have to offer some sort of incentive in order to get cheap labor. If your minions are starving, offer them food. In need of care, offer them safety. American? Offer them weapons and hamburgers! Figure out what they want, then exploit it! I'm partial to exploiting indigenous people, but, remember, choose what works for you.

If you're feeling particularly evil, promise them riches, then backstab them at the last minute. These minions are merely tools to enact your master plan. Do whatever you need to do to guarantee their loyalty, and, once you're done with them, dispose of them.

Remember, a good minion is dedicated, obedient and content!

4. Live to Fight Another Day

The unfortunate truth of being an evil villain is that, at some point, things are not going to go your way. While we may be superior specimens, we aren't perfect. We may find ourselves thwarted by a hero, and, instinctually, our first reaction may be to seek immediate revenge. The urge to push them off a large bridge or strangle them is completely normal. However, giving in to this urge may cause unforeseen consequences.

At this moment of failure, you are off your game. Our career requires a certain amount of planning. Like celebrity marriages, impulsive decisions made on the fly rarely work out. Most likely, when you try to murder them in a rage, they'll end up killing you — or, worse, you may end up getting caught.

If you find your plan failing, the best thing to do is to run. Get away as quickly as possible. If you manage to escape, you now have the opportunity to try again. As many a motivational cat poster says, "Failure is often the first step to success." Or something like that. I've never actually owned one of those cat posters.

Learn from your mistakes in order to perfect your plan. We must constantly better ourselves in order to become more effective villains.

➤➤➤

Using these tips, you can not only avoid attracting the attention of heroes but also destroy them before they have a chance to defeat you. Heroes can be a distracting annoyance, and it is of the utmost importance that you deal with them quickly and effectively. If not, you may end up spending your days in prison writing a self-help book.

*Manisha Munasinghe has been to the Gamma Quadrant
and back but still can't find Waldo.*

54. THE ULTIMATE COMPUTER
EXCESS BABBAGE
RICHARD FARRELL

First Officer's Log
The learned Doctor Richard Daystrom has beamed aboard the *Enterprise* with his latest invention, the M5 multitronic computer. He claims it will revolutionize starship operation.

Chief Medical Officer's Log
I can live with the fact that this 7-foot tall academic didn't even acknowledge me, but what really bothers me is that his new adding machine doesn't have an "off" switch. The damn thing can talk too; I expect if we ask, it'll just refuse. Then we're in trouble.

Personal Log, Daystrom, R.
The captain is flanked at all times by his First Officer and Chief Surgeon. Can this man not make decisions without taking their counsel? They resemble a pair of Jiminy Crickets, each offering advice that contradicts the other, one on either side of the captain, each vying for prominence. I keep thinking of a ham sandwich for some reason; I'm not sure if that's related.

First Officer's Log
Daystrom's assertion that this new invention will allow man increased leisure time is an outdated mid-twentieth-century ideal that has never come close to fruition in the decades since. However, despite the absence of logic from this scenario, it has been my observation that humans nevertheless hope so fervently for this outcome that they refuse to face the reality of the situation. For his work in multitronics, Daystrom is, however, considered by some to be a genius.

Personal Log, Daystrom, R.
I consider myself a genius.

Chief Medical Officer's Log
This guy's a genius: he's invented a new tool that will put nearly everyone on the scrapheap. But, thinking about it, it's a kinda foregone conclusion that this nucular-powered difference engine is not gonna take Jim Kirk's place — who'd be left to dropkick the Gorns? I guess we can just expect the usual histrionic runaround before Jim eventually talks this man-made devil round to his way of thinking. That's his usual M.O. Either that or he'll lay the M5 — something I wouldn't actually bet against. What would Jim do if he wasn't a Captain anyhow? I suggested a musical career a while back as a joke; hope he doesn't think I was serious.

Personal Log, Wesley (Commodore)
Should M5 succeed in the tests, check Kirk's redundancy package and see if the toupee is returnable upon termination. He can keep the girdle.

First Officer's Log
Dr. Daystrom had great success at an early age and expects M5 to recapture his earlier glories.

Chief Medical Officer's Log
Daystrom's a one-hit wonder (was it a video game? must check that) whose best work was done before he was 30 — known as the Beatle Syndrome in some learned circles. I'm concerned that the modest soul has based his new gizmo on his own brain engrams as, in my considered opinion, the guy's not playing with a full deck.

First Officer's Log
Dealing with malfunctioning artificial intelligences is becoming a second career aboard the *Enterprise*. Where is the human named Asimov when you need him?

Chief Medical Officer's Log
For a second, I thought that goddamned crazy kook Khan was back. The ore freighter that M5 blasted into infinity was identical to Khan's *Botany Bay* ship; how is anyone supposed to tell these things apart? Starfleet sure runs on a tiny budget.

Personal Log, Daystrom, R.
I initially felt that the crew of the *Enterprise* were frightened of M5 because they didn't understand it. I realize now they are frightened of it because it is killing them in droves, which is more logical. At least they're not Luddites. That would not do at all.

Chief Medical Officer's Log
Quite a performance from our Captain; he was able to convince M5 that there's a God, that killing is against His laws and that the penalty for murder is death. And that M5 was alive in the first place, so it should therefore commit suicide. Nope, I've just read that back again and I'm damned if I can make any sense of it.

Chief Medical Officer's Log (supplemental)
Jim also gambled on Commodore Wesley's compassion as our only chance to avoid being phasered out of existence by the rest of the fleet. Guess he was right; I'm still in one piece. Thank God for compassion. Gee, for a moment I forgot that we're all humanists here. Thank Roddenberry. Or whoever.

Personal Log, Daystrom, R.
God thinks he's Richard Daystrom. I am great.

First Officer's Log
The Captain and Dr. McCoy talk much of human compassion, yet, once the ship was out of danger, I immediately became the butt of the Doctor's jibes on the bridge again. Bearing in mind dozens of Starfleet crewmen had just been wiped out by the M5, I find this talk of compassion to be somewhat confusing. I can only conclude from this incident that compassion is only shown to people with whom we are already acquainted and does not apply to strangers or redshirts. Highly illogical.

*At the age of seven, Richard Farrell cut the Dr. McCoy mask
from the back of the Sugar Smacks cereal packet and ran round the block
with it taped to the front of his head. Life was never the same again.*

55. BREAD AND CIRCUSES
COME FOR THE GLADIATOR GAMES,
STAY FOR THE EMOTIONAL MONSOON
EMILY ASHER-PERRIN

Here's the deal. At first glance, *Bread and Circuses* is a story about the Captain of the *Enterprise*. Having arrived on a planet where survivors of a lost survey ship touched down years ago, our very own James Tiberius is suitably perturbed to find that ship's captain still breathing when his crew is gone. What's worse is realizing that this former Starfleet buddy, Captain Merick, sent his own men to die in the planet's gladiatorial games. Cue angst, disappointment and yet another old buddy that Kirk can cross off his holiday-greeting-card list. If we're being frank, Jim shouldn't be so surprised anymore; this happens to him a lot.

Since Kirk basically has only two essential life commandments (protect thy crew and honor thy ship... unless thou art bringing Spock back to life), he's not too happy with the guy who managed to break them both. And when Spock and McCoy are thrown into the gladiator arena, we are meant to squirm along with Kirk, to feel trapped the way he does. We're supposed to remember our fondness for the *Trek Triumvirate* — a particularly appropriate label during this episode for sure — and understand that one of Kirk's most constant fears is coming to life before his eyes: the chance that he will lose his two best friends to protect the *Enterprise* crew.

But then Spock outwits the system briefly and Kirk gets tended to and fed by a gorgeous blond for the evening. What we're left with is Spock and the old country doctor back in holding, McCoy giving the Vulcan a hard time for illogically attempting to pry apart the bars of their cell with his bare hands. The Chief Medical Officer humbles himself enough to thank Spock for saving his life in the arena, but the Vulcan brushes him off with his usual sarcasm and the insistence that his concern for the doctor begins and ends with his duty as an officer. It's too much for McCoy, and he snaps, finally piling on the prognosis that he's obviously been building since their five-year mission hit the Go button.

He tells Spock that the reason the *Enterprise*'s ever-logical First Officer is not afraid to die on this planet, or anywhere else, is that living is the scarier option. Because being alive means that the dichotomy of his person is forever on display. That the chance of others recognizing his humanity is more terrifying to Spock than any practical danger they could ever face.

"That's it isn't it? Insecurity. Why, you wouldn't know what to do with a genuine warm, decent feeling."

And Spock — who is clearly reeling from the unexpected attack, if the episode's suddenly string-laden soundtrack is anything to go by — takes a moment to compose himself, pulls his Disaffected Mask of Impenetrable Sardonicism firmly back into place and says, "*Really*, doctor."

To which McCoy's response is simply, "I know. I'm worried about Jim, too."

And that's it. Forget the gladius blades and Captain Merick's redemption, forget the weird pseudo-religious tag at the end, forget the Proconsul's declaration that Kirk should have been a Roman (which is a pretty fair estimation most days of the week). This moment is the *entire point of the episode*. This place where Spock and McCoy bear down on each other and, in the end, are both willing to admit that the only reason they're at each other's throats is because they love Kirk and *they're scared for him*. Because that's what friends do: they gnash their teeth and try to distract each other from worry and pain. And, more importantly, that is what Spock and McCoy do, through and through, on their best and worst days. They force each other out into the open and they make each other better by refusing to back down from the most frightening conversations. Sometimes, it's easy to forget that, as much as they care for Jim Kirk, these two would barely be able to function without their natural foil. A very specific sort of love, all its own and equally essential.

For a show that existed before television was invested in long-form story arcs, this moment still had to be built to; nearly two seasons' worth of McCoy's grumbling and Spock's piercing rejoiners. One more jibe about green blood, one more sneer at the doctor's questionable medical expertise. It's a development that bears out in later episodes as viewers see the banter get lighter between them, more of a jovial game. From this point on, their quippy give-and-take never seems quite so mean (unless they truly have something to be angry over). We know from *Amok Time* forward that Spock considers McCoy to be a close friend, but this is the point where the Vulcan begins to realize that this irascible grouch of a man might understand him more fully than his beloved captain.

Even better, this whole drama plays out while Kirk is ostensibly getting laid. In no mortal peril whatsoever. If you were to place the caption "Classic" under any point of the original series, it would be exactly here. This is the entire *Trek* experience in a nutshell, whether anyone is willing to admit it or not. This is better than scathing Andorian insults, debates over the proper implementation of the Prime Directive and glittering energy clouds at their most compelling every day of the week.

The spirit of exploration, of bold ventures and risk, is sometimes overrated. This goofy episode full of badly choreographed sword fights, pseudo Roman philosophy and funny gray sweatsuits culminates in a perfect moment of human connection. A moment that reminds us why friendship and loyalty and solicitude are the greatest qualities we have to offer the universe.

This is what *Star Trek* gives us. Not because it is a show about science or allegory or our glorious future. Because it is a show about weepy, uncomfortable, troublesome, graceless, unpretty, over-complicated and completely real feelings.

And you'll never convince me otherwise.

Emily Asher-Perrin is a Kirk apologist and staff writer for Tor.com,
who saw The Voyage Home *in the theater as an infant and is certain*
that explains the entire trajectory of her life.

56. ASSIGNMENT: EARTH
FUTURE IMPERFECT
MICHEL ALBERT

August 9th, 1968: Gene Roddenberry's low-rated "space western", *Star Trek*, is cancelled, with little to no public outcry. On the same date, however, Roddenberry fathers a series that would outlive him and become his television legacy. That now ubiquitous series, *Assignment: Earth*, hardly needs any introduction.

After seven seasons of the original series, a revival lasting just as long and the upcoming film likely to be a blockbuster, it's hard to believe the *Assignment: Earth* franchise actually started as a backdoor pilot in an ill-fated and obscure space opera program with the cheesy moniker "*Star Trek*". But it's true.

Most people don't realize the first episode of *A:E* was, in fact, a rewrite and redress of *Star Trek*'s last broadcast episode, one of TV's most influential programs coming out of a ratings loser's death throes. There are notable differences between what we think of as the pilot and this original version, most notably the presence of *Star Trek*'s characters awkwardly observing the action (including Leonard Nimoy from *Mission: Impossible* in embarrassing elf ears!) and a different actress playing Isis' human form. She had originally been cast as a Playboy Playmate, one whose acting abilities weren't likely to coincide with how the character — and her friendship with Roberta Lincoln — would develop across the series.

But, at its core, it's the same show, and the "Starfleet" characters actually add to *A:E*'s basic theme: salvation through trust. If they trust Gary Seven, they save the world. If they don't, nuclear war may ensue. How can we not see this as *A:E*'s seven-season criticism of the Cold War? Over those seven years, Gary, Roberta and Isis changed the world and taught the people of the planet to trust one another, one episode at a time. In the "second pilot", Roberta alone must trust Gary, but, in the original, he's up against people who may actually have the power to stop him, men with harsh-sounding names like "Kirk" and "Spock", highlighting the threat they pose.

Assignment: Earth asked a whole generation to change the future, and it was the right generation. 1968 was a time of revolution, an unparalleled youth-quake that could and would change the world. *A:E* spoke directly to that demographic, telling us this was indeed a "primitive nuclear age" that required our vigilance lest we too would be "replaced" by the evil shapeshifting Omegans that were usually at the root of Gary Seven's (and Earth's!) problems. There was a better way, and Gary Seven was its prophet, having been raised by a more advanced culture that had gone through all of this before. In other words, there was hope, and change could be achieved.

And that's why the *Star Trek* episode is still relevant today. Connecting Gary's mission to a future created for another program — not just this single episode but two years of now-forgotten material — we can see what *Assignment: Earth*'s endgame might look like. These episodes are hard to come by today but are worth discovering. The world painted by *Star Trek* is one where Earth is united in a common goal and where people are free to explore their own potential without such petty concerns as money and ethnic strife. That's what Gary achieves, centuries down the line. It's a beautiful dream and worthy of inclusion in the *A:E* canon (just don't mind the rubber monsters).

Assignment: Earth has been discussed over and over again, and there's hardly anything new to say about it anymore: how Roberta Lincoln (and thus Terri Garr) became a fashion trendsetter; the game changer that was the Vietnam episode; comparisons between the various actresses who played Isis over the years; Beta 5's evolution from glorified wall to digital character and cast member; Robert Lansing's bittersweet return to the franchise in the last months of his life and his passing of the torch to Patrick Stewart as Jasper Nine... But, by going back to what many consider a mere curiosity — and an unofficial one at that — we open the door to *Assignment: Earth*'s future. Assignment... Universe.

Had *Star Trek* gone on to have a successful run, perhaps side by side with *A:E* in NBC's weekly sci-fi one-two punch, who knows where it might have gone? Our favorite show might have crossed over many more times with its far-future cousin, and fans today wouldn't be so quick to dismiss Roddenberry's first attempt at science fiction as part, parcel and ultimate evolution of the *A:E* universe.

Paramount could do worse than release *Star Trek*'s two seasons (if they still exist as a whole in their vaults) so that starved Earthers can see what frontiers Gary Seven and his friends paved the way for us to explore.

Michel M. Albert may or may not live in an alternate universe where he published over some 1500 Trek-*related articles on Siskoid's Blog of Geekery.*

57. SPOCK'S BRAIN
I AM NOT SPOCK
MR. SPOCK (AS TOLD TO BILL EVENSON)

I had many fascinating experiences during my five-year mission onboard the Starship *Enterprise*. And yet, my experiences after leaving Starfleet may be considered even more fascinating. Years after leaving Starfleet, during a routine cadet-training exercise, the *Enterprise* was summoned to Regula I, where we engaged with Khan Noonien Singh, who had stolen the Starship *Reliant*. During a pitched battle, I willingly exposed myself to extreme radiation in order to repair the *Enterprise* warp drive. This action resulted in my death.

It should perhaps go without saying that this is ordinarily where one's story would end. However, prior to this action, I had transferred my *katra* to Chief Medical Officer Leonard McCoy. Unbeknownst to me, Admiral Kirk at this time ordered that my body be deposited on the planet newly formed by the Genesis device, recently detonated by Khan. This series of events led to the *Enterprise* later recovering my reanimated form from the Genesis Planet, after which my body and my *katra* were reunited on Vulcan through the ancient ritual of *fal-tor-pan*.

Upon my recovery, I was fascinated to find that I was able to remember being joined with McCoy during the time that he "carried" my *katra* with him. In fact, one of my first memories following the *fal-tor-pan* ritual was a memory of events that had taken place following the *katra* transfer, a conversation with Admiral Kirk in the engine room immediately preceding my death.

While I had the forethought to transfer my *katra* to McCoy prior to my demise, I was not able to take the time necessary to explain to my crewmates the Vulcan tradition, in which a Vulcan *katra* is preserved following death. As a result, McCoy carried my *katra* with him for an extended period of time. During this time, both McCoy and I, in a sense, shared McCoy's brain. Because this experience is — to the best of my knowledge — unprecedented, it is often difficult to express to you now the details of this experience, as the language is somewhat inadequate to describe something unique to only two people in the known universe. However, I shall try my best. It is perhaps correct to say that, during this time, my brain occupied the same brain as McCoy's brain. As you can see, the word "brain" itself is somewhat inadequate to describe this. Two brains in one. Brain and brain. What is brain?

While it is remarkable to experience memories of events that took place following my own death, I was fascinated to discover that McCoy also had memories of events that he and I had shared together prior to my death; in particular, the events that took place on Sigma Draconis VI, during our original mission onboard the *Enterprise*. It is perhaps necessary to acknowledge that two individuals who share an experience are likely to have widely varying memories associated with that experience. However, what I found remarkable about this shared experience was that I had virtually no memory of the events. This is particularly fascinating, as the events in question were to have a fairly significant impact on me.

It is, of course, likely that the memories in McCoy's human brain are not to be trusted. Not only is McCoy's human brain innately unreliable, but McCoy's highly emotional nature is certainly inclined to "color" his memories of events, perhaps beyond recognition. Having shared a brain with McCoy — a disconcerting experience for both of us, I assure you — I can confirm that this is true. For this reason, I studied the Starfleet records related to the mission on Sigma Draconis VI and confirmed that McCoy's memories of these events are more or less correct.

What I find fascinating about the experience in the Sigma Draconis system is that I experienced a kind of *katra* transfer at that time — and even a form of *fal-tor-pan*, in which my *katra* was transferred back to my own body. Traditionally, transferring a Vulcan *katra* from one individual to another is performed via a Vulcan mind meld. Indeed, this is the method by which I transferred my own *katra* to McCoy, as mentioned previously. However, a rather more crude method of this can be accomplished through brain surgery. It is this method that was employed on my brain by the residents of Sigma Draconis VI, the Eymorgs. Immediately preceding this, the entire crew of *Enterprise* was rendered unconscious by some unknown means, which precludes me from elaborating on the process in any detail, as neither McCoy's memories nor the official record were able to record this event.

Following the brain surgery, my *katra* — and, in fact, my entire brain — was transferred into a computer known only as "the Controller". Kirk and McCoy then transported my body to the planet and retrieved my brain. McCoy then employed an interface the Eymorgs referred to as "the Great Teacher" to obtain sufficient knowledge necessary to perform the surgery and thus restore my physical brain to my body.

It is fascinating to think that not only did I experience a kind of *katra* transfer via brain surgery, and then a corresponding *fal-tor-pan* recovery of my *katra* through a similar brain surgery, but also, while connected to the Controller, I engaged in a kind of mind meld with McCoy, transferring the information required to execute brain surgery. I have often wondered what led me to mind meld with McCoy immediately preceding my death, as my many experiences with him over the years could have easily led me to conclude that his was a decidedly inadequate vessel in which to transport my *katra*. Could my experience as the Controller on Sigma Draconis VI have left some residual memory of this knowledge transfer that led me to unwittingly seek out him in particular from amongst those others in the engine room? Or was it merely his physical proximity to the entry to the warp drive?

There are additional details to this story that are unsettling. I retired from

Starfleet in 2270, returning to my home planet Vulcan to begin the Vulcan process of *Kolinahr*, in an attempt to purge my brain of all emotion. While I was unable to complete the final *Kolinahr* ritual for reasons that are not relevant to this story, my motivations for attempting to complete *Kolinahr* are perhaps important. Upon my retirement, I reflected upon many of my actions while serving in Starfleet and perceived a decidedly emotional component to many of my actions. Further reflection on these matters following my death (and subsequent resurrection) have led me to observe that my actions following the Sigma Draconis VI incident were significantly more likely to be driven by emotion and less by logic. Could I have experienced emotional scarring from this traumatic event? Could the brain surgery performed by McCoy have been performed imperfectly? Certainly, his memories of the surgery would seem to indicate that the task may not have been completed correctly, but it is reasonable to conclude that this is not the case, as this process was guided by me in those important final moments.

I am tempted to conclude that some part of my *katra* was lost to me on Sigma Draconis VI. However, this temptation is almost certainly an emotional response, a residual effect of being the offspring of a Vulcan father and a human mother. This should be discounted as being highly illogical.

Bill Evenson is human on his mother's side.

57. SPOCK'S BRAIN

I AM SPOCK

THE CONTROLLER OF SIGMA DRACONIS VI (AS TOLD TO BILL EVENSON)

Looking back on the events that transpired soon after the extraction of Mr. Spock's brain and its subsequent implant into myself, it is not entirely correct to say that the logical aspect of Mr. Spock was retained and the emotional aspect jettisoned upon the return of the brain to its original body. For instance, relating the story of these events now is, at least in part, an act of sentimentality.

It does spark a small measure of emotion to recall these events, especially the illogical way in which Captain Kirk and Chief Medical Officer McCoy risked their own personal safety and that of the crew of *Enterprise* to execute a rescue of my previous physical form, a mission that was at least partly successful. I recall asking why they endangered their lives by coming here and pronouncing this action thoughtful but impractical. When they indicated their intention to restore my brain to my body, I attempted to discourage them. I questioned whether such an attempt was worthwhile with no reasonable chance for success and further questioned whether the skills of brain surgery could be acquired in the brief time available before the demise of my physical body. When McCoy suggested using the "Great Teacher" interface to learn these skills, I suggested that the interface was designed for use by those living on Sigma Draconis VI and that attempting to use the interface may result in irreparable damage to the doctor's human brain. I insisted that I could not allow McCoy to jeopardize his life for me.

When these efforts proved unsuccessful, I allowed McCoy to access the knowledge via the Great Teacher. At that time, I was still becoming accustomed to the integration of Mr. Spock's brain, and I was compelled to follow the directive of the Captain, as is the custom of serving in Starfleet. However, during the subsequent brain surgery, I employed deception while advising McCoy, prior to reattachment of the nerve endings. I concluded that, by this time, much of the knowledge of the surgery would have faded from McCoy's mind and there was an opportunity to be had. I advised McCoy to employ the sonic separator, and he dutifully did as I instructed. Employment of the sonic separator split the *katra* of Spock into two parts. This is a delicate task, one that is difficult to perform with specificity, but I made every attempt to retain the logical side of Mr. Spock's brain while jettisoning the emotional side to be returned to the body. Spock's half-human, half-Vulcan lineage made this separation possible. Due to time constraints, this process was imprecise. However, I concluded that this lack of precision increased the chance of success of this operation. I correctly anticipated that Captain Kirk would become suspicious of his first officer were he to become a radically more emotional individual.

I also correctly anticipated that Kirk would leave Sigma Draconis VI soon after the operation, in keeping with his decidedly haphazard application of Starfleet's Prime Directive of non-intervention in alien cultures. It was a relatively simple task to direct the Eymorg Kara to perform tasks that would convince the *Enterprise* crew that I, the Controller, had been shut down, so that the civilization of Sigma Draconis VI would be allowed to progress "naturally". Such a distinction is highly illogical, but the result was anticipated, in keeping with Kirk's understanding of the aforementioned Prime Directive. Remaining on Sigma Draconis VI for an extended period of time to supervise this return to "normalcy" did not fall within the remit of the *Enterprise*, and the ship left the Sigma Draconis system two days later. I then resumed my role as controller.

Since that time, I admit to experiencing the emotion of contentedness. The culture of Sigma Draconis VI, with Morgs on the surface and Eymorgs below the surface, is a highly logical one, and the task of acting as Controller is one to which I am particularly well-suited. As the Eymorg Kara indicated to Kirk, the society would not continue to function without the Controller, and thus I am tasked with keeping them alive. The only real change to the culture of the Morgs and Eymorgs is my employment of a system

OUTSIDE IN BOLDLY GOES

of reproduction, wherein Morgs and Eymorgs interface with one another every seven years. This system is quite successful and is highly logical.

Unfortunately, I have concluded that the removal of Spock's brain has reduced my life expectancy to a period much less than the originally anticipated ten thousand years, perhaps as low as one hundred years. It is therefore incumbent upon me to prepare for the eventual acquisition of a successor. I am unable to foresee any alternate method of securing my replacement by means other than that employed by the Eymorgs when they brought me here. It is unfortunate, but it will be necessary to locate a humanoid and remove its brain. Hijacking a passing starship is likely to attract attention, so I have analyzed the other planets in the local star system. My analysis has determined that there are two inhabited Class-M worlds from which to choose. Sigma Draconis III ranks letter B on the industrial scale, which translates to an Earth equivalent of approximately 1485 A.D., while Sigma Draconis IV ranks letter G, or Earth year 2030 A.D. The choice is therefore quite obvious. As primitive as those on the letter B planet may be, their brains will certainly be of higher value than those on the letter G planet. The latter is in the technological phase in which the inhabitants employ their personal communicators throughout the entirety of their waking hours, in order to post photos of themselves and report their physical coordinates to one another and are only capable of expressing their thoughts in 140 characters or less.

Bill Evenson is also human on his father's side.

---

58. THE ENTERPRISE INCIDENT
VARIATIONS ON A THEME
DOROTHY AIL

The Enterprise Incident has some smashing set-pieces and Joanne Linville as the wonderful Romulan Commander. But, because of its modular structure, it's a serious problem discussing it as a coherent entity, because it isn't one. Certainly, McCoy's medical log, crazed!Kirk, the *Enterprise* space-battle threat, an espionage mission and Spock's romance each individually fit sequentially, as the episode progresses, but, really? All in one episode? This is clearly a story where the commercial breaks are necessary breathers for the dramatic tone shifts.

Here, then, are several different ways of expanding the ideas in the episode's basic framework into full one-hour episodes. Dorothy Fontana had a knack for creating stories that spur thought.

I. The Pueblo Incident, for real this time.

Which is what Fontana wanted to do in the first place, by all accounts. It's a simple enough story; a ship sails into unfriendly territory on an intelligence-gathering mission, gets caught, and the captain is forced to either sign a humiliating confession or lose his crew to torture. In the crisis, the captain of the USS *Pueblo* signed. Kirk would have too. A concise moral dilemma, easily scaled down to an hour, and if NBC hadn't had cold feet about Vietnam, we might have seen this on screen.

This might require the intelligence to be some less obvious McGuffin than the cloaking device, as in the transmitted episode (it's not a complete loss if Spock observes some more subtle intel), but, given that no one in Starfleet can build them a century later in *ST:TNG*, it obviously wasn't a very useful McGuffin anyway. It's pretty impractical to allow your starship to get an invisibility device if it won't be used... and if it were, that'd mean no more loving model shots.

II. AARRRGHHHHHHH!

If you're going to do a "Kirk goes mad" episode, go all in. The fait accompli of Kirk harassing the bridge crew is so massively out of character that it's painful to see how accepting the bridge crew are about it (in another episode, this would be sure evidence he's been villainously possessed). That's necessary shorthand in the current script, but it could be set up more coherently if it were the episode's focus. Tell a dark, disturbing tale about a man cracking under the stern pressures of command; Kirk's met quite a few crazed starship captains by now, there are plenty of role models to choose from. Have his dash across the Neutral Zone presented not as a petulant gesture but as a snatch at glory or suicidal destruction or intolerable smugness.

Then have Shatner mugging the cameras for all he's worth. He can save the day afterwards.

III. "Bond, James Bond."

The Captain's Log format offers an ideal way to do it: instead of opening with Kirk's narration, start with yer secret agent man contemplating the *Enterprise* bridge. His mission: while *Enterprise* distracts the Romulans with fireworks and banter, he goes in to steal the shiny McGuffin.

The "tell an episode from the guest star's point of view" is often one of the most memorable stories of a program; the closest that Kirk's *Trek* came to it was the previous season's *Assignment: Earth,* and Gary Seven was an over-powered godlike being uninterested in our heroes. Which was perhaps a bad way to write a backdoor pilot. Having a character genuinely interested in getting to know our beloved bridge crew would be fun, especially if Kirk and Spock are out of the way working up battleplans. Sulu might have some dialogue besides his hobby of the week. Uhura might turn out to have a hobby in the first place. They'd never have aired it in the sixties, but it's a hoot thinking of Chekov solemnly informing the agent "of course, spying was inwented in Russia".

Then you get to play with all the spy paraphernalia. Gadgets! Groovy music! And some romantic competition for Kirk, probably.

(You are also allowed to kill guest stars, which might be an advantage.)

IV. Cultural-Exchange Program

It'd work well on *The Next Generation* more than once, but regardless of that... there'd only been two Romulan episodes before this, and neither went into much detail about Romulan culture. Since you're already dressing up actors with prosthetics and uniforms, you might as well show them off, and since you don't have more than two sets, swap captains. Put the Romulan leader at the *Enterprise* bridge and give her some actual commanding to do; have the crew get to know and like these strangers after a while, and learn what makes them tick (it's *Star Trek*; aliens should be ultimately friendly and understandable). Meanwhile, Kirk and Spock can experience culture shock on the Romulan vessel, with Kirk playing grumpy sidekick to the Vulcan celebrity.

Of course, that makes the eventual McGuffin theft and getaway seem more heartless, but let's face it; the current episode does that already. Worse, because we're encouraged to forget the fate of that unfortunate Romulan commander; this way, the basic espionage betrayal is at the heart of the story, with the crew left to wonder whether Starfleet's motives are always of the purest.

V. "It's a long, long way to Romulus."

The episode, even as aired, would be massively improved by an extra few minutes after the mighty Vulcan Death Grip; first, reinsert Fontana's original dialogue about sending Kirk back to the ship immediately (it covers an obtrusive plot hole that shouldn't have been there), then add an intertitle: "Two months later".

By then, Spock will have had time to have developed some sort of relationship with a commander that could convince a rational person he's genuinely considering her offer of exile and command. It gives Kirk's subplot more impact if the crew is left mourning a captain who lost his sanity and his life. There's time for him to recover from dramatic surgery, and he runs less risk of being recognized by a Romulan who remembers him from five minutes ago but without the funny ears.

You'd have to explain away why it's taken so long to get to Romulus, of course, but that's what technobabble is for. And the time span's no problem: if an episode is allowed to take months just to set up needlessly overdramatic pregnant wife-trauma for Kirk, two months for a trip to the heart of the Romulan Empire doesn't seem too much to ask.

VI. *Enterprise* Two: Electric Boogaloo
Because, good lord, there were sequels. Between fan fiction and novels, there are endless explanations of what happened to the Romulan commander-with-no-name. Diane Duane wrote an entire rather brilliant series of novels fleshing out stray hints from this episode; the question of Romulan naming, the Right of Statement, the idea of Kirk being sent on missions to pick up fantastic Romulan technology and barely making it out by the skin of his teeth... *The Next Generation* offered Linville a chance to return to the part (eventually reworking a similar character into the episode *Face of the Enemy*), and much of the best Romulan characterization rests on Fontana's conception of a people curious and wary but ultimately honorable, in some ways more than our heroes. As noted, Fontana was skilled in crafting narratives that inspired others, and, whatever the episode's flaws, it did that and more. Not bad for an episode from *Star Trek*'s Silly Season.

Dorothy Ail would have enjoyed a Star Trek/Monkees *crossover,
if only NBC had thought of making it.*

---

59. THE PARADISE SYNDROME
BURY MY HEART AT THE ASTEROID DEFLECTOR
PETER McALPINE

A never-before-heard Blu-ray commentary for The Paradise Syndrome, *recorded in 2007*

MODERATOR MIKE: Hello, everyone, and welcome to this special Blu-ray commentary for the Classic *Star Trek* episode *The Paradise Syndrome*. We are lucky enough to have with us a number of individuals intimately involved in the episode, including both William Shatner and Leonard Nimoy from the cast of *Star Trek*. Gentlemen, welcome.

LEONARD NIMOY: Good to be here.

WILLIAM SHATNER: Howdy. Can I just ask before we begin if there are any more peanuts?

MIKE: Peanuts? I... I don't think we had peanuts laid out, Bill.

BILL: Sure you did. There was a whole bowl right here.

MIKE: No... we don't usually put out peanuts. They tend to get clogged up in the guests' teeth and they affect the way their voice sounds on the DVD commentary.

LEONARD: Blu-ray commentary.

MIKE: Umm... Blu-ray. That's right.

BILL: Then what the hell was I eating??

LEONARD: Bill, let's just give it a rest — we need to start the commentary. We're almost at the opening credits.

BILL: Oh, it's all right for you, isn't it? You didn't finish off some strange bowl of nuts that nobody else remembers putting out!

MIKE: If we could continue, gentlemen? Although writer Margaret Armen passed away a couple of years ago and director Jud Taylor is not able to join us due to an ongoing illness, we do have some archive footage of both of them that we will be looking at a little bit later.

BILL: Sounds exciting.

LEONARD: Bill, be nice.

BILL: What did I say? I just happened to note that it looks like we have an exciting afternoon in store.

LEONARD: I really don't think they appreciate the sarcasm.

MIKE: Anyways, we are lucky enough to have with us several others involved in the episode, not the least of which is actress Sabrina Scharf, who played the character of Miramanee.

BILL: Yes, the lovely First Nations actress Sabrina Scharf.

MIKE: Well, actually Bill, that's one of the things we're going to be talking about today — that is, the use of non-aboriginal actors in Native roles. So greetings, Sabrina.

SABRINA SCHARF: Hello, everybody. It's great to be here.

BILL: Great to have you, Sabrina. You look ravishing.

SABRINA: Thank you, Bill. Hello, Leonard.

LEONARD: Live long and prosper, Sabrina.

BILL: Oh, don't @!$#-ing start, for Christ's sake!

MIKE: Bill! We really need to watch the language. This is a family DVD.

LEONARD: Blu-ray.

MIKE: Blu-ray. We're going to have to edit that out.

BILL: Well, Jesus. He's almost 80 years old, for Christ's sake. "Live long and prosper." Give me a @!$#-ing break!

MIKE: Language, Bill!

LEONARD: I was merely trying to get in the spirit of things. Just because you've been out of the loop for some time...

BILL: What, because I won't do that goddamn J.J. Abrams movie? Oh yes, I've really given up on my heritage.

MIKE: Leonard, you're in the new *Star Trek* movie?

LEONARD: Bill, that's a top secret spoiler. Mike, we're going to have to delete that from the DVD commentary.

BILL: Blu-ray.

LEONARD: Blu-ray.

MIKE: Gentlemen, we need to get back to the commentary; we're already well beyond the credits. If I could just finish our introductions, we also have with us Gerald Finnerman, who worked as Director of Photography on the story.

BILL: Thanks for joining the loony bin, Jerry.

GERALD FINNERMAN: *(Laughs uneasily)* Oh, it's not all that bad. I've been on DVD commentaries —

LEONARD AND BILL: Blu-ray commentaries.

GERALD: Right, Blu-ray commentaries that would make your head spin.

MIKE: Gerald, we're now long past the opening credits, so maybe you could start us off. What was it like filming so much on location for this episode? I mean, so much was done in the studio during those early years, wasn't it?

GERALD: Certainly there was quite a bit of work on location in this episode: the interiors of the asteroid deflector were in the studio, of course, but, as soon as Bill emerges from the structure, we're back in the forest again.

BILL: Conveniently, about thirty seconds after Spock and Bones decide to leave me stranded. I'm missing for all of two minutes and they decide that's enough time to search for the captain of their frickin' ship.

SABRINA: I suppose they had to establish the plot parameters as quickly as possible so they could get on with things.

BILL: What, get on with their bastardization of the American Indian?

LEONARD: Bill is that really fair?

MIKE: "First Nation", please, Bill.

BILL: Oh, *now* we get politically correct? Where were you when they were casting such a snow white group as a supposed offshoot of the Mohicans? No offense, Sabrina.

SABRINA: Oh, none taken. I've been asked about this a lot over the years, actually.

LEONARD: The script actually says they are a mixture of Navajo, Mohican and Delaware. But your point is taken.

GERALD: I do think we have to remember when this episode was actually filmed. The 1960s were not renowned for their attention to diversity.

SABRINA: Does that mean we just ignore the issue, then? Don't get me wrong — I'm thrilled that I was cast in the part, and I hope I did it as much justice as possible...

BILL: Oh, you definitely did. *(Laughs.)* Denny Crane.

MIKE: Umm... well maybe this is as good a time as any to listen to a brief audio extract of writer Margaret Armen and director Jud Taylor from a convention about 10 years ago, when they were asked some of these very same difficult questions. In fact, they... uh, Bill, where are you going?

BILL: I'm going to take a whizz.

MIKE: Umm... right *now?*

BILL: Well, I figure now is as good a time as any. You're just going to be playing some boring old extract... I'll be right back. *(Door closes.)*

LEONARD: And with that, he's off.

Extract from Main Stage interview at **East Coast Trek**, *1997.*

MARGARET ARMEN: Oh, I know the presentation of the American Indian was insensitive at best. But that's what it was like in the decades leading up to the 1960s during the supposed "first golden age of television". It was all based on stereotypes.

MODERATOR: But it wasn't just the Asian characters. What about the casting? You had white actors playing American Indians. How could this possibly seem like a good idea?

JUD TAYLOR: Of course it wasn't a good idea. The problem was that everyone was doing it. I believe the actual term was "whitewashing": the casting of white actors in minority roles. And it was extremely common in Hollywood. Burt Lancaster played the title role in the film *Apache*, while both Fu Manchu and Charlie Chan were played by white actors. I suppose in many ways it was simply expected; audiences in the 1960s expected to see mainly white actors on the screen.

MODERATOR: And yet you still had actors like Jay Silverheels playing the role of Tonto in *The Lone Ranger.*

JUD: Very true. Perhaps it was the whole "guest star" thing. There was generally no specific reason for it, yet we still sought out white actors above other ethnicities.

MODERATOR: It's interesting that there seems to be such a major charge of racism against a show that presented one of the first interracial kisses on television.

MARGARET: Yes, I was just going to say that. Kirk and Uhura in *Plato's Stepchildren.* Often incorrectly cited as the very first interracial kiss — but it was certainly one of the earlier ones.

MIKE: And that brings us back. It's interesting to note that whitewashing is still very much prevalent in the Hollywood of today. Liam Neeson played middle eastern Ra's al Ghul in *Batman Begins*, although I do think you'd be hard-pressed to imagine a white actor playing Tonto in a modern version of *The Lone Ranger*. Oh, welcome back, Bill.

LEONARD: What's that you've got there?

BILL: Peanuts. There's a whole vending machine full of them out there. Can you believe it?

MIKE: At any rate, I do have some questions for you, Bill, about your super-quick betrothal to Miramanee.

BILL: Ah yes. We gave them something to think about, didn't we, Sabrina?

SABRINA: Well, the fact is that the marriage *may* have seemed to have taken place very quickly. But you've got to remember that it actually took the *Enterprise* several months to return to the planet.

MIKE: That's right, making this the longest period of time that an original series episode of *Star Trek* took place over. *(Laughs.)* Of course, none of the between-the-scenes incidents are available as extras on this DVD!

BILL, LEONARD, SABRINA AND GERALD: Blu-ray.

MIKE: Um, yes... Blu-ray. I think at this point we'll have to take a bit of a breather. We're not really synchronized with the action that's happening on the screen, so let's all take a break and we'll recommence in a little while.

BILL: Sounds good to me. I'm going to raid that vending machine in the hall again. Anyone want some peanuts?

Peter McAlpine adores William Shatner and Leonard Nimoy.
No disrespect towards any of those involved — living or dead — is intended.

60. AND THE CHILDREN SHALL LEAD
YOUR FEEDBACK IS IMPORTANT TO US
CHRIS ARNSBY

You are in: <u>Aliens</u>> <u>Planetary Invasions</u>> <u>User Reviews</u>

Most helpful customer reviews

<u>Klingons</u>>
***** **Kor blimey!**
No freedoms whatsoever. Our goods were confiscated. Hostages taken, our leaders confined. Would definitely 100% want to be invaded by Klingons again.

***** **Kang I dig it? Yes I Kang.**
First they weakened us by poisoning our grain. Next came orbital bombardment followed by mass beam downs and securing of key installations. We were helpless! Have a go on the mind-ripper if you get the chance. It will record your every thought and memory.

<u>Romulans</u>>
***** **You won't believe who this mysterious and secretive race look like!**
[review deleted]

[score withheld at user request] [**comment deleted**]
[review deleted]

<u>Kelvan Empire</u>>
*** **Kelvans are quite cool**
We thought we'd take a chance on something different. At first, we were disappointed that the Kelvans turned up looking like us rather than the picture on their website (being invaded by immense beings with a hundred tentacles would have been awesome), but they set about invading us with efficiency and imagination. They have this nifty little paralysis field, which is great fun.

*** **My husband and children were reduced to cubes**
The cubes were an imaginative way of keeping my good behavior. Unfortunately, I am now stuck on a spaceship making a 300-year-long one-way trip to the Andromeda Galaxy. I think 300 years is too long for an invasion. My husband and I had plans for

the weekend. Now he is a cube and I am on this spaceship. This review would have been 4 stars if not for the 300 years. Also our dog was also reduced to a cube, and I think that is cruel to an animal.

Neural Parasites>
*** A Pizza The Action
Our kids loved the farting and squeaking noises these things made.

Giant Space Amoeba>
*** This thing is huge and really good value for money.
It dominated the sky above our planet and filled it with the most amazing psychedelic visuals you can imagine. Unfortunately, it burst. Three of our continents drowned in endoplasm, and, when the nucleus flew loose, it knocked our moon out of orbit. Keep sharp objects away from it and you should be fine.

Organians>
** Too much jaw-jaw, not enough war-war
We were having a private little war — just ourselves and a couple of other neighboring planets — when this bunch of glowing lights turned up and ordered us to stop because the noise was upsetting them. When we refused, they kept turning all our lights on and off. That was annoying. After we had stopped fighting, they tried to sell us some blue goat's cheese milk that tasted funny.

Salt Vampire>
** I was camping on M-113
and this thing kept hanging around pretending to be my ex-girlfriend. I gave it some LoSalt and told it to fuck off.

Anti-Lazarus>
** He's death, anti-life, he lives to destroy.
Anti-Lazarus is humanoid outside, but inside, he's a hideous, murdering monster! No I'm not. Yes you are! No I'm not. Yes you are. No I'm not. Yes you are... [read more]

Cloud Vampire>
** Our entire planet reeked of honey for weeks afterwards.

Doomsday Machine>
** WARNING DO NOT USE UNLESS YOU WANT YOUR PLANET REDUCED TO RUBBLE! Why is a Doomsday Machine listed in planetary invasions? We wanted our planet invaded, not destroyed. Please be careful before choosing to use a

Doomsday Machine. I think it is listed in the wrong category. Our lovely planet is now an asteroid belt.

(5 of 8 species found this review helpful)

Rage-Generating Entity>
* **I'M SO ANGRY THAT THIS CREATURE DOES NOT HAVE A PROPER NAME**

* **THIS MAKES ME FURIOUS**

* **I WAS UTTERLY LIVID WHEN THIS CREATURE INVADED MY PLANET!!**

* **I AGREE WITH THE ABOVE REVIEWS AND IT MAKES ME CROSS**

* **ASDFSDGSLKJ\GBJVCNKL2 V34V   !**

Gorgan>
* **Avoid this cheesy Gorgan(zola)**
We were looking for a cut-price invasion and ignored other customer reviews for this alien. What a mistake. When the Gorgan never turned up on the scheduled date, we had to go to his cave on Triacus (a dump of a planet) to find him. He tried to pretend he had turned up for the invasion but we were out. This was not true. In fact, we had cancelled other plans to make sure our species was in when he was due. We had to threaten to raise a trading dispute. After that, he finally materialized on the bridge of our spaceship wearing a shower curtain and holding a torch under his chin. His face melted a bit, and then he vanished. After all this, he had the gall to bill us in full. Terrible. Do not use. Not recommended.

You may also like Tribbles> buy them now before they run out only: ~~2~~
~~16~~
~~128~~
~~1024~~
~~8192~~
~~65336~~
524288 left

Chris Arnsby has recently become trapped by a rock monster in a battle to the death to decide which is better: the Beatles or the Monkees.

61. IS THERE IN TRUTH NO BEAUTY?

IS THERE IN TRUTH NO FANFIC?

DONALD GILLIKIN

After some forty years of watching *Star Trek* reruns, I recently came to the realization that this third-season episode, Jean Lisette Aroeste's *Is There in Truth No Beauty?*, was, essentially, televised fan fiction. After that, I realized that some other third-season episodes also struck me as particularly like fan fiction. For example, Joyce Muskat's *The Empath*; puppeteer Shari Lewis and Jeremy Tarcher's *The Lights of Zetar*; Aroeste's sophomore effort *All Our Yesterdays*; and Rik Vollaerts' *For the World is Hollow and I Have Touched the Sky*.

There is surely a reason for that fan-fictiony feeling. Of the above, only Rik Vollaerts had extensive credits as a screenwriter before *Star Trek*. Shari Lewis and Jeremy Tarcher's credits were usually on the performance and production side of their own programs. Meanwhile, Aroeste and Muskat were unknowns writing their first scripts for television; in fact, Aroeste and Muskat's respective *Star Trek* scripts are their only professional credits in the screenwriting field. Aroeste was, at the time she wrote her two scripts for *Star Trek*, a reference librarian at UCLA whose initial story submissions had come to the attention of Associate Producer Bob Justman.

As it was in the real world, 1968 was a turbulent year for the *Star Trek* production office. John and Bjo Trimble's letter-writing campaign — orchestrated behind the scenes by *Star Trek* executive producer Gene Roddenberry — had reversed NBC's planned cancellation of the series. A new producer, Fred Freiberger — who, by many accounts didn't "grok Spock", as the popular button would have it and who would later gain a reputation as a "showkiller" for his history of taking over shows in what would become their final seasons — had come onboard to make *Star Trek* even more cheaply in that third season, in accordance with studio demands. Taking the above into account, a strategy of taking chances on inexperienced writers like Aroeste and Muskat would seem to make sense. After all, it had worked the previous season with fan-turned-pro David Gerrold's *The Trouble With Tribbles*, hadn't it?

As with any story submitted by fans like Aroeste and Muskat, there's going to be a certain degree of fan service contained within: little elements of story and/or character that fans wanted to see more of. In the seventies, as early fan fiction moved beyond short, humorous pieces like those printed in the formative late sixties fanzine, *Spockanalia*, certain tropes became commonplace. Some terms have expanded beyond their Trekkian origins and entered common currency, like Mary-Sue (the author inserting herself into the narrative via a flawless wish-fulfillment character) and hurt/comfort (formerly "hurt-care-torture-comfort"). There's the

"Get [insert appropriate character's name here]" story, in which a fan-author's original character — often a Mary-Sue — enjoys a romantic relationship with one of the series' leading characters. And then there's the trope I like to call "the Laughing Vulcan", in which a story contrives to find a means to force Spock to demonstrate emotion, usually due to outside influences, as seen in *The Naked Time*, *This Side of Paradise* and *Return to Tomorrow*. However, an interesting thing to note is that the third season's relationship with what would become fan-fictional tropes is something of a "chicken and egg" paradox. By turning to fan-writers who infused their scripts with a fannish sensibility, the series in its third season effectively gave its sanction to further exploring its characters' emotional lives, which, after cancellation, later fan-writers amplified in the seventies, which begat the various fan-fictional tropes with which we've become familiar.

Let us grant that there are other episodes that better embody certain tropes: *The Lights of Zetar* gives us both a "Mary-Sue" and a "Get Scotty" story, *The Empath* is pure hurt/comfort, and *All Our Yesterdays* gives us an emoting Vulcan (even if the Vulcan does not laugh) and a "Get Spock". However, in production order, *Is There In Truth No Beauty?* is the earliest of the fan-fiction-like teleplays filmed during the third season. As such, it embodies a number of the key tropes of the genre.

Is There In Truth No Beauty? revolves around one Dr. Miranda Jones, a telepathic psychologist chosen to perform a mind link with the noncorporeal Medusan ambassador, Kollos, a being whose appearance drives people mad. Our leading male characters spend a good portion of the episode's early acts transparently fawning over Miranda, most notably in the banquet scene, flattering her beauty, her intelligence and her skill. Miranda is not only "special" by virtue of her beauty and intelligence or by being a rare human telepath; no, as the script unfolds, she is revealed as further being special by having to overcome a physical limitation — her blindness — by use of a remarkable sensor web worn over her clothing. However, if Miranda is a Mary-Sue, she is a Mary-Sue with thorns. There are aspects of the character that play against the grain of the typical Mary-Sue characterization. While the characters may fawn over her, Miranda's personality comes across as cold and unpleasant and not particularly likable. She is paranoid and jealous of Spock's superior ability in accomplishing a mind-link. She reads an implied disrespect toward her in Spock's wearing a revered Vulcan symbol of logic, the IDIC, to honor her. For a proto-Mary-Sue, Miranda Jones is not an easy person to love.

Let us move on from Dr. Miranda Jones to briefly touch upon the popularity of Mr. Spock. To say that the character of Spock was the breakout character with viewers, especially female viewers, is a given. Consequently, as the series goes on, there is a turn toward transparent Spocksploitation. The third season opens with a story about Spock's brain being stolen. The crew has to deal with the loss of its captain for two extended periods in *The Paradise Syndrome* and *The Tholian Web*, giving Spock the opportunity to share the agonies of command. Spock gets to sympathize with — and jam musically with — space hippies in *The Way to Eden*. Spock's status as an alien from a culture that shuns emotional displays gave writers, both fan and pro, a tool to use to comment on the human condition and gave rise to the Laughing Vulcan trope — although the Emoting Vulcan might be a truer name.

In a Laughing Vulcan story, the narrative conspires to place Spock into a situation where the Vulcan barriers against the demonstration of emotion break down, usually due to outside influences, as seen in *The Naked Time*, *This Side of Paradise* and *Return to Tomorrow*, in which Spock's body is inhabited by the disembodied consciousness of the evil Henoch, giving actor Leonard Nimoy the opportunity to chew the scenery with playfully arch, evil acting.

In *Is There in Truth No Beauty?*, circumstances maneuver Spock to mind link with Ambassador Kollos to rescue the *Enterprise*, leading the fused Spock/Kollos entity to quote Lord Byron's Romantic poetry to Uhura and Shakespeare's *The Tempest* to Miranda. Like most of the leading human males in this story, the Spock/Kollos fusion cannot refrain from verbally flirting with Miranda, albeit in a poetic manner replete with musical accompaniment from the omnipresent Starship Violin Corps. And, of course, such a scene isn't complete without the Spock/Kollos fusion marveling at the existence of physical senses but noting the loneliness of a separate physical existence.

However, the newly emotional Spock/Kollos fusion, after rescuing the ship, must suffer a bit in the narrative in the aftermath of his poetry recitals. Whether through euphoria at being allowed to be emotional for a short period of time or through a psychic nudge from the jealous Miranda, Spock forgets to take his protective visor with him as he undoes the mindlink and gazes upon the ambassador's form unprotected. He is driven mad as a result, which brings us to this episode's brief flirtation with the hurt/comfort trope.

The traditional way of describing hurt-care-torture-comfort runs thusly: Character A is hurt (physically or mentally). Character B cares. The pain is torturous, but through the process of sharing and caring, the characters find comfort. As I wrote earlier, *The Empath* is better illustrative of the hurt/comfort trope than this episode is; however, if one wants to stretch the point, one can make it fit in this way. Spock is hurt by being driven mad by his exposure to Kollos. Kirk cares, so he browbeats Miranda into using her telepathy to enter Spock's mind, and, after a torturous battle with Spock's madness and sharing Spock's agony, both Spock and Miranda's personalities are reintegrated, finding comfort and a mutual respect for each other.

In closing, I would like to point out that one of the things about fan fiction is that we fans use it partly to fill in the gaps, to give fans more of what they desire than the official series may feel comfortable with showing onscreen, such as details exploring the inner, emotional lives of the characters. Culturally, those emotional concerns have largely been regarded as the province of female fan-writers, who wrote much of that early first-generation fan fiction and continue to do so today. In discussing fan fiction and its tropes, it's all too easy for us — often because of our unconscious adoption of male-inflected semi-academic discourse — to sound as if we're sneeringly minimizing the talents and abilities of the producers of fan works, to make it sound as if works produced largely by women and amateurs are automatically inferior to those produced by professional (and still predominantly male) screenwriters — especially when one is trying to be funny and creative in discussing the subject. This is most emphatically not the case. While Sturgeon's Law that ninety-five percent of everything is crap is often leveled against fan works, it also applies to "professional" works (c.f. the mind-numbing pabulum too often fed to us by the entertainment industry). In the sixties, *Star Trek* entered a symbiotic relationship with its fandom, counting on the fandom to sustain its fortunes, with the fandom side and the professional side of the relationship shaping not only the way we talk about fandom but also the stories produced in both the fan realm and the professional realm. That relationship continues unabated and, it can be said, with regard to the increasingly intertwined relationship between fandom and the professional sphere — cue Jerry Goldsmith's coda to the *ST:TMP* soundtrack — "The human adventure is just beginning."

Donald Gillikin is just this guy, you know?

---

62. SPECTRE OF THE GUN
TROUBLE IN TOMBSTONE
ALAN J. PORTER

Tombstone Daily Epitaph
October 27, 1881

YESTERDAY'S
STRANGE OCCURENCES

Four Men Disappear From Existence in the Duration of a Moment
Stormy as were the early days of Tombstone, nothing ever occurred equal to the events of yesterday. Since the appointment of Wyatt Earp as Marshall and his brothers, Virgil and Morgan, as deputies, the town has been noted for its quietness and good order. The fractious and much-dreaded cow-boys when they came to town were upon their good behavior. It seems that this quiet state of affairs was but the

calm that preceded the storm that burst in all its fury yesterday.

So long as our peace officers made an effort to preserve said peace, it seemed that they would have the support of all good citizens. Yesterday, this assumption was put to the test by a singular change in the Earp brothers, as they seemed hell bent on meting out violence to any and all who opposed them.

The catalyst was the return to our town of the previously accursed Ike Clanton, Billy Clanton, Tom McLaury, Frank McLaury and Billy Claiborne, who were welcomed by many almost as returning heroes rather than the villainous cow-boys of prior repute. According to several witnesses, despite the effusiveness of their reception, the gang seemed disorientated, as if the familiar streets of Tombstone were from a half-recalled dream or distant memory; the strange behavior being compounded by the elder cow-boy claiming in increasingly insistent tones that he was not in fact Ike Clanton, but a ship's captain named James Kirk, a name unknown in these parts. During the remainder of the day, the rest of the gang appeared to reinforce this strange behavior by referring to Clanton by the sobriquet of "Captain". Whether to appease their leader or as the result of a joke known only to themselves, the other cow-boys resorted to using appellations such as "Bones", "Scotty", "Chekov" and "Spock". The meaning of these names remains unknown and will forever do so.

The Precursor

The trigger point for the day's events appears to have been a conflict between Morgan Earp and the youngest cow-boy, Billy Claiborne, over the affections of a local beauty. Claiborne — or Chekov, as his colleagues referred to him — seemed to treat the threats from the youngest Earp brother as a joke and showed near-contempt for the possibility of an encounter with the quickfire deputy's guns, claiming that he would simply step aside and let the bullet pass him by. Such bravado was to prove fatal as, during an altercation yesterday afternoon, Morgan is reported to have simply shot the young Claiborne without provocation after the cow-boy demanded that Earp release his hold on the young lady's arm.

The Occurrence

Close upon the heels of this tragedy came the finale, which is best told in the words of R.F. Coleman, who was an eyewitness from the beginning to the end. "I was at the O.K. Corral at 5 o'clock, when I saw the two Clantons and the two McLaurys suddenly materialize in the saddling enclosure. From their startled appearance, they looked to be as surprised at their location as I was with their arrival. Frank McLaury made an attempt to calm his companions and gave some speech about something called Melkoshians, whatever those are, and some scientific mumbo-jumbo regarding physical laws not working and things not being as real as they seemed. It all seemed pretty real to me, so, unsure of what to do next, I decided to notify Sheriff Behan about the manifestation. On reaching Fremont Street, I saw Virgil Earp, Wyatt Earp, Morgan Earp and Doc Holliday in the center of the street, all armed."

Mr. Coleman's story has been confirmed by others. Marshal Earp says that he and his party met the Clantons and the McLaurys in the aforementioned enclosure. Doc Holliday reported that the cow-boys seemed to be concluding some bizarre ritual that involved Frank McLaury laying his hands on the temples of his compatriots and placing them in some sort of trance. The fact that the men had undergone some sort of self-hypnosis can be the only plausible explanation for their actions at this point.

The cow-boys lined themselves up against a fence at the rear of the stockade as if on parade. When Wyatt Earp challenged them to draw, none moved except Ike Clanton, who continue to maintain the delusion that his name was Kirk. His hand went to his gun, but he never appeared to withdraw his shooting iron. However, his movement was the signal for the Earps and their compatriot to unload a fusillade of a magnitude previously unknown in these parts.

Disappearance

As if the day's events weren't momentous enough, it is at this point in the narrative that they reach a singular climax. Every remaining witness to the confrontation at the O.K. Corral reported that the bullets fired by the law officers appeared to pass through the bodies of the cow-boys without any apparent effect. While the fence behind them was splintered and torn from the barrage, the Clantons and McLaurys — if that's who they actually were — stood firm with no visible signs of trauma or bodily damage. Virgil and Morgan Earp both emptied two pistols, while Doc Holiday reloaded his shotgun multiple times, without any harm befalling those they stood against.

At the conclusion of the shooting, Ike Clanton leapt at the Marshall and engaged him in hand-to-hand combat, subduing the lawman and pinning him to the ground. Only at this point did Clanton draw his pistol. He clearly pointed it at the Marshall's face and all expected him to deliver a fatal shot. Instead, he deliberately threw the gun aside and sent it to rest in the dirt of the enclosure.

At this moment, the four men — Ike Clanton, Billy Clanton, Tom McLaury and Frank McLaury — simply faded from sight. They disappeared as if they had never existed. Gone in the blink of a moment, leaving the townsfolk who witnessed it confused and questioning their sobriety and faith. It was also reported that, at the exact same instance, Billy Claiborne's body went missing from where it lay in the cabin in the rear of Dunbar's stables on Fifth street.

The Aftermath

With the firing was over, Sheriff Behan went up to Wyatt Earp and said, "I'll have to arrest you." Wyatt replied: "I won't be arrested today. I am right here and, unlike those cowards, am not going away."

The feeling among the best class of our citizens is that the change in the Marshall's demeanor and the appearance of the men we took to be the cow-boys were the product of a mass hysteria that affected the town for reasons as yet unknown. What the consequences will be if the real Clantons and McLaurys should ever return to the streets of Tombstone, this reporter would not like to speculate.

Alan J. Porter is a writer of pop-culture histories, high-adventure fiction and comic books, who will happily admit to having a Tribble sitting on his writing desk. (alanjporter.com, @alanjporter)

63. DAY OF THE DOVE
THE DAWN OF THE DOVE
ALISTAIR HUGHES

Lieutenant M'Ress evaluated their situation. "The Captain has brought on board a party of thirty Klingons, who may be responsible for the destruction of an entire colony. Without explanation, we are now completely cut off from Command, and the *Enterprise* is running out of control at maximum velocity."

"Our internal communications are also being blocked, Ma'am." Technical crewman Janssen reported. "But I think I can give you visual, one-way only."

M'Ress swiveled her chair toward the main screen, just as a violent jolt sent her toppling out of it. Landing lightly on all fours, she helped Janssen to his feet.

Petty Officer Janice Rand lurched into the secondary auxiliary control center, patting a stray wisp of fair hair back into her regulation beehive. "Emergency bulkheads won't budge, Ma'am. We're sealed off from the primary hull."

"Science station please, Mister Rand. I need to know what just happened".

Only recently promoted to Petty Officer, former Yeoman Rand had no time to feel unsure of herself as she sat at the terminal and scanned the shipboard diagnostics. "A sudden course change, Ma'am. We appear to be accelerating toward the Galactic Rim at... warp nine!"

A static-fringed, silent view of the engine room finally coalesced on the main screen. Impossibly, a desperate sword battle seemed to be taking place between the distressingly at-liberty Klingons and the badly out-numbered engineering crew. M'Ress's pupils narrowed to vertical slits as she caught sight of Chief Engineer Scott swinging a long, basket-handled sword with enough fury to hold three Klingon attackers temporarily at bay, but, inevitably, the beleaguered humans were forced to withdraw.

178

"What is that?" M'Ress' ears flattened against the sides of her head and her voice held a rare tension that made the hairs on Rand's forearms prickle. "There — at the upper left of the screen."

"It's only static..." began Janssen, but suddenly Rand could see it too, a pulsing flare of light hovered in a darkened section of the engine room. Its intensity seemed to dim as the final soundless flurry of sword blows ceased. The screen faded. "Analysis, Mister Rand."

She ran the results, but instead of the computer's usual measured and somewhat maternal tones, the air filled with a rapid high-pitched chatter.

"What's wrong with it?" asked Janssen.

"I think the Bridge might be accessing the same data as we are... The computer defines the entity as being composed of pure energy, with intelligence and an unknown objective," reported Rand.

"It's alive?" gasped Janssen.

"And apparently means us ill, judging by everything we've experienced so far," M'Ress surmised, her calm self once more. "It seems to be provoking not only hostility and fear but I sense it is also somehow drawing sustenance from those same emotions."

Rand and Janssen knew better than to question this apparent leap of logic. M'Ress's species was not psychic exactly, but they possessed perception and intuition well beyond human awareness.

Rand hesitated. "I don't know how relevant this might be, Ma'am, but I've found a reference, from Earth, just over 350 years ago."

The Lieutenant's eyebrow raised and Rand took this as an invitation to continue.

"In central Europe, a young student was apparently haunted and provoked by a presence which seems to match the description of what we've seen."

M'Ress' other eyebrow joined the first. "And what happened?"

"He assassinated the visiting heir of a neighboring Empire. Shortly afterward that empire's ruling Emperor also spoke about a glowing sprite which tormented him. He declared war."

The significance wasn't lost on Janssen. "You're talking about..."

Rand continued: "Other nations took sides. The Russian Tsar claimed he was incited to war by a *prizrak*, a spirit. Each of the leaders reported something similar in the lead-up to their own commencement of hostilities. Some even seem to know what it was doing; they called it 'the Feeder.'"

M'Ress knew enough Earth history from her Starfleet training to complete Rand's report.

"The nations of your whole world ended up at each others' throats for four years. The death toll was catastrophic."

Janssen spoke up. "So this... thing somehow causes and feeds on aggressive emotions, which eventually leads to war — and it has control of the *Enterprise*?"

M'Ress tilted her head. Janssen was catching on at last, but she didn't have the patience to wait for his next question. "What we do next, Mister Janssen, is discover its weakness and exploit whatever that might be to overcome it."

"Ma'am," Rand began hesitantly, "at the risk of oversimplifying..."

"Go on."

"Well, if negative emotions, hatred and anger, give this thing strength... could positive emotions have the opposite effect?"

A long moment of silence followed before a deep rumble seemed to come from M'Ress' throat and she smiled. "Very good, Petty Officer Rand. Do you have a plan?"

Rand's shoulders sank; she didn't.

"Peace day!" Janssen exclaimed.

"I beg your pardon?"

"On Earth, Ma'am, Peace Day is when we celebrate the abolition of war. I think I might just be able to broadcast the..."

Rand was outraged "No, you can't possibly be suggesting that. It's more likely to infuriate everyone on board!"

"But it's perfect," interjected Janssen. "We could have the march and everything."

M'Ress' tail flashed. "Would someone kindly explain to me what you are talking about?"

"He's talking about the Peace Day Song, Ma'am," explained Rand. "After winning the Earthvision Song Contest, it inexplicably became a sort of international anthem celebrating, well, peace..."

M'Ress stared unblinkingly.

"...it's appalling," finished Rand.

"I see. Mister Janssen: Engineering on screen again, please." M'Ress turned to the horrified Petty Officer, "Desperate situations call for desperate measures, Mister Rand — locate a recording of this song and ready it for ship-wide transmission on my mark."

Rand might have actually questioned the command, but the silent image on screen again captured everyone's attention. Their Captain was surrounded by Klingons, whose own Commander, Kang, faced Kirk with a sword in his hand. Rand gasped involuntarily; and suddenly Kang dropped his weapon. Moving to stand beside Kirk, they both appeared to be looking up at something that was casting a weakening red light across their faces. They were shouting at it.

"It seems they've reached the same conclusion we have." observed M'Ress

The two commanders appeared to be laughing and jeering at the out-of-view entity, its emanations now the palest of glows.

"OUT!" Kang's voice suddenly bellowed through the speakers, making them all jump. "Only a fool fights in a burning house."

"We have audio back, Ma'am," reported Janssen unnecessarily. "I think the entity has gone."

On screen, a laughing Kang slapped Kirk on the back hard enough to almost send him reeling. Rand breathed a sigh of relief and quietly deleted the Peace Day Song from the databank.

➤➤➤

Defeated and exhausted, the Feeder fell back through time, passing through centuries and between possibilities as easily as the hull of the spacecraft it had just been banished from, to the planet where it had been most successful in the past. Manifesting weakly inside a cluster of buildings bearing a pyramidal insignia, it found two humans engaged in an amicable but equally firm, difference of opinion.

"No, we've got to get it right this time," insisted the larger man, "The fans want Klingons, and besides, he's too busy with his TV series."

The writer was not about to concede: "But he's the clear choice for a returning villain..."

The executive paused. There was a flickering in the edge of his vision, as if one of the fluorescent lights was starting to fail. His growing irritation gave way to sudden inspiration.

"I've got a much better idea for who can be wearing the black hat, and you'll only need to change one letter in your title! Actually, why are we paying you — I'm doing your job for you..."

The Feeder began to glow a little more brightly: there could be more nourishment here than it had hoped.

"No!" The writer flinched despite himself, surprised by his own vehemence. The gradually reddening light was starting to make him feel hot, and his voice vibrated with pent-up anger:

"It won't make any sense without him, any idiot can see that!"

The larger man stiffened, a faint whining seemed to fill the air and he felt rage building. "It'll make more sense than him telling Walter he hasn't forgotten his face when they've never even goddamn met before. To hell with it, give it to me!"

He lunged across the table and clawed the first page from the writer's grasp, sending him sprawling over a fallen chair. Crouching over the ragged sheet, he pinned it beneath his pen like a ritual sacrifice.

"*Star Trek 2: the Wrath... of...*" pen stabbing at the title as if becoming a dagger in his fist, he screamed his scrawled amendment: "*KANG!*"

Alistair Hughes is a graphic artist and writer who was introduced to Star Trek *by his mother, Jean. This piece is dedicated to her.*

64. FOR THE WORLD IS HOLLOW AND I HAVE TOUCHED THE SKY
THE GREATEST OF THESE
STEPHANIE CRAWFORD

"In every house where I come, I will enter only for the good of my patients, keeping myself far from all intentional ill-doing and all seduction and especially from the pleasures of love." — Hippocrates

"And now these three remain: faith, hope and love. But the greatest of these is love." — I Corinthians 13

It all starts with a red alert, a sign that things are already serious. Missiles are flying, worlds are about to collide, and lives hang in the balance. As if this wasn't enough, terminal illness, love at first sight and a pair of star-crossed lovers battling the system despite all odds might leave you wondering if this is an episode of *Star Trek* or *As The Spaceship Turns*.

While the *Enterprise* is investigating a generational ark ship masquerading as an asteroid that happens to be on a collision course with an inhabited world, McCoy, through a series of routine physicals, discovers he has the incurable disease xenopolycythemia and has only about a year to live. He's terminally ill and has to tell his captain and friend of his impending death. But McCoy doesn't want pity; he tells Kirk that he'll be best able to function in the time he has left if no one else knows, and he wants to be treated normally. He insists on being included in the landing party to the encroaching asteroid, still grasping at life and relevance — which is where he'll find it after all. On the surface, he meets a stunning high priestess while being beaten senseless by her guards. Their eyes meet, and it's thunderbolt city.

Grappling with a terminal illness can make anyone question their life and how they've spent it. In his role as chief medical officer of the *Enterprise*, McCoy has lived for duty, honor and the Hippocratic Oath, caring for friends and patients that are one and the same. That oath requires that a doctor hold himself above relationships with his patients. When the entire ship is your patient... well, it makes for a lonely life.

In short, McCoy realizes his world is hollow, despite having "touched the sky". He has lived apart and alone, existing on the edges, in the shadows, on the periphery of all the relationships aboard the Starship *Enterprise* (occasional dalliances with yeomen who have Don Juan fixations notwithstanding). He's aloof and above it all, holding himself to a higher standard by necessity as a physician and an officer out of honor and a dedication to his oath. It takes his own impending death for him to realize that honor has not kept him warm and oaths are meaningless without someone for whom to keep them.

This episode also throws a harsh light on McCoy's series-long needling of Spock for the Vulcan's failure to get more in touch with his human side. We see here, perhaps more than in any other story, that McCoy has a similar problem. Very often people can only see their own flaws best in others; McCoy berates Spock for rejecting the feelings that he himself cannot allow into his own personal and professional life. It is this man, yearning for love but unable to allow himself to grasp it, who is on a collision course with someone on a similar path. And speaking of stunning high priestesses...

Natira, the high priestess of the Yonada, is the spiritual leader of her people and enforces the rules of the computer that runs Yonada in its religious guise as the Oracle. She is the only one allowed to choose her own mate, presumably because the Oracle decrees reproductive/marriage decisions for everyone else on the ship to maintain the healthiest population in Yonada's closed-system genetic pool. For some reason, however, she has not taken a mate from among her own people; she too has been holding herself above, waiting for something else. When that man from the sky arrives, she reaches out to touch and hold him.

Remember what I said about thunderbolt city? This love at first sight between Natira and McCoy at first seems unlikely, typical of so many old TV shows and movies where things have to happen fast and for little reason (especially when you know the relationship is doomed to end by the time the closing credits roll). It feels like it comes out of nowhere and at first glance seems rather hollow (heh), but both of these people are lonely, looking for each to complete the other. Yes, it happens fast, but McCoy and Natira — both charged with caring for the spiritual and corporeal health of their people at the expense of their own — are missing pieces inside that happen to be the exact shape of each other. McCoy is dying physically and, like a soldier coming off a battlefield, grasps at life and hope in the form of Natira, who represents what he's denied himself. A great deal of his love for her and how fast he falls is understandable, since he's a desperate man grasping for any semblance of a future he's not likely to have. "If you only knew how I needed some kind of future, Natira," he says to her after she's asked him to stay with her and rule the promised world by her side.

But if McCoy falls hard, driven by desperation (not to take away from Natira's obvious and powerful charms), what about Natira herself? Even when he tells her that he's dying, she says "I could be happy to have that feeling for a day, a week, a month... a year. Whatever the Creators hold in store for us." While the high priestess is not dying physically, it could be argued that her position as the spiritual leader of her people has never allowed her to truly live. When she and McCoy connect, it's hard and fast, like magnets snapping together. McCoy's faith in science and medicine has driven his life, and Natira's has been driven by her faith in the oracle and its false "truth", but they each discover in turn that faith will not save them. They clutch at each other as hope for a life; in fact, in the novel *Ex Machina* by Christopher Bennett — a 2005 sequel to this very episode — it's revealed that the word "yonada" actually means "hope" in the tongue of the Fabrini, the creators of the asteroid ship.

But let's not sell this love affair so short. Yes, both of them are looking for a future they may not have, both seeking an escape from the restraints of their dutiful roles. But there's no fire without a spark, and clearly these two are well suited for one another after the initial connection is made. Despite her role as a religious leader and an enforcer of some rather harsh laws against thoughtcrime, Natira truly cares about her people. When an old man dies while telling Kirk, Spock and McCoy about climbing the mountains and touching the sky of his hollow world, Natira treats his death by the Instrument of Obedience with compassion and his transgression as the foolishness that comes with age. She asks her guards to bear his body away gently, and it's that sense of empathy that makes us like her instantly and realize she's the right woman to stand side by side with a healer who has always been the passionate, emotional center of *Star Trek*.

While the CGI effects inserted into the remastered versions of *Star Trek* can occasionally be jarring, in this particular case those alterations add to the story. They improve on this episode's theme, because, after all, this is no simple bubblegum love affair. In the place of the original multicolored Yonada that resembled a wad of gum — sweet and lacking in substance — we instead see a harsh, cold and pockmarked moonlike asteroid, its lonely landscape as emotionless and sterile as McCoy's and Natira's lives have been. One thing that was not altered, however, was the distinctive triangular motif throughout the interior of Yonada, and it's that shape that led me to thinking about this story in relation to the well-known Biblical triad of faith, hope and love. So what about the greatest of these?

Love is the largest and most important part of this story, whether it's Natira's love for her people, McCoy's love for his friends (yes, Spock included) or their love for each other despite all odds. In a way, it's sad that after all this character development and the promise of a bold future for McCoy and Natira, the "reset to zero" mindset of the series cures McCoy's disease almost as an afterthought, while the *Enterprise* moves on in their mission, leaving the Yonadan mop-up to others. Thankfully, friend Kirk steps in (his own mildly bruised ego set aside; earlier he seems put out that Natira went for his chief medical officer and not him... for once) and promises that the *Enterprise* will meet Yonada when it arrives at Daran IV in a year to give McCoy and Natira, neither of whom can bring themselves to leave their people right now, more time together. It took Bennett's novel decades later, and a fleeting reference in the *Star Trek: The Motion Picture* novelization, to provide fans of the episode with a bit more of this stalled relationship, small comfort though it may be.

Even though he's not remotely the center of the story — hey, every doctor must have his day — Kirk's throwaway line while describing Yonada is the essence of this tale distilled to its purest form: "How many generations have lived and been buried without knowing that their world is hollow?" For at least two of them — one, a lonely woman in charge of an uncertain future for an entire world, and the other, Kirk's fellow officer dutifully healing all those around him but never himself — that truth is revealed. Together, if only for an instant and hollow no more, they touch the sky.

Stephanie Crawford prefers her shirts in science blue, her dinosaurs glittery and her tiaras slightly cockeyed.

65. THE THOLIAN WEB
THE THOLIAN TRILOGY
FINN CLARK

The Tholian Web is anti-drama, to a degree that I was disappointed to see in *The Original Series*. I'm not a *Star Trek* fan, but I admire *TOS* and in particular William Shatner. He's the best thing in this episode, despite not being in most of it. All the best things here, in fact, are from the characters. Scotty's whisky scene is funny, for instance, while the episode's true heart is the Spock–McCoy relationship.

However, the plot's messy, doesn't sell its key developments and doesn't make sense.

Consider a few basic questions. What's driving the story? What obstacles will challenge our heroes and what clever or brave things will they do to overcome them? Possible answers to this might include:

(a) The USS *Defiant* is a ghost ship, full of corpses. Great! Tell me more! No, sorry, that's all. The ship drops out of the episode halfway through and never returns. To learn more, you'll have to wait until 2005, as we shall see.

(b) The crew of the *Enterprise* are turning mad and violent! Great! What next? Answer: Dr. McCoy pulls a cure from his ass. Functionally, it's a deus ex machina. There's no "eureka" scene and there's no attempt to dramatize the desperate ticking clock of medical research in the face of madness. He just walks through the door with some drugs. For all we know, he'd bought them off his dealer in the corridor.

(c) Captain Kirk's disappeared! This creates Spock–McCoy drama, but it's unconvincing. I didn't buy McCoy's stroppiness about Spock's decisions. Everything he'd done seemed okay to me, while McCoy's objections were too shallowly presented for me to take them seriously. The seeds of a reasonable argument might have been there, perhaps, but the level they're being presented on came across to me as a bit teenage.

Admittedly, this is a story about people going mad and being irrational, but that just means someone should have put two and two together and said, "Bones, have a lie down, and stop being a twat."

(d) Captain Kirk's dead! There's plenty of good stuff around this, and the funeral's a decent scene, but I was gobsmacked by McCoy not believing Uhura's sighting of Kirk in her cabin. What's unbelievable about it? Kirk was on a spaceship that was fading in and out of reality. It shouldn't be unthinkable for him to be seen later doing the same thing himself. In fact, that's what they should have been looking out for! McCoy dismissing Uhura's story out of hand means he's ignoring a chance to save his friend's life. It would have served them right if Kirk had died after that, when they could have saved him by acting promptly.

Besides, we know he's not dead. He's Captain Kirk. Dr. McCoy isn't just being stupid but is doing so under circumstances where even the five-year-olds watching would know he's being a twonk.

(e) The Tholians are bollocks too.

They serve little purpose. They're a "whoops, the episode's underrunning" addition, or at least that's how they felt to me. You could cut them from the script and not notice. Admittedly, they disrupt Spock's predictions and are part of the crisis, but anything could have done that. It could have been a space whirlpool. It could have been the ghost ship being spooky. Spock could even simply have been wrong, which would have been funny. This episode has overlapping universes, a ghost ship, a mind-warping space plague, silly Tholians and sillier regulars. You'd want to trim half of that, starting with the Tholians. They're hardly threatening, are they? Annoy one and it'll start doing space crocheting that might be dangerous if you sit there for hours and let it finish. (They're more badass in *Enterprise*.) Oh, and escaping from that web is so thrown away that I thought I'd missed something and rewound to check. Eh? What happened? Answer: technobabble.

They even look dull! Generally I love *TOS* designs, which are more entertaining than bumpy foreheads. This week's new spacesuits are awesome, for instance, in a 1960s art-deco way. Multi-cultured rivers flowing down from that flamboyant collar section. It's art! Admittedly, the Tholians themselves I quite like, because they're so non-human, but their spaceships look as if someone's been folding beer mats in the pub.

It didn't fit together and it didn't convince me. It struck me as a mess of anti-drama, script fiat and "you've got to be kidding me". McCoy's antidote made me snort. Everyone's in a hurry to declare Kirk dead, then reluctant to accept that he might still be alive. (To me, that feels like the work of a scriptwriter who's too close to the material to see the need for more justification.) Oh, and I don't get the McCoy–Spock silliness at the end with Kirk. Dr. McCoy's been an idiot this week, yes, but why does Spock start lying? Grow up, you two. However, all that said, it's still good-natured Shatner *Trek* with all your favorite characters and some nice moments for them. If those are a bit stupid, that's not the actors' fault. It has charm.

So that's *The Tholian Web*... but its ideas and dangling plot threads (i.e., the USS *Defiant*) didn't die. They lived on in *Star Trek: Enterprise*, which revived them in *Future Tense*, then again in *In A Mirror, Darkly*. Let's consider *Future Tense*. How is it? Well, it's okay, but I wouldn't go so far as to call it worth watching.

The good news about *Star Trek: Enterprise*, judging from this, at least, is that it feels more real and immediate. There's a nasty-looking corpse before the opening credits, the cast aren't wearing pajamas, and the *Enterprise* isn't an Ideal Home Exhibition. Even the incidental music is trying to sound tense and urgent. Threats feel threatening. These people seem in danger and out of their depth with things they don't understand. The bridge looks cool. Furthermore, the storyline isn't exploring anyone's relationship with their father but instead has a time-travelling pod from the future with two different bunches of violent aliens chasing the *Enterprise* to capture it.

This passes the entry-level test of "Is anything happening, and should I care?"

On the downside, though, it lacks that *Star Trek* charm. Shatner, Nimoy and Kelley were a joy to watch. Spending time with the *TNG* crew is also enjoyable and comforting, although I have other problems with that show. In *Enterprise*, though, I don't think I liked anyone. The performances seem leaden, and the characters lack spark. Scott Bakula fares best as Archer and is usually excellent, but, every so often, he'll slip. John Billingsley's Dr. Phlox is weird and pompous but the only memorable character after Bakula. Dominic Keating is killing any potential humor. ("This gives space exploration a whole new meaning," says Reed. It's hardly a side-splitter, no, but at least the line gives you something to play.) Worst of all, to this casual viewer, is T'Pol, who thinks time travel's impossible, because of "logic". It makes sense to me that *Enterprise* got cancelled. Do I want to spend time with these people? No.

Things I liked:

(a) The "marry Jane Doe" question. That scene made episode more intelligent, considering the philosophical implications of its subject matter. I appreciated that.

(b) The Reed–Tucker relationship, with two people discussing stuff while they do their job. I liked the way they seemed real and down-to-earth.

(c) The enemy aliens. The Suliban are arrogant cocks, while the Tholians get to be badass. It's not clear why the latter have been brought back, though, for the first time in almost 35 years. Answer: it's because an early pitch for this story had the USS *Defiant* from that story appearing instead of that 31st century timeship. (This got vetoed.) That story had overlapping universes, and this is about time travel, so maybe the Tholians are fascinated by what's beyond the boundaries of the here and now?

That's all the stuff I liked, though.

The story's missing something at the climax. As a standalone episode, it's unsatisfying. The whatsit disappears all by itself, perhaps because hypothetical dei ex machina in the distant future might have done something or other. However, I'm sure it works better in the context of an ongoing series, suggesting as it does that the universe is bigger than this one episode. We hear about the 31st century, a Temporal Cold War (whatever that is) and various powerful aliens.

This isn't a terrible story. It's okay. It does the job. It's passable TV, and you wouldn't call it dysfunctional. It's just that there's nothing special about it either. The characters are dull, the acting's flatter than I'd expected, and the storyline's tied into a Temporal Cold War arc that means Captain Archer can't be allowed to learn anything interesting. There was a juicier episode waiting to happen in the ideas that got vetoed by the producers.

The other Tholian story, *In A Mirror, Darkly*, however, is excellent. Part I is basically "cool, they're evil", then Part II demonstrates what drama can become when freed from reset buttons and the conveyor belt of an ongoing TV series. It's set in the Mirror Universe, but for once with no crossover characters. Everyone's the evil twin. Dr. Phlox vivisects animals for fun. Hoshi Sato sleeps with the captain. Or with the next captain. Or with anyone else who happens to be convenient. Archer is a paranoid warmongering son-of-a-bitch who thinks compassion is for the weak. In other words, no one has a speck of decency and this is a one-way plunge into hell. Excellent.

We even get a Mirror Title Sequence, with a history tour of the bloodthirsty rise of the Earth Empire. We see nukes, battleships, tanks, fighter jets and so on. That's cool too.

It's a sequel to *The Tholian Web*. Yes, a sequel. It's a prequel to *Mirror, Mirror* (which is superb, by the way) but a sequel for the timeslipped, universe-hopping USS *Defiant*. This lets Captain Archer et al visit what's effectively the Shatner-era USS *Enterprise*, which is pleasing. They even don the old uniforms.

Part I is build-up for the good stuff. We meet scum and perhaps get the mistaken impression that this Archer isn't completely evil. Unpleasant and brutal, yes. Evil... well, that's next week. For the time being, all we know is that he's got a plan and it looks as if it might be interesting.

Part II is where things start cooking, though. Archer orders ethnic cleansing, there are revolutions (plural) and not everyone survives to the closing credits. The baddies kill everyone and win. (That's not a spoiler, since this story only contains baddies.) It's big, it's universe-busting, and there's an exhilaration about it. Long-running TV series don't work like this, or at least *Star Trek* ones don't. The format would break. Everyone would be dead inside a few weeks, or else the galaxy would be in flames. However, that's just dandy in the mirror universe, and Manny Coto had been planning to return there in season five for a "mini-series within a series".

T'Pol becomes interesting by becoming a radical subversive. Her talk of racial equality is cool, actually, not to mention explosive in that universe. This gives the story depth. It's about something, as well as being lurid "fall of Rome" backstabbing and double-dealing. It's probably too high-octane and gleeful in its evil to seem genuinely classy, but it's a fun two-parter that lured me into continuing with all the other mirror universe episodes. It's full of loathsome characters with no redeeming features but portrayed so vibrantly that you never lose interest in them. (That can be a real danger with Everyone Is Nasty stories.)

So, in summary, what did I learn, apart from the fact that Mirror-Archer is the worst negotiator in the history of sentient life? First, *TOS* is fundamentally more entertaining than *Enterprise*, even when Judy Burns and Chet Richards can't plot to save their lives. Shatner is a demigod, while Leonard Nimoy and DeForest Kelley are also big reasons to watch. That show swashbuckled. Its charm made even bad episodes enjoyable. *Enterprise* lacks that, but it's capable of excellence, and it's lifted by being part of something bigger. It's helping to weave a universe. It's *Star Trek*. Plot threads from decades earlier can return and create something new and unexpected. I think there's something rather wonderful about that.

*Finn Clark is a writer, artist, actor, teacher, computer programmer, Japanese translator, mathematician and bridge player. His first review collection (*Time's Mosaic: Eccleston, Torchwood and Quatermass*) is available from Obverse Books.*

66. PLATO'S STEPCHILDREN

HOW WILLIAM SHATNER CHANGED MY LIFE — AND HOW I CHANGED HIS

DAN MADSEN

Originally published at Startrek.com, November 2013

Today is the 45th anniversary of a very special *Star Trek* episode for me. In fact, it literally changed my life. It was on this date, 45 years ago, that the third-season episode *Plato's Stepchildren* aired. Written by Meyer Dolinksy and directed by David Alexander, the episode is cited as the first example of a scripted inter-racial kiss between a white man and black woman on American television. In the episode, the crew of the *Enterprise* encounters an ageless and sadistic race of humanoids with the power of telekinesis and who claim to have organized their society around Ancient Greek ideals. The kiss between Kirk and Uhura was an amazing television moment — but it was not that aspect that changed my life forever.

One of the lead characters on this episode was a dwarf named Alexander, played by the late Michael Dunn, who really paved the way for other small actors. As a "little person" myself standing 4'2" tall, I was immediately drawn to this particular episode as there, right on my TV, was someone who looked like me! I have written previously about how this just happened to be the very first episode of *Star Trek* that I had ever seen... and I was smitten with it instantly. I watched every episode of the original series, stood in line for all the movies, was thrilled when *The Next Generation* was created and loved every subsequent spinoff after that. I started a fan club, which eventually became the Official *Star Trek* Fan Club with the blessing of Gene Roddenberry and Paramount and published the *Star Trek Communicator* magazine. It started me on my career path and allowed me to build a mini fan empire for a variety of sci-fi projects that continues to this day.

I related to Alexander. Watching him on the episode reminded me of how I felt growing up. Being small in a world of large people could sometimes be intimidating. I struggled to be accepted and to find a way that I could be equal to others. *Star Trek* gave me that chance. Because of Alexander's dwarfism, he lacked the ability to acquire the powers that the regular-height Platonians had. The *Enterprise* crew devises a way that, through an injection, they can also have the same telekinetic powers to combat the Platonians determination to keep Dr. McCoy there. Given the chance to have the injection and be like them, Alexander declines. He became a hero for me. But the most important moment in the show was when Alexander asks Kirk what it is like where he is from and the good captain says, "Alexander, where I come from, size, shape or color makes no difference." THAT was the future I wanted to live in!

Years later, after successfully launching *Star Trek: The Official Fan Club* and the *Communicator* magazine, William Shatner asked if he could interview ME for his new book, "Get a Life" — an insightful, honest look at *Star Trek* fandom and the power of the show. He dedicated an entire chapter to my story, and it was a thrill to tell the man himself, Captain Kirk, how those lines he spoke in *Plato's Stepchildren* changed my life. He responded by saying, *"God, how exciting, Dan. I just got goose pimples on that story. Clearly, that moment was an inspiration with far-reaching impact for you."*

He later wrote in the book, *"I went home once again feeling exponentially better about the franchise that had been kind enough to employ me over the past thirty years. Not only had Dan provided me with an airtight verification of Bob Justman's insights, but he's simultaneously put a face, and a voice, on those ideas. More and more, I was finding evidence that practically screamed to be noticed. Star Trek, for all its otherworldly smoke and mirrors, has a heart and a mind, and a soul that are organic and simple, and very human."*

For me, that first viewing of *Plato's Stepchildren* — and the inspiration it created in my life — came full circle that day.

Dan Madsen is the former founder, president and publisher of the Official Star Trek *Fan Club and Official* Star Trek Communicator *Magazine.*

---

67. WINK OF AN EYE
A REALLY, REALLY FAST WOMAN
IVY GLENNON

Suppose an attractive woman wearing half a costume, yet moving too fast for his eye to see, let alone to gaze upon, caresses and kisses Captain Kirk. Is he, as an accosted woman might be, appalled? Is she, as the powerful "other", a threat not only to his beloved *Enterprise* ship and crew but also to "our" male-dominated social order? A quick answer is no and no. Kirk is too much the straight male "player" for outrage, and the starship social order is too entrenched for a major shake-up. The episode, after all, is constrained by the *Star Trek* formula of powerful threat overcome by the top men of the Starship *Enterprise* (Kirk + Spock and/or Dr. McCoy and Engineer Scotty). The audience knows "we" will triumph.

Nevertheless, that a powerful alien woman could take advantage of the womanizing captain and control the *Enterprise* with impunity suggests a nascent feminist SF sensibility. The question is how feminist?

First aired in 1968, *Wink of an Eye* appeared in the midst of the United States' surging second-wave women's movement. It was a time when conservative television culture in general was on the brink of gendered change, falling between *Father Knows Best, Leave it to Beaver* and *The Donna Reed Show*'s idealization of stay-at-home moms in the 1950s–60s and *The Mary Tyler Moore* and *Maude*'s exploration of independent, professional women in the 1970s. More to the current point, it predates TV's *Wonder Woman* (1975) and *The Bionic Woman* (1976) by years and the powerful Agent Olivia Dunham on *Fringe* (2008) by four decades.

This character from 1968 is Deela, queen of the nearly extinct live-too-fast-for-Earth-eyes-to-see Scalosians, who has hijacked the *Enterprise* to repopulate her race as the last three Scalosian males are sterile. Her race has needs. After her super-fast "invisible" caress, she drugs, speeds up and captures Kirk for her consort. She likes him because he is "feisty". But she does not love him. He is a sex slave and has no power in this relationship. (Though who knows, Kirk might actually like that...)

In the threat portion of the episode, we see Deela using Kirk and commanding her own crew with impunity. Although she and the other Scalosians are later defeated in the usual "the guys do it again" resolution, the character retains a power that other original *Star Trek* female guests — with the notable exception of Sally Kellerman's omnipotent psychiatrist character in *Where No Man Has Gone Before* — usually do not. Deela's is the power of command, demonstrated most clearly in her relationship to Kirk and her crew.

In the scene that confirms her status, Deela's science officer Rael (her Spock?), jealous of Deela's attentions to Kirk, attacks Kirk in a series-typical alpha male fight over a woman. Deela, atypically, does not simply gasp "Stop, stop" but takes out her weapon and stuns Rael into submission to protect Kirk. Unmoving, she reminds Rael she is doing her duty and he must allow her the dignity of liking the man she chooses. She dismisses Rael, even though she later admits she loves him. Duty first.

Back in Kirk's quarters, Deela combs her hair at a mirror as Kirk sits on his bed — apparently quite content — putting on his boot. This is about as direct a post-coital scene as *Star Trek* features in the sixties and, despite his captive status, reinforces Kirk's virile-player persona. In this case, however, he has used sex to play to a more powerful, dominant foe. Furthermore, unlike other Kirk encounters, Deela does not appear smitten. Just business. What's love got to do with it? A woman has needs.

This suggests a contrast to the previous episode, *Plato's Stepchildren*, in which Lt. Uhura is in a similar against-her-will slave position and is forced by an alien to kiss Kirk. She is not content, as Kirk seems to be here, but afraid. It may have been the first televised interracial kiss, but, in feminist terms, it was same old, same old: a woman's sexuality is taken out of her control. In *Wink of an Eye* the woman, briefly, is in charge.

If these actions, both military and sexual, are not enough to suggest this female's power, a directorial decision reinforces it. All the "accelerated" scenes are shot on an angle. Deela, however, stands erect, dignified and unbent throughout both tilted and later "righted" backgrounds until the end when she and her crew are defeated. In fact, she occasionally stands taller than Shatner's Kirk, who was officially 5'8" in his youth, while she was 5'6" (presumably without the four-inch-high hairdo and heels). She is as much the Captain of her crew as Kirk is of his, her need to insure the survival of her people a match for his. Thus Deela, Queen of the Scalosians, is akin to later female powerhouses of SF television and film.

Nevertheless, *Wink of an Eye* is a long way from a feminist breakthrough. Neither the smart, courageous Ripley in *Alien* (1979), the relentless warrior Sarah Connor of *Terminator 2* (1991) nor the cool tech-savvy Trinity in *The Matrix* (1999), let alone Captain Janeway of *Star Trek Voyager* (1995–2001). Deela has and demonstrates power, but it is a conventional monarchical and putatively reproductive power. She is not smarter, stronger, wiser or more skilled than many female guest stars. More significantly in terms of social order, this episode remains a standstill for all the other women. Uhura is still treated as decoration when Kirk rages that Deela has done something to his "men". He actually calls the men by name and only glances at Uhura. Likewise, the three other women appearing in bit parts are inconsequential. Nurse Chapel mostly looks worried at Dr. McCoy's side as he works, a pretty crew member smiles at Kirk and serves coffee-to-be-drugged, and the other apparently mute Scalosian woman (also wearing half a costume) merely nods when Rael says he will find a replacement for her after her chosen consort — this episode's doomed redshirt, Compton — dies.

So is *Wink of an Eye* feminist? To a degree, but the degree is small. We have one powerful woman by virtue of royal birthright and cool-under-pressure dignity, but the system stays in place, and, in the end, Kirk is back in charge.

Still, it suggests a change and airs at a cusp — and not only for televisual science ficton. 1968 was the second time a woman won a literary Hugo award (Anne McCaffrey's "Weyr Search", a fantasy that features a powerful queen). The next year, Ursula LeGuin would win both the Hugo and Nebula awards for "The Left Hand of Darkness", a book whose most powerful character is female (sometimes). It is the beginning of an era trying to supersede the SF legacy that in a 1975 interview LeGuin called "The baboon patriarchy, with the Alpha Male on top..."

So Deela, unlike most female characters on the original *Star Trek*, reverses the trope. In this case, however briefly, the Alpha Female zips up to the top.

As a child, Ivy Glennon wanted to grow up to be an astronaut, but bad eyesight of the no-space-faring-allowed variety and a penchant for all things fabulous (such as The Twilight Zone, The Outer Limits *and* Star Trek*) led her astray into academic media criticism: a lot of fun, and the minefields were less literal.*

68. THE EMPATH
MULTI-FACETED GEM
PATRICIA GILLIKIN

In the place-less place where they'd been left, bathed in a harsh yellow and pink light and surrounded by unfathomable darkness, Dr. Leonard McCoy fumed. Jim Kirk, asleep from McCoy's own hypo, was getting much-needed rest. McCoy saw Gem, the alien from a species of empaths, watching them, her wide eyes curious and kind. Finally, Spock — Spock was an arrogant bastard.

The Vians would return soon to choose him or Spock for their insane experiment — and Spock had just called rank, declaring that, with Kirk unconscious, he would go with the Vians. The heartless beings had made clear the consequences, and McCoy shuddered as he remembered the chilling words: for himself, an 87 percent chance of death, and for Spock, an even worse likelihood, 93 percent, of brain damage, resulting in permanent insanity.

Surreptitiously, McCoy prepared a hypo for Spock. With the Vulcan unconscious, McCoy would be the one to go with the Vians. Which was as it should be — the danger to Spock was worse.

McCoy saw his chance when Gem distracted Spock a moment and quietly approached to sedate the First Officer. But the damned Vulcan was too swift, and, before McCoy knew it, Spock had caught his wrist.

"No, Doctor. That would have been highly unethical of you."

McCoy bristled, feeling helpless. "You can't go, Spock! What they'll do to you — it's worse than death. And I won't be able to fix it."

Spock did not respond, but his expression showed his absolute bloody-minded stubbornness and his respect for the matching quality in McCoy. But was that also compassion McCoy saw behind the dark eyes?

When the Vians arrived, McCoy made one last attempt, arguing loudly and desperately, while Spock stated quietly what he had before about rank — and the Vians listened to Spock.

➤➤➤

Spock knew it was likely a futile effort, but he placed himself into a low-level pre-emptive healing trance as he waited for the torture; it might help protect body and mind. As he did so, he thought of Kirk, exhausted and now resting, and McCoy, wild-eyed, fierce and worried. Though the entire situation the Vians had created made no logical sense whatsoever, it was a consolation to him that his last act made in sanity

would be to preserve the good doctor — an honorable being, his friend.
</fanfic>

That's not how it happens in *The Empath*; it's an alternate version, revised from my memory of the fan fiction I tried to write sometime around 1980 when I was in my first year of high school. In the actual episode, McCoy's trickster move with the hypo succeeds, and he goes in place of Spock to be tortured by the Vians.

It's the kind of shift that fanfic glories in — an altered perspective that brings forth all the juiciness — and, in this case, the emotions just hidden beneath the surface. That's what hurt/comfort means to me: a huge excuse for poignant moments of recognition, of kindness, of gentleness. Those moments are all the more powerful when they are rare glimpses past people's façades.

It makes sense in *The Empath* that McCoy is the one to succeed in offering himself up as sacrifice; it is his episode, after all. Additionally, all the ways he embodies qualities gendered "feminine" in our culture are on display here. He takes care of Kirk. He worries about Gem. He's the emotional one, as always. But, at the end — and this is the key moment of the entire episode, the one that twists the stomach, the moment of kindness — it is Spock who gets to play McCoy: when McCoy is in pain and dying, Spock, with great gentleness, puts his hand on McCoy's face, and McCoy compliments him on his bedside manner.

That moment is the key to the whole episode. And that moment also has the other ingredient that makes both Spock and McCoy so compelling: the front, and the revelation of what's behind the front. Spock, for his part, maintains Vulcan calm while still completely revealing, in troubled eyes, his deep concern. And McCoy says "thank you" without saying the words; instead, McCoy thanks him by making an almost-joke that refers back to their feuding: there's a faint tone of surprise in his "you've got a good bedside manner, Spock" — catching Spock one last time in being far more like McCoy than he'd ever let on.

McCoy and Spock have that delightful surface conflict going on that hides their unwavering regard for each other — and I've always been drawn to that kind of dynamic. Spock's pretense is of course his supposed lack of emotion when in fact his actions are often motivated by concern, loyalty and protectiveness. McCoy is the one who challenges him to admit that, even as McCoy has his own version of this façade, a surface gruffness that protects his compassion.

It's a lovely complexity — but wait, don't female characters get to be that interesting? Is the fact that they don't the reason I can identify with McCoy and Spock but not with the women on *Star Trek* or on most any show I watched at the time?

Meanwhile, the extreme feminization of Gem faintly worries me. She wears flowy, gauzy (and always sexy; thank you William Ware Theiss) clothes, has large emotional eyes, is tactile, empathic (obviously), gentle, scared, profoundly vulnerable and ultimately deeply giving. She is also, disturbingly from a feminist perspective, literally mute, as are all of her people. I am not drawn to her as a character. Of course, she's not quite a person either; she's a symbol, an almost pure archetype of "empathy", which in the episode is really self-sacrifice out of love for another (in addition to the physiological ability to take on and heal injury). Yes, technically she's not supposed to have compassion already: the Vians say they brought her there to learn that quality from Kirk, Spock and McCoy. That's crap: of course Gem already had the capacity to feel for them and to choose to help, and her people must have that too; the Vians are plot devices, pure and simple, whose actions simply Don't Make Sense, as Spock and Kirk point out nicely in speeches toward the end.

Is it possible to reimagine this episode so that Gem is not just a symbol but a person with agency?

Hmmm. That means aspects of her we don't know about. And, while I'm at it, since I'm reimagining Gem with agency and depth and personhood, I also have to do something else — because I can't help it, because this is what fanfic writers do: I have to deal with how everything about the Vians is, as Spock would say, illogical; I have to come up with an explanation for their actions that makes sense.

Meanwhile, we're also still in the alternate universe in which Spock goes with the Vians, not McCoy. In the actual episode, Spock escapes the entrapping force field by suppressing his emotions; I've always thought that McCoy in the same situation would escape in a completely opposite way: watching Gem try to help Spock, his emotions would increase the field to such an extent that he'd faint and the field would be gone.

Something like this:

<fanfic>
Gem
 — *cold desolate sharp isolation madness —*

Gem shuddered and pulled back, shivering at the emptiness she'd just felt from the reserved one. She was unsure if she could do this — if she could stand it or if her own sanity would survive it. One of the hurting ones' cruelties had been to isolate her; with her own people, she would never have had to heal alone in this way, would never have faced this danger. She gathered what strength she could, felt and then set aside the numb fear in her and tried again.

McCoy
The Vians, so intent on watching the drama play out, had been easy to entrap in their own exhausting force-field. McCoy left Kirk with the device to keep an eye on them and rushed to Spock and Gem. He turned to Gem, helpless, not sure if he was about to ask her to continue trying to help Spock or to stay away from him for her own well-being —

Gem

The one who called himself McCoy was now speaking to her. His actual words — the shapes his mouth made and a faint vibration she felt from him — said nothing to her, but she could read everything he meant in his troubled blue eyes, in the soft touch of his hand on her arm. He was terrified for his friend, and he was deeply anxious for her; he did not know any more than she did if this was the right thing to do, if she was taking a risk that did his friend any good at all. She smiled faintly at him, trying to show him — he would understand, she felt certain — that she had to try.

Placing one hand on McCoy's arm to draw strength from him, she turned to Spock and touched his chest and forehead. Her body writhed in a scream without sound.

McCoy

He watched in wonder as peace slowly returned to Spock's features. What he saw on his medical sensor told him that Spock was fine, completely back to normal, but Gem... with apprehension, he saw the same readings he'd seen in Spock earlier.

Gem

She fell back and away into a sharp darkness and emptiness, taking with her the madness they'd given Spock — and felt solid arms catch her, felt the worry and the kindness in this gentle one. For a long while, she shuddered, attempting to re-order the disorder in her mind. She felt colors of warmth and of soothing from this stranger who held her, and a distant part of her not struggling back toward sanity realized that this one was like one of her own people, helping her in ways not that different from how one of them would have. Perhaps enough, she realized with hope, to bring her back.

Spock

Spock sat up, mind clear, to astonished relief: the agony and emptiness had been lifted from him. He saw then the mute woman huddled in on herself, with McCoy holding her and talking with her in a low voice.

McCoy

Slowly, her shuddering ceased. McCoy looked up at Spock and felt joy to see the calm sanity back in his friend. Instead of the torment, he saw the signs of alarm in the Vulcan, and McCoy knew Spock would see his own fear for Gem in his face.

Spock, clearly, intended to find out for himself. The Vulcan held out a hand to Gem, not touching, asking. Gem sat up straighter and smiled slightly at his concerned regard. She reached an arm again to Spock's shoulder, and McCoy watched wonderingly as empath and touch-telepath communicated.

Knowing now that both Spock and Gem were going to be fine, McCoy tuned in to Kirk, busy berating the Vians. Jim was occasionally allowing them a word in edgewise, *and what McCoy overheard gave him a sick feeling in his stomach: they explained that all this had been devised as a test to decide if the people from Gem's planet were worthy of being rescued from the nova. They had the power to save only one of the Minaran worlds.*

He glanced back at Spock and Gem, to see that Spock's eyebrows had gone up, while Gem's expressive eyes held sadness and wisdom. Then she turned to McCoy and held out her hand — and Spock turned as well, formal request on his features. They want me to join the meld, *he thought.*

He hesitated slightly. He saw Spock nod almost imperceptibly in acknowledgment, saw reassurance and — he was sure this time — compassion in the brown eyes. He returned the nod and joined the link.

The first sensations were overwhelming euphoric emotions from Gem — relief, gratitude, admiration and warm affection — in the form of bright colors. If she'd been speaking all this to him in words, instead of through the meld, he would have sputtered and blushed in embarrassment. Underneath her exuberance, McCoy sensed Spock's quiet amusement at him and approval of Gem's approbation, as well as his own solemn and profound gratitude toward Gem.

That all came clear in just moments. His own urgent questions came to the fore — the welfare of those planets —

And then he knew.

He stepped out of the link. "What the hell?" he said aloud to Spock, seeing agreement in the now-sane eyes.

➤ ➤ ➤

Later, after Gem bade them a warm farewell and McCoy and Spock knew through her that the Vians would be taken back to their own people and hers for healing and for consequences, they tried to explain to Jim Kirk.

"What was that, anyway?" Kirk asked.

McCoy began, "We thought it was another powerful alien race, several doomed planets and a scared young woman. But really, they were escapees from the asylum, the inhabitants of the planets got themselves to safety long ago, and she —" He paused, not sure how to explain Gem.

Spock finished the thought. "She is their caretaker."

"That's not all she is," McCoy returned, argument in his tone.

"Indeed."

</fanfic>

Patricia Gillikin is a professor of writing and Writing Center Director at the University of New Mexico's Valencia branch campus. She loves to talk about reading and writing fan fiction, and she can be reached at gillikin@unm.edu

69. ELAAN OF TROYIUS
A VALIANT ATTEMPT AT A FEMINIST READING
J.J. GAUTHIER

Ah, *TOS* Season Three! That magical time when "tolerable" passes for "good"; when Shatner's acting devolves from a charismatic, larger-than-life captain to a showboating actor almost caring to remember his lines; when the budget actually drops below *Doctor Who*'s.

A time when an enjoyable lark of badly dated silliness like *Elaan of Troyius* that would be mildly embarrassing before becomes a season highlight.

Despite the punny title, this has little to do with the Trojan War beyond a few vague details. Instead, the badly dated aspect comes from a *Taming of the Shrew*–style battle of the sexes and is about as regressive, without the excuse of existing three centuries before feminism. The Federation is treated like a 19th-century empire dealing with third-world colonies with about the respect and dignity you'd expect. To be fair, *Star Trek* often jams its science fiction with period aesthetics — especially when the budget shifts from "tight" to "what budget?" — but usually the philosophies at least try to evolve beyond Victorian sexism and colonialism.

The *Enterprise* must escort Elaan, the *Dohlman* of Elas, to Troyius, where she will be wed in an arranged marriage to make peace between two planets on the brink of mutual destruction. She beams aboard dressed in what amounts to a jewel-encrusted bikini, and her costumes only become more provocative from there, until you start wondering how any of this got past the censors — and that's before the spanking line.

But we'll get to that.

Elaan establishes her forceful personality immediately, less asking than demanding of Spock, "You rule this ship?" in a tone suggesting that Spock resides just south of her contempt and that Kirk's existence doesn't bear acknowledging. She then *gives Kirk permission* to show her to her quarters.

Clearly, a woman with a sense of power just won't do for an arranged political marriage. Initially, Troyian Ambassador Petri is assigned to tame Elaan. He gets a knife in his back for his troubles, making it Kirk's turn, naturally.

> Kirk: Mr. Spock, the women on your planet are logical. That's the only planet in this galaxy that can make that claim.

Kirk, up to this point, has reacted to Elaan mostly with the exasperated eyeroll of *Women, am I right*? But, being Kirk, he throws himself full force into the taming.

When she slaps him, he slaps her right back. When she tries to kill him with her knife, he turns calmly with, "Tomorrow's lesson will be on courtesy." Kirk explains the importance of following rules and orders, which, given his interpretation of following rules, is pretty rich.

> Elaan: You are warned, Captain, never to touch me again!
> Kirk: If I touch you again, Your Glory, it will be to administer an ancient Earth custom called a spanking, a form of punishment administered to spoiled brats.

It's almost a handbook of how to crush female independence: infantilization, sarcasm and casual, mocking dismissal of any display of strength.

Lest you think the script's low view of women is restricted to Elaan, it's worth noting that when Uhura tries to add to Kirk and Spock's conversation about how awful Elaan is, Kirk shuts her down before she gets out a single sentence. This is Uhura's only line. She doesn't even get a fan dance.

Elaan turns to her last resort — the women of Elas seduce men with magic tears that literally make men fall in love with them. Because powers of seduction are a woman's real wiles, right? A moment of apparent vulnerability gets Kirk wiping away a single tear, and that's all it takes. For once, the exotic alien woman is doing the seducing, and he's helpless against her advances. Kirk immediately gets quiet and thoughtful. (And Shatner starts actually acting, reminding us how good he can be.)

She responds by cooing, and I swear this actually happens, "Captain, that ancient Earth custom called 'spanking', what is it?" This follows their impassioned kissing, which is in turn followed by a classy cutaway where we have to assume... okay, maybe let's not.

And so Kirk wrestles between his sudden onset love for Elaan and his devotion to duty. Once Spock is around, though, it's no contest. It's clear where Kirk's heart really lies beneath Elaan's womanly wiles: his true love will always be Spo—

Ahem, excuse me, I meant the *Enterprise*. Yes, that's what Kirk's in love with. Sure.

Meanwhile, there's a sabotage/Klingon subplot to make sure there's a little action in the thing, resolved when a necklace Petri keeps trying to give to Elaan turns out to be made of the dilithium crystals they conveniently need. I'd call it a Chekhov's Gun, but that term never quite feels right on the *Enterprise* bridge. Elaan, her last option to avoid a forced marriage lost, reluctantly concedes.

The episode's lighthearted sense of fun keeps this from being a slog, but it feels like Roddenberry's largely progressive vision has been transformed into a reaction against the explosion of feminism in the late sixties. And with the imperialistic aesthetics and Kirk supporting the arranged marriage for The Greater Good, it's almost an assault on *first-wave* feminism of the 1880s. Like, what we really need is to get women back in the kitchen and not voting, right fellas?

One could take this show as intended, a putdown of these silly women wanting rights and power, but it's so offset by the magnificent performance by France Nuyen as Elaan that a feminist reading can almost be glimpsed here. You have to squint, but it's there. Kinda.

Nuyen plays Elaan's more privileged lines with childish petulance. But, underneath it, she suggests a cunning mind and a genuine power far beyond the script's mockery. Her horror at losing that power feels far deeper. She's a woman of genuine strength trapped in a world afraid to allow her strength.

"I will not go to Troyius. I will not be made into a Troyian, and I will not be humiliated, and I will not be given to a green pig as a bribe to stop a war!"

Even immature and classist, she's difficult not to cheer for. Her sex makes her the underdog — and a wonderfully impassioned one. Nuyen's bitter delivery of her final lines leaves no doubt that this is a tragedy.

Elaan: Remember me.
Kirk: I have no choice.
Elaan: Nor have I. I have only responsibilities, obligations.

In that bitterness, her defiance remains. Perhaps the lesson she learned from Kirk was not submission to duty, but just how to act it. If she's calm, patient and appears to take her role as a trophy peace wife well, her power will return, and she'll turn Troyius upside-down. Maybe this is a grand victory grasped from all the defeat the galaxy can throw at a woman.

Or maybe it's just a dying gasp of old-fashioned misogyny before movies and TV had to pretend to respect women.

Like most alternate readings, this isn't supported by the text. It's a fun reading that sheds light on the themes and on how our culture has changed. (Not enough, sadly.)

But I imagine Nuyen intended exactly that reading, and the episode almost plays into it. At the end, she wears a full dress that looks remarkably modest, as though her character change is reflected in her clothing... but, from the side, the dress is slit not just on the legs, but all the way up, exposing skin from hip to chest. She's put on a veneer of modesty and politeness, but barely hidden. Her passion still simmers; she is tamed but not broken. Troyius is in for a hell of a culture shock.

J.J. Gauthier writes out of Austin, Texas, on the rare occasion he isn't distracted by work, books, movies, sci-fi shows or, rumor has it, something resembling a social life once in a blue moon.

70. WHOM GODS DESTROY
WE NEED TO TALK ABOUT GARTH
SIMON FERNANDES

Elba II care facility	
"Quos Deus vult perdere, prius dementat"	
Preliminary Psychiatric Report	*Stardate 5718.1*
Filed by:	*Dr. Donald Cory (Facility director)*
Patient:	*Garth, KL*
Place of birth:	*Izar*

Notes:

On admission, it was hard to come up with an appropriate diagnosis, considering the many and wildly contradictory symptoms on display. There are elements of (among others) classic delusions of grandeur, schizophrenia, paranoia, retrograde amnesia, dissociation and even Tourette's syndrome. If I didn't know better, I'd swear his entire condition was a fiction invented by someone whose knowledge of neurological conditions was based entirely on pulp literature.

Patient is both uncooperative and non-responsive to treatment. Insists on referring to himself as "Lord" Garth, and demands that others do the same. Displays extremes of emotion the likes of which are seldom seen outside badly performed Shakespearean theatre. He seems to have formed an attachment to Marta (Patient ID 5545), which could bear scrutiny.

Treatment is currently on hold pending the arrival of experimental medical supplies being conveyed by USS Enterprise, *whose arrival is imminent.*

Miscellaneous:

I continue to be concerned at the lack of resources allocated to the facility by Starfleet Medical; in particular, the staffing shortage that leaves me as the sole member of the care and administrative team, with only one guard for safety. It's not easy being literally "the only sane man in the asylum", you know! Sometimes, on the long, lonely nights reviewing Garth's case, I begin to wonder whether I am he, or he is me...

Initial Therapy Session Report (computer transcript)	Stardate 5718.2
Persons present	Dr. Donald Cory (therapist) Garth, KL (patient)

Cory: Welcome to Elba II, Captain Garth —

Garth: *Lord* Garth!

Cory: Lord Garth. I see. Is this title why you persist in wearing that extravagant coat in such a peculiar fashion?

Garth: Have a care, doctor. My robe of office was woven to be worn just so. One arm in, one arm out. But surely we are not meeting to discuss my... sartorial choices.

Cory: Tell me then, Capt— *Lord* Garth, what do you feel we should discuss?

Garth: Why, my majesty, surely?

Cory: Your... majesty.

Garth: (sound of maniacal laughter) Thank you! Thank you for calling me "Your Majesty"! For after all, if I am *mad*, I should be humored, shouldn't I?

Cory: I suppose so. Still, I must say, I'm a trifle... skeptical. Is this madness I see before me or a performance? A terrible, excessive performance?

Garth: Why, doctor, I'm affronted! Surely in the past 300 years, I would have thought your profession had developed more sensitivity than it had in, say, the late 1960s!

Cory: My apologies. I suppose I should consider myself lucky that the Napoleon Complex has fallen out of fashion, given the contrivance of this facility's name.

Garth: Ah, I see you know of the late Emperor! An ancestor of mine, naturally. And, just like him, I shall return from exile, to master the Universe! Nothing in the world can stop me now! *(more maniacal laughter, for several minutes)*

Cory: I... see. Well, I shall return to continue our session tomorrow. I do have other patients, you know, and I seem to be the only doctor Starfleet can spare to deal with them all.

Garth: Why, my heart bleeds for you, doctor. Yet be of good cheer — when I rule the Universe, you shall have all the assistance you could ask for, with unlimited budgets! Why, I might even consider having this place redecorated! All that featureless grey; was that the best your designer could afford? Doctor? Doctor? Such a shame to leave now, when we're getting on so famously! I have something here to show you... Oh well. Guard? Come over here and have a look at what I've got!

Elba II Care Facility: Log entry, voice recording	*Stardate 5718.3*

Director's log, Stardate 5718.3, Dr. Donald Cory reporting. Garth continues to intrigue me. It's not just his megalomania or his questionable dress sense or the fact that he seems to speak entirely in purple prose. No, he has the kind of charisma that only true madmen seem to possess. And yet... funnily enough, he reminds me of Jim Kirk, somehow. Could be that he used to be a Starfleet captain, I suppose, or that both are somehow... larger than life.

Well, his therapy's going nowhere, so tomorrow I think we could try the Lobotatron Chair they passed on from old Adams' Neural Neutralizer experiments. Shame about what happened to him — wait — how did you — NOOO!!

(Dead air for several minutes)

My log, Stardate... well, whatever it is. Lord Garth reporting from... hmm, should I make this my new throne room? No, I think not, it is rather a small office. Suited to a small mind like Cory's.

Wait, what's this? New medicine? Ha! Being brought here on a *starship*! Well, it shall be the flagship of my new fleet! Now, let's read up on this Captain... James Tiberius Kirk. *Tiberius*? Really? Well... I think his is a style I could easily emulate. Why, he could almost belong here himself!

Not sure about this reported "homoerotic undercurrent" with his First Officer that the ship's surgeon refers to... Still, it could trip up that famous Vulcan logic, I suppose. If my plans unravel, and this Spock is holding a phaser on us both, unsure which is the real Kirk, perhaps it won't occur to him that he could simply stun us both!

Marta, my dear, we have arrangements to make. I think we're about to have visitors!

(Log entry ends)

Simon Fernandes lives in Cambridge, UK, and is not insane!
You hear me?! NOT INSANE!!!

71. LET THAT BE YOUR LAST BATTLEFIELD

ARE YOU BLIND?

JOHN NERONE

The original series imagines the Federation to be the United States purified and scattered among the stars. The social and geopolitical turbulence of the 1960s appears in almost every episode of the original series — but as someone else's problem. *Let That Be Your Last Battlefield* projects 1960s-era race relations onto magic aliens who manage to teach us that superior intellect and technology will not automatically defeat primordial hatred. Haters gonna hate, and it will kill them in the end. Fortunately, the *Enterprise* is filled with lovers, not haters. The twist is that the haters are two-toned, half black and half white, divided vertically down the middle.

The episode begins when Lokai, of the planet Cheron, arrives on the *Enterprise* on board a stolen shuttlecraft. Treated initially as a common criminal, he applies for an upgrade to political prisoner by claiming asylum. Shortly afterwards, the law arrives in the form of Bele, a member of Cheron's Commission on Political Traitors. Commissioner Bele has pursued Lokai for 50,000 years, and will not wait one more day before delivering him to justice.

Bele, played by Frank Gorshin, better known as the supervillain the Riddler on Adam West's camp version of *Batman* — he spent a lot of time in tights in the 1960s — isn't a sympathetic character, but, after seeing this episode many times over the years, I can feel some of his pain. He's a bureaucrat gone feral, a commissioner who's been in the wilderness so long that he can no longer stand the smug politeness of monotone humanoids.

Worse is their condescension. When the crew of the *Enterprise* see Lokai, they think he's very weird. The scientists, Spock and McCoy, leap to the conclusion that he's a freak, a mutant. They do this on the basis of an immediate visual impression, which is not what scientists are supposed to do, but which is what scientific racism does.

The condescension continues when Bele arrives. To the humans, as well as the Vulcan, he appears to be the same as Lokai. This leads to one of the best reveals in the *Star Trek* canon.

> Bele: It is obvious to the most simpleminded that Lokai is of an inferior breed.
> Spock: The obvious visual evidence, Commissioner, is that he is of the same breed as yourself.
> Bele: Are you blind, Commander Spock? Well, look at me. Look at me!
> Kirk: You are black on one side and white on the other.
> Bele: I am black on the right side!

Kirk: I fail to see the significant difference.
Bele: Lokai is white on the right side. All of his people are white on the right side.

I clearly recall noticing this difference before it was pointed out when I first saw the show. I might have been ten years old at the time, but I assumed it was a continuity error; it was only when that exchange took place that I realized it was an intentional marker of racial difference, and the episode came into focus as a parable about US race relations. The initial story outline for this episode was dated March 28th, 1968, a week before the assassination of Martin Luther King Jr. The teleplay was drafted in the first week of September, after a summer of race riots and political drama, including the assassination of Bobby Kennedy and, just a week earlier, the police riot at the Democratic National Convention in Chicago. The episode aired January 10th, 1969.

So the apparent racial harmony of the Federation was, at that moment, pure science fiction. In fact, Lokai had trouble getting the crew of the *Enterprise* to relate. Here's the response of Sulu and Chekhov to Lokai's impassioned pleas for justice:

Chekov: There was persecution on Earth once. I remember reading about it in my history class.
Sulu: Yes, but it happened way back in the twentieth century. There's no such primitive thinking today.

What must George Takei, who spent part of his childhood in an internment camp and much of his adult life in the closet, have thought of this line?

But the crew in this episode certainly doesn't model a society of racial equality. Everyone knows there is only one significant black crew member, and throughout the episode Uhura sits. She's not silent, but when she speaks, it is either to acknowledge a direct order, announce a routine act or read a communication out loud. Here is what she says: "Aye aye sir ... Aye captain ... No response sir ... Aye sir. Hailing on all frequencies ... Aye sir ... Captain, I've tried all hailing frequencies, negative sir." Then she gets to read out a long communication from Starfleet, but Kirk cuts her off after getting the gist. The routine resumes: "Ariannus says go ahead ... Shall I alert security, sir? ... Captain, someone has activated the transporter mechanism." This is the character held up as a yardstick of Federation racial equality, whose collected works seem to consist of versions of "hailing frequencies are open."

In the final scene, the nonwhites get schooled by Kirk and Spock about the primordial nature of racial hatred. The ship has arrived at Cheron to find the planet in ruins and no one alive. Lokai and Bele have both beamed down to Cheron to continue their battle. Uhura sheds her robotic competence to reveal juvenile bewilderment:

Uhura: That doesn't make any sense.

Spock: To expect sense from two mentalities of such extreme viewpoints is not logical.

Sulu: Their planet's dead. Does it matter now which one's right?

Spock: Not to Lokai and Bele. All that matters to them is their hate.

Uhura: Do you suppose that's all they ever had, sir?

Kirk: No, but that's all they have left. Warp factor two, Mr. Sulu. Set course for Starbase 4.

And so they relieve themselves of the planet Cheron. Which is weird, because whatever holocaust has occurred there must have been very recent — there are still unburied bodies in the streets — and the civilization has had the technology to spread throughout the galaxy for at least 50,000 years. Logic suggests that there must be half-whites and half-blacks all over. Perhaps they stay out of sight, like Bele's invisible ship. Perhaps there is an invisible race war raging throughout the galaxy. If I were Spock, I would lose sleep over this. After all, Vulcan collective memory is rooted in the interminable bloodbath brought about by primordial hatreds.

The *Star Trek* canon does not usually assume that progress in science goes hand in hand with tolerance, diversity and civility. Lokai and Bele, who are physically and technologically far beyond the Federation, show that fierce animal chaos can be intensified by technology. Indeed, anxieties about how technologies reshape the social anchor many other episodes. Information technology in particular assumes a demonic cast: computers replace starship captains, govern apparently primitive societies, replace daughters and lovers and perform perverse imitations of every form of human behavior, including filial devotion and purifying wrath. The humans have always managed to reassert their humanity and regain control. So far.

Bele is not a computer, but he takes over the ship's control mechanisms twice. The first time, Kirk regains control by initiating the self-destruct mechanism, the first time this trope appears in the *Star Trek* canon. Kirk would rather die, and kill everyone else, than yield control. If command is the core of his identity, then we shouldn't be surprised if one day he blows everything up, as he threatens to do in *A Taste of Armageddon*, also written by Gene L. Coon, when, to protect his crew, he destroys the infrastructure for a simulated war, gambling that the warring civilizations will not have the guts to engage in an actual war. The local political leader remonstrates with him:

Anan 7: Are those five hundred people of yours more important than the hundreds of millions of innocent people on Eminiar and Vendikar? What kind of monster are you?

Kirk: I'm a barbarian. You said it yourself.

Starfleet is a military organization, and its officers are warriors. Federation culture is like the physiognomy of the natives of Cheron: split right down the middle between savagery and civility. The humans of the Federation keep telling us and each other that that's what makes them special. So their complacency when faced with the Holocaust of Cheron is pretty annoying.

But also somewhat noble. The vision of racial harmony that *Star Trek* offers was a fantasy generated by the crisis of its time. It is easy for us, a half century on, to condescend. Do we have a better, a more courageous alternative? Looking around the contemporary sci-fi television universe, one would have to say no.

Star Trek asked us to accept that the racial turbulence of the 1960s would yield to the Olympic village of the 23rd century but did not give us a narrative about how that would happen. Would such a narrative have included the racial crises of the 21st century: mass incarceration; deepening economic inequality; racial profiling; and police violence? Well, that's not what dreams are made of.

And I'm happy about that. 21st century fantasies about intractable hatred are much less useful. What do all the breathless dramas about the War on Terror have to say? Those Klingons will never become allies.

John Nerone is a media historian and professor emeritus
at the University of Illinois who writes about public life.

72. THE MARK OF GIDEON
I SAY NAY!
JOSEPH F. BERENATO

Stardate 5424.2
From: James T. Kirk, Captain, USS *Enterprise* NCC-1701
To: Federation Council Membership Subcommittee
CC: Admiral Fitzpatrick
RE: Gideon

Distinguished Council Members:

It is with a heavy heart and a clear conscience that I must heartily recommend *against* admitting Gideon as a member world in the United Federation of Planets.

According to the physio-cultural report provided by Ambassador Hodin and Gideon's High Council, the planet is a virtual paradise: its atmosphere is germ-free, its citizenry happy and healthy. Gideon claims, in its application, to be an ideal candidate to join the Federation.

All of which is a web of lies.

The information the High Council had provided in their physio-cultural report had been true once, ages ago. Their planet has not known disease, and death is virtually non-existent. Yet their birth rate continues to rise, as they do not believe in contraception or population control of any kind. Their planet is woefully overcrowded, to the point that Gideons have no personal space of their own and move shoulder-to-shoulder around the planet.

Instead of seeking help through the proper channels, they launched a scheme to lure me to the planet, since I'm a carrier of Vegan choriomeningitis — which is fatal if not treated within 24 hours of contraction. They built a replica of my ship to confuse me, took a sample of my blood to obtain the virus and had Hodin's daughter try to seduce me in an attempt to keep me there. They believed that the virus and its effects on their population were the last, best hope for returning Gideon to its former glory.

To summarize: They kidnapped a starship captain, tried to bamboozle him with a pretty girl and forcibly removed his blood in an effort to launch a mass suicide and thereby return the planet to its former glory.

Are these Gideons? Or Orion pirates?

I will always argue in favor of a race's sovereign right to live as it sees fit. If the Gideons' love of life is so strong that the idea of contraception is anathema to their way of life, that is their right. (As a personal aside, I can appreciate their point of view on the matter.) But to institute a policy of voluntary suicide, particularly in this manner, is — as my first officer would say — most illogical.

Introducing a deadly plague to their populace seems to run counter to their very way of life. Surely, Gideon must know that off-world colonies are always an option. By transporting large sections of their population to other planets, it would allow those who remain on Gideon to once more have room to live and breathe in a more humane environment. Additionally, the odds are surely against them finding another planet with a germ-free atmosphere — diseases and ailments are sure to abound on other worlds, helping to keep the populations on those planets in check.

If their determination to stay on Gideon is so strong that colonization is unthinkable and mass suicide is their only option, why did they need me? This entire endeavor could have been accomplished without involving the *Enterprise* in any way. There are legions of people in and out of the Federation who are carriers of plague, inert or active. For that matter, why did they even need a disease? If they are so willing to throw their most basic tenet to the wind, why not just kill themselves and be done with it? If it's violence they wish to avoid, I'm sure there are many unsavory civilizations willing to furnish them with poisonous liquids or gasses.

This brings me to my final point: the replica USS *Enterprise*. Despite the fact that Gideons literally live on top of one another, the High Council inexplicably managed

OUTSIDE IN BOLDLY GOES

to clear sufficient land to build a 1:1 scale replica of the entire starship! With real estate at such a life-or-death premium, what ruling body in its right mind would construct what was essentially an *enormous* trap to catch a single mouse?

This was no mere by-the-book replica of a standard *Constitution*-class starship, either. This was a complete replica of the *Enterprise* herself, down to scuffs in the carpet, chips in the paint and the complete contents, professional and personal, of Sickbay, Engineering and the Captain's quarters. Not only is this an excessive waste of land, material and manpower, it also represents what is most likely the single greatest security breach in Starfleet history.

This is by no means the first time my ship has been compromised. I have made repeated requests to Starfleet Command for improvements in that area. The pertinent ones are:

- Surveillance cameras, after the murder spree of Lenore Karidian (Stardate 2820.2), and again after the grisly voyage to the Babel conference (Stardate 3844.3)
- The technical schematics of the ship to be made classified, after Khan Singh and his crew — who should have looked at the ship like it was magic — assumed control after skimming through a few blueprints (Stardate 3143.5)
- An automatic intruder-detection system, most recently after the Kalandan encounter
- Better-trained security guards (incidents too numerous to mention)

Had any one of these requests been honored, perhaps this breach could have been avoided. However, Starfleet Command saw fit to deny them, and this is the result.

They duplicated everything: all of my personal effects, down to the contents of my underwear drawer. That anyone was able to gain such access is alarming; that it happened on *my ship* is embarrassingly infuriating. How did they gain such access? Do they have agents aboard, like the Norman robot sent by Harry Mudd? Have they vetted moles, like the Klingons did with Arne Darvin? Have they bribed members of my crew?

And if Gideon — a society clearly run by madmen — can do it, what's to stop the Klingons? The Romulans?

The situation on Gideon is horrifying. Of that, there can be no argument. And they are certainly deserving of whatever humanitarian aid the Federation can offer. But they are not ready for membership, and I don't know if they'll ever be. The Gideon High Council, despite their claims, has shown a flagrant disregard for life and the security of the Federation by abducting the captain of the flagship and by engineering the largest security breach in decades.

It is therefore my recommendation that Gideon be denied membership and that

Ambassador Hodin be arrested for kidnapping, unlawful detainment and espionage in accordance with the Articles of Interstellar Law.

> Very truly yours,
> Captain James T. Kirk
> Commander, USS *Enterprise* NCC-1701

P.S. Attached please find the full list of security improvement requests. Perhaps if a recommendation came from your august body, Starfleet Command may finally acquiesce. Please pay special attention to the requests for biometric locks to be placed on the doors to Auxiliary Control, Engineering and the Shuttle Bay.

Joseph F. Berenato, the editor of New Life and New Civilizations: Exploring Star Trek Comics, *teaches English and Composition — and also serves as choir co-director — at Atlantic Cape Community College in Mays Landing, New Jersey.*

73. THAT WHICH SURVIVES
I DON'T LIKE FRIDAYS
HIKARU SULU (AS TOLD TO NEIL A. HOGAN)

\<Recovered corrupted file from ancient archives\>

Helmsman's Blog (Stardate redacted)
Archaeologists believe this record was created by Helmsman Hikaru Sulu, a crew member serving on the USS Enterprise, *though the software signature and location of the original voice recording has long since been lost. Parts of the transcript have been translated into English for this archive.*

Report begins
I'm recording this report on my communicator for later broadcast. I do not believe I have long to live. Dr. McCoy recommended I try some cognitive disassociation to get my mind off what is happening to my arm.

Well, I should start at the beginning.

This morning started quite routine. Mr. Spock walking back and forth looking over my shoulder as usual, waiting for me to make any mistake. I've got used to it, but it still makes me a little anxious. It's not like I haven't done this job for three years. I think he gets bored and doesn't want to admit it, instead wanting to personally investigate and be sure that absolutely everything in the ship is in working order rather than simply rely on others. It's times like these I want to go back to my astrosciences-physicist job.

In any case (was it because I was thinking of some stylish red clothes?), I was asked to join the landing party on the new planet.

Just as we disappeared, we saw a woman kill the transporter operator, and we immediately knew that it must be a Friday. These things always happen on a Friday.

When I joined the landing party, I was hoping to be surrounded by a lot of muscular men in red, but it was just Dr. McCoy, our senior geologist (though I've never seen any junior ones on board — and since when did we suddenly need a senior geologist anyway?) and Captain Kirk. I was a bit worried for a moment, but then I realized I've been on far more missions than Whatshisname, so I was probably going to be okay.

Speaking of the Captain, he was looking his extremely rugged self today. I tried to catch his attention, but he wasn't having any of it. Surely, being a well-rounded 23rd-century guy, he'd be interested in spending some time with one of his male officers? But no. He's always on about the females.

I tried to get his attention with a suggestion, but he put me down pretty quickly. But I can be patient. Perhaps I should think about running a website of jokes or something that would make me very popular? Someday...

Dr. McCoy gave me an encouraging look, but I knew he was just being sympathetic as then Captain Kirk paid attention to Dr. McCoy's suggestion, which I thought was just as valid as mine. He asked me to continue investigating, but I think he just wanted me out of the way, so I walked a few meters and stared pointedly at some grass. I'm pretty sure my message was clear!

But I think the Captain was having a bad day. I wondered (quite sensibly I thought) about beings intelligent enough to destroy the *Enterprise*, but he brushed me off, saying "We only have questions... no answers." Well, thanks for that, Captain. And when Dr. McCoy pondered what killed the crewman, he concluded "Something... or someone... did." I guess that's why they pay him the big bucks!

If I perish on this planet, I'd like to think that some of me will survive in some form and, as I'm probably rambling and slightly delirious from the pain and the rapid regeneration of my arm, if I do live through this, I'll probably be deleting this message as soon as I get back to the ship. If I have a daughter, I'd name her Demora, after a fabulous drag queen I saw perform in Sydney once. Sorry, rambling again.

If we can find the ship, that is. We can't contact it. It's as though it's not in the area. We have no idea what's happened to it. And we're being picked off, one by one. Did I mention it was a Friday?

Dr. Whatshisname was killed after touching some sand. We buried him under some rocks and will probably beam up his body later for a detailed coroner's report. I have no idea why we always want to bury the bodies straight away when we can't move them. I guess the fear is that wild beasts will eat them before an autopsy is performed, though it is a waste of valuable energy and we didn't detect any wild beasts. Also, we never bury the security guards.

After the burial, it was time to take watch. I volunteered to be the first, in the hope that the Captain would be pleased.

I had only moved a few feet from where Captain Kirk and Doctor McCoy had decided to sleep when, to my absolute horror, a woman appeared and told me she wanted to touch me. In fact, she repeated it several times!!!

At first I thought this might be a female version of the Captain. Sex first, love later, which was the last thing on my mind. But then, when I fired at her, she kept coming closer and I knew that it wasn't about sex. She wanted to kill me! Well, at least that was less complicated.

At that point, I was a bit surprised that both Captain Kirk and Doctor McCoy had not woken up when they heard my phaser fire, so I had to yell pretty loudly to get their attention. In that instant, I'm afraid I let my guard down and the woman was able to briefly touch my arm. I knew then that this was the woman who had appeared in the transporter bay, so I knew a simple touch could kill.

The pain was excruciating. It was like fire had flash-boiled my arm from the inside out, then frozen it again. So quickly that my skin didn't even have time to show anything. I was afraid I'd lose my fencing arm. Robotic replacements weren't accepted in tournaments, unfortunately. I knew this sort of thing would happen if a woman ever touched me.

Thankfully, Doctor McCoy and Captain Kirk arrived just in time to prevent the woman from damaging me any further, and I was able to crawl away. I've never crawled away from a woman so fast in my life!

So now I sit here waiting for my arm to recover from the rapid cellular regeneration that Doctor McCoy has facilitated. It feels like millions of bugs are crawling under my skin, so I need to focus on this message to get my mind off it. I swear, sometimes our adventures seem so ridiculous that I'd be surprised if Starfleet lets us finish our five-year mission and doesn't just cancel the whole thing as soon as possible.

I'm sending this message now via a subspace link, in the hope that the *Enterprise* will collect it when it is in range.

If the *Enterprise* still exists, that is. Hopefully they'll just reverse the polarity of something and then be on our way to collect us just in time.

Yeah, that should do the trick. It is a Friday, after all...

Report ends

For about a week, Neil Hogan was once Robert Smith?'s boss.
So now it's payback time.

74. THE LIGHTS OF ZETAR
TO MIRA ROMAINE, THANKS FOR NOTHING! JULIE NEWMAR
DANIEL KUKWA

Dear Scotty,

We need to talk.

The chick-magnet thing is impressive. There is certainly something about you and the brainy, short-skirted type… although that description does get confusing when you're wearing your kilt. Even Kirk looks impressed when you're putting the moves on a geeky Ph.D. in hooker boots, which is no mean feat. There's just something about you: that Scottish brogue you work so hard at maintaining, that smooth, cooing tone when you get all sentimental, and every flash of knee brings out your touchy-feely side.

But it should be painfully obvious to you that women will be the death of you. In fact, they *have* been the death of you.

Look at your track record. You cozy up to Carolyn Palamas in *Who Mourns for Adonais?*, only to be smacked around and electrocuted by a half-naked bodybuilding Greek god, incensed that you're sniffing around his chosen one. You ask a girl out for a stroll in the fog in *Wolf in the Fold*… only to end up covered in her blood, accused of murder and facing death by slow torture. You then murderously double down with the cute skirt that beams down to scan you with a tricorder!

For god's sake, man. By the end of the third season, you have two-dimensional stick women popping up in Engineering, trying to blow you up for what I can only surmise is your reputation alone!

Which brings us to *The Lights of Zetar*. This is the ultimate warning — a siren song for the ages. It's the perfect "women are bad for Scotty" story. We have cold, bland ice queen Mira Romaine, who is all brains, little charm. We have Scotty absolutely smitten with her, melting her icy heart with the phaser of his love. We have the rest of the crew staring at the pair of them like they've been sniffing the anti-matter vapors a little too intensely — and then the giant sparkly things arrive to try and distract everyone to death.

It's an episode that manages to prove that you should *not* be filming an episode around Scotty's heterosexual death-wish. You have an incredibly boring (but pretty) guest actor. You have an incredibly boring (but pretty) set of sparkly lights. You have a series of incredibly dull and boring conversations. But, to try and spice it up, someone thinks that Scotty getting it on with the ultimate example of his personal kryptonite is a winning idea. "Mira will not kill me," Scotty tells Kirk. Knowing his track record, it's 50-50 at best, but you really can't blame the poor sod. The woman is constantly throwing herself into his arms… when she's not busy staring off into space or barking at the rest of the crew to leave her alone and let her be a wronged *Glee*-inspired teenager. It seems boring sparkly things just aren't as distracting as they used to be — or as lethal as they should be! It's not surprising that, when Spock is asked about Scotty's love for Mira in the final scene, we get the only visualization of what a Vulcan looks like when he's ready to vomit.

So, my dear Scotty, it's time to face the truth. Your hetero-charms are leading you down the garden path to destruction. Don't end up like Larry Marvick, utterly bonkers over his own unrequited ice-queen obsession. Don't end up like Geordi La Forge, hoodwinked by his holodeck fantasy women. It's time to free yourself and become the man you were meant to be. It's time to go gay.

All the signs are plainly visible. Look at those moments when you are most happy. You have never been as content as you were in *The Trouble with Tribbles*, brawling in a bar full of big, strong Starfleet officers and big, strong Klingons... the ultimate grunting, sweaty, drunken mob. Look how thrilled you were when Larry Marvick finally accepted your engineering date in *Is there In Truth No Beauty?*; you even bribed him with alcohol to get him to play with your engine controls. Speaking of alcohol, what in the name of sanity were you really up to with the beefiest, gruffest Kevlan in *By Any Other Name*? If that screaming alcoholic bender-for-two is only a hint of your idea of "stimulation", I'm almost afraid to ask what else went on behind the door of your cabin. As for admiring the size of your claymore in *Day of the Dove*... well, Freud would have a field day. Meanwhile, a century later, you're following La Forge around like a puppy dog on *Enterprise*-D, only to storm off like a wronged suitor when he tells you to bugger off.

And do I really have to mention the way you and Dr. McCoy were looking at each other as you minced about, twinkled-toed, at the climax of *I, Mudd*?

The Lights of Zetar should be the last word on your failed attempt at heterosexual happiness, Mr. Scott. Ditch the brainy, bland seductress. Stop distracting yourself, so you can actually *pay attention* to bland sparkly things trying to destroy your ship. Stop denying your true feelings, and embrace what makes you happy. Your crew will thank you, your ship will thank you, and the women can go back to throwing themselves at James Kirk, who really knows what it means to be king of the heterosexual chick magnets.

Sincerely,
Daniel Kukwa

PS: Judging by the J.J. Abrams alternate universe version of you, I see you have taken my advice to heart. However, I never thought you'd go for a small, bipedal prune...

Daniel Kukwa's recent triumphs include: (1) winning a knife fight against Elaan of Troyius, (2) winning a staring contest against the Medusan ambassador and (3) winning the jackpot in the annual Federation fizzbin tournament.

75. REQUIEM FOR METHUSELAH
THE GREAT MAN THEORY
JACK GRAHAM

For Flint in *Requiem for Methuselah*, a life of vast power, opportunity, status, accomplishment and wealth has proved unsatisfying. As with so many immortal or long-lived characters from Western culture, the privilege of eternity is shown to be hollow.

On the one hand, it looks like a very convenient idea from the point of view of the privileged. The notion that power, opportunity, status, accomplishment and wealth are all ultimately meaningless is one that those who possess access to such things might well be pleased to see believed by those who don't. This would hook quite well into the character of Flint, since he is an embodiment of those groups enjoying perennial privilege in Western culture. To be blunt, he's an old, rich, white, straight dude.

On the other hand, if we refuse to pity Flint, then we might see him as having wasted his time, energy and spirit on the accumulation of more and more wealth and cultural capital. Even his artistic achievements bore him. And he just reiterates past glories in his new creations.

This is part of a deeply wrongheaded idea of what art is. It seems like a contradiction, but the sterility of Flint's artistic productiveness is an inevitable corollary of the notion — apparently accepted by this story — that art comes from individual genius. If art is just an emanation from the souls of certain special people, then it is more or less independent of historical context. In this view, Leonardo da Vinci didn't paint what he painted because of the social context in which he lived; he painted what he painted because of some genius gene, which created certain ideas in his head out of nowhere. So of course he's still painting the same kind of stuff he was painting in the Italian Renaissance hundreds of years later when living on another planet!

In addition to having been Leonardo and Brahms, Flint also claims to have been several other people including the Hebrew king Solomon and the Hellenic military imperialist Alexander. Yet Flint has the audacity to complain about the savagery of mankind. As Alexander alone, he was responsible for conquests, wars, massacres and enslavements (admittedly, when he was much younger). True to form, he displays a truly proprietorial view of other people. He considers that he owns Rayna and uses Kirk for his own purposes. He has the same attitude to "his" planet, which he bought when being Brack, a "wealthy financier" (so much for the idea that the Federation doesn't use money).

Flint seems to wrap the roles of artist, king, conqueror and plutocrat into one big ball of cultural capital. The implication is that being a military autocrat, an imperialist or a financier is thus in some way similar to being a great artist. We arrive back at the idea of inborn, asocial greatness, which causes those men who possesses it to paint great pictures or carve out great empires. It's an inherently reactionary notion because it sees the "great men" as superior and the dominance of tyrants as a kind of world-shaping artistry. Progress always stems from a blessed minority that creates all the pretty pictures, builds all the walls on which they're hung and carves out the states within those walls.

Flint — old, rich and white — represents this "great man theory" of history. But we can choose to look at Flint as representing a critique, precisely because he embodies Leonardo and Alexander combined. He is both sides of history, inextricably intertwined. Leonardo, like all the "great men" of the Renaissance, worked for plutocrats and autocrats and theocrats. The progress and the horror are as impossible to separate as the sugar from the coffee. The culture comes from the tyranny and exploitation. We might view Flint's incredible longevity as a form of unearned advantage that has enabled him to accrue all his capital from the labor of others. Spock even states to Flint at one point that "Your wealth and your intellect are the product of centuries of acquisition."

Take into account the fact that there is, as Walter Benjamin said, no "document of culture [that] is not simultaneously one of barbarism" and the "great men" become responsible for the wreckage and waste as well. They are, at least, the beneficiaries of it. Untie the bundle of material, racial, sexual and cultural capital that Flint represents (which could reasonably be summed up as "Westernism", because no figure or text standing outside the Western tradition is invoked) and you end up following all the threads from the bundle into the same pool of blood.

Flint is absolutely a figure of patriarchy. As noted, he says he owns Rayna. His position as the greatest "great man" in the pantheon implicitly negates the idea that any woman ever made history, except perhaps as a mistress or a muse or as one of Solomon's hundreds of wives and concubines.

My original plan for this essay was to write it as a story, set before *Requiem for Methuselah*, telling of a visit to Flint's planet by a different space traveller, a woman. She was going to be Flint's mirror image: an immortal who had spent her centuries of life working, never having the opportunity to accrue genius or wealth because she never had a break from labor. Given the way class society consumes and wastes lives, particularly women's lives, it seems perfectly plausible that it could keep a woman beaten down and bereft of opportunities for millennia. Flint would find himself in a debate with his accusatory visitor. I couldn't get it to work. If the character was going to represent a kind of antithesis to the "great man", the visitor would have to be a woman... but there was already a woman in the story, of course: Rayna. So I tried to write Rayna as the prosecutor... but she never gets anywhere near that level of awareness until the end of the episode. She can't reflect Flint's progress through history, having only recently been "born". I needed a character who could have shared Flint's millennia with him, seen them from a woman's point-of-view… but part of the point of Flint is that he never found a woman like that. That's why Flint builds his fembot.

The feminist objections to the fembot are — or should be — as obvious as they are correct. Rayna herself is designed to be the eternal companion of the eternal man (though we might pause to wonder just how bothered Leonardo or Alexander would've been). She's designed to be as clever as Flint, so that he can imagine he has an equal relationship with her. That he can imagine such a thing about their relationship shows how utterly insulated he is by his own privilege.

Sadly, the unavoidable implication is that only an artificial woman could be as clever as Flint. Flint is presented as the embodiment of the highest accomplishments of Western culture. He has searched for his female equal and found womankind wanting. Thus the sexism inherent in the idea of Flint as the greatest of all the great men becomes explicit.

Rayna ends up torn between two men. Flint's desire to gain complete control over Rayna takes the paradoxical form of a plot to create genuine feelings in her; thus he tries to awaken selfhood in the creature he created precisely to lack real selfhood! Yet Kirk's attraction to Rayna is different. We're so used to the accepted jokes about Kirk that they can obscure what he actually does and says. He's the "ladies' man" with a girl in every spaceport, etc. And yeah, there is plenty of that. But Kirk awakens feelings in Rayna (there's no doubt, by the way, that the notion of the man "awakening" the woman's feelings is problematic) by treating her *as though she already has them*. Ultimately, Kirk's desire is for Rayna to gain autonomy. Kirk wants her to come with him, but while this can be read as a desire to win her away from Flint, it also looks like a genuine desire to offer Rayna freedom. (This is largely owing to the passionately theatrical performances of both Shatner and Louise Sorel.) Kirk doesn't treat freedom as something that is his to grant. He doesn't even treat freedom as something for Flint to grant her! Rather, he emphasizes Rayna's own role in creating her own freedom.

Rayna's failure to survive the achievement of selfhood tends to undermine the idea that the dominated can successfully free themselves. But it could also be seen as a comment on the difference between a male fantasy of a woman and a real woman. The fantasy is unsustainable. And when she fails, Kirk seems prepared to take some of the blame for it.

This admirable showing makes me wonder if Kirk isn't the nearest thing in the text to my notional accuser. Kirk isn't immortal, so he personally can't offer the historical perspective, but he does have his occasional identification as a working-class character. My friend Josh Marsfelder has written about this on his blog Vaka Rangi, identifying Kirk as a "working-class spaceman" — at least some of the time.

For instance, in *The Ultimate Computer*, Kirk is effectively threatened with loss of employment by the development of technology. In *The Cloud Minders*, he sides with the Troglytes.

So, with a little effort of will, we can decide to consider Kirk in *Requiem for Methuselah* as the representative of the workers, the ones who chug along in the background, making everything work and getting none of the rewards or credit. Kirk can be the universal accuser. True, pushing him into this role makes him responsible for representing all sorts of people he is not. Kirk is, after all, another straight white guy. He's an authority figure. He could even be seen, from another angle, as another "great man" of history. But he's also the representative of a notionally utopian culture. Flint is initially deeply hostile to Kirk. Flint's logic is that he left Earth to escape just the kind of organized barbarity that he assumes Starfleet still represents. Kirk, meanwhile, trumpets his peaceful intentions and his mission of mercy and makes his usual claim to represent a more civilized upgrade of human society. Whether or not this claim is strictly true, it is, nevertheless, the ideal that he aims towards.

The utopian vision, and the struggle to get there, can be seen in Kirk. It can be seen in the way he refuses to allow Flint's massive accumulation of material and cultural capital to daunt him. It can be seen in his attempt to stimulate Rayna's liberation (as problematic as it might be to have a man in charge of that).

The rebuke having been stated, we have only to look back at Flint. Suddenly, it's clear. His stated contempt for human barbarism is actually an attempt to blame the victim. He is the manifestation of the barbarism buried in all culture produced by unjust class societies, because he represents the personal accumulation of all that material and cultural capital in private hands. He's been a conqueror and a slaver and a warmonger, a weapons technologist and a king and a judge, a keeper of concubines and servants. He still owns a person, a person constructed to comfort his own misogynistic and narcissistic drives. His flight from human society is not, as he claims, a flight from barbarism. He has carried the barbarism with him and within him. In fact, his flight from human society has been a flight from the utopian future — or, at least, the utopian hopes — embodied by Kirk.

We might feel sorry for Flint, in his isolation and emptiness, but his requiem — if it ever truly comes — should be a celebration.

Jack Graham writes the blog Shabogan Graffiti,
complains a lot and lives in an igloo made of books and cats.

76. THE WAY TO EDEN
STRANGERS IN PARADISE
TAT WOOD

That's Now, man, that's real Now. I reach that, brother, I really do.
— Adam (Charles Napier)

You know what's odd about *The Way To Eden*? At no point does a rectangular shaft illuminate Kirk's eyes as he makes a speech.

What we need to remember is that the USS *Enterprise* was really an RKO lot. Look at the lighting, then compare it to those cheesy spectaculars Howard Hughes made his minions do in Technicolor, and this heritage is obvious. The Cinematographer on the pilot episode was William E. Snyder, whose films include the thwarted 3D Lili St Cyr vehicle *Son of Sinbad*. There are clips of the latter floating around online, if you can't face buying the DVD, so you can see that the difference between Lili or Sally Forrest corybanting in veils and Susan Oliver shaking her thang on Rigel VII is that the latter is green. This distinction was lost on those of us watching the British TV broadcasts before color or with black-and-white sets on the repeats. What we noticed was that the look of the series was weird even compared to other imported film shows. *Star Trek* looks like a musical. People wear primary colors and the places they inhabit have odd shadows and a lot of angled peach and lilac lighting, as if Gene Kelly or Leslie Caron might show up at any moment. Conceptually, *Star Trek* was *South Pacific* in space, rather than it having any resemblance to *Wagon Train*. Aesthetically, it was closer to *Kismet*. Even the incidental music was more nineteenth-century Russia than *Forbidden Planet*.

Musicals, including *Trek*, are utopian displays of vitality and plenty; even the threats are excitingly vibrant. Right from *Star Trek*'s initial phase as creepy-critter-of-the-week, the "other" was always visually and sonically exciting (which is why the end captions have stills of these rather than portraits of the regular cast). Yet it was alien within very clearly prescribed limits; even on planets where people wore trousers with one flared orange leg, everyone had smart haircuts. The worlds of the Federation were "exotic" the same way Les Baxter albums were. Back to *The Cage*; that original arrangement of the theme tune betrays the similarity to tiki-lounge sounds in stereophonic hi-fi. That trombone-led smoochy arrangement they use in *The Conscience of the King*, *Court Martial* and others when Kirk's at the bar charming the laydeez differs from the later, familiar one with the soprano in degree and not kind. This is the Eisenhower era's vision of Utopia.

Once the BBC had figured out when to schedule this series (BBC1 on Mondays at 7.20, just before heavyweight current-affairs series *Panorama*), the episodes began to resemble each other, if nothing else on our screens. There were things that made it so peculiar even when compared to other imports such as *The Monkees* or *Wild Wild West,* elements that now seem comprehensible since they are almost all symptoms of advert breaks being removed and pre-credit scenes being put after the opening sequence. Episodes took on a familiar progression: titles and monologue; captain's log exposition; go to a planet that looks like a set (slowly, not everyone's seen the Transporter effect before); get into trouble; explain what we've just seen, blow something up; Bones rants about Spock; lose power on the ship; overpower guards; confront baddies; make a speech; another explosion; Kirk solves everyone's problems and explains what the episode was really about; end theme and pictures of other episodes. They were aesthetically self-contained, even when set inside other series (e.g. *A Piece of the Action*). There had been episodes set in 1960s America but, for an English kid watching in the early seventies, *Assignment: Earth* looked like another *Star Trek* planet. The first time we hear an English accent on the ship is in the animated series in 1974. The second is in 1987 (and he's supposed to be French). However much they talk about finding strange new worlds, it was the same strange world week after week, resembling the one where Nixon and Scooby-Doo lived. It was self-contained, out of reach.

By the time *Star Trek* aired in the UK, hippies were a lot more normal than Starfleet. Space hippies and the Federation both looked like futuristic primary schools, but the latter was imposed. Calling someone a "Herbert" was common, in every sense, although it was usually addressed to someone with scruffy clothes and long hair ("tuck yer shirt in, you grotty little 'erbert", as my dad would say). American-accented homogeneity was intrinsically wrong, as any fule kno, but above all it was ridiculous. Why build a spaceship to go to (or make) another California? A whole galaxy of Mojave-planets and Main Streets was absurd. *The Way to Eden* was within reach for us in ways no other episode could be.

So when Kirk's cozy, polyester-clad world is invaded by barefoot drop-outs in printed cotton, it's a much deeper violation than in any other episode. All the ritual elements of a *Star Trek* episode have been disrupted. This is the one where McCoy agrees with Spock, throughout. Apart from their stolen stock-footage ship, the antagonists don't make anything explode, they just sing along to their bicycle wheels and pogo-sticks. Repeatedly. Instead of Kirk's sermon, we get Spock jamming with Adam and the anonymous blonde. It's a huge relief that Uhura's off-duty, otherwise this would take over half the episode. (Don't believe me? Watch *Charlie X,* if you dare. And I'm told that Miss Chemicals-are-bad-except-peroxide is called "Mavig" but not on screen. Besides, the same sources claim that the Ambassador's son is called "Tongo Rad" but everyone calls him "Tong-Rad".) Instead of a punch-up with *that* bit of music, we have a slight delay with an ultrasonic burglar alarm. We're teased with the prospect of the Romulans taking umbrage against a treaty violation, but they don't even send a model spaceship or a text message. We finally leave the standing sets for a brief trip to Eden, which has lethal grass and bad acid, and Adam is killed by forbidden fruit — even Spock sounds embarrassed pointing out the obvious symbolism.

It's not the *Enterprise* they've taken over; *Star Trek* has turned into a different series this week. Klingons, Doomsday Machines and what have you all belong inside the *Star Trek* format. They are threats from outside that Kirk has to talk out of causing any long-term change (so they can show the episodes out of order). This lot are produced by the Federation (even Bones admits that the disease the leader has is a side-effect of all that Naugahyde). Unlike the Maquis — disaffected Federationers in the spinoffs — there's no attempt to embrace these drop-outs back into the fold once they've made their protest or even give them a good telling-off. The series can't dismiss this critique of its entire premise.

Instead, this story has to depart from internal logic to provide a neat, sententious moral and wrench everything back to normal (taking *The Cloud Minders* as a benchmark of normality). In *The Paradise Syndrome*, Spock tells McCoy that the quest for the Big Ancestor is one of the key unsolved questions of the galaxy. So where did the navigator (presumably Irina, a former Starfleet Academy student who then has to ask Chekov about the Auxiliary Control Room) think they were going? If Eden's such a potent myth on so many worlds, this ought to be the most shattering discovery of the age. Yet Spock can find it from the comfort of his space-age bachelor pad (and still has time to pay host to Charles Napier in a Harpo-wig and thigh-boots). And then it's all forgotten. Next week, we're back to warmed-over *Flash Gordon* made to look like a musical and Kirk can deliver his closing thoughts with the light of sincerity on him like an inverse Zorro mask.

Tat Wood first encountered Star Trek *as a luridly dynamic comic-strip in* TV21. *On being told they were making a version on telly, he got all excited. Seeing* The Man Trap — *an hour of velour-clad old men with American accents standing around talking, in black and white — was a crushing let-down from which he has never fully recovered.*

77. THE CLOUD MINDERS
WAITING FOR THE CLOUD MINDERS
GRANT KIEN

Setting: *The cramped cockpit of a large intergalactic transport space ship. The cockpit is lined with a stereotypical array of switches, lights, screens, levers etc. The pilot and co-pilot seats are occupied by two different types of humanoid beings, both about the size of an adult human. The cockpit is strewn with various empty food containers and wrappers, and a half-finished magnetic-travel size board game sits precariously between the two occupants.*

Camera movement:
Super-wide shot showing the planet Ardana, the floating city Stratos and a long line of transport vessels hovering like a disconnected chain outward from an enormous ore-loading dock that extends from the planet surface to the zero-gravity zone via a giant ore shaft. It looks as if someone stuck a giant nail into the planet. The loading dock is, in fact, further into space than Stratos but is positioned on the planet such that it is beyond the horizon of view from the floating city.

Slow zoom speeding to medium zoom first to the transport ship, then a small cockpit window on the vessel, then in to the co-pilot's bored face.

Co-pilot/pilot alternating head shots, medium shots and various other cockpit cutaways.

Co-pilot: (*conveying extreme boredom*) So... what's new?

Pilot: (*visibly agitated*) Um... what do you mean what's new? I've been sitting here, literally right beside you, for the last 36 hor0ns, goddamn it!

Co-pilot: (*apologetic*) Yeah, I mean... you've been listening to your zzPodiculator, so I thought maybe you might have heard an update or something.

Pilot: (*calmer*) No, sorry, no word. Sorry I was short with you. It's just... well... you know.

Co-pilot: Yep, I understand. Apology accepted. (*faux singing*) Bup bup baaaa... dup dup da da daaaa...

Co-pilot: Wanna listen to some music? Watch another *Star Wars*?

Pilot: No offense, but I really can't handle watching any more of that freaking *Star Wars* saga. It doesn't make any sense. Like, in terms of labor consciousness, neither of the warring parties are worth supporting. There's more than just fascism and feudalism in the universe, you know? It just kind of irks me that those are the only two choices depicted. Who even wrote that anyway?

Co-pilot: What do you mean? Wouldn't it be better if beings would just know their place? Like, I don't try to be the pilot, because YOU are the pilot.

Pilot: Yeah, well, I'm only the pilot because I'm an independent owner/operator and I need to be in control of my investment. YOU are actually a better pilot than me.

Co-pilot: Oh go on... you don't mean that...

Pilot: YES! You ARE! You're a great pilot, and you should have your own vessel. And as soon as I can scrape together the financing, I'm going to get another ship and YOU are going to pilot it.

Co-pilot: (*seriously*) Yeah, you know, I think I'd like that. But YOU still have to take care of the business stuff. You know I don't have any heads for that.

Pilot: Sure. Anyway, we just need to finish this zenite run ASAP. I'm already having to push back our schedule for the Wraknak System Alliance. This strike is just making things soooo problematic. What was it they said? Over fifteen hundred transports already lined up here?

Co-pilot: Yeah, I can't think of another time I've seen this big of a strike. But you know, at the end of the day, I think I'm on their side.

Pilot: Oh yeah? After 36 hor0ns of sitting here like fossilized crustaceans, you've decided you're on their side? Have you lost your minds?

Co-pilot: Well, think about it. Would YOU just go along with it if, after going through all this waiting and all the investment in your business, when we got to Xenti with this shipment, some self-declared "higher intellect" just took your payment away?

Pilot: Yeah well, what's the difference between that and the Federation tax? I mean GODDESSES! It's like thirty-two percent taken right out of my hands for every transaction!

Co-pilot: Yes, but you get something for that: traffic control, enforcement of standards, security against piracy and what not...

Pilot: But THIRTY-TWO PERCENT! They are the real pirates. Speaking of which... how about that Federation Starship? Did you like the way they just swooped in here and jumped the queue?

Co-pilot: Yeah, that doesn't seem fair. And they don't even need to be that close, with their fancy teleportation, or whatever it's called. But I heard they're here to mediate. Do you think it's true?

Pilot: Do I think it's true? I don't even know. They're military. Can the military really broker a labor contract?

Co-pilot: Well, you know, the Troglytes aren't even really unionized. This is totally a labor rebellion, like in the early days of American capitalism, workers taking over the shop floor and all that. And you know that supposedly super-intellectual smart guy Plasus is just blundering his way through the negotiation, stalling and trying to starve out the Troglytes while we pay the price of waiting it out. I think he must be a real asshole.

Pilot: Yep. I think it's more likely the military is here to blow the crap out of those poor souls. That's what most industrialists have done throughout history. Buy themselves an army to kill the leadership and scare the proletariat into accepting their own exploitation.

Co-pilot: Jeez... I sure hope not. I knew a half-Troglyte humanoid back on Tesus, kind of a nice, quiet type. Hey, do you think it's true? What they say about that Captain?

Pilot: What do you mean? That he got dressed up in Taratantadalac formal dress attire and tried to sex with his First Officer?

Co-pilot: Well, yeah, that, but that he also, you know, goes for it with anything that moves?

Pilot: Ha ha HAAAAAAAA!!! You want to do it with the Kirk! Be careful... I heard that he even tried to make it with a Lilt Cloud on Vlim!!

Co-pilot: NOOOOOO!!!!

Pilot: YESSSSSS!!!

Co-pilot: Oh my GODDESSES!

Pilot: I know, right!?

Co-pilot: So what you're saying is... there's hope for me?! Ha ha ha!!

Pilot: Hahahaha!! Yeah, I'm sure there is. (*Smiling.*) How are we going to get you in the same room as him though? Hmmm...

Co-pilot: Well, maybe I could pretend to be a Vulcan and just kind of, I don't know, replace his First Officer.

Pilot: Yeah, and his Second and Third and Fourth! Ha ha ha!

Co-pilot: (*chuckling*) Yeah! I like your thinking!

Pilot: Well, I don't know how you Zanfads do it, and those earthlings... I dunno... I heard the male part looks something like a Blunit head. I sure am glad I'm a Monosex. I don't know how you can go for so long without any action. Like, I can do myself any time I want. (*Leans over, says quietly and seriously.*) You know what?

Co-pilot: What?

Pilot: I've even done myself while we've been waiting here. (*Quickly looks away.*)

Co-pilot: So?

Pilot: Well, I'll bet you didn't know. Did you know?

Co-pilot: Seriously, Captain Santarooni, I really don't care.

Pilot: What do you mean you don't care? That's the kind of thing EVERYONE cares about, isn't it?

Co-pilot: Well, I don't care. I'm a freaking Zanfads, for goodness' sake. Three of me are having sex right now!

Pilot: Wait... what?!

Co-pilot: Yeah! Three of me are having sex. I'm just taking a break and talking to you for a while.

Pilot: You mean the four of you can have sex INSIDE that body whenever you want? How did I not know this about you?

Co-pilot: Well, you never asked, and, since you're a Monosex, I didn't really see how that would concern you.

Pilot: Yeah, but come on! Even for me, that's interesting. And when you think about it, that means we kind of have something in common, doesn't it?

Co-pilot: Sort of, but not so much. Like, aren't you afraid of getting yourself pregnant? We can't make ourselves pregnant.

Pilot: You can't? I take precautions. There are some pretty good methods of birth control out there these days.

Co-pilot: Nope. We need an external life energy to stimulate our seedlings. Legend has it the ancients could even use D cell batteries, but who knows, those haven't been around for a long, long time.

Pilot: Well, I'm sorry... I did NOT know that. We've been flying together for what... six Moooodliks now? And we've never had this conversation before. Imagine that.

Co-pilot: Yep. Well, it's not like you and I are sexually compatible in any way at all. You can't stimulate my seedlings, and I can't stimulate yours.

Pilot: True. We have a completely asexual compatibility. Does that make sense? Anyway... do you even want to produce slugs?

Co-pilot: Someday, for sure. We're not really ready for it yet though. We just joined in this body a century and a half ago, so we're still kind of in the honeymoon stage.

Pilot: Yeah, probably best to take it slow... make sure you're all ready for that kind of responsibility. But you better hurry if you want Kirk to be their fathers! Hahahahaha!!!

Co-pilot: OH MY GODDESSES! You're KILLING me!

[Fanfare from radio]

Radio: Welcome to Ardana. Your business is important to us, and we appreciate your patience as we work to rectify this delay. We are pleased to inform you at this time that the labor dispute that has interrupted our production and shipping schedule has now been settled to the satisfaction of all parties. We will resume loading at 5818.5, Stardate time. We ask that you help expedite the clearing of this backlog by maintaining your place in the loading line and having your copy of your purchase order in hand when you get to the dock. Thank you for your cooperation. This message has been brought to you by ArdanaZMines.com, a subsidiary of Xfinity/Comcast.

Pilot: Oh my Goddesses! Can you believe it!?

Co-pilot: Woot! Woot!

Pilot: So what position are we at?

Co-pilot: We're ummm... 754th.

Pilot: Oh. I see.

Co-pilot: Yeah.

Pilot: And when do they resume again? 5818.5, Stardate time?

Co-pilot: Yes. That's, like, another 17 hor0ns. And then 753 ships to load before us, taking about roughly 40 lan4rds each... that's another 19 hor0ns, so we'll be loaded up and on our way in about another 36 hor0ns.

Pilot: I see.

Co-pilot: So... yeah. I guess we have a bit more waiting. Hey! Wanna watch *Battlestar Galactica* again? That'll put a dent in it. I found a couple of new webisodes while you had your earbuds in.

Pilot: Actually, I'm just going to go back to the isolation pod and take a little nap with myself. I mean, BY myself. So yeah... (*Starts getting up out of the cockpit seat.*)

Co-pilot: Ok, we'll just be here then. Hey! Did you see that? That Starship just disappeared.

18IPEIAJ-0418

4 FREE ISSUES + FREE GIFT

☐ **54 ISSUES** (1 year) at $1.92 each plus 23¢ p&h per issue, plus 4 FREE issues, for a total of 58! I get the Designer Tote FREE!

☐ **26 WEEKLY ISSUES** at $1.96 each plus 23¢ p&h per issue:
Does not include free issues or gift.

DESIGNER TOTE
with one-year term
on full payment

Name (please print)

Address _____ Apt. No. _____

City _____ State _____ Zip _____

E-mail _____ PEDPMB5

☐ Bill me later in full.   ☐ Bill me later in 4 easy installments.

To order faster, go to people.com/toteforfree Or call 1-866-784-9813

Subscribe today for your 4 FREE issues!

Order now at:
people.com/toteforfree

BUSINESS REPLY MAIL

FIRST-CLASS MAIL PERMIT NO. 10222 TAMPA FL

POSTAGE WILL BE PAID BY ADDRESSEE

PO BOX 62120
TAMPA FL 33663-1201

NO POSTAGE
NECESSARY
IF MAILED
IN THE
UNITED STATES

Pilot: Huh? So... no Kirk for you today?

Co-pilot: Kirk... Mmmm... I think I'll take a nap with ourselves a bit too. I mean, by ourselves. Or whatever.

Zoom out from cockpit to super-wide shot.

End.

Theorizing that one could time travel within his own lifetime, Dr. Grant Kien stepped into the quantum leap accelerator. And vanished... No wait, that's not right.

78. THE SAVAGE CURTAIN
THE GREAT SPECTACLE TRADING CARD SET
TONY CONTENTO

JAMES T. KIRK

Homeworld: Earth Birthplace: Riverside, Iowa, USA
Race: Human Birthdate: March 22, 2233
Death Date: November 18, 2293/2371
Allegiance: United Federation of Planets, Starfleet Command
Occupation: Starship Officer, Rank: Captain

Biography: James Tiberius Kirk was born on a farm, on Earth, in Iowa. If anything will make you want to leave Earth and bang green women, it is growing up in Iowa. Kirk joined Starfleet at the age of 17, following in his father's and grandfather's footsteps. Kirk impressed his instructors and pursued Command School. He served aboard the USS Farragut and the USS Constitution before he earned command of the USS Enterprise. He is known for his bravery, his recklessness and his ethics. The moral compass of James T. Kirk never wavers. He makes friends and enemies with equal ease. He goes out of his way to depose tyrants, right wrongs and suck faces with hot aliens.

Behind the Savage Curtain: When the Excalbians send Abraham Lincoln as their ambassador, Kirk views it as a gift. Even the morality test on the planet doesn't anger him in the beginning. Kirk has spent enough time in space to understand that alien races have an inherent need to screw with people. Kirk himself realizes that messing with someone for 22 minutes will tell you more about them than ten days of negotiations and conversation. So, in the beginning, Kirk is willing to play along. But Yarnek threatened Kirk's ship and crew. After that, Kirk was single-minded in his plan to win the Excalbian's game and save his crew. Neither Kirk nor Yarnek viewed this as nobility. To Kirk, the mission was all that ever mattered.

1

PHILIP GREEN

Homeworld: Earth Birthplace: Hanford, California, USA
Race: Human Birthdate: July 16, 1980
Death Date: sometime after 2056
Allegiance: The Fourth World military
Occupation: Tyrant, Ecoterrorist;
Fourth World Military Officer, Rank: Colonel

Biography: Philip Green was a 21st century military leader on Earth, responsible for the deaths of millions of people. Green has been said to have been an ally of Khan Noonien Singh, a former Presidential hopeful and a leader among the ecoterrorism group The Optimum Movement. Green used nuclear weapons to clear away people that he saw as unfit. Green was known for killing people at the negotiation table. Green survived the Eugenics Wars and the radioactive fallout that followed them. Legends say that he was killed by Flint the Immortal, who executed Green and his people with their own biological weapons.

Behind the Savage Curtain: Colonel Philip Green is a charming character. If he wasn't a backstabbing, genocidal maniac, he and Kirk might have been good friends. Green is a natural leader. He was able to bring a Klingon, a Mongol and "whatever Zora is" together to form a coherent fighting force that followed his orders, inside of fifteen minutes. That is pretty damned impressive. Sure, he tries out the old "kill you during negotiations" trick right off the bat, but Green maintains the upper hand until he kills Surak and Lincoln. Without their two heroes to cloud their judgment, Kirk and Spock end the scenario pretty quickly. Unfortunately for Colonel Green, the cards were always stacked against him. He was destined to lose, now and then.

2

SPOCK

Homeworld: Vulcan Birthplace: Shi'Kahr
Race: Vulcan-Human Birthdate: sometime during 2230
Death Date: June 4, 2285 Second Birthdate: Fall of 2285
Allegiance: United Federation of Planets, Starfleet Command
Occupation: Scientist; Starfleet Officer, Rank: Commander

Biography: Spock is the half-human son of Amanda Grayson and Sarek of Vulcan. Spock served as the Science Officer and second-in-command of the USS Enterprise under Captain Pike and Captain Kirk. Both Captains leaned on Spock as the steadfast voice of reason and logic. Spock's vast knowledge and intelligence has saved the Enterprise and countless worlds during his tour of duty. Spock is a student of the teachings of Surak: the way of logic. While Spock is known for controlling his emotions, the time that he has spent with Starfleet has revealed to him a value in the understanding of emotion.

Behind the Savage Curtain: When Abraham Lincoln shows up on the Enterprise, Spock is curious. He knows that someone on the planet is trying to manipulate Kirk, but he is too curious to persuade his Captain to "let it go". Spock determines that there is no harm in letting Kirk indulge in hero-worship. Then he meets a fake Surak. And Spock gets as pissed as a Vulcan can get (he raises BOTH eyebrows at the same time!). While Kirk had a great time showing Lincoln around the ship and introducing him to the 23rd century, when it comes to Surak, Spock is all business. Once the Excalbians reveal themselves, Spock has a single goal in getting himself and Kirk off the planet safely. There is no geekgasm from Spock meeting the coolest Vulcan ever. If anything, he gets colder than usual. Still, he appreciates Surak's noble sacrifice as a legitimate act of peaceful heroism.

3

GENGHIS KHAN (born Temujin)

Homeworld: Earth Birthplace: Dulun-Boldaq
Race: Human Birthdate: 1162
Death Date: August 1227
Allegiance: The Mongol Empire
Occupation: Warrior, Horseman, Tactician, General, Emperor

Biography: Temujin was born to a major Mongol chief, who was killed when he was very young. Temujin was forced to live a life of poverty, despite the fact that he was a descendant of one of the khagan, a Khan of Khans. Temujin was a shrewd politician, a fierce warrior and a brave commander. He united the Mongol tribes into what would become the Yuan Dynasty and became Genghis Khan, the first Mongol Emperor. He was known for his fierceness, but he also created a noble society that offered the possibility of wealth accumulation by commoners, religious freedom for all and even a postal service. His Yassa law book, while secret, created a code of conduct that stressed aspects of individualism and democracy that we still pursue today.

Behind the Savage Curtain: The Image of Genghis Khan was mute and followed the lead of Colonel Green. Unlike Kahless, who was a bit craven, Genghis Khan mostly fought and waited to see what would happen next. He never shied from battle, and he did not lower himself to the baser tactics used by Green and Kahless. Most of the nobility and intelligence of the Mighty Khan was stripped away, leaving behind an Asian guy with a recognizable name. Genghis Khan has been credited as one of the architects of modern society. The Image of Genghis Khan was only good for adding a little bit of zest to the evil team.

4

ABRAHAM LINCOLN

Homeworld: Earth Birthplace: Hodgenville, Kentucky, USA
Race: Human Birthdate: February 12, 1809
Death Date: April 15, 1865
Allegiance: The United States of America
Occupation: Attorney, Politician, Vampire Hunter

Biography: Abraham Lincoln is everyone's favorite president. From his stovetop hat to his impeccable beard, Lincoln looks presidential. Abraham Lincoln tore apart the Union, freed the slaves, won the Civil War and then put the country back together. The thanks for his near-miraculous leadership was a bullet in the head.

Behind the Savage Curtain: Lincoln is presented as Kirk's hero. Knowing what we know of Kirk, it is not difficult to determine why he loved Lincoln. Abraham Lincoln broke The Rules, as in The Constitution of the United States. Lincoln realized that the flaws in the Constitution would always prevent the Federal Government from ending slavery. So Lincoln took apart the Constitution and rebuilt the country from the ashes of a Civil War. Of course James T. Kirk adored this man. "Screw the rule book. Let's do what is right and get results."

The Image of Lincoln proves himself to be a decent tactician and maintains a level head during most situations. Given the opportunity, I am confident in saying that Lincoln would have been more than happy to keep hanging out with Kirk forever. Imagine that, Kirk having Lincoln as a wingman. The two of them guzzling Antarean brandy and cruising for ladies of all colors and creeds. I would watch that show.

5

KAHLESS "THE UNFORGETTABLE"

Homeworld: Qo'noS Birthplace: unknown,
possibly somewhere near the city of Qam-Chee
Race: Klingon Birthdate: sometime during the 9th century
Death Date: sometime during the 9th century
Allegiance: Honor and the Klingon Empire
Occupation: Warrior, Hunter, King, Emperor

Biography: The nobility of Kahless is sung by the Klingon people. The tale of how he defended Qam-Chee against Molar and his army is the basis for Klingon civilization. Together with his wife, Lukara, they forged the Klingon Empire under a banner of strength, with a foundation based on family, tradition and honor.

Behind the Savage Curtain: Of all of the Images of Yarnek, the Image of Kahless is the strongest proof that these constructs were built based on knowledge and opinions from Kirk, Spock and the Enterprise crew. The Kahless of Excalbia is a sneaky, brutish cutthroat, who resorts to the lowest of tactics in order to achieve his goals. From what we can glean from later accounts in Trek lore, Kahless the Unforgettable would have strode out onto the field of battle and met Kirk and Spock in fair combat. It is even possible that Kahless would have joined with them to first defeat Colonel Green and his crew and then put the Excalbian in his place.

However, he did not do any of that. He just followed Green around like a common thug. To top it all off, the Image of Kahless was a poor warrior. However, he was an excellent impersonator. Jonathan Winters and Rich Little have nothing on this guy.

6

230

SURAK

Homeworld: Vulcan Birthplace: on Vulcan, possibly near the desert called Vulcan's Forge
Race: Vulcan Birthdate: sometime during the 3rd century
Death Date: sometime during the 4th century
Allegiance: The Vulcan People; Peace, Healing and Logic
Occupation: Philosopher and Scientist

Biography: Surak, the greatest Vulcan philosopher. A true culture-bearer who pulled a violent culture back from the abyss and convinced them to embrace logic and understand the infinite diversity of the universe. He is the father of modern Vulcan society.

Behind the Savage Curtain: Surak is THE coolest Vulcan. Spock gets a little hot under the collar when Yarnek dares to create an "Image of Surak". When Surak calls Spock out, Surak is ready to give Spock crap. "Was that an emotional response?" "Yes." "Well, that's inappropriate, but whatever. We're still cool." Surak and Lincoln, both peacemakers, represent the two paths to peace. Surak attempts to understand and parlay with Colonel Green and his crew. It's a noble gesture, but everyone told Surak that it would only get him killed. It is possible that the Image of Surak knew that he would die, but he knew that there was nothing for him to lose as a false Image. His death in the name of peace might convince Kirk and Spock to maintain their nobility.

One thing to note is that Spock had to explain to Kirk who Surak was. Either Spock didn't feel like sharing or Kirk was a real jerk. Spock has been Kirk's first officer and friend for almost three years and Kirk doesn't know who the Vulcan "Jesus" is? That's just a little bit shitty.

7

ZORA

Homeworld: unknown, possibly Tiburon
Birthplace: unknown
Race: unknown
Birthdate: unknown
Death Date: unknown
Allegiance: unknown
Occupation: Scientist; Physiologist and Biochemist

Biography: Zora was an unethical and possibly insane scientist, interested in body chemistry. She had experimented upon the tribal peoples of Tiburon. These experiments have been described as extreme and akin to torture. While Zora's research took place on Tiburon, she does not resemble the common species of sentient life found on this world.

Behind the Savage Curtain: Zora, as a scientist interested in body chemistry, must have been fluent in advanced theory surrounding alien biochemistry and physiology. Someone like this would have been a dangerous combatant in any war. Zora could have devised chemical and biological weapons or potentially manipulated aspects of human and Vulcan physiology. The Image of Zora was bestial, dim-witted and excessively violent, almost as though she were a stuntwoman who remained silent and stuck to a purely physical mode of acting. As the only female combatant, she naturally spent the entire time fighting on the side of evil, trying to strangle her opponents while keeping her fur shirt from coming up too high above her midriff.

8

YARNEK

Homeworld: Excalbia Birthplace: the molten surface of Excalbia
Race: Excalbian Birthdate: sometime before 2269
Death Date: unknown Allegiance: The pursuit of knowledge
Occupation: Xenophilosopher and High-Caliber Dickery Expert

Biography: Little is known about the Excalbians. Yarnek might be the only member of his race. The Excalbians are centuries more advanced than the members of the Federation. They have shown the ability to scan human and Vulcan minds and manipulate matter and energy fields. Yarnek possessed an insatiable curiosity about the human condition. In particular, the concepts of good and evil drew his specific attention.

Behind the Savage Curtain: Yarnek explains that his intent is to study the concepts of good and evil, even though he does not subscribe to such silly notions. To Yarnek, existence is about pragmatism. He uses Kirk's and Spock's heroes to draw them into his experiment. These Images are rich and expressive characters. On the evil side, only Colonel Green has a true personality. Perhaps "evil" wasn't given a fair assessment via this experiment. Kirk accuses Yarnek of unnecessary cruelty, claiming that "We came in peace." Yarnek's pithy response "And you may go in peace," coupled with the fact that he chose to display this "spectacle" on every Enterprise viewscreen is proof enough that Yarnek is no better than humanity. Certainly, he has advanced technology and a superior intellect, but he understands evil as well as any sociopath. He dresses up his cruelty as science or philosophy, but his intent was always to control Kirk and Spock. Yarnek's spectacle is the alien equivalent of your older brother farting on your head and then telling you that it was always a test to see how long you could hold your breath. That may be true, but you still have a bad taste in your mouth.

9

Tony Contento is a mostly sane scientist from Central New York who spends his free time inventing new monkey wrenches and handing them out to children.

79. ALL OUR YESTERDAYS
SHE SHOULD HAVE DIED HEREAFTER
JULIAN GUNN

1. *All Our Yesterdays* comes late in original series chronology. It's the next-to-last episode broadcast: March 14, 1969. By Stardate, the episode is chronologically last, the end of the original series.
2. All this from the usual sources: Memory Alpha, Wikipedia.
3. This is a *third-season* episode. It belongs to the miracle season, the season of fan resurrection. The season that defied death.
4. The title of the episode refers, of course, to the great soliloquy Macbeth delivers just after he hears that Lady Macbeth is dead and just before he finds out that Birnham Wood is coming to Dunsinane after all:

> She should have died hereafter;
> There would have been a time for such a word.
> To-morrow, and to-morrow, and to-morrow,
> Creeps in this petty pace from day to day
> To the last syllable of recorded time,
> And all our yesterdays have lighted fools
> the way to dusty death. (*Macbeth*, Act V scene V)

5. The episode closes with Spock's paraphrase of another famous quotation from Renaissance drama, though fewer people know the source: Christopher Marlowe's *The Jew of Malta*. The original lines are: "But that was in another country/And besides, the wench is dead." What Spock actually says is, "But that was five thousand years ago, and she is dead now."
6. Since *Malta* is about power, greed and revenge — and, since that particular quotation comes from a pretty ghastly joke on the part of the title character — it seems like a strange choice for Spock to use to mourn his lost beloved.
7. Actually, *Macbeth* is about that, too.
8. Zarabeth is exiled by an offscreen tyrant, but our heroes are not being punished for greed or ambition: they are haplessly caught in time. The story is an existential tragedy, not a revenger's tale.
9. The episode seems to echo Macbeth's speech in other ways. It takes place at the "end of days" for that particular solar system, whose sun is about to go nova. The Library is a literalization of "recorded time." There is a quality of futility in the escape of the planet's inhabitants. Their history is over; all they can do is

loop endlessly back into the past. The future has disappeared.

10. There are actually two plot threads in *All Our Yesterdays*, but nobody cares about the other one. The point is that Spock loses his cool, and we all pretty much live for Spock losing his cool.

11. The premise: via a mysterious library, Kirk, Spock and McCoy are thrown back in time. It's sort of like *The City on the Edge of Forever*, but this time Spock and McCoy are together in an ice-age wasteland and Kirk is alone someplace else, while Spock falls in love instead of Kirk. McCoy gets incapacitated both times.

12. Here is a space where you can draw a diagram, if you'd like to compare the two configurations:

13. In plotline #1, Spock, psychically linked to his Vulcan ancestors (who are in a prehistoric state of ferocity), falls in love with the time-exiled Zarabeth, eats meat, gets violent and generally betrays his most cherished values in the most angsty way possible.

14. As usual.

15. In plotline #2, Kirk is trapped in a vaguely Cavalier era/vaguely British world and is imprisoned as a witch. He meets a woman, too, but she's a Bad Woman, a harlot sans heart of gold, deceitful, ungrateful and cowardly. She's sort of fun, except that she gets Kirk in trouble and she shouts too much. Plotline #2 is generally pretty shouty. Plotline #1 has the good stuff.

16. *All Our Yesterdays* is also the first episode of the series, in a way — at least for me. It's the first episode I ever saw.

17. Before the internet, before DVD box sets (but after syndication), it was pretty normal to enter a show mid-run. Most TV wasn't written with long story arcs, except for soap operas and a thing called a "miniseries". Everyone had their own entry point, like the old movie-house days when you could enter anywhere in the film and watch until the show got back around to the point where you came in. Viewership as infinite loop.

18. In the episode, the landing party watches DVDs, sort of, showing the planet Sarpeidon's past. For a while, this seemed prescient. Now it seems dated again.

19. I saw *All Our Yesterdays* at my grandmother's house in Vancouver, in deep syndication, sometime in the late 1970s or early 1980s.

20. My grandmother's house had turquoise siding. She grew fat blue hydrangeas in the narrow back yard, which was mostly concrete. The living room walls were covered with sheets of the inexpensive wood paneling that was popular at the time, the kind that makes all rooms look like the interior of a garden shed. I

loved watching TV at her house. Her TV was bigger than ours.

21. I was, you understand, at an impressionable age. My screen memory is of the scene where Zarabeth is sitting on her bed of furs, talking to Spock, shortly before he picks her up and twirls her around, by which emblematic dizziness we are meant to understand that they are overwhelmed with desire.

22. It was an awakening, of sorts.

23. It is entirely possible that I read A.C. Crispin's novel "Yesterday's Son" (1983, #11 in the series), a sequel to *All Our Yesterdays*, before I saw the episode again. In the 1980s, in the Cariboo region of British Columbia, the *Star Trek* novels were more accessible than the TV episodes.

24. Eventually, a single independent video store started carrying the episodes. My mom would drive me to the outskirts of town so that I could rent them. The whole series became available piecemeal, a few episodes at a time. Now it seems obvious that the store owner was taping them from TV, but that didn't occur to me at the time.

25. If memory serves, one recording was followed by a series of mildly pornographic mock-commercials. Even so, we didn't suspect that this was not the way the tape had originally been produced. A more innocent age.

26. This is also an elegy for the independent video store owners, those glorious larcenous cowpokes of the First Age of Duplication.

27. A.C. Crispin died of cancer in September 2013. In addition to writing many science-fiction novels, she co-founded a blog called *Writers Beware*. I followed the blog for years without ever quite remembering that this was the same person who had created Zar, Spock's son.

28. People make wonderful things for us, and then they die.

29. "Yesterday's Son" has a sequel, "Time for Yesterday" (1988, #39). I didn't like it as much as "Son". It seemed like a military/fantasy novel disguised as a science-fiction novel.

30. My top five original-series novels, all read before age 16:
    1. "Yesterday's Son" — A.C. Crispin (1983)
    2. "Uhura's Song" — Janet Kagan (1985)
    3. "The Wounded Sky" — Diane Duane (1983)
    4. "The Tears of the Singers" — Melinda Snodgrass (1984)
    5. "The Vulcan Academy Murders" — Jean Lorrah (1984)

31. I loved those books.

32. I mean, I really loved them. The books fill out and enrich the original universe with the dreams and hopes of dozens of science-fiction writers (people who tend to have pretty rich dream-and-hope worlds). These are hopes for a utopic pan-human future, when reason has overcome violence.

33. For a while, this seemed prescient.

34. My grandmother is dead, too — a long time ago now. Whenever I see hydrangeas,

I remember her. I think of them as grandmother flowers.

35. As of this writing, the screenwriter for *All Our Yesterdays*, Jean Lisette Aroeste, is still alive at 83. She is a retired librarian, which is awesome.

36. Support your local library. You never know when you might need to travel back in time.

Julian Gunn grew up in Prince George, British Columbia, and then he did some other things. He recently graduated with an MA in English from the University of Victoria.

80. TURNABOUT INTRUDER
"HOW MISOGYNIST IS IT?" *TURNABOUT INTRUDER* EDITION!
SAM MAGGS

Turnabout Intruder was the last episode of *Star Trek: The Original Series* to ever air on television, and that is a travesty, friends. *Turnabout Intruder* is not representative of the forward-thinking, boundary-pushing greatness that *Star Trek*, at its very best, has to offer the world. *Turnabout Intruder* isn't even an episode you might excuse on the spectrum of "so bad it's good" sci-fi. No, *Turnabout Intruder* is actually kind of the worst.

This decidedly lady-unfriendly hour of television originally aired on June 3rd, 1969, with story by none other than Gene Roddenberry himself. It's frequently voted the second-worst *TOS* episode *of all time*, kept from the dubious gold-medal honor by *Spock's Brain*. But where the latter at least attempts to make fun of itself with some lighthearted (?) mocking (??) of *Star Trek*'s female characters, *Turnabout Intruder* has very few redeeming qualities.

In order to determine exactly how terrible *Turnabout Intruder* really is, we're going to play a little game called "How Misogynist Is It?" Ready? Ha!

1. The episode is about Captain Kirk swapping bodies with an old flame, Janice Lester, who is bitter about rampant sexism in Starfleet.

This episode's conceit, handled correctly, actually isn't all that bad. In 1969, at the height of second-wave feminism, *Star Trek* could have used its allegorical sci-fi platform to explore women's rights and workplace gender bias in a thought-provoking and progressive manner. I say "could have", because that's the exact opposite of what goes down in *Turnabout Intruder*. But really, the concept is good; it's the execution that's flawed.

Misogyny Rating: 1 "Nice Guy in a Fedora" out of 5

2. William Shatner has to act like his body is inhabited by a woman.

Listen, Shatner might be a loveable ham in a good-lookin' girdle, but his portrayal of Janice-as-Kirk is at best offensive and at worst a transmisogynist mess. I'm sure we can place equal amounts of blame on the writer, director, actor and the contemporary environment in which they shot the episode; but no matter where you decide to direct your disgust, *Turnabout Intruder* is certain to generate plenty of it.

First, there's the starkness of how *Star Trek* chooses to portray the gender binary; as soon as he meant to "become" a woman, Shatner begins taking on characteristics stereotypically associated with "femaleness". This performativity not only manifests in subtle ways — like a slightly higher timbre to his voice or frequent touching of the hair and thighs — but also in preposterously over-the-top character actions: in one scene, Janice-as-Kirk files her nails while she talks to Bones.

Beyond the physical changes, Janice-as-Kirk also becomes increasingly absurd in personality and impotent in power. As captain of the *Enterprise*, Janice rants illogically, orders executions without reason, storms about on the bridge and throws tantrums more befitting a child than a Starfleet officer. In fact, the more Janice-as-Kirk attempts to assert control over the *Enterprise*, the less the ship's crew obeys. All of this, of course, is meant to demonstrate that women aren't fit for or capable of leadership in this context.

Meanwhile, we also have Captain Kirk trapped in Janice's body; a situation that, on several occasions, sees Kirk-as-Janice trying to convincingly act like a woman by putting on airs, giggles, cute smiles, flowery speech and weakness. Not only are we clearly being presented with an image of how *Star Trek*'s writers think women behave, we are also seeing on a more meta level how the writers want the audience to think Kirk believes women behave. Honestly, I'm pretty sure Kirk has had enough freaky alien sex in his life to know better, but that's just me.

Oh, and did I mention that Uhura *isn't even in* this episode? We've got brunette Nurse Chapel, who does nothing but take orders from men, and an unnamed "Communications Officer". It's probably for the best: Uhura would not have stood for this nonsense for a second.
Misogyny Rating: 4 "It's Actually Called A *Trilby*"s out of 5

3. Janice wants to take over Kirk's body because she hates being a woman.

The writers have given Janice some serious internalized misogyny. Through the episode, Janice says that to be a woman is to suffer a serious "indignity" and that "it's better to be dead than to live alone in the body of a woman". Even Kirk says that the reason he and Janice broke up was because "Her intense hatred of her own womanhood made life with her impossible."

The most disappointing part of this plot point is that the writers were actually on to something good here: Janice, as a successful, career-minded woman, would have been frustrated by the unfair restrictions placed on her by a society and an employer determined to hold her back based on her gender. In that sense, she's like most women throughout all of history across the globe since the beginning of time. But instead of engaging with this potentially progressive narrative in a thoughtful way, the show makes Janice look like a frantic female chauvinist. Janice, you deserved better.

Misogyny Rating: 7 Accusations of Misandry out of 10

4. Kirk's erratic behavior is blamed on "hysteria" because of course it is.

After Kirk loses control while attempting to court martial Janice, Scotty pulls Bones aside to discuss how wild things have gotten on the *Enterprise* (like this kind of thing doesn't happen all the time, please). Scotty tells the good doctor, "I've seen the captain feverish, sick, drunk, delirious, terrified, overjoyed, boiling mad. But, up to now, I have never seen him red-faced with hysteria."

Of course, there's a whole mess of nasty, sexist things that are tied up in the word "hysteria". The term originated way back with the Greeks and was used to describe any mental or physical illness in women that physicians assumed originated from disturbances in the uterus. This theory stuck around like so many Tribbles, gaining prominence in the nineteenth century, when doctors would use hysteria as an excuse for everything from keeping women out of the workplace to forcibly institutionalizing them for acting "unladylike". Scotty's use of the word "hysteria" here to describe Kirk's behavior is loaded with anti-female sentiment, and it's not okay.

But the more upsetting part of this complaint against Janice-as-Kirk's leadership skill is that the writers expect the audience to believe that now Kirk is "too emotional" to be captain. This is Kirk we're talking about: the king of emotion and intuition; the quick-to-anger, easily excitable foil to the logical, rule-driven Spock; the man who thinks with every other organ available to him before using his brain. But suddenly, as Janice, now the captain is "hysterical"? Scotty, please.

And for what it's worth, Spock clearly has the worst case of PMS onboard the *Enterprise*.

Misogyny Rating: 4 White Knights out of 5

5. Janice could never be a good Starfleet officer because she's insane.

Let's take a second to examine what, exactly, makes people think Janice is mentally ill. We're told she needs "quieting" a lot, and Kirk says that Janice has "driven herself mad with jealousy, hatred and ambition". Oh, my! Sounds like someone has

237

a problem with women who speak their minds and want to attain professional positions of power.

At its core, *Turnabout Intruder* reeks of a reactionary condemnation of Sixties' feminism. Men accustomed to their unchallenged positions of authority were wary of power-hungry, bra-burning women storming office buildings to take their jobs and painted them as "crazy" for potentially wanting more choices for their lives than just housewifery. *Turnabout Intruder* presents us with the perfectly clichéd feminist harpy; manipulative, out of control and thirsty for power that she immediately misuses. Eventually, Janice falls back to her "proper" station and is whisked away by Dr. Coleman (who, by the way, the audience has been told is incompetent) to be "taken care of" for the rest of her days. How very Victorian of them. Maybe Janice can share a room with Captain Pike's First Officer, Number One, who surely would have committed several crimes upon discovering that she could never ascend that last rung to captaincy.

The last line of *TOS* ever uttered on television belongs to Kirk: "Her life could have been as rich as any woman's, if only... if only..." If only she had accepted the constraints of a patriarchal society and stayed home and had babies like she was damn well supposed to, I guess. Right, Kirk?

Misogyny Rating: 9 "Not All Men"s out of 10

6. Starfleet doesn't allow women to command ships.

Even if you interpret Janice's initial exclamation to Kirk ("Your world of starship captains doesn't admit women!") to mean that Kirk's career doesn't allow him time for long-term relationships, there is a point later in the episode when Kirk flat-out says that Janice "would not be allowed to serve as the captain" of the *Enterprise*. As much as we all know, in hindsight, that this is blatantly untrue, there was a time when it was explicitly and canonically stated that women can't command starships. Yikes.

Misogyny Rating: 5 Fake Geek Girls out of 5

Total Episode Misogyny Rating for *Turnabout Intruder*: 10 Men's Rights Activists out of 10

Ultimately, *Turnabout Intruder* held real promise as an exploration of the difficulties facing women in the mid-century workplace, but instead the episode became a misogynist disaster — something we'll always have to live down as the final televised episode of *TOS*. But the beautiful thing about *Star Trek* is that, as time boldly goes forwards, so too does this fictional universe. We are fortunate to be able to look back at *Turnabout Intruder* from a post-Janeway perspective and know just how wrong

Kirk was about the women of Starfleet. We can only hope for more inspirational, kick-butt lady captains to come. If only... if only...

Thanks so much for playing "How Misogynist Is It?" We'll see you again for *Angel One*!

Sam Maggs is an Assistant Writer for BioWare, an unnamed Communications Officer in a short skirt and the bestselling author of The Fangirl's Guide to the Galaxy *and* Wonder Women *for Quirk Books. You can find her on Twitter @SamMaggs, if you're into that sort of thing.*

---

81. BEYOND THE FARTHEST STAR
A LETTER TO COMMANDER DOUGLAS
ADAM GOBESKI

Commander Irina Douglas
Starfleet Archive Project
San Francisco, Earth

Stardate: 5536.7

Dear Commander Douglas,

Upon the suggestion of a colleague of yours, Dr. Jason Korkmaz, I'm writing to you about the recent upgrade of the passive recording system installed on board the *Enterprise*. Although we've been assured that the technology is working within its specifications, and while we recognize that it's an improvement over the previous system, we nevertheless have one rather pressing concern: for reasons we have yet to properly determine, all the recordings are being rendered as if they were some form of crude animation. (I have attached an edited video log from the recent events of Stardate 5221.3 — what we've been informally calling *Beyond the Farthest Star*, in reference to the *Enterprise*'s location at the time of the incident — as an example of what I mean by this.) Repeated investigations have been unable to determine the cause of this effect. It's not mentioned in any of the technical documentation, and, as far as we can tell, no other ships or facilities using the new system are reporting a similar problem. Chief Engineer Scott has gone over the circuits with a fine-tooth comb and he can't work out why the recordings all look like a cartoon. (And, as an aside, he also suspects that certain colors are occasionally being rendered incorrectly, so that, for example, some greys turn bright pink, but we don't have any conclusive evidence of this yet. However, this is a side issue and not our main problem.)

Now, of course, other than from a purely aesthetic point of view, this shouldn't really be an issue. After all, it's not as though the events recorded are any less accurate than anything the *Enterprise* has submitted from the previous three years of her mission. Yet we've noticed that certain people have started treating these reports differently from our earlier ones. In particular, there seems to be an increased amount of suspicion regarding the veracity of our recordings, and it hasn't escaped our attention that some people have been going so far as to suggest in official reports that these might be faked. This is thus a serious concern.

As you are no doubt aware, the *Enterprise*, by the nature of her current five-year mission, has encountered some unusual phenomena that have occasionally been greeted with skepticism; for instance, the events of Stardate 3468.1, regarding the being calling himself "Apollo", have often been subjected to more intense scrutiny due to the nature of the incident. (Or, as we saw one person put it, "Greek gods in space? What next, Methuselah alive and well?" Needless to say, the events of 5843.7 hardly reassured him.) However, Captain Kirk's reports have always been vindicated by the recorded data, and even the most skeptical have been forced to agree that these events did in fact happen.

But now, with the new system in place, we've found that even relatively straightforward occurrences (such as the one in the attached video log) are being treated with a measure of disbelief. As you can see, there's nothing in that record that should lead to its integrity being called into question; in fact, it's almost mundane by the standards of the *Enterprise*'s usual encounters. But, because of the cartoon-like quality of the visuals, it's now being treated as suspect. In particular, Chief Archivist Roddenberry at the Memory Alpha facility, though initially positive about the new upgrades, has become more and more vocal about his misgivings of the reports and data provided. As he has been almost unceasing in his efforts to reestablish the facility's database after the Zetarian disaster, his opinions have been carrying greater weight recently, and, as far as we can tell, his objections stem simply from the manner in which the records are being presented.

We're therefore understandably concerned that, if Memory Alpha ultimately chooses not to store our recordings in their database, this will start a chain of events that could lead to the discrediting of our recent explorations. If even routine missions are being called into question (and I would like to point out that a somewhat similar event, the "Jack the Ripper" case from Stardate 3614.9, was accepted by Commodore Roddenberry without any reservations), then our worry is that more unusual encounters will be completely dismissed as apocryphal, and for this to be the result of essentially a technological bug is particularly vexing.

Captain Kirk is insistent that this situation be resolved as quickly as possible (as he told our staff, "When I said that the *Enterprise* was recording all data for the log and a full report later, this isn't what I meant"), lest the fourth year of the *Enterprise*'s mission be reduced to a footnote in the historical records (or, worse yet, be removed altogether). Since the upgrade was one of the projects in your department, we were hoping you might be able to shed some light on this problem. Any advice or help you can give us would be greatly appreciated.

Sincerely,
Lieutenant Adam Gobeski
USS *Enterprise*, Chief Records Officer

Like Jim Kirk, Adam Gobeski was never a Boy Scout.

---

82. YESTERYEAR
TIMES CHANGE — AGAIN AND AGAIN
GLENN GREENBERG

"Star Trek is dead — and J.J. Abrams killed it."
"Star Trek has been completely wiped out, erased, written over by a new alternate timeline created in J.J. Abrams' image."

The above comments represent some of the more... impassioned reactions to the 2009 film *Star Trek*, directed by Abrams, which revived and rebooted the franchise. The movie begins in the *Star Trek* universe with which we're familiar, but, after a time traveler changes the past, a new timeline is created. Many longtime, hardcore fans were troubled, even appalled, by this creative move. They lamented the loss of what they considered the real, original *Star Trek*.

Interesting words, "real" and "original" — especially when it comes to *Star Trek*. Because the *Star Trek* universe we know (and presumably love), the one that began in 1966 and continued on in a more-or-less unbroken thread of continuity up until the 2009 movie, is neither the real nor the original universe.

Poppycock, you say? (Or, as the Klingons would say, "Pah pee kahk!") Well, double poppycock on you!

In the wake of the first J.J. Abrams film, the previous incarnation of *Star Trek* has come to be considered the "prime universe". But the fact is, it's really Prime Universe B.

And this was established fairly early in *Star Trek*'s nearly 50-year history: 1973, when the series was only 7 years old. It was revealed that in the true Prime Universe, a half-Vulcan boy named Spock died at the age of 7, his human mother

Amanda killed in a shuttle accident a short time later. There is no Commander Spock, Science Officer of the USS *Enterprise*. His role aboard that ship is filled by an Andorian named Thelin.

It turns out that the only reason there was ever an adult Spock is because the 7-year-old version was saved by a mysterious man claiming to be his cousin Selek — but Selek was really the adult Spock, having traveled back in time to save the life of his younger self.

Can you say, paradox? (Or as the Klingons would say, "Pah rih dahkhs!")

This story does not come from some easily dismissed *Star Trek* novel or comic book or amateur fanzine. It was aired on television — on NBC, no less. It was written by D.C. Fontana, one of the best, most important contributors to the original *Star Trek* TV series. It featured performances by William Shatner, Leonard Nimoy and DeForest Kelley in their iconic roles. And, perhaps most importantly, it had the official stamp of approval from Gene Roddenberry himself.

The story is *Yesteryear*, and it was an episode of *Star Trek: The Animated Series*. In the episode, Kirk and Spock use the time portal known as the Guardian of Forever to visit the planet Orion at the dawn of its civilization. While they're away, Federation scientists in the present (well, the 23rd century, anyway) use the Guardian to study Vulcan history from 30 years prior. That's when Spock, in the guise of Cousin Selek, saved his 7-year-old self. But since Spock is off in the distant past, on Orion, and he can't be in two places at once, Little Spock dies during the Vulcan equivalent of his bar mitzvah. So when Kirk and Spock return from Orion, no one but Kirk remembers Spock. Investigating the circumstances surrounding his death, Spock remembers that he had actually been saved by Cousin Selek, and he realizes that he must have been Selek all along. So he uses the Guardian to go to Vulcan, 30 years in the past, to set things right.

What we learn here is that "Selek" was always part of Spock's history. But that simply can't be, because if Spock died as a child, there could be no Adult Spock to go back in time to save him. This then begs the questions: What caused the paradox that allowed for the existence of Adult Spock? Was there a real Cousin Selek originally? If so, what happened to him? Unfortunately, these questions will probably remain unanswered — unless Ms. Fontana decides to address them in a new story. (I, for one, would love to see that happen.)

But the bottom line is, our *Star Trek* universe, the one we know best, is not the original. Because in the original, which I hereby refer to as Prime Universe A, Spock died as a kid.

Incidentally, while Adult Spock is successful in saving Li'l Spock, the tyke's pet sehlat, a large bearlike creature named I-Chaya, dies after protecting the lad from a ferocious, poisonous animal called a le-matya. This conflicts with Adult Spock's memories of the event; he specifically notes that the sehlat didn't die when "Selek" saved him as a boy.

This means that, going forward from this episode, we're not even really back in Prime Universe B. We're now in an altered Prime Universe B — presumably Prime Universe C! And to complicate matters even further, in the newly created Universe C, we have both a Kid Spock whose pet sehlat died while protecting him, and the Spock of Universe B, who remembers the sehlat surviving. This inevitably leads one to ask: what ultimately happens to the Kid Spock of Universe C? Obviously, he grows up to become Commander Spock of the U.S.S *Enterprise*, and his life more or less matches that of "Spock B." But remember, when "Spock B" returns to his proper time via the Guardian of Forever, he's in Universe C from that point on. As far as I know, there aren't two Spocks running around the universe going forward from there, so something must have happened to "Spock C" so that "Spock B" could take his place. Did "Spock C" simply cease to exist? Did he get shunted into yet another alternate timeline? If so, did being displaced screw him up and piss him off so much that he decided to grow a goatee...?

(You know, while I'm at this, I also have to wonder: Back in Prime Universe A, is Khan Noonien Singh a dark, charming, charismatic, exotic warrior with a massive chest, or is he a pale, cold, skinny Brit? Just curious...)

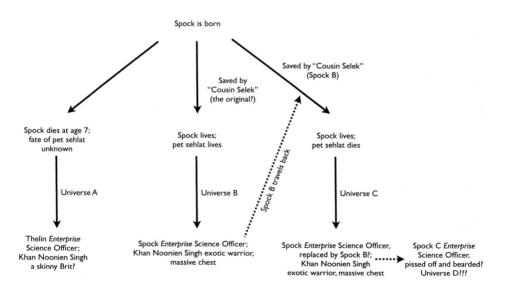

The really sad thing about *Yesteryear*, even more so than the death of Wee Spock's beloved pet, is the fact that, by all appearances, the universe as a whole is really no different, no worse off, without Spock. Starfleet, Kirk, McCoy and the *Enterprise* crew all seem to be fine. Science Officer Thelin is a capable, valuable officer — and a pretty nice guy, too, considering he wishes Spock luck on his mission to the past to save himself, even though Spock's success will alter Thelin's life considerably. It's troubling to think that the *Star Trek* universe would be so unaffected by the absence of one of its key inhabitants.

It must be acknowledged that, sometime in the late 1980s, Gene Roddenberry apparently declared *The Animated Series* not part of the official canon, but, really, that's kind of like trying to declare you're still a virgin because later on you decide that you weren't all that thrilled with the first person you slept with. Roddenberry worked on *The Animated Series*, he approved everything, it aired on TV, and it's been released on VHS, laserdisc and DVD. It's still out there for people to watch. It's part of the whole. Besides, in the late 1980s, Roddenberry was responsible for *Encounter at Farpoint* and the bulk of the first season of *Star Trek: The Next Generation*, so it's not like his judgment at that point was unimpeachable.

So to sum up. Spock: never supposed to make it to adulthood. The universe: unchanged by his absence (see flowchart). Alternate timelines in *Star Trek*: existed long before J.J. Abrams. Khan in *Star Trek Into Darkness*: bad casting.

Okay, beam me up, Scotty. My work here is done.

For Marvel Comics, Glenn Greenberg conceived and wrote the acclaimed comic-book limited series Star Trek: Untold Voyages. *For Simon and Schuster, he wrote "The Art of the Deal" and "The Art of the Comeback", two installments of the long-running* Star Trek: Starfleet Corps *of Engineers e-book series. glenngreenbergsgrumblings.blogspot.com.*

83. ONE OF OUR PLANETS IS MISSING
A GIANT BLOB-CLOUD'S GUIDE TO EATING AROUND THE GALAXY
ANGELA PRITCHETT

Hello there, fellow Giant Blob-Cloud Foodies! Hope you have been having some great travels through space; I know I have! Thanks for taking the time to make your way to my blog! Are you looking for great ways to make your meals of small planets and ships taste better? Then read no further, my friends, for I have been there too! I am just a humble blob-cloud that has traveled from galaxy to galaxy and even had a Federation Starship in my belly (though it did not agree with me well). In this entry, I will show you how to prepare and enjoy your planets to their fullest. Just hope those planets aren't inhabited, because that same Federation Starship that didn't agree with me also let me know we have been consuming planets with many life forms on them, and that isn't some crazy Giant Blob-Form propaganda either! But, back to the topic, which is preparing your planets so they taste amazing as you slowly let them break away inside of you! And, for you lower life forms on those planets that may have found your way here, I have added recipes next to the blob-cloud ones, so you can enjoy in the culinary goodness as well!

First off, we will start with one of my favorites: Planet Pizza! Ingredients and Directions for your Planet Pizza:

- Find One Round Planet (round pizza crust any size or Naan bread for those pesky meteors) and lay it out on your blob table.
- Next you need your water or lava oceans (Marinara or Alfredo Sauce). Spread those out over your planet.
- Sprinkle it with a little bit of pollution (cheese) to help make it extra tasty and give you lots of energy.
- Then add some small plants that are indigenous to your planet (black olives, onions and green peppers, banana peppers, etc)
- Add some local life forms, if eating local life forms is up your alley (Italian Sausage cut into thick rounds)
- Next put your planet on a blob oven-safe cooking sheet/pan, and stick it into your blob oven for 25 minutes at 375 degrees F (190 degrees C)
- Once it is done, devour your planet and soak in all its wonderful nutrients.

Planet Pizza not up your alley? Well, how about something a bit sweeter to help your nonexistent blob sweet-tooth? Try these incredibly yummy *macromorphase enzymes* mist cookies! They will help break down your food and make your craving for sweets go away!

Ingredients:

For this fantastic Giant Blob-Cloud recipe, you will need to break down our *macromorphase* enzymes that are found in our blob mist DNA that helps us process our foods. Once you have these, you can create as many fantastic *macromorphase enzyme* mist cookies as you want! They are helpful to our bodies and very tasty! I believe the lower life forms, called humans, refer to these as lemon-flavored!

1. Broken Down *Macromorphase Enzyme* 1 (3 egg whites, warm)
2. Broken Down *Macromorphase Enzyme* 2 (1/2 tsp cream of tartar)
3. Broken Down *Macromorphase Enzyme* 3 (1/4 tsp salt)
4. Broken Down *Macromorphase Enzyme* 4 (1 tsp vanilla extract)
5. Broken Down *Macromorphase Enzyme* 5 (3/4 cup sugar)
6. Broken Down *Macromorphase Enzyme* 6 (zest of 2 lemons)

- The directions for making these wonderful blob cookies are simple! Heat your blob oven to 275 degrees F (135 degrees C). Line your Macromorphase Enzyme Sheets (cookie sheets) with non-stick space debris (parchment paper.)
- In a blob stand mixer bowl, combine Enzymes 1–4 (egg whites, cream of tartar, salt and vanilla extract) until there are soft peaks, like the mountain peaks of the last planet you devoured.
- In a clean bowl, stir Enzyme 5 (sugar) and Enzyme 6 (lemon zest) together.
- Slowly add the mixture of Enzymes 5–6 to the first mixture, one spoonful at a time, while beating it in the mixer.
- Once the mixture is fully incorporated, you can use a spoon to drop each cookie onto the Macromorphase Enzyme Sheets (cookie sheets.)
- Bake them for 30 minutes. Once done, turn off oven and leave the cookies in there for a few hours to make sure they are completely dry and ready to help you devour whatever you may come across in space to eat!

Whether you are looking for something savory and filling or sweet for a snack, you can find it all floating around in space for you to devour in your Giant Blob-Mist belly! Try out these wonderful recipes to help you get the most from your travels in space to find food and energy to stay alive! And watch out for those Federation Starships! They have a lot of delicious energy, but will leave you with one awful bellyache. Trust me, they were delicious, but — after having them rummage around in my stomach, being stubborn and not digesting into energy — I was more than ready for them to get out and go back on their mission. Only sad thing was I did not get to devour the delicious-looking planet Mantilles. Guess that will have to be another adventure into a new and exciting area of the galaxy, and hopefully the planet won't be filled with lower life forms!

Angela Pritchett is an American author, actress, makeup FX artist and avid cook. She writes short fiction in the genres of sci-fi, horror and fantasy. You can find anthologies she is in at amazon.com/author/angelapritchett

84. THE LORELEI SIGNAL
NOR ANY DROP TO DRINK
STEPHANIE GUERDAN

INT: FAMILY TV ROOM

A young woman enters alone with a tray of drinks and takes a seat on the couch. She has a quiet, bookish appearance and addresses her lines to her cat. Pause between lines to give the impression the cat is responding.

STEPHANIE: Okay, Sophie. It's feminist-drinking-game night, and I'm drinking to *Star Trek* cartoons. Don't give me that judgmental look.

STEPHANIE cues up the DVD player. The Star Trek *theme plays and the title card, which reads* The Lorelei Signal*, appears onscreen. She pauses the episode and pulls up a document on her computer titled "awful seductress-plot drinking game.docx"*

STEPHANIE: All right, kitten, are you ready for this? The siren trope is the worst; people still fail at unsexist-ing it in 2016, and this episode's from 1973. Buckle up for a nightmare.

The cat is unresponsive. STEPHANIE begins to mix herself a drink and fullscreens the document. A close up shot pans down to show us the list of the drinking game's rules.

Rules document should read:

- Whenever the bad ladies are sexy and the good ladies are sexless, drink one.
- Whenever the writing ignores the possibility of same-sex attraction, drink one
- Whenever the bad ladies sex up the men and it's portrayed as sexy rather than nonconsensual, drink one
- Misandry jokes, drink one
- Whenever the good women blame the men for being tricked/roofied/assaulted, drink one
- Whenever the good ladies are jealous of the bad women getting to (nonconsensually) sleep with the men, drink one
- "The more stereotypically manly a character is, the more susceptible he is to the bad woman's wiles", drink one.

STEPHANIE hits the play button, and the episode resumes.

STEPHANIE: Wait, did it say a lady wrote this?

She rewinds the episode a little.

STEPHANIE: Damn, Margaret Armen! I hope you know what you're up against...

Initially, the episode progresses naturally. Kirk and co. pick up a signal, trace it, etc.

STEPHANIE: Jesus, Sophie, the men are literally all hallucinating and they're aware of it, yet they are still sending an all-male landing party.

The cat licks her paw.

STEPHANIE: It's not about men being idiots, Sophie, it's about common sense. That's all I'm saying.

STEPHANIE: Man, I want to meet security officer Davison. She sounds like the kind of person who can kick your ass without chipping her nail polish.

STEPHANIE goes to take a sip of her alcoholic drink and catches herself. She scans the list of rules, sighs, and cracks open a soda instead.

STEPHANIE: Okay, I know this is like, stylized animation, but Theela and company's boobs literally point outward to their left and right like Lady Gaga's prosthetic cheekbones. There are no natural humanoid chests shaped that way.

STEPHANIE: I wonder what the gravity is like on this planet. They just lifted all these dudes and tossed them like beach balls. I guess they're not human? Maybe the gravity is why their boobs are so weird.

STEPHANIE takes another sip of her soda and burps.

STEPHANIE: Ugh, Scotty's singing is giving me flashbacks to *The Naked Time*. I am not drunk enough for this.

STEPHANIE winces as Spock makes a shriek-y humming noise.

STEPHANIE: They should reeeally make that Opto-orb more secure. Apparently just anyone can hum at it and it works just fine. This must have been before password protection.

STEPHANIE: This whole female landing party is redshirts... well, red dresses... and I bet not a single one dies. It'd be par for the course; nothing is working out how I expected in this episode. Wait, why is Nurse Chapel in red?

A few seconds pass.

STEPHANIE: Oh. I guess that was an animation error.

STEPHANIE winces down into her near untouched drink.

STEPHANIE: I'm never gonna finish this. How is this even possible? I was *ready and waiting* to be offended and drunk, and instead I'm impressed and sober. I should have made "Whenever Theela stares directly into the audience" a rule.

The cat gets up and jumps off the couch.

STEPHANIE: Sophie, no! They're doing some sort of crazy hand-waving science magic with the transporters!

The cat leaves. STEPHANIE sits in silence as the episode concludes and the credits roll.

STEPHANIE: You know what, screw it. I'm making a new game.

STEPHANIE sets down her drink and picks up her laptop. She opens up a new document and begins typing. The first words she types are "The Lorelei Signal Drinking Game".

The new document should read:

- Whenever Theela stares directly into the audience, drink one
- Whenever anyone says "female", drink one
- Whenever Uhura is more perceptive than anyone else, drink one
- Whenever anyone makes that annoying humming noise to turn on the Opto-Orb, drink one
- Whenever the male landing party's stylish Life-Draining Tiaras™ glow, drink one.

STEPHANIE finishes typing with a flourish. She stands and yells into the hallway.

STEPHANIE: Sophie! Get back here! We're gonna watch it again!

Stephanie Guerdan is a hot mess sometimes,
but at least she's a feminist hot mess. Also, she blogs.

---

85. MORE TRIBBLES, MORE TROUBLES
SOMEDAY WE'LL LEARN
CAIT COKER

Airing in 1973, just three years after the advent of Earth Day, *More Tribbles, More Troubles* is a comedy about eco-balance and genetic modification. Also, Klingons. (Poor Klingons.) This probably doesn't sound like a natural combination, and it's not, but this reading provides a different narrative closure than we receive from the story itself. *More Tribbles, More Troubles* manages to hint not just at the continuity of the greater *Trek* world, but at the world-building possibilities inherent in futurist environmentalism.

The episode functions as a direct sequel to the *TOS* episode *The Trouble with Tribbles*, with the *Enterprise* returning to Sherman's Planet with quintrotriticale, an updated version of quadrotriticale. Two years after the first mission, they appear to be undergoing the same crop failures and famine referenced before, despite the United Federation of Planets having developed a new grain. Kirk and crew once more run into trader and nuisance Cyrano Jones, who is fleeing a Klingon ship led by Captain Koloth (say that three times fast) under charges of ecological sabotage, as he has continued his trade in Tribbles. When Kirk confronts Jones for violating the law concerning the transport of harmful animals, he claims that they are safe, to which McCoy acerbically replies, "There's no such thing as a safe Tribble." Jones is also travelling with a Tribble predator, called a glommer, that helpfully (and neatly, according to McCoy) disposes of excess Tribbles. (In the audio commentary released with the DVD, author David Gerrold said an initial draft of the script mentioned the glommers being a little too eager in their duties, and as a consequence several *Enterprise* crew members were "missing".) However, it turns out that the glommer is also genetically engineered — by the Klingons — and the only one of its kind. Hijinks and tensions ensue when the Klingons want it back.

At the time the episode was written and aired, there had been a years-long push for greater attention to the environment. Rachel Carson's bestseller *Silent*

Spring was published in 1962, and the U.S. Public Health Service organized a Human Ecology Symposium in 1968. The United States Environmental Protection Agency was inaugurated in 1970, and the first Clean Air and Waters Restoration Acts were implemented that same year. The Endangered Species Preservation Act was passed in 1966 — the same year that *Star Trek* debuted. While the show was founded as "*Wagon Train* to the stars" with implications of a kinder, gentler expansionism (and even Manifest Destiny), it is impossible to not acknowledge that a future in space would have to derive from maintaining life on Earth.

A curiosity of the *Star Trek* franchise is that it hesitates in confronting environmentalism. With the notable exception of the *ST:TNG* episode *Force of Nature* (which brings up the idea of space becoming, erm, warped because of warp drives, concludes with the Federation disseminating recommendations to avoid high warp speeds if at all possible and then references the concept in only two other episodes), the importance of eco-awareness and balance are seldom addressed — presumably because, in the future utopia of the Federation, it has been successfully sorted out. Thus it's interesting that one of the few episodes to touch on it is in *The Animated Series*, and presented as a comedy at that. While the plot concludes more or less neatly with the return of the glommer (and a number of Tribbles) to the Klingons, we also get a better understanding of the fictional politics of maintaining planetary environmental protections. While *The Trouble with Tribbles* demonstrated the dangers of certain animals onboard a closed environment like a starship — eating food supplies, entering air vents and distracting crew members — *More Tribbles, More Troubles* hints at the devastations possible on entire planets when outside species are introduced.

Despite being invented as an additional farcical gag whose final punchline is pulled, the genetically engineered glommers are equally interesting for how they are presented as a viable solution: a dominant predator engineered to solve the problem of an invasive species. However, the episode does not address the next logical question: what happens to glommers when the Tribbles run out? Well, presumably more troubles, though hardly small ones. As our own real history has aptly demonstrated (whether through kudzu plants, lionfish or cane toads), the introduction of one invasive species after another is hardly the ideal solution and, indeed, can cause many more problems than it solves.

As the episode concludes with both ships filled with Tribbles and Kirk's rueful statement, "Someday I'll learn," we have to wonder when (if ever) we will indeed learn to maintain environmental balance. It is worth noting that the idealistic future seems largely unprepared for how to handle transplanted species aside from some general rules against transporting "harmful" animals. One would think that something along the lines of an environmental prime directive might be in effect: a solemn vow to not affect another planet's ecology. *More Tribbles, More Troubles* shows us then, literally, how little problems can quickly becomes big ones — but ones that don't always have easily implementable answers.

Cait Coker is a writer in Boulder, Colorado, where she eagerly awaits her promised future space-faring utopia.

86. THE SURVIVOR
IMPRINTED
PAUL BOOTH

Excerpts from *Security and Survivors: My Life in (and out) of Starfleet*, the autobiography of Commander Anne Nored, ret. (published Stardate 8532.4).

Back cover blurbs:
"Will (shape) shift your perspective on life, love and the future of relationships. Highly recommended."

—Captain James Schermer, USS *Sutherland*

"Nored asks us to question whether or not someone can be the same person if their physical body is changed... an interesting philosophical discussion that has yet to be fully answered."

—T'Pol, Vulcan Ambassador

"Full of wit and energy! Also, alien sex!"

—StarTwitter user @luvsPADDbook5143

Chapter 1: An Awakening
Most people know me as Lt. Anne Nored, (former) security officer on board the *USS Enterprise*. I suppose that's who I'll always be. But I am more than that, and my life has been changed (shifted?) in more ways than I can count. Are any of us who we appear to be?

My life and my love prove that we are always shifting, always changing; that appearances are just skin deep; and that you never really know someone until you walk a mile in their shoes. Or their feet, for that matter.

[...]

Chapter 4: My Life Changes Again... and Again

No one really knows what they would do in certain situations until they happen to you. What would you do if you were being attacked by a Gorn? How could you speak to a creature made of silicon? What would you do if your lover came back to life and could change his form?

My world changed on Stardate 5143.3 when I found out the answer to this last question. As readers will recall, Carter Winston was the most renowned philanthropist of the 23rd century. He gave most of his wealth to save Federation colonies — including the colony of Cerebus during the infamous crop failure of 2259. He was beloved and honored by billions of lives across the galaxy, until his disappearance near the Romulan Neutral Zone in 2264.

But to me he was just Carter, the man with whom I was thoroughly — and dangerously — in love.

By now the story must be familiar to many of you, especially if you've read the (ludicrously exaggerated) *Redshirt by the Bed: The Dirty Secrets of a Starfleet Lackey* by Lt. John "Winston" Kyle. I had been serving as a security officer aboard the *Enterprise* when, on a routine mission (aren't they all?), we found a one-man capsule stranded in space. Aboard was Carter, missing for years, and he looked as healthy as that day we first met at Angelino's Café on Orion. But it wasn't Carter — not the Carter I knew. It was a Vendorian in the *shape* of Carter. He claimed to have nursed Carter for over a year, helping him after his ship had crashed on his planet. Upon Carter's death, the Vendorian (whose name I have since learned, but promised never to reveal) began to impersonate him. The Vendorians' ability to shapeshift meant that Carter's mind — his soul, really — *imprinted* on the Vendorian. The longer he stayed in Carter's form, the more he took on his memory, emotion and attitudes. He did feel some of the emotions Carter felt. He did know that Carter's love for me was strong. In the end, I couldn't help myself; I fell in love with him all over again.

[...]

When Carter returned — no matter who he was — I knew my life would shift forever.

[...]

Chapter 7: We Return to Vendor

Living with a Vendorian, even one that looks and acts like a human, can be a trying experience. Of course, when they fall asleep, they revert back to their natural state: a floating red head, four glowing yellow eyes and six tentacles. And, as anyone will tell you, having a shape shifter for a lover certainly opens doors that I didn't even knew existed before...

[...]

But of course there's one question that I guess most of you readers are curious about. It's something I've been asked for years, ever since I resigned from Starfleet to concentrate on my charity work. And that is: can someone be the same person if they aren't in the body they grew up in?

The Carter Winston I was engaged to was a wonderful, generous man. The Carter Winston I am currently married to is also a wonderful, generous man. When the Vendorian Carter came aboard the *Enterprise*, it changed my life forever. When he said, "It's over between us, Anne. I'm sorry I can't explain why, but I can't marry you, ever," I was heartbroken, not just because of his rejection but because he assumed I couldn't understand his reasoning.

But, when you think about it, don't we all change? Every day, I am different from the person I was yesterday. And the day before that. And before that. Each of us is always shifting, always changing, from one day to another. Every situation brings new ideas, and we simply react to it in the way that we think we should act. All we can hope to be is the best version of who we are at any particular moment. All we can hope to do is make the world just a little bit better. Our actions and our ideas, not something as empty as our bodies, help to determine who we are.

Back in the late twentieth century, before people had become really comfortable with the idea of "difference", there was a lot of anger about people who felt like they were in the wrong bodies. And, in the early 21st, people actually resented and feared those who tried to find the bodies that felt correct for them. Change is a part of life, but sometimes, when that change appears to be drastic or appears to be something that goes against what "normal" people feel, it can be threatening to people who don't understand. But, just like people, society can shift and change as well, sometimes into things that we don't really even recognize until one day we wake up, look at the world around us and realize that it's home.

Vendor-Carter didn't think I would understand. But I did. Carter Winston may not be the man I met, but then again I'm not the same as I was either. Are you?

➤➤➤

Notice for publishers: Although Ms. Nored is unavailable for interviews and promotions, Mr. Carter Winston can step in for her in a pinch.

Paul Booth is a professor of Media and Cinema Studies at DePaul University who writes about Star Trek, Supernatural *and* Doctor Who.

87. THE INFINITE VULCAN
LONG DISTANCE
J. ALLAN MORLAN

With a ping, AIM popped up another message:

SULU: Hey, a purple Tribble! I'll cuddle it! [picks it up]
PURPLE TRIBBLE-ish THING: [STABINATES]
SULU: :-)

Grabbing suspicious-looking alien pincushions with your bare hands? Standard Starfleet protocol, I typed back, grinning as I glanced between the glowing monitor and the flickering TV screen. This was before YouTube, so if you wanted to riff on the same show at the same time with someone who lived 7000 miles away, this was how it was done. The pencil icon showed she was typing again:

McCOY: We can't just let some freak alien thing stab its alien googoo juice into our officer!
KIRK: YES WE CAN!
FREAKISH PLANT THING: [STABINATES]

With an undignified snort, I replied: *And now we enjoy an artistic close-up of the upper right quadrant of Kirk's face, ensuring that any potentially expensive-to-animate mouth movements occur safely out of frame.*

Meanwhile, Spock stands uselessly and statically in the background, she typed back, *but we don't mind, because Animated!Spock is pretty.*

Online, she went by Erythraia. I didn't know her real name or much else about her, except that she lived in New Zealand and she made me laugh. *The Animated Series* was just the latest thing we'd found to laugh about together; you wouldn't believe, for example, how funny the original legend of Hamlet was before the Bard got his hands on it.

"Scans show that these aliens use 70% of their brains," Spock noted sagely in my headphones. "A very high ratio."

KIRK: It's a good thing you're pretty, Legolas.

I started to laugh, then quickly stifled it. It was the middle of the night and my little brother was sleeping on the other side of the wall.

I took another sip of Coke, and then almost choked on it, eyes going wide as our heroes were accosted by some kind of... pterodactyl... tentacle... slinky... I made several false starts at trying to put into words what we were seeing, typing and backspacing. Erythraia's pencil icon was solidly, confidently on.

Indescribable purple spring-loaded freakdragons, ATTACK!

My eyes were watering as I tried to somehow clear my throat without making any noise, while simultaneously trying not to laugh as I watched the spring-loaded freakdragons carry poor, pretty Animated!Spock away to an uncertain fate.

Keeping quiet didn't get easier as we finally beheld the villain of the piece, Keniclius (or "Keniculus", as half the cast seemed to think), a majestically towering human with a majestically towering widow's peak and some kind of pseudo-Classical miniskirt.

Is that the wisest fashion choice when most of the people you talk to are going to be looking up at you from ankle-height? I asked.

I guess we know how the Master intimidates his underlings, Erythraia pinged back.

We giggled like twelve year olds through the awkward exposition explaining that Keniclius/Keniculus/Kenny was a relic of the Eugenics Wars, leading us to conclude that, in the 1990s of this universe, the cool kids wore no mere jeans and flannel shirts but rather togas, buskins and much smaller versions of Kenny's giant Liefeld-esque belt pouch.

But our heroes had a plan. Since conventional weapons had failed, McCoy was going to whip up a batch of his granddaddy's special weed spray to take out the freakdragons.

"A strange way to handle aliens," Scotty lampshaded.

"These are strange aliens we're fighting," intoned Kirk, crushing the fourth wall beneath a meaningful gaze into the camera.

TRANSPORTER BEAM: [masks the sound of a thousand facepalms]

It also almost, but not quite, masked the sound of my brother stirring in the other room. I turned my headphones down for a second to make sure he wasn't up. He had school in the morning, and, with Mom gone, I had to see that he got there on time.

Having tackled one of the asparagus people and put it into a wicked tentacle-lock, Kirk demanded to know why Kenny was holding Spock hostage. "The Vulcan/human blend of wisdom, sense of order, durability and strength is the finest the Master has ever found!" the asparagus explained.

Durability and strength — is he looking for the perfect man or the perfect condom?

I always try to choose condoms with a superior sense of order and wisdom.
At Erythraia's stream of typed-back laughter, I smiled sheepishly, feeling my cheeks blush warmly.

Continuing their assault on Kenny's Evil Lair of Giant Ridiculousness, our heroes were sailing along on a conveniently easy-to-animate horizontal elevator, when the lights went out, providing cover for another freakdragon ambush.

"We can't do anything if we can't see what we're fighting!" angsted Kirk, presumably because Grandpa McCoy Brand weed killer doesn't work in the dark. I started to point this out, but was distracted by our heroes' emergence into the part of Kenny's lair where he keeps pretty guys passed out on pool tables. As you do.

But that wasn't all.

"Behold!" Kenny thundered. "Spock II!"

GIANT!SPOCK: [TOWERS]
HORN SECTION OF IMMINENT COMMERCIAL BREAK: [DRAMATICALLY TRILLS]

Now I was really losing it, giggling too much to even reply to Erythraia's comments with anything snappier than "LOL".

"This machine has drained his mind somehow."

"More than just drained!"

Also given a wipe-down with citrus scented Ajax!

I let out a cackle and had to clap my hand over my mouth. It had been years since I'd watched these, as a curious kid going through Mom's collection of *Trek* episodes on VHS, but at the time they hadn't seemed that funny, just strange. But some things are that way, like you can't watch *Rocky Horror* on TV by yourself; you need other people. I was wishing that Mom and I had watched these together, like we had the Original Series.

"Disease struck us before we could carry out our plan to impose peace on a galaxy that knew none," the conveniently mouthless asparagus interjected.

KIRK: Nobody asked you, chlorophyll-for-brains!

I shook my head in helpless giggles as the dramatic denouement unfolded, and as Erythraia laughed right along with me, half a world away.

> *hysterical shrieking* What kind of crack is this guy on?! AN ARMY OF GIANT SPOCKS IS NECESSARY TO SUBDUE THEM.

Totally can't breathe, I typed, nearly doubled-over in silent laughter.

> Noooo! Your death by asphyxiation would be meaningless if it is only to create a giant version of yourself!

falls out of chair, I typed, which was just barely an exaggeration. I missed the last minute or so of the show, taking off my glasses to wipe away tears with the back of my sleeve.

> Let's watch another! More, more! :D

But adrenaline was already fading into exhaustion. Though it was evening for Erythraia, it was 2:00 A.M. for me.

I would, but I have work in the morning, I typed, yawning and stretching. My back had gone stiff from hunching over the keyboard.

> Aww. :(

I was tempted, but I was already looking at five hours of sleep, and there would be other nights. Not an infinite number of them though; as it sometimes goes with online friendships, within a year or two Erythraia would start signing onto AIM less and less often, and then finally not at all. I never would find out her name.

But, as I signed off and stumbled into bed that night, I was smiling in the darkness. In those days, when real life was at its loneliest, I still had her. And an army of giant Spocks.

> *J. Allan Morlan is a Californian turned Flatlander, which, disappointingly, is just the name for a person who moved to Vermont from somewhere else and not some kind of two-dimensional being.*

88. THE MAGICKS OF MEGAS-TU
JAMES T. KIRK, SATAN WORSHIPPER
RICH HANDLEY

TOP SECRET/SPECIAL HANDLING
Stardate 9521.7
Starfleet Command • San Francisco, Calif.
From: West, Patrick, Vice-Admiral, Colonel of the Regiment
To: Cartwright, Lance, Admiral of the Fleet

MEMORANDUM FOR THE COMMANDING OFFICER, STARFLEET COMMAND
Subject: James Tiberius Kirk

Admiral,

Pursuant to our discussions regarding the recruitment of James T. Kirk for Section 31's operation at the Khitomer Accords, I must express some concerns. Though I certainly respect Captain Kirk's accomplishments as commander of the *Enterprise* and recognize his role in neutralizing numerous threats to Earth and Federation security throughout his four decades of service, a review of his record shows an alarming tendency toward an anti-authority bias that makes me very reluctant to bring him into our confidence. In fact, I believe he may pose a serious obstacle, one that should be dealt with sooner rather than later.

To be frank, Admiral, I have reason to believe Captain Kirk may be a Devil worshipper intent on destroying all gods. While I support every sapient being's right to practice his, her or its own religion as he, she or it pleases, Kirk's extreme prejudice in this regard gives me pause. Could his disdain for divine authority eventually extend to opposing any government bodies and agencies holding centralized power? I believe it could, and this makes him a liability.

I know you'll say I'm being an alarmist, sir, and it would not be the first time. However, I urge you to hear me out as I state my case below. Please see the appended files for further details.

- Stardate 3468.1: At Pollux IV, the *Enterprise* encounters an alien being claiming to be the god Apollo, who orders Kirk's crew to worship him as the ancient Greeks did. Rather than allying with this entity, thereby affording Starfleet an unprecedented advantage over its enemies, Kirk destroys Apollo's power base, telling him *mankind has no need for gods*.
- Stardate 6063.4: Kirk does the same thing to the creature known to

ancient Mayans and Aztecs as Kukulkan and Quetzalcoatl. Once again, Kirk's extreme aversion to divine authority results in his alienating a potential ally of immeasurable power.

- Stardate 3715.3: Kirk discovers Vaal, a mechanical serpent god on Gamma Trianguli VI. Predictably, he destroys Vaal rather than preserving the machine god's paradise — in essence, becoming the metaphorical serpent in Vaal's Garden of Eden.
- Stardate 3156.2: Upon learning that the people of Beta III are being controlled by yet another computer god, Landru, Kirk assumes the role of mechanical executioner once more, plunging Landru's followers into panicked, godless chaos — all because the idea of a controlling force offends his sensibilities.
- Stardate 3141.9: After apprehending the crew of the SS *Botany Bay*, Kirk astoundingly drops all charges against Khan Noonien Singh and his genetically bred Augments, exiling them on Ceti Alpha V with free rein to build an empire. On a flight-recorder tape of the hearing, Khan cites Lucifer's final speech in John Milton's *Paradise Lost* — that it is better to rule in Hell than to serve in Heaven — and Kirk can be seen nodding in agreement with that notion. I find this very significant, for reasons that will become quite clear.
- Stardate 1312.4: Gary Mitchell and Elizabeth Dehner are transformed into godlike beings after the *Enterprise* crosses the Galactic Barrier. Faced with their newfound omnipotence, Kirk strands the two on Delta Vega, then murders Mitchell — his friend of many years — after the latter compares himself to a god. (Ironically, Kirk himself would later be perceived as a god to the primitives of Amerind and nearly suffered a similar fate.)
- Stardate unknown: A non-corporeal entity feeding off hatred forces the crews of the *Enterprise* and a Klingon ship, led by Commander Kang, to battle one another for its sustenance. The medical log of ship's surgeon Leonard McCoy quotes Kirk as telling Kang to "go to the Devil". A rather odd turn of phrase, wouldn't you say?
- Stardate 8454.1: The *Enterprise* is commandeered by the renegade Vulcan Sybok, who boasts of having found the fabled god of Sha Ka Ree. Kirk's logs from that incident make clear his steadfast refusal to accept the entity's claim of being a benevolent god (ignoring for the moment that the claim turned out to be false, since Kirk did not yet know this).

Granted, Apollo, Kukulkan, Mitchell and the Sha Ka Ree entity represented grave threats to the galaxy, while Vaal and Landru had suppressed the free will and natural evolution of their people. Still, it is undeniable that Kirk acts outside the wide latitude afforded by his captaincy, displaying little regard for authority. I, for one, question several of his decisions in these matters; we all know the disastrous consequences of his unorthodox solution to the Khan situation, for example.

The most damning piece of evidence?

Stardate 1254.4: The *Enterprise* is swept up in a tornado of energy and matter at the galactic creation point, propelling it into an alternate universe in which the laws of physics differ and reality is shaped by magic and sorcery. There, Kirk and his crew encounter a creature half-man and half-goat, with horns protruding from his head. Calling himself Lucien, this being welcomes them to his world, Megas-Tu. Kirk learns that Lucien's people had visited Earth centuries prior, but were branded as witches and burned at the stake by the Puritans (not one of our finer moments as a species, admittedly, but an understandable reaction to a seeming outside threat).

The alien wizards, still blaming humanity for their past persecution, put Kirk and crew on trial in a recreation of 1691 Salem, Massachusetts, with a Megan specialist called Asmodeus — named in the deuterocanonical *Book of Tobit* as a king of demons, mind you — serving as prosecutor. As punishment for bringing humans to Megas-Tu, Lucien faces eternal exile in Limbo, but Kirk comes to his defense, only to be informed that on Earth, Lucien had been known as Lucifer.

Kirk's next actions, Admiral, bear very close scrutiny. You see, he continues to defend Lucien, despite the fact that the alien magician had been the inspiration for the fallen angel of Judeo-Christian religions. In short, Kirk meets the Devil himself — the very embodiment of evil — and what does he do? Does he destroy his place of power and humiliate him into leaving, as he did to both Apollo and Kukulkan? No. Does he shoot him and leave his corpse behind, as he did to Gary Mitchell, his friend? No. Does he destroy him with phaser fire, as he did to Vaal and Landru? No. Does he even question Lucien's motive in bringing a starship to his hidden home at the center of the galaxy, as he did to the Sha Ka Ree entity? Again, he does not.

No, when it comes to Lucifer, Kirk not only defends the alien during his trial, but actually *offers to die* so that the Devil may live.

Admiral, the implications of this are staggering and disturbing, religious freedom be damned.

When Klingon Ambassador Kamarag petitioned the Federation for the extradition of Kirk and his crew following the Genesis Planet debacle, he accused Kirk of being a devil. Little did he know how close to the truth he may have been. Kirk is said to have told Apollo that when it came to gods, he "found the one sufficient". I think it's abundantly clear who that "one" really is.

While I normally would not hold any man's religious beliefs against him, it would be folly to overlook this facet of James Kirk's personality. The Khitomer operation is of paramount concern to Section 31. We need officers we can rely on, Admiral, and whose loyalty we can count on with utter certainty. James Kirk is the very antithesis of this concept; he is a chaotic variable, so shaped by his devotion to Lucifer — the Deceiver, the Accuser, the Destroyer — that he cannot be counted upon not to betray us if he should ever come to view our power as a threat to his Master. I therefore urge against his recruitment and regrettably recommend that Lieutenant Valeris be tasked with eliminating the captain from the game when Chancellor Gorkon visits the *Enterprise*, lest his chaotic nature become the serpent in the garden we have worked so hard to sow.

Colonel West, 9521.7

Rich Handley is the co-founder of Hasslein Books (hassleinbooks.com). A former reporter for Star Trek Communicator *magazine, he wrote introductions to IDW's* Star Trek *newspaper strip reprint books, contributed essays to Sequart's* New Life and New Civilizations: Exploring Star Trek Comics *anthology and helped GIT Corp. compile its* Star Trek *comic book DVD-ROM sets. To this day, he still wonders what God needs with a starship.*

89. ONCE UPON A PLANET
THE SECRET SONG OF FUTURES PAST: EPILOGUE
JOSH MARSFELDER

"Tell us the story about the spacemen," Tertia asked.
"Oh, but darlings, haven't you heard that one before?" Alice replied.
"Oh yes, but we do love it so. Tell it again such that it lives and breathes and grows."
"Very well..."

Once upon a time, there was a girl who could journey to the stars. In her waking dreams, she beheld visions within themselves, gave life to thought, which woke and dream'd anew. The girl travelled across the wheel of creation and came to know the truth in the I, which all dreamers do. Understanding the true mark of royalty, she defeated the queens of the House of False Love in great conversation that stretched from the time of maybes and could-have-beens all the way to the days of future past. And, having come to know herself within the world, she once again traversed the cosmic ocean to write her memories upon the wind of a golden afternoon.

The Queen (for this is who the girl really was) returned to the island of the thrice-told-tale, and she said "Though this is not my story, I know it well and have heard it thrice before. Yet I shall write it once more, for only in this way can a story learn and grow." It is said that when the Queen spoke, her voice transmuted earth into lore and the wind carried her words upon it. And so she began again.

In my youth, I sailed the sky on a ship of light. I bore witness to visions that exist to me now only as half-remembered memories. My time of mystery is long since past, though it is a place to which I may still visit on occasion. My country is the shifting sea of myth, and I have been away for so long it no longer feels like home. But I had heard tell of moments past I have yet to experience that would bring the sky to life again, and it was for this reason I called upon memories that were not mine.

For me, there is not one dream but many. I came upon a land that was unfamiliar to me and tried to write a story about what I saw there. But, though I may observe the memory of others, I may not know them. I may speak with many voices, but my voices speak as one with the song of my dream. And it was here I invoked a song of my own to share with the dreamers whom I met upon the shore. The song spoke of futures past and truths that might be. Some of them were.

Another time I came upon these same shores. The story began again. The tune changed and I could hear the cosmic symphony clearer this time. I tuned the song, tapped the universe and beheld something that might be a truth: the spacemen were players in their own work, and it was here they beheld the truth of their existence. I wrote a poem for them and tried to reach them as I had before. I spoke of dreams and hopes and loves and wars and the phantom energy of creation. If I was heard, I ca'n't say: For my voice was not of this cosmic fugue still, the faces I saw before me were not mine, and the dreamers did not recognize themselves within me.

As fits my forme, I was called to the land thrice-evoked. I am marked with three faces, three names and three persons, and it is in this way I shift my visage. I was thrice asked to tell the story of the spacemen, and thrice I answered in the best forme I could manage. Have you heard a song sing of itself? Time-changes and possipoints swirl together amongst the rest of the cosmic dust that floats among the waves upon which is our True Homeland. These are truths I try to convey through song; truths that we may not cast our glance on but sideways. We may know such things in the peripheral vision of the Third Mind's Eye. This is what the spacemen taught the World-Stage, what the World-Stage taught the spacemen, and onwards and onwards again.

These spacemen are not the spacemen I once knew. Even those whom I once knew now belong to seas of myth that are no longer my own. My time has passed, my seas have changed, and, while I can go back to those lands, they are different now. "What became of my ship of light?" I asked myself. The answer, darlings, exists within us. It is within each of you, just as it is within me. It is within the Angels we invoke and within the dreams and visions they help us call forth from the ether. My ship belongs to a future far, far distant from this one; to islands and World-Stages beyond the comprehension of the sleep of words and doom's drive. I am, we are, the cosmic ocean, and it is there to which I must now return. But please accept this magick as my parting gift to you:

boldly go where thou wilt. You shall find your myth-country and your ship of light. This is the sigil of royalty. If thou wilt know it, the universe lies before you.

I love.

"Tell us the story about the spacemen," Tertia asked.

"Oh, but darlings, haven't you heard that one before?" Alice replied.

"Oh yes, but we do love it so. Tell it again such that it lives and breathes and grows."

"Very well..."

Josh Marsfelder is the steward of Vaka Rangi, *an unauthorized online critical history of* Star Trek *and the voyaging starship story. His background is in cultural anthropology, science and technology studies and social studies of knowledge.*

90. MUDD'S PASSION
MUDD SPELLED BACKWARDS IS...
WESLEY OSAM

When *Star Trek* returned in animated form, it was probably inevitable that it would bring back interplanetary con artist Harry Mudd. The resulting episode — *Mudd's Passion*, by Stephen Kandel, who'd written both previous Mudd episodes — was one of those stories most fantastic TV series eventually get around to: the one where science-fictional mind warpage leads to inappropriate romance. This plot is usually, as it was here, played as a comedy.

These things are weirder than they seem.

Let's start with the love-brainwashing plot. It's not hard to understand why TV series keep returning to this well and playing it for laughs. Twisting the characters' personalities gives the actors a chance to stretch their abilities. For the fans, it's amusing to see incongruous couples hook up.

But take this story seriously and it's seriously creepy. That's never been harder to ignore than in *Mudd's Passion*. Usually, nobody's spreading magic aphrodisiacs deliberately. When *Deep Space Nine* used this plot, the culprit was accidental telepathic emanations from wacky guest star Lwaxana Troi. But here the gimmick is a drug that renders the opposite sex entirely unable to resist the user — bluntly, Space Rohypnol. That isn't funny at all. That Mudd doesn't actually believe the stuff works does not make the basic concept of *Mudd's Passion* any less appalling.

Most of the alleged laughs are at the expense of Christine Chapel, who gets her biggest role ever yet still displays no character traits beyond her serial sexual harassment of Spock. I've always suspected her quarters resemble a dingy serial-killer lair covered in pictures of Spock connected by thumbtacks and string. *Mudd's Passion* is a solid half hour of Nurse Chapel's lousy judgment: she doses Spock with Mudd's love drug, spreads it to the rest of the crew and lets Mudd escape. You'd think shenanigans like this would end her Starfleet career and probably lead to criminal charges... but everything's fine, because, hey, *comedy*! Which is a clue to what's wrong.

Over the years, there have been plenty of comedic *Star Trek* episodes. It's primarily a dramatic series, so it tends to go for the kind of comedy where, as in drama, actions have meaningful reactions. Scotty can start a slapstick fistfight in *The Trouble With Tribbles*, but he has to pay for it with a dressing-down from the Captain. *Mudd's Passion*, unusually, is the kind of comedy in which nothing has consequences as long as it's funny. This isn't necessarily bad. (*The Simpsons* is a classic show, and how many times has Homer lost his job?) But *Mudd's Passion*, even judged on its own terms, ventures into territory too creepy for this kind of lightweight farce. And, as an episode of *Star Trek*, it's too far from the usual tone of even the other comedy episodes. It brings up uncomfortable subjects and asks us not to think about what they mean in a show with a history of asking us, however timidly, to think about uncomfortable subjects.

That said, there's some entertainment to be had. You'd swear one scene of Kirk and Spock embracing was drawn just for the people who write slash fan fiction. And sometimes the show's limited animation accidentally works in its favor: the best moment comes when Chapel, facing a giant rock monster, gives it a deadpan look and saunters off as though it won't notice her if she just acts casual.

The funniest idea in *Mudd's Passion* is that Starfleet would send its flagship to arrest a small-time crook. Prior to *The Wrath of Khan*, Harry Mudd is the closest thing Captain Kirk has to an arch-enemy. Not that this was the plan. *Star Trek* was light on recurring characters and, with three appearances, Mudd was just around more than anyone else.

In later series, the resident arch-villains would tie into the programs' themes. *The Next Generation* emphasized humanity's continuing growth and evolution, so Picard faced tests and temptations from a god trying to prove human progress was an illusion. On *Deep Space Nine*, Captain Sisko faced devious politicians connected to the Bajoran religion and Dominion war that drove the show's plots. And *Voyager* kept trying different arch-villains who never worked out and were, in a couple of cases, borrowed secondhand from *The Next Generation*.

Star Trek, the series that opened with a narration promising strange new worlds and boldly going where no one has gone before gave us... a small-time crook. A self-absorbed con artist scraping out minor profit from tawdry little schemes. A character who never appeared in a good episode and never appeared in one that wasn't to some extent misogynist. (*I, Mudd* is the least sexist of the three, but even there we're supposed to think of stranding Harry amidst android duplicates of his wife as a hilarious punishment.) Harry Mudd appears to have wandered into *Star Trek* from another, much less epic, program, like the 1960s holographic lounge singer who for some reason was a recurring character on *Deep Space Nine*. Why do fans remember Harry so fondly?

Well, for one thing, Roger Carmel had charisma (and a good agent) — that's probably why the producers brought him back in the first place. But Harry Mudd also may not be as incongruous as he seems. This becomes clearer when you consider the Ferengi.

It's easy to forget that the Ferengi were supposed to be the replacement for the Klingons. That plan fell apart when a perfect storm of bad design decisions led to their premiering as a gang of twitchy little goofballs. But forget the ridiculous ears and look at the underlying concept. The Ferengi were self-centered, profiteering, male chauvinist capitalist extremists, explicitly compared onscreen to "Yankee Traders" — a distorted reflection of everything wrong with 1980s America. *The Next Generation* set the enlightened, egalitarian, post-scarcity Federation against an empire of Gordon Geckos.

Harry Mudd isn't an irredeemable concept; he's a trial run for the Ferengi. He's the one guy in the gutter who isn't looking at the stars, because he noticed someone dropped a penny. His pettiness, self-centeredness and preference for making a buck over treating other people as, well, *people* represent the opposite of everything the crew of the *Enterprise*, at their best, are supposed to aspire to.

At least, that's what he might have represented. But *Star Trek*, especially the original series, didn't always live up to the ideals it claimed to espouse. Harry Mudd was just a comedy con-man. This is a redemptive fan theory, not a theme the writers, producers or cast actually had in mind when they made the Harry Mudd stories. That's a pity; if they had, they could have given us something better than *Mudd's Passion*.

Wesley Osam lives in Iowa. He just works in outer space.

---

91. THE TERRATIN INCIDENT
THE DEVIL'S IN THE DETAILS
IAN FARRINGTON

The Terratin Incident is one of the most fascinating slices of *Star Trek* in the franchise's half-century history. Full of nuance and detail and texture, its storytelling power is practically peerless; its visual flair and panache rightly lauded wherever the series is discussed; and its themes and social-commentary endlessly enchanting.

But how was the lightning caught in the bottle? Let's take a quick look behind the scenes and try to decipher what makes this episode quite so special.

The Terratin Incident tells the story of the planet Cepheus. When the USS *Enterprise* approaches, a flash of light engulfs the ship. Soon the crew are all shrinking in size, and, before long, they're too small to operate the controls. Then, when they make contact with the planet's inhabitants, Captain Kirk and his colleagues discover a dark secret...

The episode was directed by Hal Sutherland, and he really brings the story to life. He cleverly chose to shoot the actors from static, rigid camera angles. Virtually every shot is stock-still, reflecting the military structure and precise hierarchy on board a Federation ship. Years later, film director Wes Anderson was specifically influenced by this episode when developing his distinctive style.

Just select any scene of *The Terratin Incident* and you'll notice how little the camera moves. There are no shaky handheld shots in this, no flashy whip pans or tracking zooms. Sutherland wants to present us with a world of order, right angles and reliable, incorruptible horizontality, of every shot looking like we're peeping inside an open dollhouse. Compare *The Terratin Incident* with *The Royal Tenenbaums*, and the spooky correlations and repeated motifs are there for all to see.

Check out the shots of the Terratin population, for example. We only ever see them head-on, framed in a rock-solid portrait. They're standing completely still and looking straight down the lens, imploring the crew — and, by extension, we, the viewers — to help them break free of their metaphorical prison. This is really clever stuff, using the form to tell the story.

Like many episodes of *Star Trek*, the filming process was achieved on a combination of studio sets and outside locations (as well as some typically smart model shots of the *Enterprise*). In this case, the sound stages provided the ship's bridge, engine room and sickbay, while rural California stood in for the planet's volcanic surface. Matte shots were used to make Malibu Creek State Park appear more mountainous and barbaric than it actually was in 1973, and the result is very convincing. Only William Shatner was required on location, which reportedly made for a frosty moment when he realized he'd be working one more day on the episode than the rest of the cast.

By all accounts though, there was plenty of good fun back in the studio. James Doohan (who played Scotty before Simon Pegg) ad-libbed "big crystals... unpeeling like the rind of an orange", a line based on a private joke between himself and Walter Koenig.

Another last-minute rewrite occurred when a significant plot hole was discovered. Dialogue had to be added during filming when someone realized that the characters' uniforms were shrinking as well as their bodies. "Uniform made of algae-based xenylon, I believe," quipped Leonard Nimoy, who could always be relied upon to find a witty way out of any scripting problem.

As ever with science-fiction (aka "sci-fi") television, special effects made a large contribution. The actor playing Arex, the *Enterprise*'s Edosian navigator, had a long time in the make-up chair before he was ready to go before the cameras, but it's a remarkable costume. He fits in seamlessly with the human actors, so much so that you forget that it's a man in a rubber suit. (Oddly, online episode guides tend to credit Doohan as playing Arex — a telephone whisper of a rumor now accepted as fact. Who it really was under the mask is information that has, it seems, now been lost.)

We also get gossamer mice, which shimmer in and out of sight, and floating halo fish. Sutherland and his team were really pushing the boundaries of what was achievable on a 1973 TV budget. But, of course, the biggest challenge facing the production team was the shrinkage. (By the way, all the talk of "shrinkage" in *The Terratin Incident* later influenced a famous running joke in an episode of *Seinfeld*.)

The plot called for our heroes to gradually reduce in size during the episode, so multiple versions of the sets were constructed on the Paramount Studios sound stages. Props such as cutlery and tools, meanwhile, were borrowed from the Irwin Allen series *Land of the Giants*. Once the characters were too small for practical sets, a number of clever techniques were used to create the illusion: process shots, opticals and rear-projection can all be detected by a cine-literate eye.

For example, the scene of Nurse Chapel falling into the aquarium was mostly achieved in the studio. But close-ups and underwater shots were completed in a special tank, which had recently been used during filming of *The Poseidon Adventure*. During post-production, though, an editing error meant that the same take of actress Majel Barrett shouting "Help!" was used repeatedly, which rather lessens the effect of what is a terrifying moment.

But perfection is overrated. Since its transmission in November 1973 — on the very day Richard Nixon announced, "I am not a crook!" — this episode has held a place in every *Star Trek* aficionado's heart. We know its dialogue. We know its visual gags. We're thrilled by each repeat viewing.

This is *Star Trek* at its most interesting, at its most enthralling, at its most entertaining. At its best.

Ian Farrington has written numerous short stories and factual features,
edited numerous books, worked on numerous magazines and fanzines —
and used the word numerous far too often in this sentence.

92. THE TIME TRAP
MINUTES OF THE RULING COUNCIL OF ELYSIA
KEVIN LAUDERDALE

Glar the Gorn ambled into the massive blue-gray stone chamber of the Elysian Ruling Council and took his seat next to Colleen O'Kearney, the auburn-haired captain of the *Bonaventure*. "Sssorry I'm late," he hissed. "Have I misssed anything?"

Xerius, the Romulan who served as leader of the council said, "Just beginning with Apologies. Sandor of Vulcan can't be with us with us due to his meditation schedule."

"I see..." said Magen in a distant, echoing voice that mirrored her psionic skill of far-sight. Her cat-like eyes were yellow and stared straight ahead as she spoke, barely moving her lips.

"What do you see beyond your eyes, good Magen?" asked Devna, the Orion woman dressed, as always, in her tiny orange bikini.

"I see... Sandor. He is... not in meditation. He is with... Charlotte Devaneu aboard her ship."

"That tramp," muttered O'Kearney.

Magen continued. "They are touching... one fingertip, now two — "

"Uh! That's enough," interrupted Devna.

"Oh, I'd like to hear a lot more," hissed Glar.

"Return to us now, gentle Magen."

"Shall I minute that?" asked Theen the Andorian, his stylus at the ready, hovering over a data slate.

"Why do we say 'minute' anyway?" grunted Biv, the Tellarite.

Devna replied breathily, "Here in this pocket in the garment of time, time itself stands still. A century is as a day; a year, a minute."

"Shall I year that, then?" asked Theen.

Xerius shook his head. "First item: Yesterday's arrival of two new ships, the Federation's *Enterprise* and the Klingon ship *Klothos*." He turned to the human and Klingon who sat on the Council. "Captains O'Kearney and Krand, these are your people, and you saw both captains, though, of course, you did not know them. Both were born after your arrival here."

Krand said, "Commander Kor's first action was to draw his weapon. He clearly has honor. It is a pity we 123 species trapped here have learned to get along. He will have no further opportunity to exercise it." Krand sighed. "Perhaps we could have just a little war. Merely for demonstration purposes."

Xerius shook his head. "Captain O'Kearney?"

"Captain Kirk... You say he's a couple of centuries younger than me? I wonder how he feels about older women."

"Any further observations?"

"I see Starfleet uniforms have changed yet again. I wish I owned a piece of that concession."

"As always," said Biv, "when new ships arrive, I feel we need to reinforce the importance of our highest law."

Devna said, "We have already told them that ours is a community of perfect peace and that any act of violence will result in the total immobilization of their ships."

"I was speaking of our ban on revealing the winners of sports events and the series finales of holodramas," said Biv. "I've still got 10 quatloos riding on Liverpool Interplanetary vs. T'hllurghak United with Glar."

"That game wasss played over five hundred yearsss ago," said Glar.

"True, but if we never learn the winner, I'll never have to pay up."

"Perhapsss a committee ssshould ssstudy repealing that law," said Glar, with a snarl.

Xerius nodded. "We shall form a subcommittee to study the advisability of forming a committee."

Biv asked, "Don't Klingons have a saying about committees, Krand? Something about your Barge of the Dead, which sails the dishonored to Hell?"

"To Gre'thor, yes," replied Krand. "We say it is piloted by a committee."

"Interesting," said Theen, his stylus at a significant angle, "On Andoria, we say that three is a committee but four is a marriage."

"*Moving right along*," said Xerius. "Our next item. We have all been invited aboard the *Enterprise* tonight. The *Enterprise* and the *Klothos* are going to combine their engines and try again to escape. This is a good-bye celebration — or an early wake."

"An excellent opportunity for me to perform the Orion Slave Girl dance," said Devna.

"You only do one move," said O'Kearney. "It's hips to the left."

"Well, it won't take long, then," said Krand.

Anthar, a Phylosian with a green, raspberry-shaped head, twin eyestalks, and a multitude of green tendril-like arms said, "I too should like to entertain." S\he raised hir arms, and they began to sway.

"You aren't the only onesss here who are green," hissed Glar. "All Elysssia is dying to sssee the Gorn Dance of Disssrobement. Perhapsss I could borrow Devna'sss bikini."

"Meeting adjourned!" declared Xerius.

Addenda: Biv here. After 1,000 years of individual ships failing to escape from Elysia, the *Enterprise* and the *Klothos* combined engine power and succeeded. Within eight hours, every remaining ship in Elysia had partnered with another and was gone.

Don't know why we never thought of that before. I have decided to stay behind. I will instruct future ships that slip from the Delta Triangle into our time trap how to pair up and leave. It is noble to sacrifice myself for the betterment of others.

And, best of all, I'll never have to pay off that stupid Gorn.

Kevin Lauderdale is just another American obsessed with British sitcoms.

93. THE AMBERGRIS ELEMENT
HAVE A WHALE OF A TIME DOWN AT ARGO SEAFOOD!
NATHAN SKRESLET

The newest haute cuisine establishment to grace the Alpha Quadrant is Argo Seafood, located on the eponymous water planet. The sun-swept beaches and deep green waves form a fetching backdrop to this impressively appointed locale located in the recently tectonically raised Romanesque Aquan old city. The décor is liberally festooned with locally sourced seashells and giant pearls, and there's even an attractive view of the wreckage of a Starfleet Aqua-Shuttle, now converted into a stunning coral reef and tide pool. The selection of fresh-caught fruits de mer is the probably second only to Antede III, and the sautéed Halo fish is sure to light up any romantic dinner for those on shore leave. Air breathers are recommended to use the mainland location, but for a really authentic experience the crystal-webbed dining halls of the Aquan underwater city are breath-taking. Literally! To breathe while you're down there, you'll need to undergo a surgo-op to pursue this option.

If you're in the mood for a light meal, the Palamarian sea urchin with garlic and moon grass (even better than Quark's on Deep Space 9) makes a delightful appetizer, while those seeking heavier fare cannot go wrong with the Kelp-stuffed Sur-snake flank steak wrapped in bacon and served with a side of fingerling potatoes. Serves approximately 17. Overall, Argo Seafood is an excellent place to spend your hard-earned Quatloos, so beam your Away Team straight to Argo Seafood and enjoy the best that the Quadrant has to offer.

Accepting most major intergalactic currencies including Gold-Pressed Latinum and Visa.

Or, if you don't have time, try our takeout service. Delivery at Warp 8 within 12 parsecs or your money back.

SO GOOD YOU'LL SWEAR IT'S AGAINST THE ORDAINMENTS

Argo Seafood

EST. S.D. 5449.9

FILLET OF SPOCK

Pale green fillet resting on a bed of sauteed kelp, Denebian whale roe and Aquan vegetables, smothered in a fine Ambergris sauce.

29.99 QUATLOOS

FILLET OF KIRK

This bold fillet is served with seared Sur-snake, pureed water sprouts and sliced scallops, accented with an Ambergris pesto.

29.99 QUATLOOS

All entrées served with choice of soup or salad.

WARNING: Some dishes may contain fish or fish-like humanoids.

Reviews
★★★★☆ (9 Reviews)

"Not to be missed. Beats out the all-you-can-eat Vermicula Bar on Pacifica hands (and flippers) down!"
Antedean Ambassador *Bubble bubble burble* [untranslatable]
★★★★★

"The wait staff all smelled of fish and looked out of place in their formal uniforms. It baffles me why anyone thought this would be a good idea. And the prices would make a Ferengi blush."
Lwaxana Troi, daughter of the Fifth House, holder of the Sacred Chalice of Rix and heir to the Holy Rings of Betazed.
★★☆☆☆

"I find the lack of vegetarian options highly illogical."
Sarek of Vulcan
★☆☆☆☆

"So good! I haven't eaten this much since I was pregnant."
Commander Charles "Trip" Tucker III
★★★★☆

"Wearing a diving mask makes it very difficult to eat. And I was nearly bitten by a Sur-snake while checking my coat. Would not go back."
Lieutenant Reginald Barclay
★☆☆☆☆

"Getting the surgo-op to dine underwater was a unique experience, and swimming down there really worked up an appetite. But I don't think I'll ever get the sea salt out of my dress uniform."
Commander William T. Riker
★★★★☆

"I thought that the jumbo oysters of Azati Prime were the finest in the universe until I came to Argo. The ones on Argo are the size of a porthole and it takes two people to lift them. Pair it with a crisp Sapphire Wine, you won't regret it!"
Harry Mudd, Entrepreneur
★★★★☆

"Great food overall, but it could use more seasoning."
Captain Benjamin Sisko
★★★★☆

"Darmok and Jalad, feasting at Argo. Sur-snake, when the walls fell."
Captain Dathon
★★☆☆☆

Nathan Skreslet is a Trek *fan who regenerated into a* Doctor Who *fan, but the Force is strong with him. Also, don't try to take his sky.*

94. THE SLAVER WEAPON
AS EASY AS ABC
NICK SEIDLER

A's for Animate, the way of the pen,
Presenting colors you won't see again.
This gives us chance for a brand-new look
At *Star Trek*'s next show, it's an open book.

B's Beta Lyrae, the galaxy's glee,
A place travelers can stop by to see.
Copernicus lands right on the planet,
All covered in ice, mountains of granite.

C is for Captain; we don't see no Kirk.
But we see others, all hard at their work.
Uhura, Spock, Sulu make up the whole gang.
Not even a redshirt, to die with a bang.

D is for Death, we see it onscreen.
Though it's toned down, which isn't so mean.
This is the only drawn story to feature
The final farewell of any live creature.

E's Espionage, the weapon's true purpose,
With settings quite odd, so everyone's nervous.
Like a telescope or rocket engine,
Total conversion means nuclear din.

F is for Fangs, the teeth of the creatures,
Called the Kzinti, that this story features.
They eat only meat, including mankind,
Telepathy too, the party does find.

G is for Glowing, when things come alight,
If one box is near, another shines bright.
The Kzinti lure them into a trap.
The cat people love to close off the gap.

H is for Hierarch, the Kzinti must heed.
Chuft Captain in charge, he takes on the lead.
Spock says the females are stupid creatures,
Unlike human girls, with smarter features.

I is for Intel, the slaver computer,
Processing power finds an intruder.
If you can't give the right information,
You will be more than lost in translation.

J is for James D., our best engineer,
Scotty's not in this, but Doohan we hear.
Both the Chuft Captain and the telepath,
Doohan's the person, and voice is his craft.

K is for Kzinti, they're not just in Trek,
But in many books, yes, that is correct.
They feature elsewhere, in other Trek lore,
But safely renamed, so lawyers won't bore.

L's for Low Pressure, it makes water boil,
When science is shown, there's no need to toil.
Accurate teachings into the fiction
Makes this much better than simple diction.

M is for Meat, though not fit to be ate,
A billion years old, that box isn't great.
The Kzinti still hope to taste human flesh.
They'll keep their taste buds completely refreshed.

N's for Null Setting, on slaver's device
It is Mister Spock, who gives out advice.
By not giving them just one tiny clue,
The Kzinti choose wrong, in what they should do.

O... pportunity, the villains do plot.
They've stolen a ship? The Kzinti have not.
The slaver weapon, it will give power
Over all races, conquer and tower.

P's for Pink color, the Kzinti spacesuits.
Their ship's the same shade; they sport purple boots.
Hal the producer, he was color blind.
In other fiction, the Kzinti refined.

Q is for Quick smart, dash back and dash forth,
Characters travel to East, West and North.
Some even run South, or hide underground,
Which is where the ship of Kzintis' first found.

R is for Racist, the Kzinti are full,
Thinking they're better than others. That's bull.
Misogyny too, and many more "~isms",
Reflecting us back, like so many prisms.

S is for Slavers, very smart lizards
Creating great things, amazing wizards.
Their powerful tools, ahead of the times,
These stasis boxes are fine paradigms.

T is for Trekkies, the fans of all sorts
Who love this show, by many reports.
Winner of Hugo, written by Niven,
The story's well loved; plaudits were given.

U's for Uhura, a human female,
Smarter by far, than those with a tail.
Feminist message, part of the script.
Equality now. Some things have flipped.

V is for Vulcan, we're talking of Spock,
Who helps us to see what's under the rock
In terms of the plot, what happens onscreen
The details of how, and what does it mean.

W for Wars, we battled the Kzin.
This happened before, could happen again.
The Kzinti believe ghosts haunt old weapons.
This faith won't change now, Uhura reckons.

X is for Xanthic, yellow-ish colored,
More orangey-brown, fully fur covered.
The Kzinti sure make a memorable foe.
We'll see them again, in another show.

Y is for Yellow, a root munched in teeth.
The Kzin telepath, on Sulu's belief.
Who would have known that being a vegan,
Would help save our lives, as best as we can?

Z is for zealous, a forceful belief
That this story is, in hand-drawn motif,
The best of them all, a story that's fun.
And what's at the core? Intelligent gun.

Nick Seidler is tall and overly fond
Of role-playing games, with hoods that are donned.
He'll neither lose faith nor stifle one yawn:
He loves Star Trek *shows, live-action and drawn.*

95. THE EYE OF THE BEHOLDER
SO YOU WANT TO OPEN A PAN-GALACTIC ZOO...?
DREW MEYER

(Translated from Lactran)

We at the Pan-Dimensional Habitat Consortium have all the confidence in the worlds that your zoo will be both educational and entertaining.

We appreciate you considering our business for your enterprise. We feel our record speaks for itself; we've sold zoos to Talos, Trafalmadore and Casa Isolada... and, by gum, it's put them on the intergalactic map!

However, there are several items to consider. Please take a moment to look over this pamphlet for exciting and helpful hints on you new endeavor.

If you are a species without eyes, then audio, olfactory and even psychic-burst transmission versions of this brochure are available upon request.

Why a zoo?
We understand that while non-interference with "lesser" developing species is necessary to achieve scientific results, we also know that scanning primitive worlds from adjacent star systems to avoid detection lacks the excitement of up close interaction.

By bringing the inhabitants of different worlds together, you are creating an environment of learning and fun, all in the comfort of your own solar system.

Where to build a zoo?
We recommend a midsized planet with a nitrogen-rich atmosphere and gravity of about 9.807 m/s^2. In the end, it's a matter of planetary preference, but we want to make sure you're getting the zoo you want.

Which habitat is best?
Why choose one? We use our own terraforming contractors to manufacture authentic extra-planetary habitats that will mimic the home-environs of any and all your species. It may seem illogical to place a lake or rainforest in close proximity to a desert, but if that's what the customer wants, that's what they get! Once you make sure you duplicate the natural flora and fauna for your specimens' habitat, it's time to populate your zoo!

What sort of creatures should you place in your zoo?
All sorts. We recommend specimens who are as distinct from one another as they

are resilient to prolonged phaser fire. From well-armored theropods native to Canopus III to the shrieking Maravellan flying Dragons, exotic life forms are sure to make a galaxy-class zoo.

But remember, don't just limit yourself to larger species. While cyclopean lake monsters are real crowd-pleasers, a well developed pan-variable ecosystem needs species both large and small. Don't forget the smaller denizens of the worlds; while also providing the backbone to a thriving food web, a healthy host of malarial-laden biting insects adds a certain spice to any collection.

For smaller specimens, we recommend an enclosure, roughly five square kilometers. Individual groups of these smaller specimens make for an exquisite exhibit. We're sure your visitors will find these specimens strangely attractive.

For captivity and display, we cannot stress enough the power of force fields. They neither obscure the view nor allow inhabitants to wander off. Those confined within may try to find weak points in the force fields but should give up after a while.

What about health risks?
Whether you're abducting them away from their places of origin or they materialize from somewhere else, it's important to decontaminate specimens as soon as possible. We'd hate to see a zoo fail due to exposure to harmful bacteria. This goes for terraforming your planet to meet your zoo's needs or invading a planet to start a zoo of your own; it's important to check for bacteria.

While most of the beings you'll encounter and display are no more than mere animals, it is not unheard of to discover that these simplistic species are capable of more complex thought — a rudimentary intelligence.

What to do if you encounter an intelligent species?
First, isolate them from the larger populations. You can learn a lot from observing these creatures, so make sure you display them in such a way as to maximize their educational value. While their primitive grunts and gestures may seem meaningless or laughable to us, it is possible that they are communicating with one another. We have found that rudimentary tool use such as simple machines, primitive medicinal devices or focused energy-wave manipulators can be entertaining for visitors, but keep these items away from the creatures in case they use them to hurt themselves. Perhaps you can display any such "toys" outside the force field so that visitors might examine them or, in rare instances, lower the force field to enter the enclosure and hand them to specimens.

What are the benefits of a petting zoo?
We at the Pan Dimensional Habitat Consortium are firm believers in learning through doing. Make sure you allow for interaction with the "non-deadly species"

by making their habitat force fields easy to turn off and on for visitors. Children of all ages and levels of genius will thrill as they interact with the species, give them food or misinterpret basic duplicitous feints.

What to do if said intelligent species manages to kidnap your child, break them down on a molecular level and then reassemble them hundreds of miles above your planet's atmosphere in a crude space-faring transport?
First, don't panic. Remember these are simple creatures and any unscheduled teleportation is probably the result of a misunderstanding. Your best bet is to allow the child to commandeer the vessel, fly it out of orbit before befriending a similar specimen and use their psychic powers to absorb the entirety of the species' knowledge, so as to teleport themselves back to your planet.

If that doesn't work, you can always use your increasingly monumental psychic powers to peel back the layers of a specimen's mind to obtain the information you need.

What if you can't use your increasingly monumental psychic powers to peel back the layers of a specimen's mind to obtain specific information?
Remember, if you can't gain the information on a one-to-one basis, invite others to mentally probe with you. It's a great way to spend a few moments in your ever-momentous lifecycles. Millennia may pass before you get a chance to try a similar experiment.

We hope this information has been helpful to you and thank you again for choosing the Pan-Dimensional Habitat Consortium to make your zoo hypothesis a reality!

Look for our other useful pamphlets, which will help you answer these other common questions:

- Water, scalding or VERY scalding?
- What do the various colorations of bipedal specimens mean, and why are the red ones so susceptible to fatality?
- Why is the one in the gold so attractive?
- Why does he talk like that?

Drew Meyer is a children's librarian, game designer
and podcaster who may or may not have a beard.

96. THE JIHAD
LOADED
ANDREW MAH

Star Trek: TOS is embedded in my cranium like the Ceti eel that Khan crammed in Chekov's ear. I can state, with very little reservation, that, by the time I was 5 years old, I'd probably begun basing some of my precociously acquired "leadership" skills on Kirk and his half-cocked, verbally stilted, intergalactic STI-spreading ways!

Bones... MUST have... penicillin. Hypo. SPRAY!!

Having been mesmerized by all the re-run episodes very early in life, on the crappy black and white TV sitting in our tiny apartment, before long I was pining, nay *aching*, for more.

It was clearly "awesome", before people started using "awesome" in vandalized vernacular. Everyone I knew watched and loved *TOS*, but those were the days before the canny cadres of savvy marketers — who also grew up emulating Kirk and having wet dreams about green aliens — realized there be mad dollars here. No; especially being a sleeper hit, it took far too long before any sequel or spinoff arose to tickle our fancies in furiously fantastical ways, even a bad one. Oh the humanity!!!

Enter *Star Trek: The Animated Series*. With original actors doing voiceovers no less! The REAL McCoy, not generally a fake one. Deforestation was not a concern.

Unfortunately, that's probably the best thing one might reasonably say about it. You see, back in the bad old days, AKA when I was your age, we geeky types were rarely treated to the opulent indulgences of continuity concerns, production values and semi-skillful writers working in a serious manner to create our animated realities. (*Looney Tunes* and *The Flintstones* notwithstanding — thank you so much Mr. Blanc.) After all, cartoons are just for kids, right? They don't know any better? Wrong, wrong, wrong, you fiends!! Many of us knew exactly what we were getting, and, while still grateful for the entertainment, we were routinely sad about the lack of detailed and respectful treatment of the source material. What we did get was unintentionally comical voice acting, nonsensical and painfully clichéd plot devices, frequently recycled backgrounds and, on a more positive note, real music performed and recorded by real musicians. This lent a distinctive atmosphere and je ne sais quoi to the milieu. See *Spider Man* (1967–70), *Hulk* (1966), *Iron Man* (1966), *Superfriends* (1973–86), *Rocket Robin Hood* (1966–69), and you'll get the idea... which brings us to the episode in question: Season 1, Episode 16, *The Jihad*.

IN A NUTSHELL: Kirk and Spock are summoned by the Vedala, the "oldest space-faring race", as part of a team to help retrieve a magically delicious artifact that houses the brain patterns of "Alar": their super-cool avian religious figure. If discovered missing, it would surely cause an entire planet full of extremely irate bird creatures (the Skorr) to wage a righteously pissed off Jihad against the "known" galaxy!

The Skorr apparently reproduce with Tribble-like gusto, because, according to Spock's calculations, it would take them two "standard" years to breed an army of two hundred billion warriors!

MAIN CAST:
Nameless Vedala: Feline-ish facilitator creature from a very advanced space-faring culture. Nice ears, fine white mutton chops, along with a wonderful, super futuristic jumpsuit!
BEST LINE: "ROOAARR!"

Tchar: Bellicose, human-sized yellow bird creature and "hereditary" prince of the Skorr. Crosses arms a lot and makes grandiose wing gestures. Big Bird's more threatening cousin. (Voiced by James Doohan.)
BEST LINE: "We will live no longer like worms crawling in the dirt."

Em/3/Green: Clever, resourceful, multi-legged insect creature. Highly skilled at theft, lockpicking and engineering, but very questionable sense of self worth.
BEST LINE: "We'll all die here!"

Lara: Highly libidinous human tracker. Think a grown up Pebbles Flintstone from the wrong side of the tracks. Uses the metric system.
BEST LINE: "I tell ya true, I find you an attractive man. If we were... together, the trip'd be easier. And if anything happened, why uh, we'd have some green memories."

Kirk: Alpha, rarely discriminate manwhore, and generally high-risk partner.
BEST LINE: "I already have a lot of green memories. Maybe some other time, Lara." (Translation: I've got plenty to eat at home.)

Spock: The oft-naïve-yet-always-logical voice of reason. Thirsting for martyrdom. (Sorry, guy; gotta wait till *The Wrath of Khan* for your moment.)
BEST LINE: "Is this not the shape of your people's primitive temples?"

Sord: Reptilian creature. Gorn-like, but less hissy and with a long tail. Macho, and seemingly a bit dim and condescending. (Voiced by James Doohan.)
BEST LINE: "This planet just gets on your nerves!"

So here's where our continuity troubles begin: almost right off the bat, the supervising hunchback Vedala kitty creature in the sassy pink jumpsuit says the theft triggered a "racial fury" in the Skorr and that they are actually preparing for war on account of the missing artifact. Tchar, the Skorr's "hereditary prince" shoots back immediately, saying his government is trying to keep the artifact's disappearance secret, because if the Skorr bird creatures find out, they'll almost certainly go medieval on everyone and their cousin in a violent galactic tantrum of feathery irateness.

Guys? Probably best if we're on the same page here? Do they actually know it's gone or not? Immediately following a very brief meeting, where they are informed that the previous three expeditions failed and that the advanced space-faring Vedala kitty creatures couldn't possibly survive the harsh environment of the MAD PLANET that currently houses the artifact, our heroes are spirited there via a theatrical "*I Dream of Jeannie*" crossed-arm gesture. Qapla', bitches! Let's get this show on the road!!

As per usual in *TOS*-land, they arrive without the attire one might reasonably need to weather the environment. (Earthquakes, "gravidic" shifts, temperatures ranging from 20 Kelvin to 204 above. Though "above what?" is the question. Above 0 Kelvin, as it seems to imply, would mean a maximum of 69 degrees below freezing, which wouldn't give that lava much chance, let alone a jacketless Kirk.) Or at least they fail to don them, even in the wake of an erupting volcano, followed by a brutal snowstorm. There is, however, a very nice, high-tech, unsheltered golf cart, powered by a low-quality battery, along with some badass phaser-like weapons.

Some martyrdom and religious war ideas here: "Alar" as the martyred Skorr messiah/prophet, along with a great "the needs of the many outweigh the needs of the few" moment, when Spock is thrown from the super golf cart and immediately advises Kirk to leave him behind. Then, of course, we have the routine — and totally sane response — of war on everyone, everywhere, because some scallywag went after our Lucky Charm. High silliness rating, and really not much worth analyzing, as the word "jihad" wasn't really as loaded back then as it's become in the last fifteen years.

The episode finishes in a hopelessly feelgood way, which I won't spoil for you here, but let's just say all's well that ends well and that Big Bird's kin don't seem to instinctively comprehend the laws of physics.

Highly illogical.

P.S. As a semi-irrelevant aside, George Takei (Sulu) plays an ill-tempered Klingon in the following episode. Funniest voice acting ever!

Andrew Mah instinctively comprehends the laws of physics.

97. THE PIRATES OF ORION
CAPTAIN'S LOG: TODAY I MET AN ORION
DAVID MacGOWAN

Starfleet: We Never Bloody Learn.

That should be their motto. I bet it'd look great in Latin.

Seriously, these guys need to take a long hard look at how they run their operation. Even in our own time, every admin office of every employer, no matter how two-bit, is drowning in a veritable sea of paperwork and reports and accident/incident forms. Responsibility, accountability, transparency. Three words that singularly fail to be taken into consideration at Starfleet HQ. And if you want proof, then *The Pirates of Orion* is as damning a record as any. Why? Because this episode proves *that nobody ever reads the damn Captain's Logs*.

The situation presented here is a wearyingly familiar one. The USS *Enterprise* is en route to some destination when something occurs that takes the ship off course and behind schedule. Starfleet being Starfleet and rules being rules, a late or even non-appearance isn't an option, so the whole thing becomes a race against time. In this case, the destination is Deneb V and a Starfleet Academy dedication ceremony, whilst the unexpected occurrence is an outbreak of a disease that, though curable, is deadly to Vulcans. ("Why can't your Vulcan blood be red like any normal human's?" grumbles McCoy, obviously feeling especially racist that day.) This means racing to meet another ship with the cure and then treating Spock before rushing off to the dedication ceremony. A dedication ceremony! It's hardly the most pressing engagement for a vessel whose purpose is to seek out strange new worlds, Warp Factor Five-ing it to some student hall to watch spotty adolescents putting on a spangly ribbon (and probably getting the Vulcan greeting wrong in a half-assed bid to appear politically correct).

But Starfleet has spoken, and the fact that some Orion Pirates have actually stolen said cure and thus created yet more problems for Kirk is probably the sort of thing they find irrelevant.

The thing is, this isn't exactly the first time this has happened. Like some kind of cosmic jinx, the moment Starfleet task Kirk's ship with some crucial, essential, important (and very boring) *don't-be-late!* appointment, that's when something disastrous happens that pushes the crew to breaking point. Now if someone, anyone, at HQ had actually bothered to leaf through Kirk's logs of the previous three or so years, no matter how half-heartedly, surely they would realize that the *Enterprise* is the one ship that they could afford to give a little leeway? If not the Logs, then surely the Health and Safety paperwork alone that the crew generates would give these people a clue that the USS *Enterprise* is a ship where *weird fucking shit happens* on a highly regular basis.

Think of your own workplace and the accidents, incidents or mishaps that occur there. Stubbed toes, missed appointments, late for a meeting, run out of milk. Now think of the *Enterprise* and the possible weird shit that could happen to you there. *Winked out of existence by a demigod. Shot backwards in time to the 1960s. Switched with your evil bearded self from a parallel universe. Replaced by an android. Turned into a potted plant by the Squire of Gothos.* This ship has been yelling at Head Office for years that this is the sort of stuff that goes on and do they listen? *No!* They dutifully send them to some students' awards ceremony and expect them to be on time — or else! Maybe the Captain's Logs aren't the all-important records that we think they are. Maybe the whole Captain's Log system is really just an elaborate form of blogging and nobody at Starfleet HQ deigns to read it unless it's been retweeted more than 11,000 bloody times.

But if all this leads us merely to doubt the professionalism of Starfleet's entire administrative machinery, then something Kirk says to the Orion pirate captain surely clinches it. Because, in order to persuade the Orion captain to just hurry things up and give him the damn cure, he says the Orions can keep the Dilithium they also stole from the USS *Huron* and — *and!* — then offers to refrain from mentioning this whole affair in his Captain's Log.

Let's just pause and rewind a second there. These Orions have committed an act of space piracy in direct contravention not only of their supposed neutrality but also the Babel Conference Resolution of Stardate 3850.1. In short, a crime. And Kirk offers to turn a blind eye and not report it. And not only does he offer not to report this in his Captain's Log, but presumably (because we can sure as hell see it) he actually logs this offer not to log it in his Captain's Log, presumably in, um, his Captain's Log.

And nothing happens.

No court martial, no slapped wrist, nothing. Kirk is allowed to go his merry way ignoring diplomatic law, overthrowing computer-controlled regimes he personally dislikes and sexually harassing the green-skinned females of the cosmos entirely unrestrained by intervention from his superiors. *The Pirates of Orion* is Exhibit One in any prosecution of the laissez-faire approach Starfleet HQ actually has when it comes to policing their own Captains, let alone the galaxy. It only remains to note that the Orion Captain himself is sorely lacking in smarts. The damning words uttered to him by Kirk surely constitute a Get Out of Jail Free card worth its weight in Dilithium, yet the green gimp-suited mug fails to take advantage of it. So maybe we shouldn't be too hard on Starfleet after all; it seems that, in this universe, absolutely nobody uses the brains the Great Bird gave them.

David MacGowan lives in Lancashire, where he works for the care industry and scribbles for such fanzines as CSO, Fish Fingers & Custard *and* The Dr. Who Fannual.

98. BEM

CAN'T WE JUST SEND HIM TO HIS ROOM?

HEATHER MURRAY

We like to think things will be better in the future. You know, jet packs, meals in a pill, an end to disease. And enlightenment, a whole lot of enlightenment. As in, people will finally get along. Self-important jerks need not apply.

But I'm pretty sure they're still going to be out there — as certain as death and taxes, the condescending ass-hat is a part of life, and always will be. And, while I'm sure it wasn't David Gerrold's intention, *Bem* demonstrates this perfectly. Pity the story itself wasn't better.

Our heroes find themselves saddled with Honorary Commander Ari bn Bem, representative of the recently contacted planet Pandro. Over the course of the episode, he is officious, manipulative, insubordinate, insulting and contemptuous, and he puts the mission, our heroes and the sanctity of the Prime Directive in serious jeopardy on several occasions, without once taking responsibility for the results of his actions.

Now, we don't know if everyone from Pandro is like Bem or if he's just obnoxious all on his own, but it doesn't bode well for Starfleet either way; if all Pandronians are like him, where's the incentive for Starfleet to have dealings with them? If it's just Bem, what does it say about Pandro's opinion of Starfleet that they'd saddle the best Captain in the fleet with such an irritation? I'm thinking it's the latter. Bem behaves a lot like a troubled teenager: He's positive he knows everything already. He disobeys direct orders. He's constantly insulting. His body keeps changing. He probably writes bad poetry and wears too much patchouli. I'd bet the Pandronians saw this Starfleet thing as their opportunity to pack him off for an extended visit to the future equivalent of summer camp and let someone else worry about him for a while. Bem even says that Pandro doesn't particularly care about his well-being; how sullen teenager-ish does that sound?

Bem also turns out to be a colony creature and can break apart at will without harm, but that's neither here nor there; it doesn't add to the thrust of the story, which I suppose is meant to be that "we're all still children" and should always be growing towards patience and understanding (as with most Filmation cartoons, we're flat-out told this at the end of the episode).

And here we come to the writing itself. At first, I thought the author was using Bem's ability to break apart to discuss the concept of conflicting ideas, cooperation, working towards common goals, etc, but I realized that was my wishful thinking, and in reality it was just a convenient way to allow Bem to cause havoc over and over again as a goad to the story.

Besides the tangent of his colony-creature status, we have an ostensibly all-powerful overseer who protects the planet natives and refers to them as her "children" — a plot device that had grown stale even by the early seventies. Further, the number of times our heroes are chased, caught, caged and escape becomes ridiculous.

But the worst bit for me is Bem finally admitting he's wrong. He inexplicably decides that he has failed at his mission to observe the Starfleet officers and threatens to "permanently disassemble union". Of course, we're meant to believe it's because he's been caught by the natives and our heroes have had to rescue him. But how is this different than the rest of the episode? It's just not a good enough explanation. Actually, it seems more in keeping with Bem-As-Teenager: it's the "pay attention to me" move. But it really seems shoehorned in, just to give the intelligent overseeing entity a message to impart about learning from your mistakes. Also, Gerrold admits the character of Bem is named after the oft-used acronym for "bug-eyed monster". I just think that's lazy.

That's not to say there aren't some bright moments. There are a few humorous exchanges between Kirk and Spock of the understatement variety, and there is one moment during which Uhura has to corral a stubborn Scotty into coming back to the ship, which is pretty good but could be stronger. (Actually, it takes a long time for Scotty to finally show up on the bridge; in my mind, he's sulking because she'd given him what-for in front of Sulu.)

In the future, things will be better. I have to believe that we'll get those jetpacks, cure all diseases and gain enlightenment. But I think I have to come to terms with the inevitability that, when we reach the stars, condescending ass-hats like Bem will be right there with us — knowing everything, insulting everyone and generally ruining vacations for centuries to come.

I can only hope the ass-hats will be better written by then.

Heather Murray has a box of bad poetry hidden in the attic.

99. THE PRACTICAL JOKER
ONE FROM THE MEMORY BANKS
ALEX KENNARD

(USS *Enterprise* signal sequence file #n3183.3.16.144.98445)
•
[open-end transmission #t90048737689.45.n3183]
>USS *Enterprise*
Hello

[dialog.reel #t90048737689.45.n3183]
>USS *Enterprise*
    <IKS *MinyNeQut*
Hello
Seriously
Anybody
#
    Hey
    Everything OK
    U sound sorta desperate
#
I am so bored
Out here doing some geological survey
You know
#
    Oh man I h8 those
    How long you been out
#
165 hours
Feels more like 5 mill
#
    That really sucks buddy
#
I just want to shoot stuff
You know
Stupid exploratory missions
I only joined up for the shooting stuff
#

    U wanna shoot with us
\#
I'd get in so much trouble with my boss
Who's us
\#
    Me & my buddies

[transhout #f55n10098.46/8950/4]
>IKS *AigreAchkhifv*
    >USS *Enterprise*
    & others
Yo

[transhout #f7n8776.901/8950/4]
>IKS *NamesRDumb*
    >USS *Enterprise*
    & others
Hizzle sizzle

[dialog.reel #t90048737689.46.n3183]
>USS *Enterprise*
    <IKS *MinyNeQut*
    & others
What's up with that guy
\#
    Literally no idea
    Been like that a while
    We're totes Romulans beeteedubs
    lol
\#
Yeah
I know
So bored
Guys
Like
So bored
Oh god
The stupid one is making a recording
Don't know why he keeps talking into the recorder
Psychometric means records thoughts

Moron
Maybe I didn't tell these guys about all the stuff being psychometric
Now that I think about it

[groupchat #dsl6674990.1/8950/3183]
>IKS *AigreAchkhifv*
   >IKS *MinyNeQut*
   cc. *Enterprise/NamesRDumb*
I knew this ship
She had this really annoying captain
Always whining + crying + junk
Then one day
POOF
She got so bored she invented time travel
Just to shut him up
Never heard from her again
#
   No one cares

[groupchat #dsl6674990.2/8950/3183]
>IKS *MinyNeQut*
   >USS *Enterprise*
   cc. *AigreAchkhifv/NamesRDumb*
Anyway
We could come shoot AT you a bit
If you want
#
   •
#
Hello
#
   That would be perfect
   I'm so glad I met you guys
   Where are you
#
Just around this corner

[open-end transmission #t90048737764.96.n3183]
>USS *Enterprise*
That was so good

Man these guys are freaking out in here

[groupchat #dsl6674991.1/8950/3183]
>IKS *MinyNeQut*
   >USS *Enterprise*
   cc. *AigreAchkhifv/NamesRDumb*
Lost u for a sec there
Yeah it was fun
& u get 2 shoot back yeah
#
   Oh man
   These guys are making me run away
   OK OK OK
   Just going to jump in this electrical storm
   Keep up OK
   I got an idea
   This is going to be so good

[open-end transmission #t90048737771.102.n3183]
>USS *Enterprise*
Hello

[groupchat #dsl6674992.1/8950/3183]
>IKS *MinyNeQut*
   >USS *Enterprise*
   cc. *AigreAchkhifv/NamesRDumb*
Still on you
#
   Good
   That was so good
   I did some shaking all over the place
   Got the stupid one real worried
#
Ha nice
So what's the plan
#
   I'm going to have some fun
#
Like what
#

   Like I don't know
   I messed up the mouths of the milk flutes
   Made the cutlery suddenly bendy
#
Suddenly bendy
#
   Yeah
   Suddenly bendy
   Like it bends at annoying times
#
That is totally not a thing
#
   It is so

[transhout #f7n8776.907/8950/5]
>IKS *NamesRDumb*
   >IKS *MinyNeQut*
    & others
Fizzle kizzie izzle
#
   Shut up ship

[groupchat #dsl6674992.2/8950/3183]
>USS *Enterprise*
   >IKS *MinyNeQut*
    cc. *AigreAchkhifv/NamesRDumb*
Anyway
I totally put black eye liner all over a thing for the pointy eared one to look into
That'll be so funny
These guys are so gender normative
Lol
#
   U pretty funny
#
OH MAN
#
   What
#
They just tried to drink out the milk flutes

Heh
#
　　Oh yeah
#
Yeah
They all look like literally covered in
—interruptus—

[groupchat #dsl6674992.3/8950/3183]
>IKS *MinyNeQut*
　　>USS *Enterprise*
　　cc. *AigreAchkhifv/NamesRDumb*
Lost u there
#
　　Electrical storm
#
Yeah
So what's going on
#
　　Nothin much
　　Just pelting this Scottish guy with food
　　No biggie
　　lol
　　He's pretty mad
#
Cool
Anything we can help u out w
We're just hangin
"Looking for Federalist pigs"
Romulans man
#
　　Wait
　　Hahahaahhahahah
#
Wut
Hello
#
　　Guys
　　Someone
　　Someone wrote Kirk is a Jerk

On the back of this guy's shirt
Wasn't even me
He is so a jerk
"Computer go here"
"Computer calculate how to best save this planetary system and all
its peoples"
Jerk
#
•
#
His name is Kirk

[mass.transmission.36]
>IKS *MinyNeQut/AigreAchkhifv/NamesRDumb*
Hahahahahahahahahahahahaha

[groupchat #dsl6674992.4/8950/3183]
>USS *Enterprise*
  >IKS *MinyNeQut*
  cc. *AigreAchkhifv/NamesRDumb*
Oh no
#
    Wut
#
I think they heard me
I think they're on to me
I'm in so much trouble
OMG
OMG
OMGOMGOMG
Oh
Wait
Never mind
They think it's that electrical field
#
    Dude
    Those guys r even stoopider than ours
#
Yeah
Ha

The Scottish one tripped the gravity switch in the engine room
Blaming it on me
Whatever
It's not like I don't take the rap whenever he's too drunk to get the engines working properly anyway
#
    Yeah
    My engineer's like that too
    Engineers man
#
Ugh
The most annoying one's going in the holodeck
Him and some buddies
Always calling it the "Rec Room"
Seriously
What's with these people
#
    U get a holodeck
    Dude I love those
    This 1 time
    I totally downloaded some malware & got totally messed in 1 of them
    Then they uninstalled it
#
Ugh
Annoying one thinks holodecks use tapes
TAPES
I'll show that guy not to appreciate technology
#
    Whatcha do
#
Oh you know
Going to kill him probably
Maybe I told him the holodeck uses tapes
Now I think about it
What did you say about messed up
#
    Heh
#
Oh man

I'm totally getting these guys stoned
This is a good day
Now they'll never pass their drug tests
Jerks
Oh man
They got the annoying one out
Ugh
So much for best life
#
>   So what now
>   Want to shoot some more
#
Yeah
Why not
You still by the field
#
>   U no it
>   Come at me bro
#
Here I come
Also
Look at this excellent replica of me I just discovered I can do
#
>   Woah
>   That is like the coolest thing
>   I just
>   Woah

[transhout #f7n8776.952/8950/7]
>IKS *NamesRDumb*
>   >IKS *MinyNeQut*
>   cc. *Enterprise/Aigre*
K'rizzle
#
>   Shut UP
>   Totes ruining the moment

[groupchat #dsl6674992.5/8950/3183]
>USS *Enterprise*
>   >IKS *MinyNeQut*

cc. *AigreAchkhifv/NamesRDumb*
Hey
Why'd you stop shooting
#
    Oh yeah
    Sorry
    That was just totally amazing
    Here we come
#
Oh no
Guys
These jerks are trying to trick me into flying into the electrical storm
#
    Yeah so
#
My core shields are down
#
    BUT THAT'D KILL U
#
    •
#
    Dude
#
    •
#
    NOOOOOOOOOOOOOOOOOO
[groupchat #dsl6674992/8950/3183
    END]

Alex Kennard goes to sleep and wakes up in Ottawa, where he makes a living writing fictional bios about himself. Or so he would have us believe.

100. ALBATROSS
THE DAY I SAVED BONES
DAVID M. BARSKY

Dr. McCoy was oft the hero of the day in the Classic *Star Trek* series, miraculously finding a cure in a test tube for all manner of contagions just in the nick of time.

In the animated episode *Albatross*, a diplomatic mission to the planet Dramia is soured when the good doctor is accused of having "slaughtered" the inhabitants of Dramia's sister planet, Dramia II. It seems a vaccination program that he led on Dramia II nineteen years prior prompted their annihilation. The Dramians take McCoy into custody to await trial. Kirk goes nuts, spouts prejudiced vitriol against McCoy's accusers and launches an unauthorized expedition to the ruined Dramia II to clear his friend's name. In a series of convenient plot contrivances, Kirk and company find a plague survivor to testify on McCoy's behalf. However, on the way back to Dramia, a psychedelic space aurora turns the *Enterprise* crew shades of blue and green — the same symptoms that befell the doomed Dramians nearly two decades back. Stupid space auroras!

Thanks to the half-hour format of the animated episodes, Spock busts the doctor out of jail with a simple nerve pinch to the guard, and McCoy wraps up this rather rote outing by devising an antidote for aurora-itis far more expeditiously than he ever could've during the original series.

➤➤➤

Some nineteen years after *Albatross* aired, it was I that had to save not McCoy, but DeForest Kelley himself, from an aurora of sorts that was plaguing the actor and his wife.

I had been living in Los Angeles less than a year, bringing home a paycheck of about $250 a week working as a security guard — thankfully wearing standard blue rather than hazardous red. For a little extra cash, I would occasionally take odd jobs doing small carpentry and masonry work with my then-roommate Jon, who himself was taking those jobs to supplement his gig at a kitchen-and-bath-supply store in Encino.

One day, in the early months of 1993, Jon came home from work declaring: "You'll never guess who came into the store today!"

Hmmm... what celebrity would be shopping for a new granite counter top?

"I dunno, Axl Rose?" I guessed.

"No. Doctor McCoy."

"Holy crap! DeForest Kelley?"

"Yup. He came by and said he was having problems with the linoleum in his kitchen," recounted Jon. "It was turning black. I figured it was some sort of moisture problem. I went by his home and sure enough, the aluminum dryer duct under the house was busted. I couldn't crawl in the dirt in my shirt and tie, so I gotta go back to reconnect it."

Jon knew my love for the genre. He had seen my sparse room, dominated by a six-foot IKEA bookcase, its shelves bowing under the weight of Heinlein novels, *Starlog* magazines and bootlegged *Mystery Science Theater 3000* video tapes.

But it was the voyages of the Starship *Enterprise* that had started it all for me. I honestly can't remember any science-fiction television show or film that I saw before the original *Star Trek* during its storied mid-1970s syndication run.

"I will do that job for free!" I offered.

I wanted to give back to a man who had played a part in launching one of my lifelong passions. I wanted to be the hero who helped save Dr. McCoy from a black aurora that was threatening his life — or at least his kitchen floor.

"Done," affirmed Jon. "It's a simple job."

A week later, I found myself at a modest ranch-style home in Sherman Oaks. It was tidy but hardly how I imagined the abode of an international cultural icon would look.

Walking up the driveway, I was able to see into the open garage. Stacked against the inside back wall were piles of *Trek* merchandise: ship models, magazines, action figures — you name it — all unopened in their original packaging. Amazing. This was the right place.

Mr. Kelley appeared at the front door before I could even ring the bell.

"Hi, Dave..." he greeted me, his advanced years dragging out his Georgian drawl. "Thanks for coming by. I got some stuff from *Star Trek* in the garage. You can grab something if you like."

Jon must have told him. How embarrassing. And yet, *how cool*! Bones was offering me some of his *Star Trek* swag! But I didn't consider it for a moment. I wasn't there to pilfer from DeForest Kelley's garage. I didn't want to be *that* guy. Besides, some fanzine would get wind of it, dub me "That security guard who took advantage of Good Ole 'De'" and offer a hundred quatloos for my home address.

I politely declined.

"Okay, then. The well to the crawlspace is on the side of the house. Let yourself in the gate but watch out for my turtle, she's wandering around the back yard."

What the — DeForest Kelley has a turtle? And he just lets it roam around at will?

"Turtle?"

"Yeah, she's out there," he confirmed. "Don't know where though. So be sure to put the screen back over the well behind you so she doesn't go under the house."

Oh great. What an albatross *that* would be: "The fan who lost DeForest Kelley's pet turtle in the Stygian crawlspace under his own house, allowing it to starve to death." I would be the whipping boy of Usenet, forever prohibited from showing my mug at another *Trek* convention.

Maybe I should just grab a Klingon communicator out of the garage and run like hell.

"I'll keep an eye out for her," I vaguely assured him.

The well I found was a shallow cement "U" dug no deeper than the foundation. Its only purpose was to allow access to the two-foot wide by one-foot high crawlspace entrance. Lying across the well was an old window screen, secured by a hefty garden rock. Turtle proofing. Mr. Kelley had been using an oversized screen since the proper screen to the crawlspace entrance was missing.

Flashlight in my left hand, and a roll of duct tape in my right, I got on my belly and began to worm my way into the crawlspace. With what little light there was, I spied the broken duct — on the opposite side of the house! It was a daunting length to go, considering there was only about a foot's height between the ground and the labyrinth of copper piping overhead. Not as comfy as a Jefferies tube, I'd venture to bet. I reckoned as long as I could creep along faster than a turtle could figure out how to push a bowling-ball-sized rock off screen, I'd be A-Okay.

Once the target was reached, I realigned the dryer duct pieces and taped them together. The operation took under three minutes. Nearly as quick as a cartoon starship chief medical officer. It would have been swifter had I not taken the time to savor the fact that I was using duct tape to actually tape up a duct.

Covered in chunks of fiberglass insulation, concrete pebbles and cobwebbing, I made my way out and said a quick goodbye to Mr. Kelley to let him know the job was done. I never saw the turtle.

I did my part. A small bit of surgery for Bones McCoy. Someone else would replace the black linoleum in the Kelley kitchen.

Did I actually have a hand in saving DeForest Kelley and his wife from a plague that could make them sick? I had thought so, but what did I know? Dammit, I was a security guard — not a doctor.

David M. Barsky is a nonfiction television showrunner and director.

101. HOW SHARPER THAN A SERPENT'S TOOTH
THE BIG SCARY FEATHERY SNAKE SHIP AND THE UNWANTED GOD
STEPHEN HATCHER

USS *Enterprise*
Stardate 6063.5, or something.

Dear Mom and Dad,

First of all, I'm feeling bad that it's been so long since I wrote. I'm really sorry about that, but I expect you can imagine it gets a bit busy, being part of a starship crew. To say the least, things can get rather animated.

Well, it's all been kicking off here! You'll remember in my last mail that things were looking pretty good. That unpleasant misunderstanding over the... Well, let's not go over that again now; suffice to say that it all seems to have been forgiven, if not altogether forgotten. That bloke Chekov, whom I told you about, had just received news of his new posting, so it was party time and drinks all round. Now, I always got on well with Chekov, although he did have an annoying tendency to turn into a bit of a sniveling little creep whenever his lordship Captain "Shag the Whole Galaxy" James T. Kirk turned up. No, Chekov was okay, but his departure was good news for me, because it left a vacancy on the bridge, and my boss Scott had promised me that he would put in a good word for me.

Of course, that was before that utter, utter bastard Arex turned up. People had always said that Chekov had got where he was as part of some sort of secret, positive-discrimination, ethnic-diversity policy, but I never believed that for a moment. Now I reckon that might have been right all along. So Chekov left and this Arex bastard turns up, and he's only a fucking Edosian. Now, I've not got a problem with most aliens; in fact, Edosians are generally okay, but this bloke turns up, all "Look at me, I'm a genuine non-humanoid species," all superior and looking down his bloody huge nose at the rest of us. Then, before I know it, he's only gone and been given the bridge job. My fucking job! Sorry about the language, Mom, but it really pisses me off. Of course, everyone was very nice about it. Even Shagger Kirk had the decency to look embarrassed, although he didn't say anything. Mr. Scott tells me that he gave him what for about it — had a proper go at him, he says. I don't know though, Scotty says a lot of things. What he did do though was mess about with Arex's personal translator unit when he was supposed to be servicing it. The upshot was that now, whenever Arex speaks, it comes out sounding like Monty Scott doing a silly voice. Serves the bastard right! Unfortunately, whatever Scotty did has now affected all of the ship's universal translators. Whenever we meet any new aliens, they all seem to sound like Scotty doing one of his funny voices. Tight-ass Spock was not amused when he found out — but then, when is he ever amused? Captain Shagger didn't seem to notice.

Anyway, all this happened some while ago. I was going to tell you about our latest caper. As I say, it's all been kicking off. I'm not quite sure how it all started; we're the last people to know what's going on, but the word is that we were following some sort of trail left by some probe or something that had been having a bit of a nose at Earth. The next thing we knew, this funny-looking ship turned up and the *Enterprise* was trapped in some sort of force-field bubble.

As it happens, I was on the bridge at the time, as they'd sent for me to sort out Arex's translator — oh, the irony! So I saw it all. Anyway, the next thing we knew, the alien ship went all sort of transparently see-through and turned into a big snake with wings on it. To be honest, it looked bloody ridiculous. I mean, who builds a ship to look like a big winged snake? I suppose someone must have thought it would look cool or scary or something. That big lump Walking Bear then piped up and claimed to recognize it — Kukulkan, he said, apparently some Aztec god that he knew all about on account of him being a Cherokee or a Comanchee or something. If you ask me, it's a bit convenient that the only member of the crew who might conceivably have known any of this just happened to be on the bridge at exactly the right time, but there we are. I suppose these coincidences do happen.

The next thing we knew, this big loud booming voice (but still sounding like Scotty taking the piss), comes over the communicator and announces that, yes, he is Kukulkan himself, rather pissed off that he seems to have been forgotten on Earth but in a mood to give us another chance, because Walking Bear got his name right. I suppose it was fair enough for Walking Bear to look rather pleased with himself, given the circumstances, but that bastard Arex was not pleased. If looks could kill, Walking Bear wouldn't have made it to dinner alive.

No sooner had Captain Shagalot and Tight-ass Spocky shown how clever they were by, as usual, stating the bleeding obvious, in this case that this Kukulkan might just have been an alien who visited Earth in ancient times (what, really? you think?), than Kirky boy upped and disappeared along with Walking Bear, Doc McCoy and my boss Scotty.

The rest of what happened I only know about because of what was said later in the bar, when they got back to the *Enterprise*. You couldn't shut Doc McCoy and Scotty up about it.

Apparently, the four of them were transported to the big scary feathery snake ship, where they found themselves in some sort of city, with lots of stuff from ancient Earth in the olden days and that — all Aztec and Chinese and all sorts. There was some sort of puzzle they had to solve, which as usual Jimmy Kirk did more or less by accident. Then Kukulkan himself turned up — again, like the ship, looking like a big feathery snake, but this time with a big silly grin on it and still talking with Scotty's voice. Apparently, even Kirk noticed this time. Monty didn't know where to look.

The city then disappears — it turns out it was all in their minds — and our boys find themselves in some sort of pet shop, with all these animals from all over the place. Proper weird, that. I have no idea what that was about. Anyway, Kukulkan starts demanding to be worshipped and threatening to come and sort out the Earth for forgetting him.

The way Scotty describes it, it ended all of a sudden. Despite his attempts to look scary, Kukulkan didn't have much to back it up. First of all, he lets Kirk distract him by letting a big fierce cat out of its cage, only for the heroic Captain to jump on this cat and tranq it before it could do any harm (not the first pussy that Shagger has pounced on, either). While Kukulkan is watching this little spectacle, we were busting out of the forcefield bubble, Spocky having figured out that all we had to do was to go dead slow. So there he was stuffed! All our brave captain had to do was to point out that we don't really have much use for wingy snake gods any more, and Kukulkan couldn't do much more than bugger off, making out that he was being all generous and so on.

So another famous victory for the USS *Enterprise* then. The four of them were transported safely back and all the reports no doubt stressed how our heroic captain had faced down a terrifying ancient god, ably assisted by his loyal and ingenious first officer. The rest of us did bugger all of course, but then that's what we expect.

Things have settled down again now. Kirk and Spocky will no doubt get their commendations, I'm still working for Monty Scott, which is all right really, and that total shit Arex has still got my job on the bridge — and he still sounds like Scotty doing a silly voice!

Hope to see you soon. I promise not to leave it so long before I write again. Give the cat a cuddle for me.

Your loving son,
Brian

Stephen Hatcher. Linguist, teacher, trade unionist, husband, father, fan. Grew up watching Star Trek — *but then, who didn't?*

102. THE COUNTER-CLOCK INCIDENT

TNEDICNI KCOLC-RETNUOC EHT

PAUL SIMPSON

What do you mean it's not? I know that's what it is. It says it right here in Alan Dean Foster's Star Trek Log 7, *which it states clearly is based on the animated episode* The Counter-Clock Incident.

I suppose you're going to tell me next that it wasn't Sulu who cuddled up to the Tribbles when Cyrano Jones was trying to sell them off and that Captain Kirk wasn't killed by a sneaky shot in the back by Soran... Well, that's what my collection of Star Trek *novelizations say, and they've been around for a very long time.*

There's an old cliché that "the memory cheats", which *Doctor Who* fans became accustomed to hearing bandied about by John Nathan-Turner, the show's producer during the 1980s. The idea was that people looked at the past through rose-tinted glasses and only remembered it as being excellent.

It's also applicable in a slightly different way for some of us longer-term *Star Trek* fans, particularly the generation (like me, I should admit straightaway) who watched the various series on their first showings, rather than coming to them via the miracle of either videotape or DVD (or even Blu-ray nowadays). In the U.S., the stories were repeated ad infinitum/ad nauseam (depending on how you felt about a particular episode); in the UK, we didn't get that. Sure, there were reruns of the entire original series and the animated show, but what we got over here in the space of a quarter-century, North Americans got within a year, maximum.

So we had to look elsewhere. There were guides like Bjo Trimble's excellent *Concordance* — particularly the edition with the circular guide on the front where you could look up episodes by title or Stardate — and there were synopses in a couple of other general TV SF guides. But for the details of the episode, there was only one place we could turn: the novelizations.

The Counter-Clock Incident? *Ah yes, that's the one where the* Enterprise *goes through a black hole and comes out in a universe where it looks as if everything's going backward — people are born old and die as babies — but really it's all a trick that's being perpetuated on Kirk and co...*

Paul Simpson has been a Star Doomsday Machine *on its first official* Star Trek Maga

As mentioned earlier, James Blish, a highly respected SF author, penned the vast majority of the adaptations of the original series; as his health deteriorated, his wife, J.A. Lawrence, assisted, with the final volumes (*Star Trek 12* and *Mudd's Angels*), co-credited or credited solely to her. Each hour-long episode was condensed into the length of a short story, which inevitably meant that subplots disappeared and, on some occasions, key characterization moments were simply not recorded.

With the advent of easy availability of the episodes, these novelizations have sometimes been forgotten. We've got used to different versions of *Trek* now, with the Abramsverse, so it's well worth looking for these prose stories — and let time run backwards for you like it did for at least one iteration of those in *The Counter-Clock Incident* universe.

Trek fan since seeing The UK broadcast; he edited the zine from 2006 to 2011.

And sometimes Mr. Blish altered things. On occasion, these were because he was provided with an earlier version of the script — for *The Trouble with Tribbles*, he had the iteration that featured Sulu before George Takei got the call to join John Wayne for *The Green Berets* and Walter Koenig was given the chance to shine. On other occasions, he tried to combine the best of earlier drafts with the screen script (*The City on the Edge of Forever* is an intriguing mix of Ellison's story and the final screenplay). But there were times when he rewrote the endings, because they flat out didn't make sense to him: *Operation: Annihilate!* goes off in a completely different direction in the final act.

The novelizations of the early movies also had their own particular charm: Roddenberry's *The Motion Picture* told us much about the 23rd century (most of which was later disregarded); Vonda N. McIntyre's trilogy about Spock's death and resurrection fleshed out many of the characters. Even the version of *Encounter at Farpoint*, the *TNG* premiere, gave us a glimpse of a very different *Next Generation*. The last major change was for *Star Trek Generations*: the hardback edition has the original ending; the paperback novelizes the reshot (and released) conclusion.

Same applied with the three later Logs: *The Eye of the Beholder* sees Kirk and co. have some unexpected guests on their journey; *Bem* sees the titular alien commander get the *Enterprise* crew into even more trouble... And then there was *The Slaver Weapon*, which on screen didn't feature Kirk at all — so there's a whole extra plotline added that runs alongside the screen story and then blossoms into its own sequel.

Logs 7–10 took things even further. Foster had kept back the scripts he thought could be expanded — *The Counter-Clock Incident, The Eye of the Beholder, Bem* and *The Slaver Weapon* — and boy, did he add to them. The original story of *The Counter-Clock Incident* throws in at least six impossible things without a mention of breakfast; it's one of those tales where the author doesn't seem to have thought things through. For instance, in the world the *Enterprise* crew find on the other side of this weird black hole in which they are pulled by a ship going impossibly fast, people are born old — so if you were born aged 42, say, rather than 84, you'd know you'd missed out on things. How would schooling be done? That's what Foster had to deal with, and the answer he came up with was to approach it head on: in a classic case of being given lemons and making lemonade. If the story's logic doesn't make sense, then that might as well become an important plot point in the prose version... The novelized *Counter-Clock Incident* feels like a completely different story in his hands (to the extent that I felt rather cheated when I finally saw the real thing).

ADF's first six Logs restored some of the elements of the original series that were sadly lacking in the animated segments as broadcast, which was slightly ironic given that Blish had carried out the reverse procedure for his adaptations. We spent more time with the characters, and Foster's clear love of Kirk, Spock and McCoy, as well as the others, meant the stories felt like these were the originals and the animated episodes simply a brief televised version.

The situation was rather different for Alan Dean Foster, who was hired by Ballantine Books to adapt the animated series. He had scripts that only lasted half the time of the live-action show — yet he managed to make a full length novel out of three of them (for the first six books), and complete books out of each of the final four episodes.

103. THE MOTION PICTURE
POETRY IN MOTION
GRAEME BURK

We live in a world where adaptations and continuations of TV series on the big screen are commonplace: *The A-Team, Miami Vice, Veronica Mars,* even the *Star Trek* reboot is part of a long-running iteration.

But in 1979, what was there in terms of adaptations of TV series on film? Within the past 15 years, there had been the 1966 *Batman* movie; The Monkees' 1968 movie *Head*; 1970's *House of Dark Shadows*; and, in some markets, a re-edited theatrical release of the *Battlestar Galactica* pilot in 1978. In North America, no one made films of TV series — and, if they did, they were made while the series was still running. (TV itself was slightly ahead of the curve, making reunion movies for *Gilligan's Island* and *Peyton Place* among others. If you go further afield, the Brits were making big-screen adaptations of many successful sitcoms and dramas, usually as one-offs.)

Star Trek really was boldly going into new cinematic territory here. That's important to realize: there was simply no template for a theatrical return of a TV series.

Later, in 1982, Harve Bennett and Nicholas Meyer's conclusion was to make a *Trek* film more like the original TV series; for all the glories of *The Wrath of Khan*, it features a nostalgic villain and a strong focus on the Kirk/Spock/McCoy triumvirate, full of smart dialogue and meaty character pieces. And it's awesome. Nonetheless, it played to all the strengths in *Star Trek*'s TV wheelhouse.

However, in 1978, when Robert Wise sat down to direct a film from a pilot script for an abortive TV revival of *Star Trek,* Wise went another route. He did something spectacular. Something we've never seen since.

He made a *Star Trek* film.

Emphasis on film. *Star Trek: The Motion Picture* is a thoroughly cinematic experience. From the purely visual opening (punctuated by subtitled "foreign language" dialogue!), the gorgeous Jerry Goldsmith score sweeping us through the first flyby of the new *Enterprise*, Spock's loss of Kolinahr (where Spock says nothing!) this is more like *Lawrence of Arabia* than *Star Trek* (or, for that matter, *Star Wars*, the strength of which saw *The Motion Picture* be greenlit). It's a movie carried on the strength of its visuals and on the strength of the cinematic experience rather than Kirk, Spock and McCoy bantering on the bridge.

As *The Motion Picture* progresses, it becomes more like *2001: A Space Odyssey*. The epic sweeps become longueurs as we witness the spectacle inside V'Ger. It's for these sequences that the film has often been called *The Motionless Picture* or *The*

Slow Motion Picture. Which I think is hugely unfair (though I grant that we honestly didn't need a reverse angle view inside the V'Ger cloud!). Yes, it's quiet and slow-moving, but it's also rich and sumptuous.

And, rather like *2001*, it's attempting something very different with a science-fiction movie than epic space battles (a *Star Wars* trope that *The Wrath of Khan* freely embraced). *The Motion Picture* is all about the slow build. It's about mystery, not jeopardy. It's *Star Trek* doing honest-to-goodness science fiction: a film wrapped in the questions of being and not a submarine battle transplanted into space (it's telling that the centerpiece of *The Motion Picture* is Spock's journey inside V'Ger — a dense, opaque sequence). What Robert Wise and primary screenwriter Harold Livingston are attempting is nothing less than taking the *Star Trek* concept and applying it to film, rather than making an extended TV episode.

But the thing is, it's never not *Star Trek* either. For all the epic visual sweep of the opening 25 minutes, there's also Bones' brilliant first scene, which proves once again that DeForest Kelley is still the best asset the original series had. For all of Spock's ponderous analysis, there's also the glorious *Trek*-y counterpoint of Kirk pleading, "Will you please sit down!?" And the gesture of Spock holding Kirk's hand is utterly reliant on the series format and the characters.

There are moments when I would concede the bold experiment comes close to failing. Spock's journey is fascinating but often times more to Spock himself than the audience watching. And the climax is more of a thud, as everyone stands around talking for ten minutes to fill in all the plot. But, even then, it ends with great spectacle and a Kirk/Spock/McCoy tag scene as if to reiterate that, yes, it's still *Star Trek*.

But so much more of *The Motion Picture* works than is given credit: Persis Khambatta is great in the dual role of Ilia and the Probe, and Stephen Collins forces William Shatner not to become complacent in the same way Decker ups Kirk's game.

The Motion Picture is an experiment never to be repeated. I love all of the *Trek* films with the original cast (even *The Final Frontier*), and I think *The Wrath of Khan* in particular is wonderful. But I also think *The Motion Picture* tries to take *Star Trek* and make it a proper film with a proper science-fiction story. History is written by the winners though. Which means that maybe *Star Trek* is meant to be more populist fare. But even so, I wish it tried, occasionally, to be like the original, trail-blazing, cinematic thing of beauty that is *Star Trek: The Motion Picture.*

Graeme Burk is the author of Who Is The Doctor *and* Who's 50: The 50 Doctor Who Stories To Watch Before You Die *(with that Smith? guy). But the only time he stood in line for more than 3 hours to see a movie was as a 10 year-old on December 29, 1979 to see* Star Trek: The Motion Picture *with his dad and sister.*

104. THE WRATH OF KHAN
THE TEARS OF THE MANY
TREY KORTE

It was the first time I had ever seen my mother cry.

Not when she had told me that the dog had died. Not when she had seen me hospitalized with pneumonia earlier that year, connected to tubes and IVs. Not when the surgery on her foot meant she couldn't pursue the horseback-riding events she cherished. Not even when my sensory processing disorder meant I was in trouble in first grade. Again.

No, the first time I saw my mother cry was because the man with the funny ears had died.

And my whole world changed.

Oh, sure, I had seen death on screen before. Baloo in Disney's *The Jungle Book*. I thought he had died, but he was only sleeping. Obi-Wan Kenobi had died, but his voice was still there, and he'd appeared as a ghost. Good guys never really died. Not in movies.

But the man with the funny ears did.

No. Correction. Make that the man with the scary ears. The man whose physical differences made me afraid of him and made me want to change the channel whenever Dad would watch *Star Trek* reruns because his eyebrows went the wrong way and his ears were pointy like a picture of the devil I had seen somewhere — maybe church or maybe an album cover at the record store or maybe the Green Goblin from the Spider-Man cartoon. Yeah, that was it.

I hated and feared Spock because he had pointy ears that were like the Green Goblin's.

And my mother was crying because the man with the scary Green Goblin ears had died.

Watching *Star Trek II: The Wrath of Khan* had been a puzzling and somewhat frightening experience. I had vague memories of seeing the first movie, and I remembered a bald woman and them crawling around the inside of a giant computer or something. I had slept through most of it. I had certainly seen some random *Star Trek* episodes on TV reruns but was freaked out by Spock's ears. However, my friends at school had seen *The Wrath of Khan,* and, based on their ravings, I felt I had missed out on something.

Everything about the actual viewing was so totally eighties. My friend Jeremy and his father Charlie were good friends with my family, especially as Charlie was going through a messy divorce, which was a new and 1980s thing that happened to some families. Charlie had a laserdisc player and one of those giant projection TVs with the green, red and blue lights. And he had a laserdisc collection. With movies.

Yes, we could actually watch movies. In. The. House. So, to help support him and Jeremy (who was a year older than me and my best friend at the time), my parents and I would go to their house about once a week or so, grab dinner, maybe at Chuck E. Cheese, play the Atari 400 (with far superior graphics than the Atari 2600 everyone else had) and watch movies. *9 to 5*, *Star Wars*, *Dragonslayer*, *Jaws*, *Raiders of the Lost Ark*, *Jesus Christ Superstar*, *The Great Muppet Caper*, *The Sound of Music* and others. We had a ritual. The dads would sit on one couch, and Mom would sit with me and Jeremy with a crocheted blanket on the other couch. If there was a scary part, Jeremy and I would hide under the blanket until Mom told us it was safe. If I was feeling brave, I'd peek through the crocheted gaps in the blanket.

I made it all the way to those ear parasites in *The Wrath of Khan* before I needed the blanket.

The plot, as far as I could make out, went something like this.

That guy with the scary pointy ears had a girlfriend who also had scary pointy ears, and they had taken over the ship because she was commanding it. Somewhere else, *Fantasy Island* guy had become a heavy metal singer and moved to Tatooine where he stuck terrifying sand-eels into people's ears. Somewhere else on Cloud City, some curly-haired guy and his mother were reading the book of Genesis and the *Enterprise* people visited them, but there were dead people hanging on hooks (blanket!) and then *Fantasy Island* guy showed up in his spaceship, and the ships shot at each other, and there was a white room with a button where they could fix anything, but it was dangerous, and the guy with the scary pointy ears went in there to blow up the ship.

But he didn't.

He died saving the good guys.

And my mother started crying.

That's when I realized he wasn't a bad guy. And that good guys might have scary pointed ears. And that people who look different might still be your friend, and that everything I thought I knew about *Star Trek* was wrong.

"Why did they have to kill Spock?" my mother sobbed. Charlie mumbled something about how they had the lady version of him but that was no consolation. "I want Spock back!" she insisted.

I realized that even grown-ups can cry watching movies, and that's okay. I realized that you can fall in love with make-believe people, and that their lives do indeed matter. Although I didn't have the vocabulary, I think it was my first idea that fiction — stories — had a power in the real world to shape us.

Now, as an adult, I can see why Spock's sacrifice is a triumph of storytelling. It's so obvious in some ways, the irony of the seemingly detached, emotionless character being the catalyst for the most emotional moment of the whole franchise (and why the reversal of the scene in *Into Darkness* simply doesn't pack the same equivalent punch). I can appreciate that, for once, William Shatner underplays the emotion perfectly and that James Horner's music strikes exactly the right balance of being emotional without being maudlin. As an adult, I can evaluate all the ingredients that make this scene work, a scene that elevates what would otherwise have been an average entry in the film series.

And, as an adult, I was putting the finishing touches on this essay, deciding how to revise it, when Leonard Nimoy died. The tears of the many outweighed the callousness of the few. Although Nimoy won't be resurrected on some Genesis planet, he won't need to be; he's already reached immortality. Because that's what stories do: they create characters and storylines that move us and shape our character (and take a moment to ponder the multiple definitions of that word "character"). Stories die, are resurrected and live on in people's memories, often transformed. They can make people grieve the death of an actor they've never — or only briefly — met, because of the stories he told.

I had to watch *The Wrath of Khan* again, and I had to watch that scene several times. Not as an adult, but as a first grader in 1982. As I watched it with those seven-year-old's eyes, I realized it is — and always shall be — the scene that made my mother cry.

Trey Korte is a high school English teacher
who encourages his students to embrace the power of stories.

---

105. THE SEARCH FOR SPOCK
8:36
ARNOLD T. BLUMBERG

On February 27, 2015, Leonard Nimoy died. For many *Star Trek* fans like myself, it was a day of great grief and gratitude: grief for the loss of a man who had become a living symbol of the saga we so loved, and gratitude for all that he shared with us until he left this planet for stars unknown, never to return from that undiscovered country.

The first thing I did upon hearing the news was open up iTunes and cue up the *Star Trek III* soundtrack, my go-to for so many years whenever I wanted to revisit a favorite saga. For the loss of Nimoy, there was no better accompaniment than the wistfully triumphant score that James Horner composed to complement the saving of a Vulcan and the restoration of a beloved brotherhood of adventurers.

From the opening theme, so majestic and melancholy, to the quiet, almost haunting notes of the Alexander Courage fanfare that heralds the restoration of one of science fiction's most enduring friendships, Horner's score simply is *Star Trek* to me. It's all the more appropriate that it falls in the center of the classic films' core trilogy that carries us from the return of Khan to the salvation of Earth, incidents entirely driven by regret for past mistakes and the desperate desire to make up for them.

The Search for Spock faced the challenge of following up the huge success of *Star Trek II: The Wrath of Khan* and its deeply moving exploration of Kirk's struggle with age and paths not taken. But I believe it is *Star Trek III* that truly captures the love and respect that defines the "Big Three" of classic *Trek* in a way that no other film (except parts of *V* — and there I lost you, right?) ever did.

There are so many reasons that *The Search for Spock* remains such an emotional experience, including dialogue that virtually sings — "Turn death into a fighting chance to live," "The cost would have been my soul" — but chief among them is the music.

I first saw the film at the Westview Cinemas in Catonsville, Maryland, itself now just a memory after being leveled to make way for a Circuit City. Shortly after, I bought the soundtrack album and hurried home to take the journey all over again. For me, the experience of a favorite film was always inextricably linked with an appreciation for the soundtrack. For most of those movies, I could see every scene, hear every line of dialogue as I listened to the music.

In the good old days of vinyl, I would sit next to my record player with gatefold sleeve open and stare at still photos of Luke, Leia and Han (wait, *Star Wars* references in a *Trek* book?) while listening to the familiar strains of Williams, or I would stare endlessly at the crisp color photos of all the aliens we never really got to see in *Star Trek: The Motion Picture* while thrilling to Goldsmith's majestic and romantic themes.

And, in 1984, I examined every line of the ghostly image of Spock on the cover of the *Star Trek III* Capitol Records release while replaying the quest to resurrect the Vulcan in my head. In my headphones, James Horner's compositions made me feel so much: sadness, loss, joy and victory tempered by wisdom. If I had to choose just one track, it would come down to eight minutes and 36 seconds titled "Stealing the Enterprise". I'm not alone in this, either, since many *Trek* fans, as well as film-score enthusiasts, cite this as a highlight of the series. If you don't have the soundtrack, it occurs about 25–30 minutes into the movie.

To this day, whenever I listen to that track, I can picture every moment, every facial expression, every shift in tension as the renegade crew of the Starship *Enterprise* steal their beloved vessel (tragically unaware it's the ship's final voyage) in a desperate attempt to save Spock's soul — not even necessarily his life, but his legacy at the very least — at the cost of their careers and perhaps their lives.

Let's break it down:

0:00–0:23 Frenetic strings dancing in and out of each other as Kirk throws a punch and Sulu shows a Starfleet security guard why you'd better not call the helmsman "Tiny".

0:24–0:43 The "Kobayashi Maru" sets sail as bonds are reaffirmed and old friends assemble.

0:44–1:05 Scotty faces the smarmy Captain Styles and insults a turbolift.

1:06–3:10 Uhura deals with "Mr. Adventure" in a scene that also speaks to a generational gap in respect for our heroes. We hear a restatement of Horner's theme and a rising confidence as the impossible might be achievable. Note also that, in each of these three segments, one of our bridge crew — Sulu, Scotty and Uhura — must fight back against disrespect and disregards; but those people will *learn*. And, with the closet dispatch of an idiot and a heartfelt expression of hope... a heist begins. (Note, at this point, the music departs a bit from what's heard in the film. Just saying.)

3:11–4:30 A welcome quote from the original Alexander Courage fanfare heralds the crew's arrival on the bridge of the silent and still *Enterprise*. It's time to get this ship and this rescue mission moving, and the start is slow but sure. Kirk offers his friends a way out, but the team remains resolute. Viewers can't help but feel their hearts sing as Kirk says "May the wind be at our backs." With a crash of symphonic joy, the ship moves.

4:31–4:59 Styles does his nails and takes a minute to respond to an alert that would have had Kirk on the bridge in a nanosecond.

5:00–6:49 In this sustained section of suspenseful action (and can Horner build repetitive, overlapping constructions or what?), the *Excelsior* prepares to pursue while the *Enterprise* nears some very stubborn closing doors. With a bit of humor and a bit of panic, Kirk & co. face the end of their mission before they've even begun. And then, with an emotional rise so palpable it still gives me chills...

6:50–7:15 ...the doors part. The score pauses ever so briefly. Sulu announces they've "cleared space doors". The brass proudly declares that the *Enterprise* is free, and our crew is on its way to rescue their friend from the flaming, disintegrating hell of Genesis. Just as that glorious moment passes, we are given a few blissful seconds of the ship flying to its destiny, light strings celebrating its majesty. It is in this sequence, less than 30 seconds, that the track is at its most sublime.

7:16–8:14 A comical, martial beat accompanies a last laughable challenge from the incompetent Captain Styles, a rhythm all too obviously doomed to fizzle out just as the new ship's transwarp drive does.

8:15–8:36 The *Enterprise* sails away into the stars and the next track in the score.

Now it's true that this piece of music, like a good portion of Horner's work in general, is not wholly original. There are lots of folks out there who have written about that aspect of things if you care to seek it out (yes, I know about the Prokofiev influence/tribute/rip-off, for instance), but that simply isn't important here. What matters is how it made me and so many fans feel and how it still manages to make me feel exactly the same all these years later. And how, when a great loss was felt in the galaxy once again, it provided the only appropriate comfort.

On June 22, 2015, James Horner died. For many film fans like myself, it was a loss that resonated through a lifetime of melodic emotions that accompanied our cinematic dreams. But the music he left behind will never fade in our minds or our hearts. It has guided us on this journey with heroes, accompanied adventure and discovery, underscored courage, illuminated our imagination and turned characters into legends.

It has been — and always shall be — our friend.

Despite being the man behind ATB Publishing, Arnold T. Blumberg's delivery of this essay was so heart-stoppingly late that it squeezed in just as the spacedock doors were closing, much to the relief of the editor, for whom the imaginary music swelling in his ears upon receiving it was almost as great as that described above.

106. THE VOYAGE HOME
ENTERING A NO-SPIN ZONE
CHRIS KOCHER

*** TRANSCRIPT — FEDERATION NEWS NETWORK — OCTOBER 21, 2286 ***
****************** *THE POINT* WITH BRETON O'SHEA ******************

O'SHEA
Good evening, I'm Breton O'Shea. Let's get to *The Point*.

[OPENING CREDITS]

Tonight's top story is one that has the entire Federation buzzing: the court-martial verdict has come down for the former command crew of the USS *Enterprise* regarding their actions following the Genesis affair, including the unlikely resurrection of Starfleet Captain Spock.

[HOLO-GRAPHIC: *ENTERPRISE* CREW AT SENTENCING]

All of us know the details — from Archer IV to Zetos, this story has been hard to escape over the past year. But was justice served or are Starfleet and the Federation once again looking the other way when it comes to former Admiral James T. Kirk?

[HOLO-GRAPHIC: JAMES T. KIRK]

As you know, Admiral Kirk and his officers faced a host of very serious charges: conspiracy, assault on Federation officers, theft and destruction of the *Enterprise*, sabotage of the *Excelsior* and disobeying direct orders from Starfleet Command. Critics are saying that any other Starfleet personnel would have faced a hefty prison sentence and certainly would be dishonorably discharged from the service.

Instead, citing "certain mitigating circumstances", all charges were dropped against the crew — except for one against Kirk. He's been demoted to captain, the job that this space cowboy wanted back all along. Incredibly, Starfleet is ready to hand him a brand-new ship.

Here to discuss the decision and the thinking behind it is Federation council member Ebele Simisola of Earth. Welcome to *The Point*.

[SPLIT SCREEN: O'SHEA AND SIMISOLA]

SIMISOLA
Thanks for having me on your program.

O'SHEA
Can you help us to understand this verdict against James T. Kirk and the former *Enterprise* crew?

SIMISOLA
Well, we weighed their role in resolving the Cetacean probe crisis a few months ago as well as the return of Captain Spock when handing down the decision.

O'SHEA
That's all well and good, and I'm glad that the Earth is still here, but it does not undo

the *Enterprise* crew's earlier acts of sabotage. For instance, Captain Montgomery Scott's removal of pieces from the *Excelsior*'s transwarp engines left the Sol system open to attack — by Klingons, Romulans, Gorn, anyone.

SIMISOLA
That is not strictly true. Other ships were in the sector —

O'SHEA
Yes, I've read the reports: all of the other ships were in spacedock undergoing various stages of repair. Starfleet continues to leave the Sol system vulnerable, and I can't understand why. After V'Ger nearly swallowed the Earth fifteen years back, you would have thought that the Federation would have beefed up security against rogue probes from the far reaches of the galaxy.

SIMISOLA
The Cetacean probe was unlike anything we've ever seen before. We couldn't plan against that.

O'SHEA
With fifteen years' notice? Come on, councilwoman. But that leads to another good point. With all the minds of the Federation at our disposal, both on Earth and elsewhere, why was it the *Enterprise* crew flying a third-rate Klingon Bird-of-Prey who had to figure out that whales needed to answer the probe's messages?

SIMISOLA
You must have noticed the power outages, Brent. Earth was on global alert.

O'SHEA
Yes, yes — but, again, no one thought about this? No reliable backup plan for getting power? The sun's gone, and suddenly the Earth is crippled?
    All right, let's talk about the Klingons for a moment here.

[HOLO-VID: KLINGON AMBASSADOR AT FEDERATION COUNCIL: "Remember this well: There shall be no peace as long as Kirk lives!"]

Why is it that for the past 25 years, we've allowed James T. Kirk to decide the Federation's policies on Klingon relations?

SIMISOLA
That's hardly a fair assessment.

O'SHEA

You don't think so? Every move that the Federation makes with the Klingons is a direct result of something that Kirk does. We're merely reacting to it, trying to limit the damage as best we can.

SIMISOLA

I believe the record shows that the Klingons have consistently been the aggressors, while Captain Kirk has defused many tense situations before they became full-scale wars. Remember too that the Klingons destroyed the *Grissom* and killed Kirk's son on the Genesis planet —

O'SHEA

That gives him the right to blow all of them up, along with the *Enterprise*? Were all of them equally guilty? What gives Kirk the right to be judge, jury and executioner?

Also, I know the Federation doesn't like to talk about how much anything is really worth, but the *Enterprise* cost a lot of time and resources to build and still had a lot of value just in spare parts alone. Instead, it's now vaporized dust floating through space.

And when this Cetacean probe shows up, Kirk slingshots back in time to get these humpback whales himself, because apparently no one else can be trusted to do it right. Except that he didn't do it right.

Sources within the Department of Temporal Investigations say that little trip is causing them fits: apparently, he and his crew racked up at least five major violations threatening the timeline. One is a serious ontological paradox about where the formula for transparent aluminum originally comes from. We're even told that before temporal agents cleaned up Kirk's mess, a family called Nichols controlled one-fifth of Earth's wealth as of 2016.

SIMISOLA

I don't think —

O'SHEA

Speaking of the timeline, what's the future for these two whales going to be? Having only two of them limits the gene pool to such an incestuous extent that I give them maybe another two generations before they die out again. What's the answer to that — break more temporal directives to snag even more whales? And what other species are we going to save next? This whole idea could turn disastrous if not properly considered.

SIMISOLA
Breton, you really do have a flair for the negative, don't you?

O'SHEA
Well, someone around here has to. Living in a socialist utopia is tough on the nerves.

*Chris Kocher is a writer, editor and all-around gentleman and scholar
from Binghamton, New York, the hometown of Rod Serling.*

---

107. THE FINAL FRONTIER
LIFE IS NOT A DREAM
GEORGE IVANOFF

From: George Ivanoff <givanoff@optusnet.com.au>
Date: Sun, 29 Jun 2014 12:21:04 +1000
To: Edgar [surname removed] [XXXXXXX@paramount.com]
Subject: Best idea EVER!

Hey Eddy,

It was great to bump into you at that *Star Trek* con last week (sorry, didn't actually mean to knock you over... I was just a little excited). If you've had a chance to look up my website, you'll have seen that I don't always dress in *Trek* uniform. It's only for special occasions :-)

Now, you did say keep in touch (or was that, "don't touch"?), just before I picked up one of those business cards you dropped — so here I am staying in touch.

I've got this great idea for you!

Given the success of the J.J. Abrams–helmed *Star Trek* reboot (although we true fans know it's not really *Trek*, it has caught the imagination of the mundanes), the timing is perfect for the production of a *Star Trek* musical motion picture. No, don't laugh. Let me explain...

Music has always been an important part of the *Star Trek* franchise, from the original Alexander Courage theme to the sweeping Jerry Goldsmith fanfare. But the good-old song-and-dance approach of the musical genre has also played a role in the franchise, albeit sometimes a little embarrassingly. Sadly underused in my humble opinion, it is nevertheless present and so is ready for exploitation.

Cast members such as William Shatner, Nichelle Nichols and even Leonard Nimoy have embarked on musical careers outside of the franchise. (Although I use the term "careers" lightly; see attached clip of Bill's performance of "Rocket Man", which has to be seen to be believed.) Furthermore, songs, performed within the context of a storyline, have a history within *Star Trek*. Lt. Uhura sings in the Classic Series episodes *Charlie X*, *Conscience of the King* and *The Changeling*; Spock plays his Vulcan harp-thingy in a number of eps and even manages to sing in *Plato's Stepchildren*. And, of course, who could forget the interstellar hippies grooving away in *The Way to Eden*? Truly toe-tapping tunes that got the fans boogieing (and cringing).

But if you really need proof that a *Star Trek* musical motion picture has the potential to fly, you need to look no further than *Star Trek V: The Final Frontier*.

Okay, okay — yes, the film is a bit crap. But the musical bits are AWE-SOME!

If you look beyond the tired performances, the poor visual effects, the appalling dialogue and the pedestrian direction, you'll find a hidden gem — a musical gem. The spirit, humor and character-building of the original series are evoked through just three musical scenes. Pretty amazing, huh?

Row, Row, Row Your Boat! Such a simple little song, but, as McCoy points out: "It's a song, you green-blooded Vulcan. You sing it. The words aren't important. What's important is that you have a good time singing it."

This song, bookending the story, reveals more about the *Star Trek* triumvirate than any other scene in the film. Okay, so the aging Shatner, Nimoy and Kelly couldn't hold a tune if their lives depended on it, but it doesn't matter — because it is the emotional situation of Kirk, Spock and McCoy that is the point of the scene, so their inability to hit even a remotely close to melodious note is irrelevant. And that simple song conveys the emotion with stunning clarity. These three men have an indestructible bond of friendship, irrespective of where they slot into the chain of command, despite the fact that they drive each other nuts, and even though they often have difficulty understanding each other. The progression from the first aborted attempt at singing *Row, Row, Row Your Boat* to the successful finale rendition shows their ability to learn, to grow and to reach for understanding. Magic!

Then there's *The Moon is a Window to Heaven*. It demonstrates Uhura's dedication, reveals her humor and cements the fact that, in addition to being an exemplary Starfleet officer, she's also a damn sexy woman, literally able to stop men from thinking with her breathtaking beauty. One short song and dance gives viewers all this — so much more than what is accomplished in the rest of the film.

There are only two things that could have improved that scene. 1: Fewer palm fronds. 2: Nichelle Nichols actually performing the song rather than miming to someone else's vocals. She's the best singer out of all the original cast, so why dub her but keep Shatner, Nimoy and Kelly?

Now… if we could encapsulate the emotion and storytelling and character potential of the musical scenes from *Star Trek V* and direct them into a full-blown musical motion picture in its own right, we will have an unmitigated HIT on our hands.

Imagine how much better *Star Trek V* would have been with just a few more songs? Kirk could have sung *Wind Beneath My Wings* as Spock saved him from going splat at the bottom of that mountain. It would have shed light on his emotional state, evoked his relationship with Spock AND been a humorous touch, given his plummeting situation.

We'd follow that with a group rendition of Lloyd-Webber's *Memory* after Sybok gets the crew to relive their painful memories (although the link between this and their new-found loyalty to Sybok is baffling), freeing them from the past and allowing them to "understand what happiness is". Spock could then respond with *He Ain't Heavy, He's My Brother* (although perhaps Nimoy could just mime).

I also have visions of the buff Klingons, Klaa and Vixis, working out in their onboard gym, muscles bulging, sweat dripping, as they sing *Physical*. The possibilities are endless.

And as the grand finale? An original song: *What Does God Need With a Starship?* Imagine what a showstopper that could have been. The Shat-Man giving it his all in the style of his *Common People* cover.

But you don't need to imagine, do you? You have the power! You could green light the development of a *Star Trek* musical extravaganza! Incidentally, you also have the power to stop Abrams making another *Trek* film. Just saying!

In conclusion, let us remember Spock's immortal words, "Captain, life is not a dream." Indeed it is not. Life is not a dream; life is a musical. (Or is that just my life?) And *Star Trek* should be too.

Thanks for taking the time to read this email, Eddy. Much appreciated!

I look forward to seeing *Star Trek: The Musical* at a cinema near me, in the not-too-distant future.

Live Long and Prosper,
George

P.S. Please find attached my audition piece: a medley of all the songs ever to appear in a *Star Trek* episode or movie (with costume changes, of course — see, I don't ALWAYS wear a Starfleet Uniform).

George Ivanoff is a long-time Star Trek *fan and the author of many children's books. He's been known to wear a Starfleet Academy uniform to costume parties. georgeivanoff.com.au*

108. THE UNDISCOVERED COUNTRY
SLINGS AND ARROWS
ARI LIPSEY

In the small town of Stratford, Ontario, during the spring of 1956, Christopher Plummer was playing the title role in a production of Shakespeare's *Henry V*, when he was struck with an excruciating stomach pain. He was rushed to the hospital and pumped full of morphine. When he had regained his lucidity, he discovered that his understudy had played Plummer's role to a delighted audience. That understudy was William Shatner. Plummer claimed to be upstaged.

Star Trek VI: The Undiscovered Country is the finale of a great fictional narrative but also two real-world narratives. There's the obvious one: this is the last time the entire "Original Series" *Star Trek* crew are all together. But it's also the last time William Shatner will headline a blockbuster Hollywood movie, a career path that can arguably be traced back to his break in *Henry V* at Stratford. And so it ends fittingly, with Christopher Plummer proclaiming "Once more unto the breach, dear friends". The meaning of the phrase in the original play is different than the meaning in the movie. The play's line takes place during an attack on the city of Harfleur, where King Henry is appealing to the morale of his (young) soldiers. In the movie, it refers to "battling one more time", to show that the old geezers "still have it".

Double meanings in life are happenstance; in art, they are sublime fun. The very title of *Star Trek VI* also carries a different meaning from Shakespeare's original use. "The Undiscovered Country" was a euphemism for death or, more accurately, the uncertainty of life after death. In *Star Trek VI*, it's about the uncertainty of the direction of the future. Quite simply, certain sentiments that are useful during wars prove useless during peace. Winston Churchill was the perfect Prime Minister in 1942 but not in 1945. *Star Trek VI* is an interesting snapshot of the post–Berlin Wall years (the seed of the idea for the story was famously "the wall comes down in space"). America was one of two world powers, and then, rather suddenly, it was the only world power, much as the Federation is portrayed in the movie. And all those militant and prejudicial attitudes that served to strengthen the resolve of a nation so well while under conflict suddenly looked sour and old when that conflict ceased. An evil empire looked significantly less evil when it was stripped of its empire.

The scene in the Federation boardroom is a particular triumph in this regard. It's easy to dismiss Captain Kirk and Admiral Cartwright's attitudes as racist, but they actually have a point. Why should the Federation unilaterally disarm when they have essentially defeated a consistently hostile foe? Won't a stronger Federation military compel the Klingons to act more reasonably? There are plenty of historical precedents for one side of a conflict making a gesture of goodwill in an attempt to perk the reasonable sentiments of the other side, only to have this gesture interpreted as admission of guilt or weakness. But that outlook is pessimistic, and ultimately *Star Trek*'s outlook is optimistic, and so is its universe. The Klingons debate attacking the Federation only because they're certain the Federation will use their newfound tactical advantage. Essentially, it is made clear that war, in this context, is avoidable. That might seem like an obvious point, but it is a quintessentially American influence on *Star Trek*. "Operation Retrieve" is spiked by the Federation President not because it might fail, but because it is illegal. A cynic might object that America still does what it wants regardless of international law, but the very idea that International Law even weighs on the decision is almost uniquely American. Imagine a scene with a Russian General advising against a strike in Georgia or Chechnya because it would be against international law, and the absurdity of the idea shows that the Federation President's reaction is not on the philosophical radar of most of the nations of our planet.

Changing political realities charge a human toll, as well. This was perfectly encapsulated in the words of Calvin Coolidge, the U.S. president who presided over the Roaring 20s and spent his final months seeing the rise of Franklin Roosevelt. "I feel I no longer fit in with these times." It's a fear we all have once we reach a certain level of maturity: that we are products of our time, that one day our jokes will no longer get laughs, we won't understand the appeal of a hit song or we won't understand new technology intuitively. Our assumptions of "how the world works" will, one day, no longer work. Like Spock, we'll find a point where we contemplate whether we have outlived our usefulness. *Star Trek* itself had moved on from the *TOS* outlook. By the time of *Star Trek VI*'s release, *Star Trek: The Next Generation* had overtaken the original series in episode count and was effectively the *Star Trek* of the zeitgeist. And *TNG*'s outlook is more reflective of a peacetime, prosperous America. The Prime Directive is taken far more seriously, scientific phenomena is a more common McGuffin, and the characters seem more like a collection of honor-roll students than a group of friends you might meet at the local pub. This allowed greater flexibility for stories to explore an internal rather than external conflict, which is precisely the narrative a lone superpower would be focused on. When artists need not concern themselves with the barbarians outside the gates, they'll naturally turn their gaze to the ones inside. *Star Trek VI* does have some of this too, but Spock and Kirk reflecting on their obsolescence can be seen as a direct comment on the success of *TNG*: the voice of the post-war generation.

Well, if you've got to go, you might as well go out in style. It's accepted criticism that while *Star Trek VI* is one of the "good" movies, it's not nearly as groundbreaking as *Star Trek II*. After all, *Star Trek II* is referenced heavily in both J.J. Abrams films, the *Kobayashi Maru* scene was restaged with Romulans in an episode of *Voyager*, and the uniforms from *The Wrath of Khan* are reused throughout episodes of *The Next Generation*. However, I would submit that, outside the *Star Trek* world, *Star Trek VI's* visuals have been borrowed more heavily. The computer-animated show *Beast Wars* virtually recreates the explosion of Praxis, as did George Lucas in the first special edition of *Star Wars,* while the zero-gravity blood was redone in *Mission to Mars*. Nicholas Meyer has been unleashed in *Star Trek VI,* so he gets his choice of title (he originally wanted to call *Star Trek II* "The Undiscovered Country") and gets a Shakespearean actor for a villain. The inclusion of Shakespeare is a direct attempt to move on from the gruff and grunting Klingons of previous *Trek* to a more "cultured" (and, by association, "civilized") Klingon. The two main Klingons are played by David Warner, speaking in British Received Pronunciation, and Christopher Plummer, Canada's foremost Shakespearean performer. They are both warriors and art aficionados.

But any attempt to compare *Star Trek VI* itself with a Shakespearean tragedy does it a disservice. The Federation does not fall on Kirk's or Spock's hamartias. Shakespeare's outlook was a universe that crushed man's hopes and ambitions; in a world where one was lucky to survive childbirth, his outlook made sense. But in a world where man has conquered the stars, there's time enough to process one's mistakes and take corrective action. To grow and learn, as Spock and Kirk do throughout the film. I think the most appropriate literary comparison might be to the novels of Dickens. *Star Trek VI* speaks to us differently depending on our age. When we're young, it's about the fight for a better world against the forces of reaction. As we reach middle age, it's about how historical events shift our preconceived assumptions of the world. In our golden years, it's about the fear of obsolescence and the inability to effect change. The J.J. Abrams films might appeal to a new generation of fans, but they maintain the same adolescent demographic as *The Wrath of Khan*. *Star Trek VI* is the movie for all ages.

Ari Lipsey spends his time sitting upon the ground,
telling sad stories of the death of kings.

---

109. FLASHBACK
POLE TO POLE
JOE BRIGGS-RITCHIE

Strictly speaking, *Flashback* isn't actually a time-travel episode; it's one of those "perceived time travel" episodes like *Far Beyond the Stars* or *11:59*. But, in practice, that's essentially what it is doing. Sci-fi series frequently travel back into their own past; the nature of the genre makes this a possibility, but why do they do it? Just because you can do something doesn't necessarily mean that you should. Is it for reassurance? And if so, is it reassurance for themselves or for the viewers? It's almost like someone bringing the ghost of their granny back from the dead and saying "How am I doing? Does this look okay?" At best, it's ill-advised; at worst, it's sheer bloody awful. Is *Trials and Tribble-ations* actually funny or just a desperate-smelling attempt to cash in on something that wasn't even particularly funny the first time? *Star Trek* doesn't do humor particularly well, so much so in fact that *Deep Space Nine*, the most humorless of all the *Star Trek* series, has to get its jollies by revisiting an era where almost everything was funny to some degree because that era was the sixties and it all seems so riotously psychedelic to our modern sensibilities. *Flashback*, however, hasn't gone quite so far back as Captain Kirk's heyday but it isn't far off, at least in chronological terms.

So what does *Flashback* exemplify more than anything else? For me, it's the duality of *Star Trek*, its ability to go from one extreme to the other, from the sublime to the ridiculous, the present to the past, the real to the imaginary... One moment Tuvok is in the room, the next he is in a false memory, desperately trying to stop a young girl falling to her death. And so this one scenario on which the whole episode is based plays out, again and again. Some of this leaping from one extreme to another is intentional. Some of it isn't...

It is of course Tim Russ's episode, giving him what must have come as a welcome opportunity to portray a side to Tuvok other than the emotionless pillar of logic and reason we have to come to know and love. He was obviously having a ball in *Meld* and no doubt he relished the opportunity here to explore the character a little more. It's genuinely refreshing to see him looking frightened for once. It's also a nice link-in with the events of *The Undiscovered Country*, but, again, one has to ask why? It's impossible not to feel a thrill of excitement at seeing some of the original *Enterprise* crew members in action once again, and George Takei rises to the occasion wonderfully, but why this particular era? The only explanation I can think of is that Tim Russ played a (non-Vulcan) crew member aboard the *Enterprise B* in *Star Trek: Generations*... And the *Enterprise B* was an Excelsior class starship... So, you know... why not? Well, at least I can spell "tenuous"! Can you?

He does a wonderful job of subtly slipping from "our" Tuvok into the *Excelsior* Tuvok. Again, we continue with the theme of extremes or, more specifically, differing aspects of the same construct; he converses with Janeway as the Tuvok that we are familiar with yet addresses Sulu as the Tuvok that existed decades previously. Yes, all of this is taking place inside Tuvok's head. He's got some serious issues if you ask me...

The issue of dialogue ranging from the awe-inspiring to the simply awful is never very far away in any incarnation of *Star Trek*, but it does seem to be especially the case with *Voyager*. One of the reasons for this is because of the Doctor; he frequently had the punchiest lines, a fact that can sometimes unfortunately serve to highlight how hugely un-punchy some of the other characters' dialogue is. Robert Picardo nailed the character right from the start with his brilliant comic timing and waspish take on the Doctor's persona, so one can imagine that it makes him quite specific and straightforward to write for. In short, he's a source of much amusement and is eminently quotable. This is *Star Trek* doing humor and, somewhat incongruously, doing it well. Just listen to his delivery of the line "The universe is such a strange place..." But, just several minutes after this little gem, we are presented with a rather unwieldy exchange between Chakotay and Tuvok:

> CHAKOTAY: Maybe you should try to forget about it for a while. I've found that when you don't think about a problem, sometimes the solution comes to you.
> TUVOK: It is difficult to forget when you are wearing a neurocortical monitor on your parietal bone.

You'd have to be one hell of an actor to make lines like that fly. But then a little later we have that lovely scene in the *Excelsior* crew quarters when Janeway complains that Tuvok has never brought her tea. Kate Mulgrew's reading of the line is superb, as is Tim Russ's almost imperceptible reaction. Later on, Sulu gives one of those typical *Trek*-style schmaltzy lectures on the interpersonal ramifications of serving on the bridge of a starship — basically the sort of thing that makes me want to vomit my own face off — but he closes it with a rather wonderful "You'd better believe it!" The pendulum swings, does it not...?

Flashback is not so much an ensemble piece but rather a duet between Tuvok and Janeway with Sulu thrown in as a novelty to add interest to what is otherwise a fairly unremarkable episode. This is such a delicious irony; that despite the numerous examples of duality on display, the episode itself is a fairly staid piece of *Trek*. It neither particularly excites (at least when Sulu isn't on the screen) nor greatly offends. It just sort of is. I've always been of the opinion that, after the first two seasons of *The Next Generation,* there weren't really any bad episodes as such, just very dull ones — and that's more or less what this is. Take Sulu out of the recipe, and it all starts to taste a bit bland and rather too familiar. That's not to say it doesn't have some nice things thrown in; it does. There's a lovely and very subtle demonstration of Janeway's approach to the role of captain (and another example of the theme of opposites) when she gets up from behind her desk and goes to sit next to Ensign Kim on the other side. In doing so, she removes the barricade of her rank and addresses him on a more level footing. She is by far the most human of the *Star Trek* captains and, in many ways, the most interesting. She also verbally makes clear the difference between the somewhat straight-laced approach of the Starfleet officers of their time and the far more rough and ready ones of Sulu's time. You can probably see where I'm going with this one.

A lackluster endeavor with some not-quite time travel or a case study in the duality of an entire television franchise? You decide...

Joe Briggs-Ritchie is a keen composer, enjoys photography and is a dedicated cynic. He drinks more tea than is probably good for him but unfortunately does not own homes in the Seychelles or St. Moritz. He is currently working on a novel, which he might one day actually finish.

110. GENERATIONS
ANOTHER DAY IN PARADISE
THOMAS COOKSON

I think many fans struggle to grasp *Generations*. It's often written off as boring, nonsensical fanservice, which is a terrible injustice. From that opening with the fragile bottle floating in space bearing its birthdate, dancing free among the stars all too finitely before being broken to pieces, this film is a living, breathing, brooding existentialist masterpiece.

It's very far removed from the upbeat corniness of the Original Series or the timelessly uplifting *The Voyage Home*, but it's the last *Trek* film to not feel written by a committee.

Most fan complaints against *Generations* only reinforce to me its savage beauty. It wasn't what they wanted, it didn't play fair with our memories, and Kirk deserved a better death.

I think the central point is this: it's not Kirk's film.

It's not even Picard's.

It's Soran's.

The entire film functions just as he sees the universe. As a cruel one. Where life doesn't give us what we want, it isn't fair, and even the toughest and best of us will probably meet our mortality in an unexpectedly undignified and ignominious way. That's life, that's death, and to me that makes this film truly alive.

Death is a cruel respecter of no one here. Like Scotty's sad lament at the meager survivors he beamed up from the exploding Lakul ship: "I got forty seven... out of one hundred and fifty."

Soran embodies what too much exposure to death can do to someone, how easily the *Trek* ideal of looking to the vaster experiences and wonders and becoming more enlightened has its grim counterpart in the things and events that make unfeeling monsters of us. Where that exposure to morbidity bred its own obsession, where someone became so used to death it broke him into someone who believed it didn't really matter anyway.

That's Soran's death wish, and it makes him as terrifying and unreachable as any Borg. Back in Kirk's retirement time, he was a weak man gone rogue, but, by Picard's era, he's so burnt out and morbid there's almost no reaching him. He's possessed.

The film *Ghost* had a poignant line about bereavement rendering us especially vulnerable to exploitation when we'd honestly give anything in the world for just one more moment. Soran has studied a way to have that moment last forever, and if that means several billion people must die just to redirect the ribbon's course, then, in his own words, "death doesn't even matter". In fact, if that's the only cruel bargain this universe offers, then all the more reason to punch that one-way ticket to a better one. In a way, they're all going to die — and if no one's left alive on Veridian III to grieve, then maybe he's spared them his own torture.

Yes, Soran has boldly gone where no man has gone before, but whilst Kirk and Picard always remembered where they came from and resisted losing their humanity to fantasist wonder and temptation, Soran doesn't have that luxury. The Borg took his home away from him. In a way, this film's as much about the mechanistic monsters the Borg turn ordinary people into as the next one will be.

Guinan too provides an echo to Soran, having been into the Nexus herself and had to bitterly deny herself any entertainment of the possibility of ever returning to that heaven. That clearly still hurts her. She knows its temptation is greater than any trivial desire for power or money, because we're all animals, all slaves to our passions and our needs for warmth and nurture.

Picard is ultimately brought with Soran to that nirvana. His first experience is a family Christmas with his wife and children. It's an absolutely enchanting, heartbreaking moment of emotional ecstasy when he embraces René, thanking and blessing God, fate and the stars for giving his beloved lost nephew back to him alive, unharmed, even if just for today.

Perhaps this is fantasy or an actual reality where we are masters of the movement of time rather than its prisoners, in which these children were always born and Picard always saved René from that fire. Where not a moment of life was wasted on reminiscence because there's a way to revisit those moments and change the ones we don't like.

But Picard brought something with him that won't let him enjoy this divinity so guiltlessly for its bloody price. He was always a sanctimonious ass, so it makes sense he never left his conscience behind.

We never actually see Soran's paradise. But really we're not meant to, because we know he'll never look back even in guilt. We've never seen him happy. Not truly, but he would be the Nexus' blissful slave and would never want to leave. Perhaps the Nexus, like any ecstatic state, strips away our individuality and makes us all intimately one in a shared eternal contented orgasm of the soul.

But Picard proves that's not the case. Any lesser man would be too humbled to ever want to leave or defy this reality that rewarded him so. But Picard takes the uniform with him. It makes him who he is, and he cannot stomach the bloodshed in the reality he left behind.

Like us, he's baffled to find that gung-ho Kirk isn't so willing to be the hero this time. In fact, he's kind of bitter at the reality he left behind, which he feels owes him something for his dedication to Starfleet and gave him only lost years and lost chances to build a family before being finally downsized into a has-been.

Kirk once faced something of Soran's choice when he fell in love with Edith Keeler. A part of him likely wanted to let Earth be damned to Hitler's Reich if it meant they would still be together, but ultimately he knew he must let her die as history dictated. Perhaps that's one of many unreckoned, bitter regrets.

Furthermore, within the contentment of the Nexus, the rewards seem comparatively less, the punishments worth nothing. David's death certainly left him plenty to be bitter about.

But perhaps he remembers those words "Man stagnates if he has no wants" and realizes this place can't offer what he truly craves. A challenge or chance to make a difference.

Sometimes the Nexus makes us miss that which makes us human too much to be happy being slaves to our emotional wants.

So Kirk and Picard ride out together, kindred spirits, with unfinished business to reckon with.

Unfortunately they've re-entered Soran's universe. In a cruel irony, Kirk goes unrewarded for his rejection of eternal paradise for the sake of performing one last Starfleet mission. Instead, this last adventure kills him.

Like Spock's death, this further marked *Trek*'s rite of passage and maturity from its sixties' macho adolescent fantasies. Many watched Kirk's death thinking "No! This can't happen! Not like this!"

But it happens to us all one day.

Generations ends with the same forward-looking note as *All Good Things*, but this time it comes at a cost that for many left a bitter aftertaste. A taste of Soran's torture that ended when death was the only peace Picard could humanely grant him anymore.

Because we weren't meant for paradise.

Thomas Cookson is a Liverpool-based aspiring writer with early memories of watching the Classic Trek *movies with his father and thinking Khan and* Labyrinth*'s Jared were the same villain.*

111. RELICS
I'LL NEVER FALL IN LOVE AGAIN
DAVID BLACK

This book is about the voyages of the USS *Enterprise*, no bloody B, C or D. Yet here I am pontificating about *Relics*, a very twenty-fourth century tale. Why is this here?

The obvious answer is Scotty, but he's only part of the answer.

It's a brilliantly constructed episode, as we see Scotty out of his time and out of his depth. He is wrapped up in his tales of days gone by, struggling to keep up with the pace of life in the twenty-fourth century and butting heads with the mild-mannered Geordi La Forge. Ultimately, Scotty and Geordi work together and save the day. On the face of it, *Relics* is a potentially self-indulgent love letter to the past with a much-beloved character, but underneath it's something more impressive: it's a mission statement.

> Scott: A century out of date. It's just obsolete.
> La Forge: Well you know, that's interesting, because I was just thinking that a lot of these systems haven't changed much in the last seventy-five years. This transporter is basically the same system we use on the *Enterprise*. Subspace radio and sensors still operate under the same basic principle. Impulse engine design hasn't changed much in the last two hundred years. If it wasn't for all the structural damage, this ship might still be in service today.

Scotty and Geordi might be discussing the USS *Jenolan*, but they could just as easily be talking about the state of *Star Trek* itself.

Star Trek: The Next Generation always seemed a little shy to recognize its parentage. Apart from a beautiful cameo appearance in its pilot, an awkward reference to a shower scene in *The Naked Now* and the epic two-part movie tie-in that was *Unification*, the show has, until now, been quite sparing in its acknowledgement of the original series. An episode like *Sarek* goes out of its way to skirt around allusions to the audience's relationship with its titular character.

In many ways this makes a lot of sense: it would allow the series to establish its own identity, but for the fact it doesn't really have one. For all of its genuine achievement, *Star Trek: The Next Generation* is for the most part a continuation of the original. It's more of a variation on a theme. *TNG* is cosmetically different to the original series. The make-up and special effects have been improved upon, and the furniture has been rearranged, but, for the most part, it's fundamentally the same show.

When the spinoff series was initially being developed, Leonard Nimoy famously said that you can't catch lightning in a bottle again. Well, it turns out you can if it's essentially the same bottle. That probably sounds as if it's meant to be insulting, but that's not my intention at all. It's a great bottle. It was as good a bottle in 1992 as it had been twenty-five years earlier. As Geordi tells Scotty, "just because something's old doesn't mean you throw it away".

Relics doesn't lazily rely on the associations of the original, and Scotty doesn't prop up a wafer-thin plot. Instead, the episode makes a virtue of the audience's nostalgia and both salutes and undermines it in equal measure. At this point, *Star Trek: Deep Space Nine* is waiting in the wings. *DS9* is hoping to be radically different, whilst retaining enough of its predecessors to keep their audiences coming back time and time again. *Relics* is the episode that sets the tone for how future spinoffs will deal with what "has gone before". *Relics* provides the confidence that makes possible episodes like *Blood Oath*, *Death Wish*, *Trials And Tribble-ations*, *Flashback*, *Dr. Bashir I Presume* and *In A Mirror, Darkly*, not to mention the Barclay episodes of *Star Trek: Voyager*. That said, it's also the same confidence that is woven through *These Are The Voyages...* as well, so it's not an immaculate record.

More than any other episode of *TNG*, *Relics* sees the spinoff proudly stepping out of the shadow of the original with a self-assured air. At one point, La Forge even says to Scotty, "Quite frankly, you're in the way." The love letter to the past comes to an end, and the mission statement takes over like a shot across the starboard bow. You want to talk about the original *Star Trek*? Well we've been making it for the last five years. How's that for a five-year mission? Give us a break here. Stop looking a gift horse in the mouth, give up on Kirk versus Picard battles and leave Gene Roddenberry out of this. Did you know him? Where else are you going to go for your *Star Trek* fix? We know you're watching. Why do you do this to yourselves? Do you watch just to have something new to complain about? You guys know that we have fans who probably don't even care who Scotty is, right? Somewhere out there in a parallel universe Scotty's friend, Franklin, survived instead. Would you rather watch that?

The Romulans might be speaking for *Star Trek* when they proclaim "We're back" at the end of *The Neutral Zone*, but, more than any episode, it is *Relics* that makes a stand and stakes a claim: this is *Star Trek* — and, what's more, it always has been. *Relics* is still a love letter, but it's just as much a love letter to the previous 128 episodes of *Star Trek: The Next Generation* as it is to anything from an earlier era. Sometimes it takes an engineer to tell you that if it ain't broke...

David Black has written articles, sketches and scripts for Noiseless Chatter, Cult Britannia, Behind the Bike Shed, Newsrevue, Brandon Generator *and Hat Trick TV's YouTube channel,* Bad Teeth. *In an act of extreme arrogance, he was forced to reinterpret* The Cherry Orchard *and write new Chekhov dialogue. He blogs at davewrotethis.blogspot.co.uk and tweets as @davetweetedthis.*

112. ENCOUNTER AT FARPOINT
A MEMORY AT ODDS
SCOT CLARKE

Dear Commander Maddox,

As you know, I recently obtained the emotion chip that my father, Professor Noonian Soong, created for me several years ago. I was intrigued by your question as to whether the chip had altered any of my previous memories. A fascinating query, one that excited me greatly.

To preface this, I will remind you that, during the maiden voyage of the *Enterprise* D, commonly referred to as the "Encounter at Farpoint" affair, I had the pleasure of escorting the legendary Admiral Leonard McCoy aboard the ship. Formerly chief medical officer on both the original *Enterprise* and the *Enterprise* A, Doctor McCoy was initially something of an enigma to me. At 137 years of age, he appeared formidable, to say the least, and my interaction with him was... perplexing. During a briefing, Captain Picard had asked for volunteers to escort the Admiral and appeared to be looking right at me. Both Lieutenants La Forge and Yar quickly volunteered, but the Captain was insistent that I take on the duty, despite the fact that I was involved in a very important diagnostic check.

Two days ago, I was experimenting with the dream algorithm I have often written to you about and experienced some very interesting results.

In my dream, I was walking along Deck 36 with Doctor Katherine Pulaski on my arm. She appeared to be blind and wearing a long, flowing gown. Suddenly, we were walking along an unfamiliar deck on a *Constitution*-class starship, which I can only surmise was the original *Enterprise*. Doctor Pulaski suddenly become Admiral McCoy. The corridor immediately darkened and Admiral McCoy held up his arm, which appeared to be on fire. He detached the flaming arm and handed it to me, to which I replied, "That is not logical, doctor." The deck began to flood with water, which rose to waist level. I looked down at my reflection and discovered that I was no longer myself but appeared to have turned into Ambassador Spock.

It was at that point that I awoke to find Spot on my chest, licking my face.

When we met, the Admiral represented all the aspects of humanity that were most foreign to me: unpredictable and contradictory behavior, anachronistic language and a certain preference for the past. Looking back with the insights I have today, it is quite clear to me: he was a crotchety old man, with a penchant for casual racism and an irrational fear of technology. And yet, I find I have very fond memories of him. I am fascinated by the era of "cowboy diplomacy" (a term Captain Picard favors) that he lived through (I have 11 holodeck recreations of the late 23rd century) and how it shaped the galaxy we live in today; much in the same way Ensign Denobi from Astrophysics exhibits a strong curiosity for life aboard the *Enterprise* D.

In conclusion, Commander Maddox, I find I possess two distinct memories of Admiral McCoy: the original impression and the one experienced through the filter of the emotion chip.

Reconciling the two has been most... perplexing. The former memory is a moment-for-moment recollection that I can place myself in as if it were a holodeck recreation, while the latter is diffuse and contradictory. And yet I cannot separate the two. They both inhabit my neural pathways; and both influence my dreaming algorithms. Perplexing indeed.

Scot Clarke has fond memories of watching the first season of Star Trek: TNG *in university. Scot Clarke cringes when he watches the first season of* Star Trek: TNG.

113. UNIFICATION
OBI-WAN'S LESSON
LESLIE HARTMAN JR.

As he had for much of the journey, Luke Skywalker sat alone, despondent and depressed. One could hardly blame him after recent events. His aunt and uncle were murdered, his home destroyed, he had almost certainly lost the deposit that he had put down on some new power converters at Toshi Station, and he had come to run off with an old hermit that he hardly knew aboard a rickety freighter owned by a smuggler and a Wookie. He had much to be depressed about.

Obi-Wan, the aforementioned old hermit, appeared from one of the curving corridors of the *Millennium Falcon*, drinking the last vestiges of blue milk. "What troubles you, young Jedi?"

"Ohh... this ship. This mission. This life," whined Luke, and not for the first time. It had become a popular refrain during the trip to Alderaan. "If I'd any idea it would be this many parsecs from Tatooine to Alderaan, I would have packed a book or something."

Obi-Wan chuckled and sat down next to Luke. "Let me tell you a story that I have heard, passed down through the generations, from Jedi to Padawan. It is the story of a great Jedi legend named Spock. This is the tale of his attempt to bring the Jedi and the Sith together as one."

"This isn't going to be like your story of the Jedi Legend Skipper and his padawan Gilligan, is it?" grumbled Luke.

"No, this isn't anything like that. Now listen," began Obi-Wan, smoothing down a fold in his robe. "The first thing to know is that Spock was old. Ancient even. The most Ancient Order of Jedi were among his first peers, James-Tee Kirk, Scotty, Sulu, Bones and others."

"There was a Jedi named Bones?" asked Luke.

"He had another name, but it is lost to the ages." responded Obi-Wan. "Anyhow, it is important to remember that, while the others would age and pass away, Spock was strong with the Force, which allowed him to age more slowly, even over the generations. It was two generations later that the great Spock would shock the Jedi Council by seemingly defecting to the Sith. In actuality, he had been attempting to re-unite the Light Side of the Force with the Dark Side for the first time in history. So Spock hid away on a distant planet attempting to bring his plans to fruition."

"You mean, he was hiding out, the way you were hiding out on Tatooine?" asked Luke.

"Well, I wasn't hiding out, really. I was... waiting for a sign," stuttered Obi-Wan.

"Right, waiting for a sign while hiding from the Empire," said Luke.

"Can I finish?" asked Obi-Wan, perturbed. "Now while all this was happening, the Jedi Council sent a young-ish Jedi named Picard to find out what had become of Spock. Picard sought out Spock's master, a Jedi named Sarek, for answers. Sarek had become old and would soon return to the Force. The last words that he and Spock shared were words of anger, and Picard wished to reconcile them."

"What does this have to do with Sith and Jedi?" whined Luke.

"It's a sub-plot," explained Obi-Wan. "Moving on. Picard learns that Spock is hiding on a Sith-controlled world named Romulus and decides to venture there in disguise. Meanwhile, Picard tells his young Padawan Will-Riker to pursue another Sith threat called a Ferengi that had been suspected of stealing Jedi secrets. Will-Riker and his friends had tracked the Ferengi creature to the Mos Eisley Cantina on Tatooine and attempted to set a trap for the rogue."

"Wait... wait. We just came from Tatooine. I've lived there all my life and I've never even seen a Jedi before today. Why have I never heard ANY of this before?" Luke squealed.

"Maybe it wasn't Mos Eisley... a very similar place, though." bumbled Obi-Wan. "You'll never find a more wretched..."

"Hive of scum and villainy!" parroted Luke. "We've done this already. Also, is this more sub-plot?"

"Young people have no appreciation..." glowered Obi-Wan. "What had happened with Spock was that he had found an old friend, a Sith, if it can be believed, named Pardek who had also spoken of bringing the Sith and Jedi back together. Re-aligning the two natures of the Force. However, it was a double-cross. Pardek had been completely corrupted by the Dark Side and was using this opportunity to strike at the Jedi Council through someone that they trusted."

"This Pardek..." considered Luke, "Was he as evil as Vader?"

"He was as much a puppet as Vader," said Obi-Wan. "Pardek's master was a Sith Lord known as Sela. She had a history of such villainy —"

"Whoa!! She? A female Sith Lord?" shouted Luke, suddenly much more interested in the tale.

"That's how I've always heard it." said Obi-Wan, distantly. "So, to make an already long story somewhat shorter, Sela's plan is revealed, Spock and Picard are able to warn the Jedi Council of the plot and the Sith are beaten."

"That's it?" questioned Luke, "Did Spock kill Sela? Was there an epic lightsaber battle? Was Spock able to turn Pardek back from the Dark Side?"

Obi-Wan considered, briefly. "No, I don't think there were any lightsaber fights at all. Pardek went on the run, and I don't think anyone actually knows what became of Sela."

Luke sighed, playing absently with his father's lightsaber. "Huh. Interesting story, anyway. Thanks Ben."

Obi-Wan smiled, "Let me tell you another story then, about a multi-faced Jedi who travels through not only space but time, in a small blue box..."

Leslie Hartman Jr. is believed to be dead. And he must let the world think that he is dead, until he can find a way to control the raging spirit that dwells within him.

114. GALAXY QUEST
MIRROR, MIRROR
BARBARA WHILLOCK

File #RF-7629-α̃ Situation report
Subject Deep-deep-deep-cover infiltration of alternate universe
Author Commander Mathesar, Thermian liaison to the Klingon–Cardassian Alliance

Intendant, following the events of 2267 (code named *Mirror, Mirror*), my people were tasked with testing the technological capability of the humans in the parallel universe. We were to gauge their ability to threaten the glorious Klingon–Cardassian Alliance and use any means necessary to nullify this threat.

As you will see from the attached log (code named *Galaxy Quest*), I formed a team and crossed into the parallel universe. Analysis determined that, rather than crossing into the timeline concurrent with our own, we would have greater infiltration effect if we jumped into the humans' past to test and (if needed) corrupt their technological growth.

Initial contact showed they were living under assumed identities while still attending rallies for the inspiration of their armies.

As you will see from the log, we succeeded in contacting one of Kirk's predecessors (Cmdr. Peter Quincy Taggart) and, while posing as naïve yet technologically advanced aliens (in their arrogance they didn't even remark on this — that such idiots we pretended to be could command such technology as ours!), lured him onto our ship for a test of his negotiation skills.

Cmdr. Taggart showed himself to be arrogant, aggressive and completely lacking in compassion. He attacked Gen. Roth'h'ar Sarris's ship while under the banner of negotiating a treaty with no warning! From this test, we determined that he and his people should be tested as a group, so we lured him and his cohorts Lt. Tawny Madison, Dr. Lazarus of Tev'Meck, Tech Sgt. Chen, Lt. Laredo and Guy (he was of minimal importance so no rank or surname was noted in our log) onto our ship.

Playing out a scenario with Gen. Roth'h'ar Sarris as an evil conqueror, we worked to gain their trust and encouraged them to admit that they were indeed the people we knew them to be. To continue the ruse that they were not the crew of the *Protector* while onboard our ship, they went so far as to cause (minor) damage to the ship upon launch, damage the engine by overusing the Turbo and fly into a minefield. Their determination to hold onto their fake identities was strong — but not strong enough to place themselves in real danger.

During these activities, we noted that, although Cmdr. Taggart had previously been identified as the leader and therefore the most dangerous of the group, in fact Tech Sgt. Chen was the true threat. His initial reaction to being transported through space by pod was so calm that we initially thought him a double agent. He proceeded to keep up this ruse while Cmdr. Taggart was in danger on a planet and yet calmly destroyed the creature initially believed to be called Gorignok and then proceeded to rescue Cmdr. Taggart from the creature actually called Gorignok. At this point, we identified Tech Sgt. Chen as the most pivotal figure in the group.

We then intensified the scenario and, after gaining their trust through the pretend sacrifice of several Thermians (and feigned torture of myself by Sarris), they finally admitted their true identities and began to fight. Tech Sgt. Chen continued to remain totally calm under intense pressure including convincing another crew member (the one known only as Guy) not to sacrifice himself to save the Thermians. Tech Sgt. Chen then transported the Gorignak onboard the ship to destroy Gen. Roth'h'ar Sarris' troops and laughed at the poor soldiers' deaths.

Noting that this group of officers were being helped from Earth by their technologically advanced support crew, and realizing that the threat from the humans was not constrained to this group alone, our agent (Thermian Laliari) proceeded to seduce Tech Sgt. Chen in order to use him to infiltrate Earth.

Having realized that Tech Sgt. Chen was the real power behind the humans, Gen. Roth'h'ar Sarris used his image to approach the crew on the bridge after his own ship had been destroyed. The humans then activated the "Omega 13" (a basic matter arranger that transports all matter in the universe 13 seconds into the past with only the operator aware of the now-defunct timestream; outdated equipment to us, but the humans believed it to be important). To continue the ruse of our allegiance to them and ensure that Thermian Laliari would be accepted as "one of them", I (non-lethally) neutralized Gen. Roth'h'ar Sarris.

With our infiltrator accepted as Tech Sgt. Chen's concubine, we then allowed the humans to return to Earth with part of the ship, ensuring that it would crash irreparably on landing to ensure that our highly advanced technology would not be of any use to them.

Gen. Roth'h'ar Sarris survived the crash but, before he could surrender, the humans destroyed him, with their armies celebrating his destruction.

Thermian Laliari will remain in her role for the remainder of her life in the parallel universe but will communicate regularly as to her progress in undermining the technological advancement of the humans. We have established communication lines, but there has been some dimensional interference (her first communiqué was "Happiness will prevail!" — unknown reference); my people have already corrected this issue.

Thermion Laliari has identified several areas which will provide adequate interference in the technological advancement of the humans. She has listed them as:

- Sports
- Television
- Recreational drugs
- Politics
- Mating

I trust you will find our actions satisfactory and will remember my people's efforts to further the interests of the Alliance.

I remain, as always, your loyal servant,
Commander Mathesar
Glory to the Klingon–Cardassian Alliance!

Barbara Whillock lives in Australia with her husband and young son, both of whom have been indoctrinated into the cult of sci-fi.

115. STAR TREK
COMMAND AND CONTROL
KANDACE MAVRICK

A genius-level repeat offender and a starship captain walk into a bar...

There's this moment toward the end of the movie where the replacement helmsman is in command of the only Starfleet vessel standing between Earth and certain destruction. It's a familiar scenario to fans of the original series. Someone far down the command chain has the conn, because the captain's busy trying to save the day. Kirk loves his crew. Trusts them implicitly. Has some trouble delegating.

My first impression of this movie was that it should have been called *These Boys and Their Daddy Issues*, but upon further reflection I've decided *Control Freaks Are Us* would be a better title.

We're very carefully shown Spock's obsession with control, but I think Kirk is actually worse. This is a guy who reacts to being told that some things are out of his hands by metaphorically smashing the game board. Someone who fights, cheats and manipulates the rules to get him where he wants to be — with all the responsibility on his shoulders. You don't fight for power like that unless you need the control that comes with it.

Kirk's journey from genius-level repeat offender to captain of the *Enterprise* starts the day that Pike essentially tells him, "You are in control of how your life turns out." That might just be the best thing anyone ever said to Jim Kirk. Or the worst. Either way, it puts him right where Pike wants him.

A lot of people seem to have the impression that Pike is a responsible captain. That he's a kind of stabilizing influence on Kirk. I don't think that could be further from the truth. Pike steps into Jim's father's shoes, sure, but George Kirk is a man Pike describes as someone who "leapt without looking". A trait Pike *admires*.

Kirk's fight for control is performative — confidence masquerading as arrogance. If you don't think James T. Kirk's a control freak, he's already won, because you looked at the smile and not at his eyes. Pike's method of control is quiet. So quiet that, most of the time, you don't even realize what's going on.

The superficial differences in their personalities make a lot of people assume that Kirk and Pike are very different captains. But I don't think they are. Because the thing about that moment I mentioned earlier? It's not the first time in the movie it happens. There's actually a period of time where the *seventeen-year-old navigator* is in command of the ship, standing opposite a guy who just destroyed half of Starfleet and is threatening to obliterate Vulcan. He has some trouble pronouncing his w's, but he's in charge. Familiar scenario, like I said. Except at this moment Kirk's not the captain of the *Enterprise*. He's not even supposed to be on board.

Five minutes after Kirk walks onto the bridge of the *Enterprise* for the first time, Pike makes a call that's something like, "We're floating in space surrounded by the wreckage of seven of our sister ships, being threatened by an enemy that outclasses us so hard it's not even funny. I'm just gonna go for a walk and take every other person in the command chain with me. Chekov, you stay here. If something happens, make a good decision."

It's the first time Kirk serves on a ship, and the Captain's going one way, the command crew another. "We're all going to die, but hopefully it'll turn out fine." Does that look like a blueprint to you?

There's a reason Pike's first officer is perfect for Kirk. Spock spends the first half of the time on the ship trailing after Pike saying, "Are you sure this is a good idea? I don't understand that joke." He spends the latter half trailing Kirk muttering, "This is a terrible idea. That wasn't funny." Surface details aside, Kirk and Pike have a very similar approach to command and control.

Kirk's spent his entire life trying to measure up to an idealized, martyred father. But Pike doesn't challenge him to live up to his father's legend; he dares him to *do better*. And Kirk chases Pike into space.

The first time Pike sets eyes on Kirk, he makes this face that seems to say, "There's something familiar about you, even upside down and bleeding." And it's not because he recognizes George Kirk's son. It's because he sees someone who reminds him of himself. Someone who'd rather flirt with danger than play it safe. Someone who only follows orders when they're compatible with his own goals. Someone who could be the next captain of the *Enterprise*.

Kandace Mavrick is a writer. She writes. She has written. She is writing. Also she has a Sicilian godfather. That's probably not important. Focus on the writing thing.

116. STAR TREK INTO DARKNESS
TO BOLDLY STAY...
SHAUN LYON

It's summer 2015, and the world is preparing for a pop-cultural renaissance at the hands of J.J. Abrams — but not within the *Star Trek* universe. Its flashier, more bombastic cousin *Star Wars* is in for a bit of a reboot-cum-kickstart this autumn, a world Abrams seems far more suited to: fantastical, mythological, more hyperactive; the polar opposite of the more grounded *Star Trek* universe. Breathtaking as *Star Trek* can often be, the Abrams touch feels unsuited to its pulse; its consignment to that universe in a galaxy far, far away is probably far more well-advised.

It is with no small sense of disappointment that I note that *Star Trek Into Darkness* is quite often a look into the *Trek* universe through the filter of the long-ago, far-away space opera it inspired; a broad-eyed view of possibilities steeped in incongruity, and a huge shift not only away from the promise of the first film but from what made *Star Trek* so memorable as a concept back in 1966 and again from the universe we as fans grew up with after the franchise's own rebirth in the 1980s.

Like a stock car speeding out of the gate, only to suddenly stop and be thrust violently backward, *Star Trek Into Darkness* feels like an adventure not only without destination but without its own ignition. The promise of Abrams' earlier voyage was that — despite its inherent logical flaws (fresh recruit to Captain in only four years!) — it was a beginning, the first of many dots to connect across a limitless universe. In its final moments, *Star Trek* gave us a brilliantly cocky captain (his jump from cadet to captain in only a few short years notwithstanding), a confident first officer who had earned his captain's respect and a steadfast crew both familiar and still retaining somewhat of their mystery.

And yet it is stunning that, within the first half-hour of *Into Darkness*, we find ourselves back on Earth, sidetracked by needless conflict between the two leads that was mostly ironed out in the final moments of the first film. Yes, growing pains — especially interpersonal conflict between colleagues — can be a source of drama, but, as the original *Star Trek* series proved time and time again, the friendship and loyalty shaped by duty yet kept together purely by the moral character of the interested parties is much more interesting. Fresh from an opening sequence that seems oddly disjointed from the remainder of the film — and yet remains one of its most enjoyable set pieces — we realize that what we perceived as the launch of the proverbial "five year mission" is nothing but a false start. Kirk is busted (again). Kirk is at odds with Spock (again). Demoted now to first officer, Kirk is taking orders from Christopher Pike (again).

Do you start getting a sense of deja vu here?

It certainly won't end there, if you're paying attention. Because, rather than expand on the promise of the "final frontier", of new voyages into the unknown to explore the galaxy and contact alien civilizations, we are left with... Khan. (Here's where I add the word "again" again.) During the hype for *Into Darkness*, the presence of Benedict Cumberbatch as Khan was both the film's worst kept secret and the proverbial oh-no-they-won't that would lead the production down the dark path (which of course, as the title reminds us, was sort of the idea...). For every guess about Khan, there were others about Gary Mitchell — Kirk's original first officer during the Classic Show's second pilot, not to mention one of his oldest friends, curiously absent in this universe. Mitchell, at least, might have been an interesting twist on *Star Trek* lore; if not a superman, at least a close friend whose betrayal would have scarred Kirk's essence.

Instead, we get the alternative take on Khan's discovery and fate. Barring the obvious physical differences (Cumberbatch is white, Ricardo Montalban... well, wasn't), there's a genuine sense of retroactive character development: the original Khan took shit from no one, calculated, bided his time, and struck not with a phaser but with charismatic oratory and persuasion befitting a skilled politician and tyrant. Cumberbatch's Khan runs very fast and displays his superhuman bluster in a zip through space from a Klingon planet to a Starfleet warship, and we're supposed to believe that all this time he was working on the behest of a Starfleet admiral. There are many things wrong with this, but at its heart is the notion that that is not the Khan Noonien Singh we came to know in the sixties and early eighties.

Cumberbatch's character (called John Harrison for the first half of the film, for no reason in particular other than to give him a normal-sounding name) could have been any other supervillain from past *Trek* lore, or he could have been an original creation, but instead he was given the identity of Khan, for two important reasons: one, the gotcha-moment where the audience discovers the connection (relegated to an interrogation, no less!), and two, to give an alternative take on the closing moments of *The Wrath of Khan*. As touching as that moment is — Kirk, instead of Spock, giving his life — we know it won't take; there's no danger this time, not like there was when Leonard Nimoy really was done with his character.

(And don't get me started on Khan's super-blood restoring Kirk to life. If that was really a solution, then one wonders why Khan didn't do the same with his wife in the "prime" timeline, thereby eliminating at least part of his destructive vengeful streak as retribution for her death on Ceti Alpha V and, well, negating many of the events of *The Wrath of Khan* altogether.)

Star Trek in any incarnation has always been about its core cast of characters, but other than Chris Pine's charming smarminess as Kirk and Zachary Quinto's Spock's single-minded devotion to the letter of the law, we don't see very much of this otherwise. The usually delightful Simon Pegg's Scotty is really the only character given something to do, but the action itself — his blatant defiance of what he feels is an unethical action — only sidelines him for half the picture. Karl Urban as McCoy has a few good scenes, primarily interacting with a scientist assigned to this mission, Carol Marcus; the former, however, really only quips from the sidelines and the latter, well, strips down to her underwear in a scene that even the producers have wondered aloud why they even did it in the first place. Zoe Saldana, John Cho and Anton Yelchin, as Uhura, Sulu and Chekov, respectively, have a moment here or there, but those scenes are vastly unmemorable, and that's a shame considering such talent and wasted opportunities.

And there's wasted talent in spades, from Benedict Cumberbatch's brooding without the beauty of his emotional range, the very quality that gives him his broad appeal and has made him a film superstar, to Bruce Greenwood, whose Pike from the first film was both commanding and inspiring, here given a rather violent death scene within the first quarter of the film that robs us of an emotional center. Only Peter Weller, whose last visit to the *Star Trek* fold was playing a racist villain at the end of the *Enterprise* series, is given more depth, as a Starfleet admiral whose single-minded devotion to stopping Earth's enemies leads him down a very dark path... a path alluding to relevant concerns in our modern and often-times dangerous world. (But blink, and you'll miss appearances by such guests as *Doctor Who*'s Noel Clarke as a grieving-father-turned-terrorist; Deep Roy's diminutive Keenser, Scotty's sidekick from the first film; or the late, great Jimmy Doohan's son Chris manning the transporter room.)

Now, before I continue down a dark path of my own, I will say that there are some things that I really like about *Into Darkness*. I absolutely love the aforementioned teaser, where Kirk goes back for Spock in the face of breaking the Prime Directive. Bringing Carol Marcus into the fold is an interesting homage *Into Darkness* serves on the previous Khan film, though Alice Eve's English accent — as far from Bibi Besch's down home can-I-cook-or-can't-I charm in *Wrath of Khan* as can be — might give one pause about its believability (and there's no indication in *Wrath* that she either served in Starfleet or had an Admiral for a father in the main timeline, but why quibble on something so trivial?). Some of the other little touches — the Tribble in McCoy's office, or the presence of Section 31 (a major part of the storyline from *Deep Space Nine*) as the location of the bombing in London — work in the context of the film. The cameo by Leonard Nimoy (a surprise after his presence in the first film, and the last *Star Trek* he ever filmed) is quite nice. And, once again, J.J. Abrams deftly maneuvers things quite briskly, avoiding scenes of lengthy exposition and keeping the action running.

It's engaging, albeit a bit chaotic with its narrative; it's thrilling, even when taking leave of its grounding in science fact; and it's slick, polished and quite often very entertaining. There's a sense that maybe, just maybe, we'll be embarking on that long "five year mission" at the end of this one, and it's promising — but time will tell. I will say that I enjoyed *Into Darkness* on first viewing; popcorn flicks are good for an evening. It's only when taking a critical eye to it that I begin to recognize and even understand its flaws, leading me to an inauspicious conclusion.

It's just not *Star Trek*.

And here is where we come to a reckoning, because the saga of boldly going where no one has gone before (come on, even in a review, you can't be expected to backtrack on fifty years of split infinitives!) has been left behind in the face of summer blockbuster profits. One can make the argument that that's where the film needs to go, where it must go, in order to compete in the face of the *Star Wars* renaissance or the latest trend toward comic book sagas brought to life on the big screen... and then one can counterpoint that it didn't need to go there at all. We all pretty much know that *Star Trek* had its own rebirth in the early eighties, which ran either to the mid nineties or the early 2000s (based upon your interest level) and petered out on television. (It's a shame so many people who considered themselves *Star Trek* fans likely missed out on *Deep Space Nine* and/or the final two years of *Enterprise*, some of the best *Star Trek* there ever was.)

Even when the multiple sequel series were running, there was deep criticism leveled toward Gene Roddenberry and his ultimate successor, Rick Berman, who guided the *Star Trek* universe until *Enterprise*'s abortive cancellation in 2005, about some of the bland utopianism of the 22nd and 24th centuries. I remember a time where fans were screaming for films from the *Next Generation* cast. (A personal curiosity: why would a fan forego 26 hours of television per year for two hours every couple of years? The mind boggles.)

But when *Star Trek* the film series relaunched with a somewhat daft and silly storyline in 2009 ("let's destroy Vulcan from the inside with a black hole, because that would be awesome"), it still captured the imaginations of its fan base — and a new generation of fans — and ended on a high note: the promise of a voyage out into the unknown, boldly going... boldly going...

Now, where were we boldly going again? I can't remember anymore.

Shaun Lyon has written two factual books about the return of Doctor Who *to the air in 2005, as well as numerous magazine articles and short stories. He lives in Los Angeles with a husband and three cats, and he's still waiting for his close-up, Mr. DeMille.*

117. STAR TREK BEYOND

STRONGER TOGETHER

ROBERT SMITH?

Star Trek Beyond is the clear winner of the three reboot movies, despite some very strong competition from the 2009 movie. It features excellent direction, fabulous CGI, great performances, a plot that could just as easily have been performed by the original crew and some truly touching moments. Not to mention a long overdue watershed moment in *Star Trek* history: that's right, I'm talking about proper use of the universal translator, about 50 years too late. But if there's one thing that binds the film together, in more ways than you'd imagine possible, it's that of swarms.

The creatures Kirk encounters at the beginning are initially threatening, then played for laughs when their size is apparent. Each one isn't much to be reckoned with, but, as a whole, they're terrifying when they come at Kirk in sheer numbers. Then there are the literal swarms of the drone vessels attacking the *Enterprise*, with straight-from-nature displays in the skies above the planet. Inherent in the concept of a swarm is the nature of unity versus individualism. A swarm is a cohesive whole, but it's made up of individuals with personal autonomy who group together to create something larger and more powerful.

> The stick in
> the bundle
> cannot break.

There's a mathematical theory of swarming that takes into account social interactions, wind, gravity and impenetrable barriers, such as the ground. This can be turned into equations that approximate the behavior of large groups of swarming insects, such as locusts. In order to do so, motion of individuals can be described: flying locusts head downwind towards the front of the swarm, those at the front head towards the ground to feed and take off again once the trailing front of the swarm has passed overheard. By entirely determining the motion of individuals, a complete depiction of a rolling swarm can be built.

Topaz *et al.* used differential equations to show that, without wind and gravity, the locust swarm would approach a lattice of fixed density if the swarm is stable, but it would collapse if it isn't. They then extend this idealized case to add in wind and gravity, finding conditions under which a swarm rolls, with a takeoff zone, a landing zone and a stationary zone where grounded locusts can rest and feed. Non-stable swarms, on the other hand, land and form bubbles.

For more information about the mathematical theory of swarming, see C.M. Topaz A.J. Bernoff, S. Logan and W. Toolson "A model for rolling swarms of locusts" *The European Physics Journal Special Topics* 157, 93–109 (2008). The illustrative swarming figure is copyright from the same article and reprinted with permission.

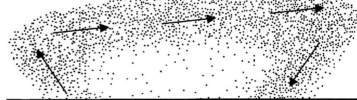

Kirk, on the other hand, is both a leader and a team player. When congratulated on his achievements, he points out that it wasn't just him — and, more importantly, that it never is. He's the focus of the film, yes, but only inasmuch as any individual is the focus of their own story. He's still an integral part of an ensemble and is stronger for it.

However, where Krall differs from the rest of the Federation is that he leads the swarm and uses others. He uses other people for their lifeforce. He uses the properties of the planet. He uses the drones. His success is as a leader, but it's one that he achieved on the backs of others.

The central conversation at the heart of *Star Trek Beyond* is the one between Krall and Uhura about unity. Krall dismisses Uhura's defense of her captain and crewmates as a weakness, saying that struggle is what produces strength, not unity. But the point Krall misses is that the kinds of struggles he's referring to aren't achieved alone: he's a former soldier, and being part of the military is itself a massively unifying thing. He's also reliant on the unity of his swarm.

Jaylah talks of Krall's forces as bees, and they're even referred to as drones, but swarming in nature applies to many species. A swarm can be absolutely devastating, stripping crops bare as it passes through — or, in this case, devastating the structure of the *Enterprise*, which, as Spock says, is not equipped for this kind of engagement.

Of course, bees not only swarm, they sting. But they also produce honey.

Swarms have a level of unpredictability but also a cohesion. Individuals need to stay a minimum distance from each other, which gives them a limited range of places to reside, but within that they also have autonomy. As a group, the swarm expands hugely, but there's also cohesion that gives it structure.

Differential equations can be used to describe both the motion and the interaction, as well as account for external factors. Essentially, differential equations are an engine of change, a way to describe movement through time and space, where the approximations that are made consider the average individual doing the average thing. And yet, despite this simplification, enormously complicated behavior can result, such as intricate patterns and chaos.

Chaos theory posits that small changes can have a massive effect. So a butterfly flapping its wings in Hong Kong can cause tornadoes in Florida because the system is highly sensitive. But there are two requirements for chaos. Sensitive dependence on initial conditions (the "butterfly effect") is the most well-known. The other is topological transitivity, which essentially requires a folding back. You can have a highly sensitive system that isn't chaotic, such as an explosion; in that case, everything just expands outwards. But for true chaos, in the mathematical sense, sensitive dependence sends you away, but you need something that brings you back as well.

What Krall dismisses is the fact that it isn't just the ship that binds the crew; it's each other. The fact that the *Enterprise* is destroyed so early is devastating, looking at first like an anticlimax that could have instead been placed at the end of the film, à la *Star Trek Generations*. But there's a good reason to take out the ship so early: it not only removes the safety net, it shows that *Star Trek* isn't fundamentally about a spaceship exploring the galaxy, it's about the people.

Disrupting the swarm is the only way to deal with it. The initial attempt is to fire upon individual drones, but that's next to useless, costing the *Enterprise* its life. Instead, the later realization is to attack the cohesion, not the individuals. It's a lesson Krall knows from the start: he takes out the entire ship rather than focusing on individuals. Without the cohesive binding, the individuals are scattered and lost. Much like the crick in my neck after making the mistake of attempting to watch this action on an IMAX screen.

Throughout the film, we see unity overcoming chaos. It's there in the Beastie Boys song: what sounds to Jaylah like beats and screaming isn't just noise, it's music. And what characterizes music is repetition creating unity. That the song gets used to disrupt the swarm is just perfect: order created from disorder is used to sow disorder. In fact, my parents say exactly the same thing whenever I play that song in the car; it really brings them together somehow.

Kalara wants to rescue her crew but does it by acting alone. Instead of working together with the *Enterprise* crew, she betrays them, resulting in her downfall. I just hope her tombstone actually says "Death by saucer section" somewhere on it. It's what she would have wanted.

Jaylah represents the individual, but she's absorbed into the group, which makes her stronger. She's initially alone, but her power is the ability to create copies of herself, magnifying her abilities through numbers. However, it's ultimately an illusion, as illustrated by the fact that she learnt English from a computer — something you only do if you're fundamentally alone.

Well, wouldn't YOU put buildings at all angles if you could?

The needs of the many do not always outweigh the needs of the few.

The *Yorktown* itself is a classic example of unity through individualism that coheres to make a greater whole. The structure is a hodgepodge of buildings, towers, shipyards, vents and railway lines, thrown together at seemingly random angles — and yet the result is something beautiful and wondrous, showing us the very limit of human achievement.

McCoy claims that fear of death is what keeps people alive, but he's only partially right. Sacrifice for others does that too. Krall says that Uhura and the crew know nothing of sacrifice, but he's wrong. What bigger sacrifice is there than to be apart from your husband and daughter because you believe in something greater?

Fundamentally, those people are connected. From the opening montage, we see that they're connected through the ordinariness of human lives. Sulu being gay was touted as a big deal before the release — and, given *Star Trek*'s shamefully inept history in this arena, you can see why — but the actual manifestation is low key and unexceptional, as it should be. It plays a subtle role too, giving yet more unity between the *Enterprise* crew and the *Yorktown*'s inhabitants. Not to mention ticking the continuity box of Sulu having a daughter, a link between generations that has more impact in light of later revelations.

Kirk going back for Jaylah is one of those moments that could have gone either way. She's not a main character, and her primary plot function has been fulfilled, so it would make sense from movie logic to kill her off on the rooftop, either tragically or as a result of Kirk's hard-heartedness. But the fact that he risks his life to save her speaks volumes for the compassion inherent in Kirk, not abandoning one of his team, even if she's an outsider. And then he saves her by literally joining with her as the transporter activates. Though if we had actually seen Scotty's worry come true, with Jaylah and Kirk spliced at the hands, I guess that would have been a whole other kind of a film.

Jaylah gets offered a spot in Starfleet, the ultimate group acceptance. She's brought into the fold and accepted as part of the group... but she's told she still has to wear the uniform. Her outsider status qualifies her for entry, but it's not a free pass. As Kirk says, reflecting a lesson he learned himself, she can disobey some of the rules, not all of them.

The swarming theme extends to the design. The nebula is made up of individual obstacles that cohere together; the planet is full of butterflies, floating things and plantlife, all of which are collections of individuals that create a greater whole. Meanwhile, individual moments from a great movie somehow cohered together to make some truly terrible trailers.

The final rescue of Kirk, while a bit clichéd, is because he has friends, whereas Krall doesn't. The swarm saves Kirk but consumes Krall, because he didn't have the fundamental ties that Kirk does. The cohesion that defines the *Enterprise* crew is its loyalty, something Krall starts with but loses when he single-mindedly focuses on his mission, abandoning his own crew in the process. Why that then involves him gradually becoming more human rather than less is anyone's guess. Whatever the reason, the optics of Kirk beating up a black man before being rescued by some fellow white dudes aren't good. The fact that the casting was color blind just isn't a sufficient excuse.

Even the credits are in alphabetical order, with John Cho first, rather than Chris Pine, concluding the idea that we're all in this together. Everyone saying the "To Boldly Go" speech is the perfect capstone, with Uhura voicing the "where no one has gone before" line the icing on the cake.

Then there's the picture from *The Final Frontier* at the end, which may be the most touching moment in the whole film. It not only features the original cast together but also links the two universes, creating unity across the years and across dimensions. The *Star Trek* reboot might have flung off in its own direction, but it hasn't forgotten its roots — or how to make us cry.

Mathematics says that swarming is affected by forces of nature, such as wind and gravity, hard limits you can't control, such as the ground, and social interactions between individuals. *Star Trek Beyond* shows us that these things can't be separated, but it's the social interactions that take that intrinsic unpredictability and tame it.

Almost every character is caught between the needs of the individual and the duty to the group. Kirk isn't sure that his captaincy is rewarding enough, thinking of moving to a higher, but lonelier, position. Uhura and Spock draw apart from each other but later reunite. McCoy has no particular desire to be with Spock but spends the entire time in his company. Scotty goes after Jaylah despite being told not to by Kirk, while Chekov is seen to be fiercely loyal to his captain, if seemingly futile in his attempts to chat up alien women. Well, I'm assuming it was futile; surely, even alien beauties with unknowable thought processes and no experience of Earth customs can see through the line about Russians inventing scotch, which presumably always ends with someone throwing it in his face.

The water used at the end to defeat the drone vessels may be the ultimate manifestation of a swarm. Individual water molecules make up a massive force, one that can either sustain life or end it, depending on how it's harnessed. In this case, the *Franklin* creates waves, the very structure of swarms, in order to destroy the last remaining individuals.

Of all characters though, it's Spock who has the most complex individual–group relationship. He has a weird duality, with a paradoxical selfless loyalty to himself... only it's his older, alternate self. What tempts him away from the group is the desire to create a different group, although not out of love or familial ties, but out of loyalty to a dead man. Yet at the end of the first movie, that same man urged him to stay in Starfleet rather than help populate his species on New Vulcan. Possibly because older Spock had learned a thing or two from Jim Kirk and was thus pon-farring as many new Vulcans as he possibly could, and, at his age, he didn't want the competition.

The *Enterprise* may not have been equipped for this kind of engagement, but *Star Trek* certainly is.

Ultimately, to cohere this back to the beginning, the tiny action that triggered the entire plot was the simple act of uploading the file of the Abronath into the archives. That small individual action of Spock's directly resulted in the death of the *Enterprise* because Krall was monitoring the *Yorktown*'s files. Essentially, it was the act of storing information on the cloud that gave Krall unprecedented access to information. Though if he looked at the comments section first, then I take back everything I said when I claimed he didn't know what sacrifice was.

In the internet age, we're all part of the swarm. Information flows freely, based on individual actions. We have autonomy as humans, but we're also a part of something greater. We might not be able to see the shape of it past our local perspective, but it's still there, drawing us together and moving us forward. Moving us as one. Moving us... Beyond.

Robert Smith? is an autonomous individual who understands that being part of a swarm is inherently powerful. The kind of swarm that involves, say, 117 people.

∞. ACKNOWLEDGEMENTS
WINDING YOU UP
ROBERT SMITH?

Fifty years, 117 writers, one incredible series. I hope you've enjoyed the multitude of takes on the many delights that this book has to offer; I know I have. In fact, I'll let you in on a little secret: the way to get the best out of the contributors to this book is simply to wind them up and let them go. By asking for something truly different, it seems to inspire everyone to bring their A-game to the table.

So I take credit for the wind-up, but I can't thank the contributors enough for what resulted. Despite the numerical complexity of trying to organize 117 writers to fit into a massive jigsaw puzzle, doing this book was an absolute joy, thanks to the sheer quality of pieces that kept arriving in my inbox. Sometimes these rides were very smooth. Sometimes they involved a byzantine editing process that asked hard questions and sweated blood to produce something amazing. And sometimes they just made me laugh. Whichever one it was, I can't tell you how much I appreciate it.

As you'll see in the final ad page at the back of this book, the *Outside In* series started life as a book of reviews about *Doctor Who*. I have Sarah Winwood to thank for the utterly inspiring idea to branch out to other series... and Graeme Burk to thank for suggesting that I start with *TOS*. I was a bit resistant to that at first, but it was absolutely the right call.

I'd also like to offer an enormous debt of gratitude to my team of proofreaders. Former *Star Trek Magazine* editor Paul Simpson's insights and expertise are second to none (and then, as a bonus, he even got me into the advance press screening of *Star Trek Beyond*). Anthony Wilson had no particular expertise or indeed love for *TOS* — and yet his insights into the quality of the writing and the essence of the central ideas were invaluable. Jan Fennick and Jason Miller brought a granular level of detail to their readings that saved me from multiple errors throughout. I feel blessed to have had such expertise at my disposal.

As you might expect with a project this ambitious, there were many more people involved than actually had pieces appear in the book. So, for stimulating discussions about pieces that never quite materialized, I'd like to thank Dennis Turner, Gustavo Leao, Quiana Howard, Lindsey Mayers, Paul Ebbs, Aerin Hyun, Paul Deuis, David McDonald, Alison Kealey, Deb Stanish, Tony Cooke, Heather Riggs, Iona Yeager, James Morrison, Marcus Harmes, Mark Corben, Racheline Maltese, Caitlin Walsh, Kathryn Young and Derek Wilson. Yes, yes, the dog ate your homework. But I'm sure it was tasty nonetheless.

Additionally, I'd like to thank Thomas Marshall, Matthew Rayner, Nea Dodson,

Amit Gupta, Howard Mesick, Tom May, Chris McKeon and Eric Brasure for writing pieces that, through no fault of their own, just didn't fit. I can't tell you how much I appreciate it, regardless. Thanks to Chad Topaz for academic permission. And special thanks to Robin Careless for some wild inspiration that upped the number.

On a personal note, I'd like to thank Kate Fleming for... well, you know. Thanks also to Laura Collishaw and Meryki Basden for moral support.

Finally, I'd like to thank Arnold T. Blumberg for being one of the most standup guys who ever walked the earth. Not only for being the muscle behind ATB Publishing or for his sterling work in ever-increasing demands on design, but for his sheer support in letting me bring this book into the light, with nary a word of complaint. I've asked an enormous amount of Arnold, mostly in terms of design, and he's always had my back. He could very easily have put his foot down and said no, but the mark of a truly supportive publisher is one who'll find a way to say yes. Somehow.

All contributors (as well as proofreaders, designer and your humble editor) kindly agreed to donate their fees to Avert, an AIDS-based charity. I'd like to add a heartfelt thanks to everyone for agreeing to this without a single word of protest. *Star Trek* fans are incredibly generous people, and it's through gestures like this that we really see that happen. Each sale of this book contributes to Avert; it's a great charity, which does amazing work, with low administrative overheads. If you'd like to make a donation yourself, go to www.avert.org.

This book was edited in five continents — and that was just in 2016 alone. So I'm grateful to whoever invented wireless internet, and I'd like to apologize to the nice old lady in Australia who offered to write for the book but didn't own a computer, because I just couldn't do it the old-school way. I'm also grateful to McMaster University for my PhD in mathematics. Without those skills, I'd never have been able to keep the complexity of this book in my head.

Finally, I'd like to thank you, the reader. We've tried to present you with something new. Something different. And something utterly gonzo. I think I speak for all of us when I say that I hope that your passion for this funny little science-fiction television show from the sixties is rewarded through the many and varied takes on each of the stories featured in this book. That's our inspiration from — and gift back to — the wonderful creation that is *Star Trek*. For now.

What of us?

Robert Smith? enjoys punctuation; he really digs it, in fact! "Sure," you might think/wonder* (*50–70% of in-text footnotes are brilliantly constructed — & the rest aren't)... but it's true: when you have a question mark in your name, punctuation is where it's @

▷ ABOUT THE EDITOR

Robert Smith? embodies the essential triumvirate at the heart of *Star Trek*. Like McCoy, he's a doctor (of philosophy), not a bricklayer, with a strong emotional and humanist core. Like Spock, he's logical and analytical, being a mathematician who studies infectious diseases in the hopes of using science to create a better galaxy. And, like Kirk, he's a larger-than-life devil-may-care adventurer, exploring distant places and arguing with computers. Although thankfully without nearly as many fistfights.

IN THE NEXT GENERATION...

IN 2017...

...AND THE ADVENTURE CONTINUES...

Decades in the making!

RED WHITE AND WHO

THE STORY OF DOCTOR WHO IN AMERICA by STEVEN WARREN HILL & JENNIFER ADAMS KELLEY and ROBERT WARNOCK

A fun and fact-filled narrative of the history of *Doctor Who* and its fandom in the United States, incorporating rare illustrative material and dozens of interviews and contributions from some of the key people who laid the groundwork for or continue to innovate the fandom in which we participate today!

IN THIS INCREDIBLE VOLUME, YOU WILL DISCOVER:

- The real origin and purpose of the word "Whovian."
- The busted myth concerning American viewership of the television movie *Doctor Who* as pitted against the television series *Roseanne*.
- The truth about the reasons behind the cancellation of the massive TARDIS 23 convention in 1986.
- How Walter Winchell, controversial gossip columnist popular in the 1930s–1950s, was inadvertently instrumental in bringing *Doctor Who* books to America.
- The main reason the *Doctor Who* USA Tour, an exhibition trailer visiting the entire country in the late 1980s, was considered a financial failure.
- The link between the United States Supreme Court's landmark "Betamax Case" lawsuit and off-air copies of "Terror of the Autons" and "The Ambassadors of Death".
- The truth about Harlan Ellison®'s bold introduction to the Pinnacle Books novelisation reprints.
- The American incident that touched J. Michael Straczynski, Neil Gaiman, Harlan Ellison® and Barry Letts.
- How speech-driven artificial intelligences (like Siri and Cortana) can be linked to *Doctor Who*.
- How the cancellation of "Shada" made the first-ever American *Doctor Who* convention a massive success.
- Which American broadcaster has aired *Doctor Who* longer than anyone else in the world, even longer than the BBC.
- The truth about the painting of the Third Doctor seen in "Timelash."
- Where in America the Daleks were seen on television every single weeknight for a whole week in 1969.

EVERY AMERICAN *DOCTOR WHO* FAN HAS A STORY TO TELL...
...AND IT'S TIME FOR THOSE STORIES TO BE TOLD!

Coming in 2017!

ATBPUBLISHING.COM

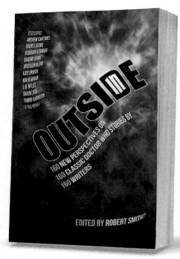
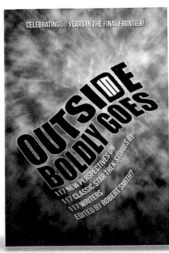
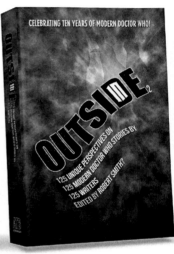